Translated Texts for

This series is designed to meet the needs of students of ancient and medieval history and others who wish to broaden their study by reading source material, but whose knowledge of Latin or Greek is not sufficient to allow them to do so in the original languages. Many important Late Imperial and Dark Age texts are currently unavailable in translation and it is hoped that TTH will help to fill this gap and to complement the secondary literature in English which already exists. The series relates principally to the period 300-800 AD and includes Late Imperial, Greek, Byzantine and Syriac texts as well as source books illustrating a particular period or theme. Each volume is a self-contained scholarly translation with an introductory essay on the text and its author and notes on the text indicating major problems of interpretation, including textual difficulties.

Editorial Committee
Sebastian Brock, Oriental Institute, University of Oxford
Averil Cameron, Keble College, Oxford
Henry Chadwick, Oxford
John Davies, University of Liverpool
Carlotta Dionisotti, King's College, London
Peter Heather, University College London
William E. Klingshirn, The Catholic University of America
Michael Lapidge, Clare College, Cambridge
Robert Markus, University of Nottingham
John Matthews, Yale University
Claudia Rapp, University of California, Los Angeles
Raymond Van Dam, University of Michigan
Michael Whitby, University of Warwick
Ian Wood, University of Leeds

General Editors
Gillian Clark, University of Liverpool
Mary Whitby, Oxford

Front cover: Based on the *Codex Sangallensis* 190, p. 132, the first page of the only surviving copy of the letters of Ruricius of Limoges.

A complete list of titles in the Translated Texts for Historians series is available on request. Recent titles are shown below.

Pseudo-Dionysius of Tel-Mahre: *Chronicle,* **Part III**
Translated with notes and introduction by WITOLD WITAKOWSKI
Volume 22: 192pp., 1995, ISBN 0-85323-760-3

Venantius Fortunatus: Personal and Political Poems
Translated with notes and introduction by JUDITH GEORGE
Volume 23: 192pp., 1995, ISBN 0-85323-179-6

Donatist Martyr Stories: The Church in Conflict in Roman North Africa
Translated with notes and introduction by MAUREEN A. TILLEY
Volume 24: 144pp., 1996, ISBN 0 85323 931 2

Hilary of Poitiers: Conflicts of Conscience and Law in the Fourth-Century Church
Translated with introduction and notes by LIONEL R. WICKHAM
Volume 25: 176pp., 1997, ISBN 0–85323–572–4

Lives of the Visigothic Fathers
Translated and edited by A. T. FEAR
Volume 26: 208pp., 1997, ISBN 0–85323–582–1

Optatus: Against the Donatists
Translated and edited by MARK EDWARDS
Volume 27: 220pp., 1997, ISBN 0–85323–752–2

Bede: A Biblical Miscellany
Translated with notes and introduction by W. TRENT FOLEY and ARTHUR G. HOLDER
Volume 28: 240pp., 1999, ISBN 0–85323–683–6

Bede: The Reckoning of Time
Translated with introduction, notes and commentary by FAITH WALLIS
Volume 29: 352pp., 1999, ISBN 0–85323–693–3

Ruricius of Limoges and Friends: A Collection of Letters from Visigothic Gaul
Translated with notes and introduction by RALPH W. MATHISEN
Volume 30: 272pp., 1999, ISBN 0–85323–703–4

For full information, please write to the following:
All countries, except the USA and Canada: Liverpool University Press, Senate House, Abercromby Square, Liverpool, L69 3BX, UK (*Tel* +44-[0]151-794 2233, *Fax* +44-[0]151-794 2235, *Email* J.M.Smith@liv.ac.uk.
USA & Canada: University of Pennsylvania Press, 4200 Pine Street, Philadelphia, PA 19104-6097, USA (*Tel* +1-215-898-6264, *Fax* +1-215-898-0404).

Translated Texts for Historians
Volume 30

Ruricius of Limoges and Friends
A Collection of Letters from Visigothic Gaul

Letters of Ruricius of Limoges, Caesarius of Arles, Euphrasius of Clermont, Faustus of Riez, Graecus of Marseille, Paulinus of Bordeaux, Sedatus of Nîmes, Sidonius Apollinaris, Taurentius and Victorinus of Fréjus

Translated with introduction, commentary and notes by RALPH W. MATHISEN

Liverpool
University
Press

First published 1999 by
LIVERPOOL UNIVERSITY PRESS
Senate House
Abercromby Square
Liverpool
L69 3BX

British Library Cataloguing-in-Publication Data
A British Library CIP Record is available
ISBN 0–85323–703–4

'Scriptis, picturis, ope, sumptibus, arte, fiuris hoc
exornastis opus ambo michique dicastis. Ambos
ergo pari faciam requie sociari'

Text processed by Ralph W. Mathisen

Printed in the European Union by
Page Bros, Norwich, England

CONTENTS

PREFACE

This little book has taken a long time to see the light of day. The translations of the letters of Ruricius were first undertaken at the University of Illinois, Chicago Circle, in early 1980, and at one point in 1981 were scheduled to be published by Coronado Press, a now-defunct publisher of several useful translations of late antique works. It is thanks to Gillian Clark and Ray Van Dam that this translation project was dusted off, expanded, and polished beginning in 1994. Without their encouragement, support, and guidance, the translations and commentaries never could have been finished. More concretely, Ray read the draft of the translations of Book I on two different occasions, whereas Gillian painstakingly reviewed all of the translations. Both of them gently pointed out several places where I had not merely veered to the left or right, but completely departed from what Faustus of Riez would have called the "royal road," and Gillian in particular is responsible for a great many literary cross-references and felicitous turns of phrase. I, however, claim responsiblilty for what surely are many remaining instances were the translations are either flat-footed or just plain wrong.

Additional thanks are due to Ian Wood, who offered extensive suggestions on the commentary section, and to Antti Arjava, Walter Berschin, Annalisa Bracciotti, Mary Garrison, Tracy Keefer, Rosamond McKitterick, Robert Patterson, Christian Settipani, and Danuta Shanzer, who have proposed invaluable suggestions on particular points of translation, palaeography, and historical fact, as well as to Elizabeth Clark, whose *John Chrysostom and Friends, Essays and Translations* (New York, 1979) provided inspiration for the title. Tracy Keefer also assisted with proof-reading the final text.

Further grateful acknowledgement is given to Cornel Dora, keeper of manuscripts at the Stiftsbibliothek in St. Gallen, who welcomed me twice to the monastic library and permitted me to study both the *Sangallensis* 190 and other manuscripts; and to Guy Lintz, of the Service Regionale d'Archéologie in France, for his valuable assistance in matters archaeological and bibliographical during a stay at Limoges.

Finally, the completion of this project would have been rendered much more burdensome without the most welcome financial assistance of the American Philosophical Society, the Friends of the Princeton University Library, and, at the University of South Carolina, the Department of History, the Research and Productive Scholarship Program, and the College of Liberal Arts Scholarship Support program.

LIST OF MAPS AND FIGURES

ABBREVIATIONS

AASS	*Acta sanctorum*
Anderson	W.B. Anderson, *Sidonius Apollinaris: Poems and Letters I-II* (Loeb: London, 1936-1965)
Aubrun	M. Aubrun, *L'ancien diocèse de Limoges des origines au milieu du XIe siècle* (Clermont-Ferrand, 1981)
BSAF	*Bulletin de la Société des Antiquaires de France*
BSAHL	*Bulletin de la Société Archéologique et Historique du Limousin* (Limoges)
BSELSAL	*Bulletin de la Société des Etudes Littéraires, Scientifiques et Artistiques du Lot*
BSLSAC	*Bulletin de la Société des Lettres, Sciences et Arts de la Corrèze* (Tulle)
BSSHAC	*Bulletin de la Société Scientifique Historique et Archéologique de la Corrèze* (Brive-la-Gaillarde)
CAG 19	G. Lintz ed., *Le Corrèze, Carte archéologique de la Gaule 19* (Paris, 1992)
CAG 46	M. Labrousse, G. Mercadier eds., *Le Lot, Carte archéologique de la Gaule 46* (Paris, 1990)
CAG 87	J. Perrier ed., *La Haute-Vienne, Carte archéologique de la Gaule 87* (Paris, 1993)
CAGR 14	J. Perrier ed., *Carte archéologique de la Gaule romaine. Carte et texte du département de la Haute-Vienne*, vol.14 (Paris, 1964)
Carm.	*Carmina* ("Poems")

CCL	*Corpus christianorum, series latina*
CIL	*Corpus inscriptionum latinarum*
Clavis	E. Dekkers, A. Gaar eds., *Clavis patrum latinorum* (2nd ed.) (Turnhout, 1961)
CSEL	*Corpus scriptorum ecclesiasticorum latinorum*
CTh	*Codex Theodosianus* ("Theodosian Code")
Dalton	O.M. Dalton, *The Letters of Sidonius* (2 vols.) (Oxford, 1915)
Demeulenaere	R. Demeulenaere, *Foebadius, Victricius, Leporius, Vincentius Lerinensis, Evagrius, Ruricius*; *CCL* 64 (Turnholt, 1985): *Ruricii Lemovicensis epistularum libri duo*, pp.312-394; *Epistulae ad Ruricium scriptae*, pp.397-405; *Epistulae Fausti ad Ruricium*, pp.406-415
Duchesne	L. Duchesne, *Fastes épiscopaux de l'ancienne Gaule* (2nd ed.) (3 vols.) (Paris, 1907-15)
ed.	Editor
Engelbrecht	A. Engelbrecht, *Fausti Reiensis et Ruricii opera*, *CSEL* 21 (Vienna, 1891): *Fausti epistulae*, pp.161-219; *Ruricii epistularum libri duo*, pp.349-450; *Epistulae ad Ruricium scriptae*, p.443ff.
Epist.	*Epistulae* ("Letters")
Greg.Tur.	Gregory of Tours, *HF* (properly, the *Decem libri historiarum* ["Ten Books of History"] or simply the *Historiae* ["Histories"], commonly known as the *Historia Francorum* ["History of the Franks"]); also *Glor.conf.* (*Liber in gloria confessorum* ["Book on the Glory of the Confessors"]), *Glor.mart.* (*Liber in gloria martyrum* ["Book on the Glory of the Martyrs"], and *Vit.pat.* (*Liber vitae patrum* ["Book on the Life of the Fathers"])

Krusch   B. Krusch, *MGH AA* 8 (Berlin, 1887): "De Ruricio episcopo
                   Lemovicensi," pp.lxii-lxxx; *Fausti aliorumque epistulae ad
                   Ruricium aliosque*, pp. 265-298; and *Ruricii epistulae*, ibid.
                   pp. 299-350

MGall   *Missale gallicanum vetus* ("Ancient Gallic Missal")

MGoth   *Missale gothicum* ("Gothic Missal")

MGH AA   *Monumenta Germaniae historica, Auctores antiquissimi*

MGH Epist.   *Monumenta Germaniae historica, Epistulae*

MGH LC   P. Piper ed., *MGH Libri confraternitatum. Sancti Galli, Au-
                   giensis, Fabaricensis* (Berlin, 1884)

MGH SRM   *Monumenta Germaniae historica, Scriptores rerum merovin-
                   gicarum*

MGH SS   *Monumenta Germaniae historica, Scriptores*

MSSNAC   *Mémoires de la Société des Sciences Naturelles et Archéo-
                   logiques de la Creuse*

ms., mss.   Manuscript, manuscripts

Pardessus   J.-M. Pardessus, *Diplomata, chartae, epistolae, leges alia-
                   que instrumenta ad res Gallo-Francicas spectantia* (2 vols.)
                   (Paris, 1843-1849)

PL   J.-P. Migne ed., *Patrologia latina*

PLRE I   A.H.M. Jones, J.R. Martindale, J. Morris eds., *The Prosopo-
                   graphy of the Later Roman Empire. Volume I. A.D. 260-395*
                   (Cambridge, 1971)

PLRE II   J.R. Martindale ed., *The Prosopography of the Later Roman
                   Empire. Volume II. A.D. 395-527* (Cambridge, 1980)

PLRE III   J.R. Martindale ed., *The Prosopography of the Later Roman
                   Empire. Volume III. A.D. 527-640* (Cambridge, 1990)

PLS	*Patrologia latina, supplementum*
TAL	*Travaux d'archéologie Limousine*
S, SG, Sg	*Codex Sangallensis*
SC	*Sources chrétiennes*
Sid.Apoll.	Sidonius Apollinaris, *Epist.* (*Epistulae*) and *Carm.* (*Carmina*)
tr.	Translator
vita	"Life" of a saint

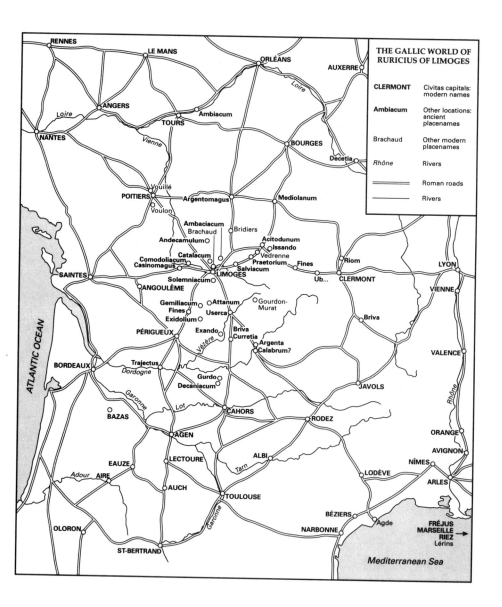

INTRODUCTION

The fifth century brought great changes to Roman Gaul. One of the most crucial was the settlement of various barbarian peoples, who, in the early years of the century, began to arrive in Gaul to stay in ever greater numbers. There has been much debate regarding the significance of the barbarian settlement in Gaul and elsewhere. Some have seen it as the primary agent of the decline of the western empire; others have downplayed the barbarian impact.[1]

Gallo-Roman aristocrats faced a very different world in the fifth and sixth centuries, and many of the changes resulted, directly or indirectly, from the barbarian presence.[2] Opportunities to pursue traditional careers were reduced. The gradual withdrawal of the Roman imperial administration, for example, meant the disappearance of most of the traditional secular offices. Even if a Gaul sought service with the barbarians, the rudimentary barbarian administrations offered few opportunities. The newcomers also appropriated much of the land and social influence. At the same time, the overall level of violence in Gallic society increased dramatically.

One of the best ways to gain insights into the personal lives and feelings of those who experienced these transformations is by reading their personal letters. There was a long tradition of letter writing in antiquity that continued into the late antique period.[3] For the Roman world, one thinks of Cicero, Pliny, and

---

[1] See, inter alios, N. Baynes, "The Decline of Roman Power in Western Europe and its Modern Explanations," *Byzantine Studies and Other Essays* (London, 1955) pp.83-96; M. Bloch, "Observations sur la conquête de la Gaule romaine par les rois francs," *Revue historique* 154 (1927) pp.161-178; J.B. Bury, *The Invasion of Europe by the Barbarians* (London, 1928); E. Chrysos and A. Schwarcz eds., *Das Reich und die Barbaren* (Vienna-Cologne, 1989); A. Demandt, *Der Fall Roms. Die Auflösung des römischen Reiches im Urteil der Nachwelt* (Munich, 1984); K.F. Drew, "Another Look at the Origins of the Middle Ages. A Reassessment of the Role of the Germanic Kingdoms," *Speculum* 62 (1987) pp.803-812; W. Goffart, "Rome, Constantinople, and the Barbarians," *American Historical Review* 86 (1981) pp.275-306; R. Latouche, *The Birth of the Western Economy: Economic Aspects of the Dark Ages*[2], E.M. Wilkinson tr. (London, 1967); F. Lot, *Les invasions germaniques. La pénétration mutuelle du monde barbare et du monde romain* (Paris, 1945); R. MacMullen, *Corruption and the Decline of Rome* (New Haven, 1988); L. Musset, *Les invasions. Les vagues germaniques* (Paris, 1965); R. Rémondon, *La crise de l'empire romain de Marc-Aurèle à Anastase* (Paris, 1964); P. Riché, *Les invasions barbares* (Paris, 1953); J.J. Saunders, "The Debate on the Fall of Rome," *History* 48-49 (1963) pp.1-17; and E.A. Thompson, *Romans and Barbarians. The Decline of the Western Empire* (Madison, 1982).

[2] See R.W. Mathisen, *Roman Aristocrats in Barbarian Gaul. Strategies for Survival in an Age of Transition* (Austin, 1993).

[3] For antiquity, see, e.g., H. Cotton, *Documentary Letters of Recommendation in Latin from the Roman Empire* (Königstein, 1981); P. Cugusi, *Evoluzione e forme dell' epistolografia latina nella tarda repubblica e nei primi secoli dell'Impero. Con cenni sull' epistolografia preciceroniana*

Fronto for the Late Republic and Principate. In the late Roman period, one encounters Quintus Aurelius Symmachus, and for the rise of Christianity, there are Cyprian, Ambrose, Jerome, and Augustine. Their collections of letters provide intimate and personal insights into the nature of the times.

Several letter writers bridge the transformation from Roman to barbarian Gaul. Ausonius of Bordeaux and Paulinus of Nola describe Gaul in the late fourth and early fifth centuries.[4] For the second quarter of the century, there are the letters of Salvian of Marseille, Eucherius of Lyon, Hilary of Arles, and others.[5] For the third quarter, one necessarily thinks of Sidonius Apollinaris, whose 148 letters have been edited and translated several times, and are the most oft-cited source for this period.[6] Sidonius represents the last days of Imperial Gaul, from Valentinian III (425-455) through Julius Nepos (474-480). Subsequently, for the early sixth century, the letters of Avitus of Vienne, Caesarius of Arles, and Magnus Felix Ennodius cover the rise of Frankish Gaul.[7] All of these individuals have received much attention in the literature.[8]

But what about the crucial last quarter of the fifth century, and the underappreciated Visigothic Kingdom of Toulouse, which had looked like it, not the kingdom of the Franks, would become the primary barbarian power of Gaul? Another letter collection, one that covers this period and region, also survives, that of Ruricius, a friend and protégé of Sidonius, who served as bishop of Limoges from ca. 485 until 507 or later. The 83 letters of poor Ruricius, howev-

---

(Rome, 1983); H. Peter, *Der Brief in der römischen Literatur* (Leipzig, 1901); and S.K. Stowers, *Letter Writing in Greco-Roman Antiquity* (Philadelphia, 1986). For the later period, see A.A.R. Bastiaensen, *La cérémonial épistolaire des chrétiens latins. Origine et premiers développements* (Nijmegen, 1964); G. Constable, *Letters and Letter-Collections* (Turnhout, 1976); A. Garzya, "L'epistolografia letteraria tardoantica," in *Le trasformazioni* (1985) pp.347-373; J. Leclercq, "Le genre épistolaire au moyen âge," *Revue du moyen âge latine* 2 (1946) pp.63-73; and N. Valois, *De arte scribendi epistolas apud Gallicos medii aevi scriptores rhetoresve* (Paris, 1880).
[4] Ausonius: K. Schenkl ed., *MGH AA* 5.2; Paulinus: G. de Hartel ed., *Sancti Pontii Meropii Paulini Nolani Epistulae, CSEL* 29 (Vienna, 1894).
[5] Eucherius and Hilary: C. Wotke ed., *CSEL* 31.1 (Vienna, 1894) p.177ff; *PL* 50.701-726; Salvian: G. Lagarrigue ed., *Salvien de Marseille. Oeuvres, Sources chrétiennes* 176, 220 (Paris, 1971-1975); F. Pauly ed., *Salviani presbyteri Massiliensis opera omnia, CSEL* 7 (Vienna, 1883); C. Halm ed., *Salviani presbyteri Massiliensis libri qui supersunt, MGH AA* 1.1 (Berlin, 1877).
[6] See A. Loyen tr., *Sidoine Apollinaire: Poèmes* (Paris, 1960) and vols.2-3, *Sidoine Apollinaire: Lettres* (Paris, 1970); W.B. Anderson tr., *Sidonius: Poems and Letters I-II* (Loeb: London, 1936-1965); P. Mohr ed., *C. Sollius Apollinaris Sidonius* (Teubner: Leipzig, 1895); C. Leutjohann ed., *Gai Sollii Apollinaris Sidonii epistulae et carmina, MGH AA* 8 (Berlin, 1887); O.M. Dalton tr., *The Letters of Sidonius*, 2 vols. (Oxford, 1915).
[7] Avitus: R. Peiper ed., *Alcimi Ecdicii Aviti Viennensis episcopi. Opera quae supersunt, MGH AA* 6.2 (Berlin, 1883); Ennodius: F. Vogel ed., *Magni Felicis Ennodi. Opera, MGH: AA* 7 (Berlin, 1885); G. de Hartel ed., *CSEL* 6 (Vienna, 1882); Faustus: A. Engelbrecht ed., *Fausti Reiensis praeter sermones pseudo-Eusebianos opera, CSEL* 21 (Vienna, 1891); B. Krusch ed., *Fausti aliorumque epistulae ad Ruricium aliosque, MGH: AA* 8 (Berlin, 1887), 265-298.
[8] See Bibliography below.

er, survive in only a single manuscript (an "unica"), have never been translated, and are rarely cited.[9] Ruricius' bibliography is, to say the least, sparse.

The neglect of Ruricius is unfortunate, for he provides a picture of life in late Roman Gaul that significantly complements the picture given by Sidonius. Sidonius, the son-in-law of an emperor, and himself Prefect of Rome in 468, contributes valuable information on the significant political developments of his day, ranging from the decline of imperial authority, to the relationships among leading Gallic blue-bloods, to the rise of barbarian Gaul writ large. Most of Sidonius' letters date to a time when Gaul was still part of Roman Empire, even if only tenuously, and are of great importance for our understanding of aristo-cratic Gallo-Roman society during the final years of imperial Gaul. But, in an intimate and domestic way, Ruricius tells of what happened afterward. What was the life of the literate Roman population like under barbarian rule? How much had changed, and how much had remained the same? What was the response of well-to-do Gauls once Roman authority had disappeared for good? Questions such as these can be approached through a study of Ruricius' letters.

Even though he was bishop of an outlying and rather modest city, Ruricius was himself a scion of one of the most blue-blooded Roman aristocratic fami-lies, the Anicii, and was married to a woman of patrician ancestry. Unlike Si-donius, however, he exhibits little interest in secular politics. Which is not to say that Ruricius was a shrinking violet. He counted among his correspondents some of the most influential individuals of south-central Gaul, including bishops Caesarius and Aeonius of Arles, Sedatus of Nîmes, Faustus of Riez, and, of course, Sidonius himself and his son Apollinaris, not to mention Julianus Pome-rius, a priest and author of Arles. But most of Ruricius' correspondents were smaller fish.

Ruricius' letters, and those that he received, provide priceless insights not only into the private and public lives of some of these persons, but also into lo-cal life and activities in Visigothic Gaul. He illustrates the means used by the Gallo-Romans to cope with their new circumstances. Indeed, in contrast to Si-donius' letters, the correspondence of Ruricius has very little to say about the Visigoths at all, and as a result suggests how little impact they may actually have had at the daily, local level.

Which is not to say, however, that Ruricius tells us nothing about political developments. Far from it. For Ruricius' correspondence clarifies the attendant circumstances surrounding the pivotal battle of Vouillé, near Poitiers, in 507, in which the Franks defeated the Visigoths and as a result became the preeminent

---

[9] In Chadwick, *Poetry and Letters*, for example, Ruricius receives only two very brief mentions (pp.16, 198). In Duckett's *Latin Writers of the Fifth Century* he is not mentioned at all. More recently, in Y. Hen, *Culture & Religion in Merovingian Gaul, AD 481-751* (Leiden, 1995), Ruricius receives nary a mention.

barbarian power in Gaul. Along the way, the circumstances of the issuance of the *Breviarium* and the meeting of the Council of Agde in 506 are clarified, and possible light is thrown upon an otherwise undated Council of Arles, whose very existence has been doubted.

Ruricius experienced the very last days of imperial Gaul, and both the apogee and the precipitous decline of the kingdom of Toulouse. His letters, which span the period from ca. 470 until ca. 507, cover the crucial transitional phase between Roman and Frankish Gaul. By the end of Ruricius' life, it was clear that the subsequent history of sub-Roman Gaul would be written not by Romans or Visigoths, but by Franks. And his miraculously surviving letter collection is of great significance for our understanding of the survival of classical culture and the development of western European religion and society

LIMOGES AND AQUITANIA:

THE FIRST THROUGH THE SEVENTH CENTURIES

Julius Caesar opened his *Commentaries on the Gallic Wars* with the famous words, "All Gaul is divided into three parts, of which the Belgians inhabit one, the Aquitanians another, and the Celts the third."[1] Aquitania was in the southwest, Belgica in the northwest, and Celtica, the largest, was centrally located. A fourth "part" of Gaul was the existing Roman "provincia" (modern Provence) of Gallia Narbonensis. During the Principate (27 BC–AD 284), there continued to be four Gallic provinces: Narbonensis, Lugdunensis (Caesar's Celtica), Aquitania, and Belgica. Each had a metropolitan, or capital, city: Narbonne, Lyon, Bordeaux, and Trier respectively. And each was divided into smaller territories known as *civitates* ("cities"), which were the centers of the local administration, economy, and society.[2] Most of the ordinary *civitates* have not received nearly as much attention, either in antiquity or in the modern day, as either the metropolitan cities or other cities of great economic or political importance, such as Marseille, Arles, or Toulouse.[3] The city of Limoges, where the Gallo-Roman aristocrat Ruricius served as bishop ca. 485-510, was such a *civitas*. In its developed form, its territory encompassed the modern French départements of Haute-Vienne, Corrèze, and Creuse. Even though Ruricius himself half disparagingly referred to its *humilitas* ("humbleness": *Epist.* 2.33), cities like Limoges formed the backbone of urbanized Gaul. Its history paralleled that of many other cities throughout the Roman world.

The History and Geography of Limoges

Limoges had its origin in the Celtic people known as the Lemovices. In the mid first century BC their territory was located in north-central Aquitania, centered on a huge *oppidum* ("fortified town"), perhaps called Durotincum, which

---

[1] "Gallia est omnis divisa in partes tres, quarum unam incolunt Belgae, aliam Aquitani, tertiam ... Celtae" (*Bell.gall.* 1.1).

[2] For city development, see P.-A. Février, "The Origin and Growth of the Cities of Southern Gaul to the Third Century A.D.: An Assessment of the Most Recent Archaeological Discoveries," *Journal of Roman Studies* 63 (1973) pp.1-28; and J.A.O. Larsen, "The Position of Provincial Assemblies in the Government and Society of the Late Roman Empire," *Classical Philology* 29 (1934) pp.209-220.

[3] For a noteworthy exception, see L. Pietri, *La ville de Tours du IVᵉ au VIᵉ siècle: Naissance d'une cité chrétienne* (Rome, 1983).

was situated on a hill at the juncture of the Vienne and the Maulde rivers, in the area of the modern village of Villejoubert, 25 km. west of Limoges proper.[4] After the Roman conquest of 58-50 BC, and the subsequent reorganization of Gaul under the emperor Augustus (27 BC–AD 14), the *oppidum* was abandoned and the city of Augustoritum was founded ca. 16 BC to serve as the new *civitas Lemovicum*, or capital of the Lemovices.[5] The site extended for 1500 meters along the right bank of the Vienne, and covered about 100 hectares. Previously part of Celtica, the Lemovices were assigned to an enlarged Aquitania that extended to the Loire river.[6] The population, or at least the elites, quickly and enthusiastically assimilated Roman culture.[7]

As a *civitas* capital, Augustoritum acquired, primarily between the mid first and mid second centuries, all of the amenities of a typical Roman city.[8] The forum area in the southeast-central section, approximately 100 by 150 meters, was built perhaps in the last half of the first century.[9] An amphitheater dates to the Flavian or early Antonine period, possibly as late as Hadrian (117-138). It was cut into the summit of small hill at the northwestern edge of the city; at 138 by 116 meters, it was larger than those at Arles and Nîmes.[10] During the later empire and the Middle Ages, it was used as a stone quarry, and nearly all the superstructure was removed. It has been partially excavated, and provides

---

[4] J.-M. Desbordes, "L'oppidum de Villejoubert, commune de Saint-Denis-des-Murs (Haute-Vienne)," *TAL* 4 (1983) pp.25-28; J.-M. Desbordes, et al., "Les remparts de l'oppidum de Villejoubert (Commune de Saint-Denis-des-Murs, Haute-Vienne)," *TAL* 9 (1989) pp.63-74; J. Perrier, Martine Tandeau de Marsac, "Le 'petit rempart' de l'oppidum de Villejoubert (Commune de Saint-Denis-des-Murs, Haute-Vienne)," *TAL* 4 (1983) pp.29-40; *CAG* 87, pp.182-186.

[5] Abbreviated as "Ausritum" in the "Peutinger Table," a second-century Roman road map. See, in general, *CAG* 87, pp.79-142; *CAGR* 14, pp.49-86; also M. Aubrun, *L'ancien diocèse de Limoges des origines au milieu du XIe siècle* (Clermont-Ferrand, 1981); Bedon, "Lemovices"; J.-M. Desbordes et al, *Augustoritum. Aux origines de Limoges* (Limoges, 1990); P. Ducourtieux, *Histoire de Limoges* (Limoges, 1925); R. Limouzin-Lamothe, *Le diocèse de Limoges, des origines à la fin du Moyen-Age* (2 vols.) (Strasbourg, 1951); J.-P. Loustaud, *Limoges gallo-romain* (Limoges, 1980); and F. Prevot, "Limoges," in F. Prevot, X. Barral i Altet eds., *Topographie chrétienne des cités de la Gaule des origines au milieu du VIIIe siècle. VI. Province ecclésiastique de Bourges (Aquitania Prima)* (Paris, 1989) pp.67-77.

[6] R. Bedon, "A propos du statut et de l'histoire de la civitas gallo-romaine des Lemovices et de sa capitale Augustoritum," *TAL* 15 (1995) pp. 31-41 at p.32.

[7] J.-P. Bost, "Elites urbaines à Augustoritum sous le Haut-Empire," *TAL* 13 (1993) pp.101-108; J.-P. Loustaud, "Nouvelle inscription relative à un notable Lemovice à Lyon," *BSAHL* 111 (1984) p.168; and J.-P. Bost, J. Perrier, "Professeur de grammaire à Limoges sous le Haut-Empire," *BSAHL* 116 (1989) pp.55-66.

[8] *CAG* 87, pp.94-118; Bedon, "Lemovices," p.38.

[9] J.-P. Loustaud, "Emplacement du forum gallo-romain de Limoges," *BSAHL* 107 (1980) p.245; J.-P. Loustaud, J.-P., J.-J. Vorioulet, "Forum de Limoges, premier approche (1976-1980)," *BSAHL* 108 (1981) pp.40-53; and *CAG* 87, p.94. The area continues to serve as the city's administrative center.

[10] *CAG* 87, pp.94-7; R. Courraud, "L'amphithéatre de Limoges. Premiers sondages: octobre 1966–mars 1967," *BSAHL* 94 (1967) pp.49-63.

virtually the only visible remains of the ancient city.

On the south side of the city, near the river, there was a theater, built, it seems, in the Antonine period and mentioned in the ninth-century *Vita Martialis* ("Life of St. Martial").[11] Public baths (*thermae*), constructed perhaps around the mid or late first century and measuring about 90 by 80 meters, abutted the forum on the northeastern side.[12] After the central section was destroyed by fire in the mid second century, the baths were reconstructed, but they then were abandoned toward the end of the third century.

A number of private dwellings have been excavated, including the so-called "House of the Ninth of March", with an area of about 3,800 square meters (40 by 96 meters) and located just south of the forum.[13] Built at the time of Nero, it contained two peristyles and at least 28 rooms; it was remodeled in the mid second and mid third centuries, and continued to be occupied into the beginning of the fourth century. About five km. northeast of the city center, at Brachaud, are the remains, some 570 meters square, of the private baths of a large villa.[14] Seven stages of construction between the mid first and the beginning of the fourth centuries have been identified; the villa seems to have been abandoned toward the end of the fourth century. Other villas also dotted the countryside outside the city.[15]

At least fifteen arteries of the urban road system converged on the area of the forum.[16] A bridge on the *cardo maximus*, the primary north-south street, crossed the Vienne from the first century; it had six arches and was "built with marvelous skill."[17] Water was supplied by a network of subterranean aqueducts from 2.5 to 14 meters deep that continue in use; a sewer system dealt with drainage.[18] Water also was provided by a system of wells, from 5-10 meters

---

[11] *CAG* 87, pp.96-7; J.-P. Loustad, "Le théatre gallo-romain de Limoges, premiers éléments archéologiques," *BSAHL* 118 (1990) pp.17-30; Idem, "Vestiges du théatre d'Augustoritum," *BSAHL* 116 (1989) pp.184-185; and J.-P. Loustaud, "Limoges, rue Sainte-Félicité, Théatre romain, Sondage," *TAL* 10 (1990) pp.148-149.

[12] Y. de Kisch, "Vestiges des thermes gallo-romains de la place des Jacobins à Limoges," *BSAHL* 102 (1975) pp.220-221; J.-P. Loustaud, "Thermes antiques de la place Franklin-Roosevelt," *BSAHL* 104 (1977) p.186, 105 (1978) p.194; and *CAG* 87, pp.97-100.

[13] *CAG* 87, pp.107-110.

[14] *CAG* 87, pp.111-113; J.-P. Loustaud, "Les Thermes de la villa gallo-romaine de Brachaud. Synthèse d'une évolution," *TAL* 3 (1982) pp.31-57; J.-P. Loustaud, J. Perrier, "Le monnaies de la villa gallo-romaine de Brachaud, 1974-1986," *BSAHL* 122 (1994) pp.4-11; A. Hochuli-Gysel, J.-P. Loustaud, "La verrerie de la village de Brachaud, près de Limoges," *BSAHL* 121 (1993) pp.21-48; G. Pichaud, "Vestiges gallo-romains à Brachaud (Limoges)," *BSAHL* 100 (1973) pp.288, 291.

[15] See, e.g., J. Mathevet, "Villa gallo-romaine da La Vaclette (Magnac-Laval)," *BSAHL* 93 (1966) p.216; and *CAG* 87, passim.

[16] *CAG* 87, p.80; J.-P. Loustaud, "La voirie d'Augustoritum," *TAL* 5 (1984) pp.57-80.

[17] "opere mirifico constructus": Geoffroy de Vigeois, *Chronicon Lemovicense*, in P. Labbé ed., *Nova bibliotheca manuscriptorum librorum* (Paris, 1657) 2.335.

[18] *CAG* 87, pp.88-91; P. Saumande, "Aqueduc du quartier des Arènes à Limoges," *BSAHL* 96

deep, that was begun in the first and second centuries and much expanded from the third to the middle of the fourth centuries.

On a wider scale, the city was part of the network of roads that knit together the cities and villages of Gaul.[19] Three major roads intersected at or near Limoges. To the east and west ran the road from Augustonemetum Arvernorum (Clermont)[20] to Mediolanum Santonum (Saintes).[21] The road linking Avaricum Biturigum (Bourges) and Burdigala (Bordeaux)[22] led out of Limoges to the north, where the next major stop was at Argentomagus (Argenton/St-Marcel),[23] and to the southwest via Vesuna Petrocoriorum (Périgueux). An alternate route branched off from the road to Clermont and arrived at Bourges by a more easterly route. Yet another road led north-west to Limonum Pictavorum (Poitiers) and south-south-east to the *vicus* (hamlet) of Userca (Uzerche), which was located on a high promontory overlooking the Vézère river.[24] There it split; one branch went south via Divona Cadurcorum (Cahors), and the other south-east, where it connected with the road between Segodunum Rutenorum (Rodez) and Anderitum Gabalorum (Javols). A road continued on from Rodez to the south and Provence.

There were a number of communities in the area around Limoges, some of which were associated with or referred to by Ruricius. Just to the north lay Catalacum (Chaptelat) and Andecamulum (Rancon);[25] and further along, on the

---

(1969), and 97 (1970) p.277.

[19] *CAG* 87, p.35; *CAGR* 14, pp.30-32.

[20] The road from Limoges to Clermont in particular has received much attention; see P. Ganne, "Un carrefour d'anciens itinéraires aux confins de l'Auvergne et du Limousin (Commune de Flayat, Creuse)," *TAL* 14 (1994) pp.115-135; M.-A. Dostes, "L'ancienne voie de Clermont à Limoges: Recherches à Saint-Agnant-près-Crocq (Creuse)," *TAL* 6 (1985) pp.97-99; J.-F. Priot, "La voie romaine de Limoges à Ahun à la Vergnolle. Le Chatenet-en-Dognon (Haute-Vienne)," *TAL* 5 (1984) pp.77-80; P. Bordier, J.-M. Desbordes, O. Hernandez, "La voie romaine du Bois d'Ahun," *TAL* 2 (1981) pp.9-16.

[21] J.-M. Desbordes, "Enquête sur le tracé de la voie antique de Limoges à Saintes entre Aurence et Vienne," *TAL* 12 (1992) pp.113-121; and J.-P. Clapham, J.-M. Desbordes, "Les itinéraires antiques de Limoges à Saintes. Etat des recherches," *TAL* 9 (1989) pp.35-44.

[22] R. Couraud, "La voie de Burdigala-Augustoritum-Avaricum dans la traversée de la region d'Ambazac," *BSAHL* 89 (1962) pp.204-206.

[23] J.-M. Desbordes, "La station routière de Praetorium dans la cité des Lemovices: Hypothèses et realité," *TAL* 14 (1994) pp.17-22.

[24] *CAG* 19, pp.186-7. Uzerche once was thought to be the site of Caesar's Uxellodunum. It had an early cult of St. Peter and was under the jurisdiction of the bishops of Limoges. Merovingian gold coins of the seventh century have the markings *Userca cas* and *User Castro* (i.e. "Userca castrum": "the stronghold of Userca"). An *ecclesiola* ("chapel") of St. Eulalia was built in 987. See L. Bournazel, G. Reboul, J.-M. Desbordes, "Les origines d'Uzerche," *TAL* 2 (1981) pp.97-104; and D. Gaborit-Chopin, "La date du recueil liturgique d'Uzerche consacré à l'école des Beaux-Arts de Paris," *Scriptorium* 24 (1970) pp.40-43.

[25] *CAG* 87, pp.67-9; *CAGR* 14, p.108; and J.-M. Desbordes, J. Perrier, "Aux origines de Rancon," *BSSHAC* 109 (1982) pp.43-52. Note *CIL* 13.1449: "NVMINIBUS AVG(ustorum)/ FANVM PLVTONIS/ANDECAMVLEN/SES DE SVO POSVER(unt)."

road to Argentomagus, lay Brigate (Bridiers).[26] A bit to the west of the city, in the direction of Saintes, was the villa of Comodoliacus (St-Junien) and the *mutatio* (road station) at Cassinomagus (Chassenon).[27] To the south-south-west, between Limoges and Périgueux, were the hamlets of Gemiliacum (Jumilhac-le-Grand) and Attanum (St-Yrieux-le-Perche);[28] and, on the boundary between the territories of the two cities, the *mutatio* at Fines (probably Firbeix),[29] on the current border between the départements of Haute-Vienne and Dordogne). Also to the south, but more easterly, between Limoges and Cahors, were hamlets such as the aforementioned Userca; Briva, or Briva Curretia (Brive-la-Gaillarde);[30] Exando (Yssandon);[31] Argenta or Argentacum (Argentat);[32] and Gurdo, later Gordonium (Gourdon), located just within the territory of Cahors.[33] Stations on the Roman roads to Clermont included Praetorium (Sauviat-sur-Vige?);[34] modern Pontarion; Acitodunum (Ahun); Fines (Giat or Voingt), on the boundary between the territories of Limoges and Clermont; and Ub...,[35]; not to mention modern Védrenne,[36] before Acitodunum; and the *castrum* (stronghold) of Issando (Issoudun),[37] just beyond. Rivers included the

---

[26] D. Dussot, "Nouvelles decouvertes dans le vicus gallo-romain de Bridiers," *TAL* 11 (1991) pp.97-102; and J. Perrier, "Partie d'un trésor monetaire antique trouvé à Bridiers," *TAL* 7 (1987) pp.175-7.

[27] J.-H. Moreau, "Cassinomagus, Chassenon," *BSAHL* 90 (1963) pp.285-6; P. Saumande, "Chassenon. Problèmes hydrauliques," *BSAHL* 123 (1995) pp.11-22; and J.-H. Moreau, "Recueil de textes et fouilles à Chassenon (Charente)," *BSAHL* 87 (1960) p.264.

[28] *CAG* 87, pp.201-202; *CAGR* 14, pp.39-40. It was the site of a Merovingian mint that issued gold *tremisses* with the legend *Sco Aredio* ("at St. Aredius").

[29] Probably not Thiviers, which is south of Jumilhac-le-Grande, for this would have put it under the jurisdiction of Périgueux: see *Epist.* 2.6 below.

[30] *CAG* 46, pp.70-76. Briva was located on the Corrèze river, where the road from Limoges to Toulouse met that from Lyon to Bordeaux. It had been occupied since the Flavian period and was the site of a pottery workshop: See J.-M. Desbordes, C. Gautrand-Moser, G. Lintz, F. Moser, *Les origines de Brive* (Brive-la-Gaillarde, 1982); F. Moser, "Les ateliers gallo-romains de Brive (Corrèze)," *TAL* 9 (1988) pp.77-89; and C. Moser-Gautrand, F. Moser, "Les figurines gallo-romaines en terre cuite de Brive," *TAL* 2 (1981) pp.17-58. In the late sixth century, Briva was described as a *vicus* by Gregory of Tours; it was under the ecclesiastical jurisdiction of Limoges and had a church of a Spanish St. Martin, believed to have been a disciple of Martin of Tours (Greg.Tur. *HF* 7.10). For discussion, see *Epist.* 2.24 below.

[31] West-north-west of Briva: see the *Vita Vincentiani* in Appendix III below.

[32] J.-M. Courteix, "Aux origines d'Argentat," *TAL* 12 (1992) pp.143-151; in the seventh century the *vicus* Argenta issued gold coins with the legends *Argenta vic*, *Argentat vic f*, and *Argentate fit*.

[33] *CAG* 46, p.85; Aubrun, *Limoges*, p.94.

[34] Desbordes, "Praetorium."

[35] The name in the Peutinger table is incomplete.

[36] P. Freytet, et al., "Le site de la Védrenne (la Chapelle-Saint-Martial, Creuse). Etude d'une villa gallo-romaine, et de son environnement," *TAL* 10 (1990) pp.33-43; and P. Freytet, "La villa de la Védrenne (Commune de la Chapelle-Saint-Martial, Creuse): Nouvelles decouvertes," *TAL* 6 (1985) pp.105-110.

[37] See Ps.-Fredegarius: *MGH SRM* 2.189. Aubrun, *Limoges*, p.125, prefers Ayen, south of Li-

Vigenna (Vienne), bordering Limoges on the east; and the Doranonia or Duranius (Dordogne) and Visera (Vézère) to the south.

During the third century and later, as in many other places in the Empire, there was a reorientation of urban life at Limoges, with an increasing focus on the development of the suburbs and countryside. The elaborate public and private buildings began to be pillaged for their building materials.[38] The population retreated from the unfortified[39] central city to a more defensible hilly region in the eastern section of the city; in the Middle Ages, the term *civitas* referred only to this area. The Limousin seems, however, to have been little affected by the "barbarian invasions" of the fifth century,[40] and the wall that eventually developed around the medieval *civitas* is first attested in the late sixth century.[41] It would seem that by the time of Ruricius much of the Roman city was in a state of advanced disrepair. New public construction, as will be seen below, was limited almost exclusively to churchbuilding.

Aquitania Prima

In the provincial reorganization of Diocletian (284-305), Limoges was included in the province of Aquitania Prima, in the diocese of Aquitania (later known as Quinque Provinciae in the fourth century and Septem Provinciae in the fifth), and in the the the prefecture of Gaul. The province was bordered by the provinces of Aquitania Secunda on the west, Novempopulana to the southwest, Narbonensis Prima on the south, Viennensis on the east, Lugdunensis Prima on the northeast, Lugdunensis Quarta (also known as Lugdunensis Senonia) on the north, and Lugdunensis Tertia on the northwest, the last three being in the diocese of Gallia. It was administered by a *praeses*, the lowest-ranking type of provincial governor. The metropolitan city was Bourges, with the other *civitates* being Clermont; Rodez; Cahors; Javols; Albia (Albi); and Reussium, the *civitas Vellavorum* (St-Paulien in Velay). Because the secular and ecclesiastical administra-

---

moges, to Issoudun.

[38] *CAG* 87, p.80.

[39] Unlike other Gallo-Roman cities, Limoges seems not to have developed an extensive fortification system in the Late Empire, despite assumptions (*CAG* 87, p.117) that the city must have had walls by c.300. See R.M. Butler, "Late Roman Town Walls in Gaul," *Archaeological Journal* 116 (1959) pp.25-50.

[40] M. Bloch, "Traces des invasions germaniques en Creuse," *MSSNAC* 27 (1938) pp.7-9; and M. Vazeille, "L'époque barbare en Haute-Corrèze," *BSLSAC* (1956) pp.108-118.

[41] "area cum domo nostra intramuranea Lemovicinae civitatis" ("the area with our dwelling within the walls of the city of Limoges"): *Testamentum Aredii* (AD 572) (Pardessus, *Diplomata* 1.136-141 = Aubrun, *Limoges*, pp.417-419); see also Greg.Tur. *Glor.conf.* 102; and *Vita Aridii* 46 (*MGH SRM* 3.590), "formidantes moenia rumpere." For later mentions, see Z. Tomieux, "Etude topographique d'un diplôme de 626," *BSAHL* 39(1891) pp.431-440; and *Idem*, "Partage de terres en Limousin d'après un diplôme de 626," *MSSNAC* 7(1892) pp.397-399.

tions both were configured in the same manner, the normal course of administrative affairs meant that the bishop of Limoges tended to have a rather greater degree of interaction with cities in its own province than with others.

By the fourth century, Aquitania had gained a reputation as both a rich agricultural area and a center of learning. Bordeaux became one of the most famous educational centers of the Roman world.[42] In the mid fifth century, Salvian of Marseille rhetorically recalled Aquitania's prosperity:

> There is no doubt that the Aquitanians and Novempopulanans possessed nearly the core of all Gaul and the richness of total fertility, and not only fertility, but also those things that sometimes are preferred to fertility: delighftulness, beauty, and pleasure. Indeed, the entire region there was so completely interwoven with vines or blooming with meadows or distinctive with cultivation or endowed with fruit or alluring with woodlands or gushing with springs or flowing with rivers or burgeoning with harvests that the freeholders and landlords seem to have possessed not so much a bit of soil as the image of paradise.[43]

But Salvian also had another agenda, to contrast the past prosperity of Aquitania with the miseries of his own time. For by then, Rome's political fortunes in the west were in decline, and the inhabitants of Aquitania were among the first to suffer the effects.

In 418, the Visigoths were settled in Aquitania Secunda and Novempopulana. Subsequently, they gradually extended their control over all of southwestern Gaul. In 475, the emperor Julius Nepos (474-480) ceded the Auvergne, and in 477, the last Roman cities in Provence were occupied. Kings such as Theoderic II (453-466), Euric (466-484), and Alaric II (484-507), modelled their administration on that of Rome. Gallo-Romans served in both civil and military offices. Under Euric, one encounters Victorius, the *comes et dux Aquitaniae Primae* ("Count and Duke of First Aquitania"); Vincentius, the *dux Hispaniarum* ("Duke of Spain"); the "admiral" Namatius who commanded Visigothic naval forces at Saintes; and the *iudex* ("Governor") Potentinus. At court, the jurist Leo of Narbonne served as a *consiliaris* ("Counsellor") of Euric, and he retained this posi-

---

[42] See Ausonius, *Commemoratio professorum Burdigalensium* ("Commemoration of the Professors of Bordeaux"), passim.

[43] "Nemini dubium est Aquitanos ac Novempopulos medullam fere omnium Galliarum et uber totius fecunditatis habuisse, nec solum fecunditatis, sed, quae praeponi interdum fecunditati solent, iucunditatis, pulchritudinis, voluptatis. adeo illic omnis admodum regio aut intertexta vineis aut florulenta pratis aut distincta culturis aut condita pomis aut amoenata lucis aut inrigua fontibus aut interfusa fluminibus aut crinita messibus fuit, ut vere possessores ac domini terrae illius non tam soli istius portionem quam paradisi imaginem possedisse videantur": *De gubernatione dei* ("On the Governance of God") 7.2.

tion under Alaric II.[44]   On a lesser, yet equally revealing, scale, the Roman
Calminius served in the Visigothic army.

In the correspondence of Ruricius one likewise finds examples of Romans
in civil offices during the reign of Alaric II, including Ruricius' friends Elaphius
(*Epist.* 2.7), Praesidius (*Epist.* 2.12 = 2.53), and Eudomius (*Epist.* 2.39; Caes. E-
pist. "Dum nimium").[45]   Eudomius, like Leo, seems to have had a responsible
position at court, whereas the others had more local duties.

Christianization and Ecclesiastical Geography

Like other cities in Gaul and the Roman Empire, Limoges felt the effects of
the growth of the Christian religion.[46]   Although it certainly was present, there
is little evidence for Christianity in Limoges before the time of Ruricius himself.
According to Gregory of Tours, seven bishops were sent to evangelize Gaul during the consulate of Decius and Gratius in AD 250; one, a certain Martial, went
to Limoges.[47]   This tale placed Limoges with Tours, Arles, Narbonne, Toulouse, Paris, and Clermont as one of the most ancient sees of Gaul.

Between Martial and Ruricius, the episcopal *fasti* ("catalogue") of Limoges
list Aurelianus, Ebbulus, Atticus, Emerinus, Hermogenianus, Adelfius, Dativus,
Adelfius II, Exsuperius, and Astidius.[48]   None of these persons, however, is
independently attested, and it may be that Limoges did not actually secure its
first bishop until the beginning of the fifth century,[49] for a list of noteworthy
bishops of Aquitania compiled at that time cited bishops from Toulouse, Vienne,
Bordeaux, Albi, Clermont, Cahors, and Périgueux, but none from Limoges.[50]
Either Limoges did not have a bishop then, or if it did, he was remarkably un-
distinguished.   In fact, the existence of a bishop at Limoges is not firmly attested until ca. 474, when Sidonius Apollinaris reported that the sees of Bordeaux,
Périgueux, Limoges, Javols, Eauze, Bazas, St-Bertrand, and Auch all had fallen
vacant.[51]   Only after the death of king Euric on 28 December 484 was another
bishop of Limoges appointed, in the person of Ruricius himself.

During the fourth century, as the city became suburbanized, the area around
the crypt of St. Martial in the northern sector developed into a large ceme-

---

[44] For these individuals, see Mathisen, *Aristocrats*, pp.126-128.
[45] See also *Epist.* 2.15 for an unnamed *iudex*.
[46] J. Becquet, "Les saints dans le culte en Limousin au Moyen-Age," *BSAHL* 119 (1991) pp.26-
59, cf. pp.58-9 (without mention of Ruricius); and M. Duchein, *Les textes anterieurs à l'an mil
relatifs aux églises de Limoges*, vol.1 (Brunel, 1955) pp.387-400.
[47] *HF* 1.30.
[48] Aubrun, *Limoges*, pp.87-101; Duchesne, *Fastes* 2.48-49.
[49] Aubrun, *Limoges*, pp. 87-121.
[50] Paulinus of Nola, *apud* Greg.Tur. *HF* 2.13.
[51] *Epist.*7.6.

tery.[52] Gregory of Tours reports that a sanctuary was built on the site;[53] and the will of Aredius, abbot of Attanum, mentions in 572 those who were "serving St. Martial,"[54] perhaps monks in a monastery associated with the church. Gregory also tells of a basilica at Limoges, probably the church of St-Pierre-du-Sépulcre, that was built by Ruricius' grandson Ruricius.[55] It measured 31 by 6 meters, and was located to the east of the crypt, allowing access to it. Gregory also notes an *ecclesia*, perhaps the church of St. Stephen, located "within the walls";[56] a baptistry was placed a few meters from its north door. Other churches included a church of St. Julian founded by Aredius;[57] and a church and monastery of St. Augustine, built by Ruricius himself and discussed below.

The Visigothic Kingdom and the Coming of the Franks

Ruricius' episcopate spanned the last years of the Visigothic kingdom of Toulouse, and his city was under Visigothic authority throughout nearly all, if not all, of his tenure. Euric's successor, Alaric II, the namesake of the Alaric who sacked Rome in 410, assumed office only shortly before Ruricius, so in this regard they were coevals. Alaric became king at the same time that Clovis (481-511), king of one of several groups of Franks, was expanding his influence in northern Gaul. In 486, for example, Clovis defeated the Roman Syagrius of Soissons,[58] and soon thereafter he overcame the Thuringian Franks.[59]

The 490s saw several poorly documented Frankish attacks upon Aquitania. An Italian chronicle notes under the year 496, "Alaric, in the twelfth year of his reign, captured Saintes."[60] Such a statement, of course, presupposes that someone else, presumably the Franks, had captured Saintes at some earlier time. A Visigothic opportunity to retake the city might have come when Clovis was forced to confront the Alamanni in the same year. During the ensuing battle Clovis was said to have promised to become a Christian if the Franks were

---

[52] J.-F. Priot, "La nécropole suburbaine et le carrefour de Saint-Cessateur à Limoges," *TAL* 1 (1979-80) pp.15-20.

[53] Greg.Tur. *Glor.conf.* 26; two of Martial's priests also were entombed there, and in Gregory's time there was an oratory on the site. Three medieval crypts survive, of which the first dates to the sixth century, the first sarcophagi having been placed there earlier (*CAG* 87, p.119); see also the *Vita Martialis antiquior*: *AASS* June V p.555.

[54] "servientes sancti Martialis": Aubrun, *Limoges*, pp.413-418.

[55] Or perhaps St-Pierre-du-Queyroix; see *CAG* 87, p.119.

[56] "intra muros": Greg.Tur. *Glor.conf.* 102; *CAG* 87, p.118: perhaps on the site of the present cathedral.

[57] *CAG* 87, p.119: situated on the modern Rue des Penitents-Blancs.

[58] Greg.Tur. *HF* 2.27. Syagrius fled to Toulouse and sought refuge with Alaric, who surrendered him to Clovis when the latter threatened to attack.

[59] *HF* 2.27, "in the tenth year of his reign," i.e. ca. 492.

[60] "Alaricus anno XII regni sui Santones obtinuit" (*Auct.prosp.haun.*: *MGH AA* 9.323).

victorious, as they in fact were.[61]

On Christmas day of this or perhaps the next year, Clovis fulfilled his vow.[62] His adoption of Nicene Christianity altered the balance of power in Gaul, for it created apprehensions among the Arian Visigoths about the loyalties of their Roman subjects.[63] Gregory of Tours noted, "At that time, many Gauls wished with the greatest desire to have the Franks as masters."[64] One affected Gaul was Volusianus, bishop of Tours ca. 489-496,[65] who, perhaps in the context of the Frankish raids of the mid 490s, wrote to Ruricius that he was "stupefied by fear of the enemy."[66] Subsequently, Volusianus fell afoul of the Visigoths: "Having been considered suspect by the Goths because he wished to subject himself to the rule of the Franks and having been condemned to exile in the city of Toulouse, he died there."[67] Given that Volusianus' death occurred ca. 496, at the very time of the Frankish occupation of Saintes, one might suppose that it was during these attacks that he came under suspicion.

Clovis soon renewed his attacks. His strategic position may have been strengthened by an alliance, perhaps facilitated by his baptism, with the Christian "Arborychi" (perhaps Armoricans) living in Lugdunensis III, northwest of Tours.[68] This would have given him safe access to the Visigothic kingdom south of the Loire. The aforementioned Italian chronicle notes, for 498: "In the fourteenth year of Alaric the Franks captured Bordeaux and transferred it from

---

[61] Greg.Tur.HF 2.30, cf. 2.37, "in the fifteenth year of his reign," i.e. ca. 496.

[62] Gregory of Tour's statement (see preceding note) that the victory over the Alamanni took place in 496 provides a *terminus a quo* for the baptism; see R. Mathisen, "Clovis, Anastase, et Grégoire de Tours: Consul, patrice et roi," in M. Rouche ed., *Clovis, le Romain, le chrétien, l'Européen* (Paris, 1998) pp.395-407. There have been many suggestions for various later dates; see, e.g., D. Shanzer, "Dating the Baptism of Clovis: The Bishop of Vienne vs the Bishop of Tours," *Early Medieval Europe* 7 (1998) pp.29-57.

[63] The Romans were Nicene Christians and adhered to the creed of the Council of Nicaea (AD 325), which taught that all three persons of the Trinity were equal. The Visigoths, and other barbarian peoples, espoused Arianism, whose primary tenet was that Christ, the Son, was in some way unequal to God, the Rather.

[64] "Multi iam tunc ex Galliis habere Francos dominos summo desiderio cupiebant" (*HF* 2.35).

[65] Gregory reports (*HF* 2.26, 10.31) that Volusianus was bishop for seven years and his successor Verus for eleven, and that Verus' successor Licinius was in office by 507 (Greg.Tur. *HF* 2.39, 43). This would put Verus' death in late 506 or early 507, with his tenure being ca. 496-507 and Volusianus' ca. 489-496. See Duchesne, *Fastes* 2.305; and R. Mathisen, "The Family of Georgius Florentius Gregorius and the Bishops of Tours," *Medievalia et Humanistica* 12 (1984) pp.83-95. Gregory's statement elswhere (*HF* 2.43) that Clovis death in 511 occurred in the eleventh year of Licinius, must be mistaken, unless, perhaps, Licinius began serving as bishop of Tours while Verus was still living in exile.

[66] "nam quod scribis te metu hostium hebetem factum" (*Epist.* 2.65).

[67] "suspectus habitus a Gothis, quod se Francorum ditionibus subdere vellet, apud urbem Tholosam exilio condempnatus, in eo obiit" (Greg.Tur. *HF* 10.31, cf. 2.26). Elsewhere (*HF* 2.29), Gregory claims that Volusianus was exiled to Spain.

[68] Procopius, *The Vandal War* 1.12.13; see B.S. Bachrach, "Procopius and the Chronology of Clovis' Reign," *Viator* 1 (1970) pp.21-31.

the authority of the Goths into their own possession, having taken captive the Gothic duke Suatrius."[69]

In 500, the Burgundian king Gundobad sent some Frankish captives "in exile to King Alaric at Toulouse."[70] This might have given Alaric a bargaining chip for reaching a settlement with Clovis. For Gregory of Tours reports that afterward, "Alaric, king of the Goths, when he saw king Clovis unrelentingly defeating various nations, sent ambassadors to him, saying, 'If my brother wishes, he might decide that, with God's blessing, we should meet.' Clovis did not reject this suggestion and came to him. And meeting on an island of the Loire, which was next to the village of Amboise in the terrirory of Tours, they ate and drank together, and having promised friendship to each other, they departed in peace."[71] One might imagine that Alaric returned his Frankish captives, and probably was happy to be rid of them. Clovis would have done likewise; indeed these perhaps are to be identified with the "people, recently captive," whom Avitus of Vienne complimented Clovis for setting free.[72]

The status quo seems to have been maintained between the two kingdoms until ca. 505, when the Visigothic position worsened. For one thing, Alaric's erstwhile ally Gundobad seems to have turned against him and besieged Arles, whose bishop Caesarius was exiled to Bordeaux after being accused of plotting to betray the city.[73] As for Clovis, he undertook another campaign against the Alamanni, in which the latter were totally defeated; Theoderic, the Ostrogothic king of Italy, settled their remnants in Raetia and ordered Clovis to let them be.[74] This then left Clovis free to resume his attacks upon the Visigoths. A sign of these new troubles is seen at Tours, where Verus (ca. 497-507) suffered the same fate as his predecessor: "And he, because of his enthusiasm for the same cause, was considered suspect by the Goths, and having been carried off

---

[69] "Ann. XIIII Alarici Franci Burdigalam obtinuerunt et a potestate Gothorum in possessionem sui redegerunt capto Suatrio Gothorum duce" (ibid. 323).

[70] "Tolosae in exilium ad Alaricum regem" (Greg.Tur. *HF* 2.33); for date, Marius Aventicus, *Chronicle* s.a. 500: *MGH AA* 11.234.

[71] "Igitur Alaricus rex Gothorum, cum videret Chlodovechum regem gentes assidue debellare, legatos ad eum diriget, dicens, 'si frater meus velit, insederat animo, ut nos deo propitio pariter viderimus.' quod Chlodovechus non respuens, ad eum venit. coniunctique in insula Ligeris, quae erat iuxta vicum Ambaciensem territorium urbis Turonicae, simul locuti, comedentes pariter ac bibentes, promissa sibi amicitia, pacifeci discesserunt" (Greg.Tur. *HF* 2.35). Gregory places this incident between the Burgundian war in 500 and Clovis' invasion of Aquitania in 507.

[72] Avit. *Epist.* 46. As in all such campaigns, and as Ruricius and his correspondents richly attest, captives, such as the aforementioned Suatrius, would have been taken as a matter of course. And if Avitus was referring to Roman captives freed on this occasion, then the date of ca. 496 for Clovis' baptism would be corroborated: see Shanzer, "Clovis," p.54, "there is ... no *terminus post quem* for Clovis' conversion other than the freeing of the *populus captivus...*"

[73] *Vita Caesarii* 1.21.

[74] Cassiodorus, *Variae* 2.41; S.J.B. Barnish, *Cassiodorus: Variae* (Liverpool, 1992) pp.38-44; and *PLRE II*, pp.233-234.

into exile, he died."[75] Ruricius would have been bishop when all these events occurred, but, except for a few vague allusions, there is no reference to them either in his own letters or in those of his correspondents.

The End of the Kingdom of Toulouse

Faced with problems with Spain, with the Burgundians, and with the Franks, Alaric attempted to shore up his Gallo-Roman support. He authorized the compilation of a civil law code based upon existing Roman law. The result, in 506, was the issuance of the *Lex Romana Visigothorum* ("Roman Law of the Visigoths"), also known as the *Breviarium Alarici* ("Breviary of Alaric").[76] It was excerpted from the two sources of Roman law: the *leges* ("statutes") issued by Roman emperors and the *ius* ("legal commentary") put forth by Roman jurists. The former included a few entries from the *Codex Gregorianus* and *Codex Hermogenianus* ("Gregorian" and "Hermogenian Codes"), originally issued in the 290s under the emperor Diocletian; 398 constitutions (less than one-eighth of the total) from the *Codex Theodosianus* ("Theodosian Code"), issued in 438 by Theodosius II (402-450); and the *Novellae* ("Novels"), new imperial statutes issued between 438 and 471. The jurists cited were Gaius, Paul, and Papinian. By providing both a synthesis and a summary of previous Roman legal statutes and opinions, the *Breviarium* reinforced the view that the Visigothic kings were the direct successors of the Roman emperors, with full authority to determine, in concert with their Gallo-Roman subjects, what previous Roman legislation was valid in the Visigothic kingdom and what was not.

The same policy of conciliation extended into the religious sphere. After some discussions at Bordeaux (*Epist.* 2.33; Caes. *Epist.* "Dum nimium"), Caesarius of Arles was released from exile, and in 506 Alaric permitted Gallo-Roman bishops to convene a church council at Agatha (Agde). They began their canons by acknowledging their dependence on Alaric: "When in the name of the Lord, with the permission of Our Lord the Most Glorious, Magnificent and Pious King [Alaric] the blessed synod had gathered, and there with our knees bent to the ground we prayed for his kingdom and for his long life, so that the Lord might expand the realm of him who had granted us the opportunity to assemble..."[77] These sentiments are a far cry from the adversarial relationship that had existed with Alaric's father, Euric, and the reference to the expansion of the

---

[75] "et ipse pro memoratae causae zelo suspectus habitus a Gothis in exilio deductus vitam finivit" (Greg.Tur. *HF* 10.31).

[76] See R. Lambertini, *La codificazione di Alarico II* (Torino 1990).

[77] "cum in nomine domini ex permissu domini nostri gloriosissimi magnificentissimi piissimique regis... sancta synodus convenisset, ibique flexis in terram genibus, pro regno eius, pro longaevitate... deprecaremur, ut qui nobis congregationis permiserat potestatem, regnum eius dominus... extenderet..." (*CCL* 148.192).

kingdom could be an allusion to the impending hostilities with the Franks. The bishops went on to promulgate 49 canons dealing with various issues of ecclesiastical administration and discipline.[78]

It is impossible to say, however, where these initiatives and good intentions might have led, for Clovis was not to be forestalled. Gregory of Tours reports that Clovis declared, "I take it very ill that these Arians should hold so large a part of Gaul. Let us go and overcome them with God's help, and bring their land under our rule."[79] Theoderic the Ostrogoth attempted to avert a confrontation.[80] He offered to mediate the dispute, and he specifically forbade Clovis from attacking Alaric. All for nought. Gundobad went over to Clovis' side and in 507, apparently in the spring,[81] Clovis undertook his threatened invasion of the Visigothic kingdom. The end result was the destruction of the Visigothic army and the death of Alaric at Vouillé, just north of Poitiers.[82]

The Franks then proceeded to lay claim to most of the kingdom of Toulouse. Clovis' son Theoderic captured Albi, Rodez, and Clermont. Clovis left Poitiers, wintered in Bordeaux, then in 508 seized Toulouse and Angoulême, returning thence to Tours. There is no mention of the occupation of Limoges. All that remained to the Visigoths, now firmly entrenched in Spain, was Septimania, a coastal strip focused on Narbonne. The Gothic kingdom of Toulouse was at an end after a brief 87-year existence, and the history of post-Roman Gaul was to be written not by the Visigoths but by the Franks.

---

[78] *CCL* 148.189-228.

[79] *HF* 2.37.

[80] Cassiodorus, *Variorum* 3.1-4.

[81] The normal time for undertaking military campaigns. In addition, a soldier of Clovis stole hay from a poor man of Tours, which would not have been worth mentioning, it seems, in the summer or fall; and the Vienne river was swollen by heavy rains (*HF* 2.37). For the battle, see also *Chronica gallica a.511* s.a.507: *MGH AA* 9.665; *Chronica Caesaraugustana* s.a.507: *MGH AA* 11.222; Isidore of Seville, *Historia Gothorum* 36: *MGH AA* 11.281-282.

[82] See Greg.Tur. *Hist* 2.39, "in campo Vogladensi decimo ab urbe Pectava miliario" ("upon the field of Voglada at the tenth milestone from the city of Poitiers"). Vouillé is in fact on the Roman road about ten Roman miles from Poitiers. But this identification has been challenged on the basis of the seventh-century *Liber historiae Francorum*, which adds to Gregory's account the words "super fluvium Clinno" ("across the Clain River") (*LHF* 17: *SRM* 2.269), and, nowadays, Vouillé lies not on the Clain, but a tributary, the Auxances. As a result, an alternate site has been proposed, Voulon, located on the Clain south of Poitiers: see R.A. Geberding, *The Rise of the Carolingians and the Llber Historiae Francorum* (Oxford, 1987) p.41. But Voulon is 17 miles from Poitiers, and not on any Roman road, thus contradicting two of Gregory's (and the *LHF*'s) criteria. The answer to this apparent problem may be that, in antiquity, rivers bore the name of their downstream section. Upstream tributaries were not necessarily distinguished by separate names as in the modern day; indeed, we do not even know what the "main branch" of the Clain was considered to be in the seventh century. Vouillé, therefore, remains the most probable site of the decisive battle.

Limoges during the Merovingian Period

The subsequent history of Limoges during the Merovingian period (ca. 511-751) is poorly known. Gregory of Tours, for example, told of rioting there in 579 after King Chilperic I had imposed new taxes: the townspeople burned the tax registers and attempted to assassinate the *referendarius* ("Referendary") Mark.[83] He also reported that in 592, "At the city of Limoges many people were consumed by a celestial fire resulting from an insult to Sunday, because the people carried out public business on that day."[84] Otherwise, Gregory only mentions the city a few times in passing.[85]

Several residents had distinguished reputations. Aredius served first as *cancellarius* ("Chancellor") of king Theudebert (534-548), and then as abbot of the monastery at Attanum. Both his will, drawn up in 572, and his *vita* are still extant.[86] Another famous native son was Eligius, who was born at the *villa* of Catalacum (Chaptelat) six miles north of the city. After serving at the Frankish court he became bishop of Noyon in 641; in 632 he established a monastery at Solemniacum (Solignac), southwest of Limoges.[87]

Merovingian and medieval Limoges was only a fraction of the size of the Roman city, with much of the space having been turned over to cultivation, a circumstance that permits fruitful archaeological excavation in the modern day. It was the site of a prolific Merovingian royal mint; attested moneyers include Rumordus, Domovaldus, Ascaricus, Saersus, Ansoindus, Saturnus, and Daulfus. A solidus of 629/639 in the name of Dagobert I bears the mintmark "Lemmovix Agustoredo" (that is, "Augustoritum Lemovicorum", the ancient name of the city). The church of Limoges also struck gold and silver in the name of St. Martial, and known moneyers include Adicisilus, Domulfus, Marcinianus, and Erdolenus.[88] Otherwise, however, little is known of the fortunes of the city during this period.

---

[83] *HF* 5.28.

[84] *HF* 10.30. The same fire burned people at Tours, and there was a drought that destroyed the vegetation in the pastures. A possible non-divine interpretation of this fire from heaven could be activity by the volcanos of the Auvergne; see R. Mathisen, "Nature or Nurture — Some Perspectives on the Gallic Famine of Circa A.D. 470," *The Ancient World* 24 (1993) pp.91-105.

[85] *HF* 5.13 (ca. 577), 6.22 (582), 7.13 (583), 9.20 (588), and 10.29 (591).

[86] *Vita*: MGH SRM 3.576-612; will: Aubrun, *Limoges*, pp.413-417; see also *PL* 71.1119ff.

[87] See the *Vita Eligii*: MGH SRM 4.730-746; and ibid. 746-749 = Aubrun, *Limoges*, pp.417-419; also *CAG* 87, p.205; *CAGR* 14, p.47.

[88] See J. Lafaurie, "Monnaies mérovingiennes. Atelier de Limoges," in *Musée municipal de Limoges. Catalogue édité à l'occasion des Journées de la Société Française Numismatique, Limoges, 7-8 juin 1975* (Limoges, 1975) pp.60-63; *Idem*, "Les monnaies épiscopales de Limoges aux VIIe et VIIIe s.," *Bulletin de la société française de numismatique* 30 (1975) pp.778-782; M. Deloche, *Description des monnaies mérovingiennes en Limousin* (Paris, 1863).

RURICIUS' FAMILY, FRIENDS, AND HISTORICAL CONTEXT

Ruricius and His Family[1]

Few events of Ruricius' life can be dated with any precision. He became bishop of Limoges by the late 480s, when he corresponded in this capacity with bishop Aprunculus of Clermont, and he could not have become bishop before 485 because episcopal ordinations had been forbidden by the Visigothic king Euric. He served until at least late 506, when he penned several well-dated letters shortly after the Council of Agde, but none of his letters can be securely dated to any later time. In addition, Ruricius eventually became a great-grandfather, suggesting that he must have lived to be about 65 or 70 at least. If he died ca. 510,[2] this would put his birthdate circa the early 440s. Given that at least one of Ruricius' sons was old enough to be a relatively senior cleric by the mid to late 480s, he could hardly have been born much later, and because he seems to have been rather younger than Sidonius Apollinaris, who was born ca. 432,[3] one likewise might conclude that Ruricius was born ca. 440/445.

Ruricius is equally uncommunicative about his place of origin. Even though he served as bishop of Limoges, he gives no indication that this was his native place. Indeed, he rarely discusses the city, and he never mentions it by name. His most explicit reference to his episcopal see is an allusion to its insignificance (*humilitas*).[4] This sentiment is similar to that of Eutropius, who ca. 460 was reluctant to become bishop of Orange because it had insufficient wealth and status.[5] Perhaps Ruricius, too, had higher aspirations.

---

[1] See H. Hagendahl, *La correspondance de Ruricius* (Göteborg, 1952) pp.3-11; B. Krusch, "De Ruricio episcopo Lemovicensi," *MGH AA* 8.lxii-lxxx; R.W. Mathisen, *The Ecclesiastical Aristocracy of Fifth-Century Gaul: A Regional Analysis of Family Structure* (diss. Univ. of Wisconsin, 1979: Ann Arbor, 1980), passim, and *Idem*, "Epistolography, Literary Circles, and Family Ties in Late Roman Gaul," *Transactions of the American Philological Society* 111 (1981) pp.95-109 = *Idem*, *Studies in the History, Literature, and Society of Late Antiquity* (Amsterdam, 1991) pp.13-26; and C. Settipani, "Ruricius Ier évêque de Limoges et ses relations familiales," *Francia* 18 (1991) pp.195-222.

[2] See below for further discussion of Ruricius' date of death.

[3] See C.E. Stevens, *Sidonius Apollinaris and His Age* (Oxford, 1933); and Ruricius, *Epist.* 1.8-9, 16 and the related letters of Sidonius below.

[4] *Epist.* 2.33; Limoges is never cited by name in Ruricius' letter collection, and appears only as a scribal comment at the end of the collection, viz. "The letters of Lord Ruricius, Bishop of Limoges, end." Other soucres connecting Ruricius to Limoges are collected in Appendix III.

[5] *Vita Eutropii*: P. Varin ed., "Vie de saint Eutrope évêque d'Orange," *Bulletin du Comité Historique des Monuments Ecrits de l'Histoire de France* 1 (1849) p.56: Eutropius complained because he was not "received by a church overflowing with wealth, puffed up with its privilege, and restless with its retinue of nobles."

Ruricius' *patria* might be inferred from the places that he does mention by name, all of which lay to the south of Limoges.[6] Gurdo, for example, where Ruricius participated in a church festival and probably owned property (*Epist.* 1.7, 1.14), is assumed to be modern Gourdon, located in Quercy, in the territory of Cahors.[7] Ruricius also tells of residing at a villa called Decaniacum (*Epist.* 2.63) which, if it is correctly identified as Dégagnac,[8] was located about 8 kilometers southwest of Gurdo and would have been Ruricius' property in that area. Mentions of other places south of Limoges, such as Gemiliacum (Jumilhac-le-Grand), the subject of a dispute with Chronopius of Périgueux (*Epist.* 2.6); Briva Curretia (Brive-la-Gaillarde), the site of a church festival (*Epist.* 2.24); Userca (Uzerche), which had a church under Ruricius' jurisdiction (*Epist.* 2.20); and the Duranius (Dordogne) and Visera (Vézère) rivers, coupled with his failure to name places elsewhere, also document Ruricius' interest in this region.

Another holding administered by Ruricius is mentioned in the late *Vita Juniani* ("Life of Junianus"), according to which Ruricius permitted the hermit Amandus to settle "in a place of great solitude, on the estate called Comodoliacus," identified as St-Junien, on the right bank of the Vienne river west of Limoges.[9] This property, however, may have belonged to the church of Limoges and not to Ruricius personally.

A discussion of Ruricius' family background might begin with the observation that the bishops of Limoges in general and Ruricius' family in particular have some connections to one of the most distinguished aristocratic families of Rome. In the late sixth century, for example, Venantius Fortunatus, speaking of

---

[6] See Aubrun, *Limoges*, p.97.

[7] Demeulenaere, *CCL* 64.305; Engelbrecht, *CSEL* 21.lxv; Hagendahl, *Ruricius*, p.5; and Krusch, *MGH AA* 8.lxiii, all identify Gurdo as Gourdon (Lot), northwest of Cahors. See also Aubrun, *Limoges*, p.94; *CAG* 46, p.85; R. Bulit, *Gourdon. Les origines, les seigneurs, les consuls et la communauté jusqu'à la fin du XIVe siècle* (Toulouse, 1925); and Abbé Gary, "Tombe à Prouilhac près de Gourdon," *BSELSAL* 22 (1897) p.78. The place currently has vestiges of Gallo-Roman construction, and there have been finds of coins dating to Constantine (306-337). But other places also have this name, such as Gourdon-Murat (Corrèze), southeast of Limoges near the upper Vézère, which became a parish during Carolingian times and has evidence of an early imperial villa: see Aubrun, *Limoges*, pp. 281,286,339; and J.-L. Antignac, "Deux fragments de poterie sigillée à Gourdon-Murat," *Lemouzi* 46 (1973) pp.256-257; and note also a "monasterium Gurthonense" at Gourdon near Chalon-sur-Saône (Greg.Tur. *Glor.conf.* 85).

[8] See M. Aussel, "Première mention de Dégagnac dans l'histoire écrité à l'occasion du passage de Ruricius," *BSELSAL* 109 (1988) pp.221-228.

[9] "in agro ... cuius nominis vocabulum Comodoliacus dicitur" (*Vita Juniani* 3: *MGH SRM* 3.377-379); see also Greg.Tur. *Glor.conf.* 101; and C. Lacorre, "Les origines de Saint-Junien: Elements de recherche," *TAL* 1 (1979/80) pp.69-81, who suggests that Amandus settled there ca. 500. The finding of a solidus of the emperor Libius Severus (461-465) nearby suggests activity in this area during the later fifth century; see *CAG* 87, pp.176-177. Note also J. Arbellot, *Chronique de Maleu* (St-Junien/Paris, 1848), pp.8-15, citing the *Vetus chronicum abbatiae Comodoliacensis seu s. Juniani ad Vigennam* of AD 1316, which describes Commodoliacus as a *vicus* or *mansus* ("lodging-place").

Ruricius and his homonymous grandson, referred to "The twin Rurician flowers, to whom Rome was joined through the parental eminence of the Anicii."[10] The Anicii were the aristocratic family of Rome *par excellence*, and family members held manifold consulates and prefectures. Now, two names that appear early in the episcopal catalogue of Limoges, Adelfius and Hermogenianus, were in fact used by the Italian Anicii during the fourth century. One notes, for example,[11] Clodius Celsinus *signo* Adelfius, the father of Q. Clodius Hermogenianus who married Tyrrania Anicia Juliana. Their daughter Anicia Faltonia Proba married Sextus Petronius Probus, whose children included 1) Anicius Hermogenianus Olybrius, who married Anicia Juliana, 2) Anicius Probinus, whose daughter Anicia Italica married Valerius Faltonius Adelfius, and 3) Anicius Probus, who married an Adelfia. But just how the Italian Anicii were related, if at all, to Ruricius and the bishops Adelfius and Hermogenianus is unclear. Only one of these Italians is known to have had any association with Gaul: Petronius Probus, prefect of Gaul in the 360s. This would be the approximate time that Hermogenianus and Adelfius[12] supposedly were bishops of Limoges, but it would be most speculative to suggest that there was any connection.

Another possible tie between the imperial aristocracy and fifth-century Limoges might be attested by an ivory diptych announcing the consulate, in AD 428, of Fl. Constantius Felix, patrician and master of soldiers from 425 until 430.[13] In 1461 half of it was used at St-Junien on the cover of a life of Ruricius' grandson Ruricius II Proculus.[14] Perhaps the Italian connections of Ruricius' family resulted in the delivery of the diptych, and its use with the *vita* may have been the result of some tradition connecting it to Ruricius' family. Curiously, moreover, the first leaf of a another consular diptych, that of Procopius Anthemius, consul in 515 and the son of the western emperor Anthemius (467-472), also turned up at Limoges, being first attested in 1708,[15] and yet another leaf,

---

[10] "Ruricii gemini flores, quibus Aniciorum / juncta parentali culmine Roma fuit" (*Carm.* 6.1): see Appendix II for full translation.

[11] See *PLRE I* and *II* for all these individuals.

[12] Others of these names also were associated with Gaul. In 511 an "Adelfius episcopus de Ratiate" subscribed to the Council of Orléans (*CCL* 148A.13-19). Ratiatum, modern Retz or Rézé, and also known as Portus Pictonum, was in the territory of Poitiers, and Adelfius may have withdrawn there after the battle of Vouillé in 507 (see above). Note also a rhetor Adelphius, of indeterminate date and provenance (Sid. Apoll. *Epist.* 5.10.3; *PLRE I*, p.14), and a *dux* Hermogenes who served in Gaul in 369 (Amm. 28.2.6: *PLRE I*, p.424).

[13] See *CAG* 87 p.177; and *CIL* 13.3.2.747-748; the first leaf survives in Paris; the second has been lost since the early nineteenth century. For diptychs in general, see R. Delbrück, *Die konsularen diptychen und verwandten Denkmäler* (Berlin, 1936). Felix: *PLRE II* no.14, pp.461-462. Virtually nothing is known of Felix' family; his name and prominence might suggest a tie to the patrician, and emperor in 421, Fl. Constantius (*PLRE II*, pp.321-325).

[14] For the name of the younger Ruricius, see the *Vita Juniani* 6: *MGH SRM* 3.378-9: "Proculus seu Ruricius"; for discussion, see Appendix III.

[15] *CAG* 87 p.140; and *CIL* 1.1.848-749; it was last attested in the nineteenth century. Also cir-

from a consular diptych of the emperor Anastasius of AD 517, surfaced at Limoges in 1773.[16] The association of no less than three rare consular diptychs with Limoges is striking, and certainly merits some explanation. One possibility is that at least some of them attest to the ties of Ruricius' family to Italy.[17]

Such, then, is the evidence connecting Ruricius, Limoges, and its bishops to the imperial aristocracy. It is very scanty, and, except for Venantius Fortunatus' terse comment, primarily by inference. Even if Ruricius was related to the Italian Anicii in some distant way, he did not correspond with anyone who is known to have been even remotely connected with them, nor did he acknowledge any kind of relation to them.

Closer to home, Ruricius also was related to some of the most blue-blooded aristocrats of Gaul through his marriage, perhaps ca. 460,[18] to Hiberia, whose family seems to have been rather more prominent at that time even than his own. Hiberia was the daughter of the Arvernian senator Ommatius, who was a descendent of a patrician family.[19] Hiberia's patrician ancestor usually is identified as one Philagrius, whom a number of Gallic aristocrats had in their ancestry.[20] One was the emperor Eparchius Avitus (455-456), indicating that Hiberia's family was related not only to the Aviti, but also, as a consequence, to the family of Sidonius Apollinaris, who had married Avitus' daughter Papianilla.[21] This family connection helps to account not only for the important role played by inhabitants of the Auvergne in Ruricius' correspondence, but also for the pursuit of career opportunities there by some of his sons, not to mention the marriage of his grandson Parthenius to the daughter of Eparchius Avitus' son Agricola (*Epist.* 2.32). And Ruricius' family ties to Sidonius and Avitus would have connected him, in turn, to other influential Gauls of the early sixth century, such Magnus Felix Ennodius of Arles, who later became bishop of Pavia (ca. 514-521), and Alcimus Ecdicius Avitus, bishop of Vienne (ca. 490-518).[22]

---

culating in Gaul was a diptych of Fl. Astyrius, who commenced his consulate at Arles on 1 January 449 (*CIL* 1.1.748).

[16] *CAG* 87, pp.140-141; it is now in the Hermitage in St. Petersburg.

[17] In this regard, one might note that it was the emperor Anthemius who made Ruricius' friend Sidonius patrician and prefect of Rome.

[18] *PLRE II*, p.960, suggests that they were married by 469, but given that they had adult sons in the 480s (*Epist.* 2.57-58), this is certainly too late.

[19] Ommatius: *PLRE II*, pp.804-805; wrongly styled by Hagendahl, *Ruricius*, p.5, as a patrician himself. See Sidonius Apollinaris, *Carm.* 11.51, "qua socer Ommatius, magnorum maior avorum patriciaeque nepos gentis", and *Carm.* 17, both translated below.

[20] Philagrius seems to have lived during the fourth century, but is otherwise unknown: see *PLRE I*, p.693; Mathisen, *Ecclesiastical Aristocracy*, p.309; Settipani, "Ruricius," p.196; and *PLRE I*, p.693; see also Krusch, *MGH AA* 8.lxii. Sidonius corresponded with a Philagrius, probably a descendent of the patrician (*Epist.* 7.14).

[21] For these relationships, see Mathisen, "Epistolography."

[22] See Mathisen, "Epistolography," p.109.

As to Hiberia, Ruricius has little to say. Bishop Faustus of Riez, however, perhaps in acknowledgement of Ruricius' love of nicknames, on several occasions referred to her as "Sarah" (*Epist.* "Propitia divinitate", "Gratias domino"), and she clearly participated in her husband's conversion to the religious life. Moreover, Ruricius' description of his villa (*hospitiolum*) as being *desertum* ("lonely") (*Epist.* 1.12) could suggest that, at least on occasion, Hiberia lived elsewhere. It may be that she spent some of her time, especially after Ruricius became bishop, with her family in Clermont, perhaps near Riom where, as will be seen, her family seems to have had property. This would help to explain the attachment of at least two of her sons, Ommatius and Eparchius, to that area.

Ruricius and Hiberia had no known daughters[23] and five sons, viz., Ommatius, Eparchius, Constantius, Leontius, and Aurelianus.[24] At least in part because of their mother's connections there, Ommatius and Eparchius resided at Clermont, where Ommatius, and probably Eparchius also, entered the clergy (*Epist.* 1.18, 2.28, 2.57-58). These two were living there more-or-less on their own during the tenure of bishop Aprunculus (ca. 485-490), so they may have been born by the early 460s. They also may be the children who were educated, probably in the mid 470s, by the Arvernian rhetor Hesperius (*Epist.* 1.3-4). And given that Ommatius was the only son to receive one of the letters in Book I, he well may have been the eldest son. Aurelianus and Leontius, on the other hand, would seem to have been the youngest. They do not appear until the early 500s (*Epist.* 2.40), at which time they were residing with bishop Victorinus of Fréjus; perhaps they were born by ca. 475 or shortly thereafter.[25]

Constantius, finally, seems to have remained at home, on the family property at Gurdo/Decaniacum. He was the recipient of two of Ruricius' letters (*Epist.* 2.24-25), both of which portray him as a typical Gallo-Roman aristocrat who enjoyed leisure and the good life; he may have been the source of Faustus of Riez' concerns (*Epist.* "Licet per") about how well Ruricius' sons would manage the family property. Constantius also may be the unnamed son who married a daughter of Namatius and Ceraunia (*Epist.* 2.1-2,4); he may have been born ca. 465/470.[26]

Some inferences can be made regarding the sources of some of the sons' names, for the names of children, and especially males, were often based upon

---

[23] See discussion at *Epist.* 2.32 below.
[24] Five sons: *PLRE II*; Engelbrecht, *CSEL* 21.lxviii-lxix; and Demeulenaere, *CCL* 64.305; but Krusch, *MGH AA* 8.lxii, names only Ommatius, Eparchius, and Constantius. It is possible that Aurelianus and Leontius, who are only mentioned in *Epist.* 2.40 (q.v.), were grandchildren, nephews, or some other sort of relative. Other "filii," such as another Leontius (actually his brother), Rusticus, and Severus, would seem to have been spiritual "sons" only.
[25] This presuming that Ruricius and Hiberia ceased sexual relations upon their adoption of the religious life, perhaps in the mid to late 470s..
[26] Demeulenaere, *CCL* 64.305, however, suggests Aurelianus or Leontius.

those of family members. Some names came from the maternal side of the family. Ommatius, for example, surely was named after his maternal grandfather, and this could indicate that he was the eldest son. And Eparchius' distinctive name would have been drawn from the Aviti; his namesake may have been the Eparchius who preceded Sidonius as bishop of Clermont[27] and who perhaps was the elder Ommatius' brother. The use of this name also could suggest that the tie between the families of Hiberia and the emperor Eparchius Avitus, already attested above, was quite close. The Arvernian origin of the names of these two sons also not only is consistent with their later careers, for, as seen above, both both entered the clergy there, but also indicates (presuming that the two were in fact the eldest sons) the importance that Ruricius and Hiberia attached to their Arvernian relations.

The names of the other three sons, however, seem to have come from the paternal side of the family. Leontius would have been named after Ruricius' brother; his name also could suggest a connection with the Leontii, one of the premier aristocratic families in the area of Bordeaux,[28] and even, perhaps, with bishop Leontius of Arles (ca. 460-490).[29] Constantius, moreover, may have been named after Ruricius' father, especially given that Ommatius bore the name of Hiberia's father. And this, as already suggested above, could indicate some family connection to Fl. Constantius Felix, the consul of 428,[30] and could add another tenuous link to the chain connecting the family of Ruricius to the imperial aristocracy. As for Aurelianus, perhaps the youngest son, his name could reflect a tie to any of several distinguished Aureliani, including, for example, one of the early bishops of Limoges, and, in the late fifth century, a patrician of Marseille.[31] The former case, coupled with an Anician tie to bishops

---

[27] Duchesne, *Fastes* 2.31.

[28] Note in particular Pontius Leontius of Bordeaux, whose estate Burgus was a veritable fortress (Sid.Apoll. *Carm.* 22; *PLRE II*, pp.674-675). And in the sixth century, two Leontii were bishops of Bordeaux: see Duchesne, *Fastes* 2.61. For the Leontii of Gaul, see Mathisen, *Ecclesiastical Aristocracy*, pp.136-138.

[29] Ruricius referred to Leontius of Arles as "tali ... parente" (*Epist.* 1.15). Ruricius certainly had more than a passing interest in the affairs of Arles, and was kept well informed: see *Epist.* 1.15, 2.8-9, 21, 31, 33, 36.

[30] A connection to the short-lived emperor Fl. Constantius (421), who came from Naissus in Illyria, would seem to be less likely (see *PLRE II*, p.322). Among other Gallic Constantii, note the priest Constantius of Lyon who ca. 480 wrote the *Life of Germanus of Auxerre*; and Constantius, bishop of Uzès ca. 442-462 (see Mathisen, *Ecclesiastical Aristocracy*, pp.280-281).

[31] Gallic Aureliani include 1) the early bishop of Limoges; 2) Aurelianus 2 (*PLRE* 2.199), *vicarius Quinque provinciarum* or *Italiae* ca. 400; 3) Aurelianus 5 (*PLRE* 2.199-200), praetorian prefect of Gaul or Illyricum attested on 29 April 473, perhaps to be identified as the patrician Aurelianus of Marseille (Greg.Tur. *Glor.mart.* 76); 4) Aurelianus 7 (*PLRE* 2.200) a *vir inlustris* and ally of Clovis in the Burgundian kingdom ca. 501/506; and 5) Aurelianus 8 (*PLRE* 2.201), a relative of Ennodius of Pavia: he visited Ravenna, was a priest by 510, and a bishop in Gaul by 512 (Ennod. *Epist.* 9.27, 6.5, 8.13, 8.35). Subsequently, an Aurelianus was bishop of Arles ca.

Hermogenianus and Adelfius, even could suggest that Ruricius had a quasi-hereditary claim upon the see of Limoges.

The most distinguished of Ruricius' progeny was Ommatius, who after serving as a priest at Clermont became bishop of Tours, where he was in office ca. 524-528.[32] Eparchius, too, although not specifically called a cleric by Ruricius, seems to have entered the clergy at Clermont. He had a rather checkered career. After being excommunicated by Euphrasius for some unnamed delict (*Epist.* 2.57-58) he may have continued as a parish priest at the *vicus Ricomagensis* (Riom) just north of Clermont, assuming he is the priest "Epachius" discussed by Gregory of Tours.[33] Gregory's description of him, "of senatorial birth, so that no one in that village was considered to be more noble,"[34] would have suited Eparchius' distinguished family origin. And "Epachius" seems to have been just as troublesome as the son of Ruricius. Gregory commented, "This feckless individual did not abstain from an excessive imbibing of wine";[35] he even conducted Christmas Eve services in an inebriated state.

Ruricius also had several grandchildren and at at least one great-grandchild. In *Epist.* 2.32 Ruricius commended to Agricola, the son of the emperor Avitus, a woman described as Agricola's "maiden" (*ancilla*), who had made Agricola a grandfather and Ruricius a great-grandfather. In the past, this passage always has been interpreted to mean that Ruricius had an otherwise unknown daughter who married Agricola and was the mother of either this *ancilla* or her husband.[36] In other letters, moreover, Ruricius spoke of his grandchildren (*nepotes*) Papianilla and Parthenius (*Epist.* 2.36-37). The traditional view identifies Papianilla as the aforementioned *ancilla*.[37] It long was assumed that Parthenius was the son of Agricola and Ruricius' unnamed daughter, and that he had married a woman, from an unknown family background, with the unusual name Papianilla.[38] But, on the basis of nomenclature and because Ruricius described

---

545-551 (Duchesne, *Fastes* 1.258-259). This just conceivably could have been the son of Ruricius.

[32] Duchesne, *Fastes* 2.306. Gregory of Tours described him as "originating from the senators and citizens of Clermont" (*HF* 10.31). For the tendency for Arvernians to serve as bishops of Tours, see Mathisen, "Family," pp.86-89.

[33] It may be significant in this regard that Eparchius' putative namesake, the bishop Eparchius, had established a monastery, perhaps on family property, "in arce Cantobennici" (Greg.Tur. *HF* 2.21, cf. 1.44), identified as Puy-de-Chanturgue, just north of Clermont on the road to Riom.

[34] "esset ex genere senatorio, et nullus in vico illo Ricomagensi, superius memorato, iuxta saeculi dignitatem haberetur nobilior" (*Glor.mart.* 56).

[35] "ab haustu nimio vini minime infelix abstinuit" (ibid.).

[36] Engelbrecht, *CSEL* 21.lxix; Krusch, *MGH AA* 8.lxvi; and Settipani, "Ruricius," p.203.

[37] Demeulenaere, *CCL* 64.305, has Parthenius as the son of Agricola and Ruricius' unnamed daughter and married to Papianilla; Engelbrecht, *CSEL* 21.lxviii-lxix, assumes that Papianilla was Ruricius's granddaughter and Agricola's daughter-in-law (*nurus*). These views are reprised in *PLRE II*, pp. 830, 833, 1318.

[38] Krusch, *MGH AA* 8.lxvi, has Parthenius as Agricola's son, whereas E. James, *The Franks*

his relation to the *ancilla* as *affinitas* ("relation by marriage"), it would seem that a more reasonable conclusion is that Papianilla was the daughter of Agricola, whose sister (the wife of Sidonius) had the same name.[39]

This reconstruction obviates the need to postulate a daughter of Ruricius. The most economical hypothesis is that Papianilla was the *ancilla* who made Ruricius a great-grandfather. For this to be the case, her husband Parthenius must have been Ruricius' grandson. This would mean that one of Ruricius' children was the father of Parthenius. Either Ommatius or Eparchius, the eldest sons, would seem to be the most likely possibility, given that Parthenius was himself a father in the early 500s and would have been born by ca. 480. Ommatius' and Eparchius' association with the Auvergne also would be consistent with the marriage of a child of one of them to Papianilla, herself an Arvernian; indeed, Parthenius and Papianilla may even have been childhood friends. Moreover, the father of Parthenius also could have been the father of Ruricius II Proculus, whose cognomen suggests an Arvernian connection.[40]

A bit more also might be said about the family connections of Parthenius, for Ennodius of Pavia wrote four extant letters (*Epist.* 5.19, 6.1, 23; 7.31) to a nephew Parthenius, an exact contemporary of Ruricius' grandson. Given that these are the only occurrences of this name in Gaul at this time, one might suspect that they refer to the same individual.[41] If so, it may have been that Ruricius' son married a sister of Ennodius, a hypothesis that could help to explicate not only the interests that Ruricius had in Arles, including even being consulted on the election of a bishop in 502 (*Epist.* 2.31), but also Parthenius' later professional success in Provence and northern Italy. Moreover, it would seem that members of Ruricius' immediate family, including not only Parthenius, but also Ruricius' sons Leontius and Aurelianus, took advantage of their ties to Provence to withdraw there at about the time of the Frankish destruction of the Visigothic kingdom of Toulouse in 507 (*Epist.* 2.34, 37-37, 41).

Like his children, Ruricius' grandchildren were a mixed bag. Ruricius II Proculus also served as bishop of Limoges, and attended church councils between 535 and 549.[42] Venantius Fortunatus reports that he built a church of

---

(Oxford, 1988) p.107, has him as the son of Ruricius and grandson of Eparchius Avitus.

[39] As suggested by Mathisen, "Epistolography", followed by Settipani, "Ruricius," p.203.

[40] Arvernian *Proculi* include a friend of Sidonius (Sid.Apoll. *Epist.* 4.23); and an ambitious priest who was killed before his own altar at Vollore ca. 525 (Greg.Tur. *Vit.pat.* 4, *HF* 3.31). For later *Proculi* at Limoges as well, note the *Vita Aridii* 27 (*MGH SRM* 3.590); and the Carolingian *Miracula sancti Martialis* (*MGH SS* 15.1.281) mentions a Proculus, "quidam homunculus ex ipsa civitate," who in the seventh century attacked the duke Lupus when he trespassed in the tomb of St. Martial.

[41] As argued by Mathisen, "Epistolography"; *PLRE II* nos.2-3, pp.832-833, however, keeps them separated.

[42] *CCL* 148A.110-111, 142-146. 157-161.

St. Peter,[43] and the "Life of Junianus" notes that "Ruricius, also known as Proculus, ordered a basilica to built" at Comodoliacus (St-Junien) where the body of St. Junianus was interred.[44] Parthenius held positions under the Ostrogoths and Franks, rising to the rank of patrician. After suspecting Papianilla of adultery with their friend Ausanius, he murdered them both; subsequently he himself was killed by a mob incensed over his methods as a tax-collector.[45] Finally, another likely relative, albeit of uncertain degree, is the Ruricius who was bishop of Bourges in the early sixth century, and who may finally have realized a family ambition to control a metropolitan see.[46]

Beyond his immediate family, some members of Ruricius' extended family can be identified through his use of the words *propinquitas* ("nearness") and *germanitas* ("brotherliness"), terms that nearly always indicated a tie of blood or marriage, rather than of religion. The former was used in letters to Celsus (*Epist.* 1.13) and Volusianus (*Epist.* 2.65); and the latter in letters to Celsus (ibid.); Namatius and Ceraunia (*Epist.* 2.1-2); Elaphius (*Epist.* 2.7); Euphrasius (*Epist.* 2.22, 29); Albinus (*Epist.* 2.46); and Aprunculus (*Epist.* 2.58).

The nature of Ruricius' tie to Namatius and Ceraunia is clear, for one of his sons married a daughter of theirs. Euphrasius and Aprunculus, moreover, were bishops of Clermont, and the latter probably was the one who gave at least one of Ruricius' sons positions in the clergy.[47] They presumably would have been related to Ruricius through Hiberia,[48] as may have been Elaphius, who seems to have lived south of Clermont, in the area of Rodez, and Volusianus, an Arvernian aristocrat who later became bishop of Tours.

Celsus apparently lived near Gurdo in proximity to, if not in fact upon, Ruricius' estate at Decaniacum. Ruricius' connection to him seems to have been particularly close, for not only are there three letters to him in the corpus, but he also is the only correspondent referred to as "tua germanitas" rather than the more formal "vestra germanitas."[49] Ruricius also called him "frater optime" and noted that they had had the same "parentes" and teachers (*Epist.* 2.12-13). Albinus, on the other hand, was a priest at Limoges. Both would have belonged

---

[43] See Ven.Fort. *Carm.* 4.5; Duchesne, *Fastes* 2.51. For an argument that this church of St. Peter was located at St-Junien, see Lacorre, "Saint-Junien," pp.74-77.

[44] "Ruricius seu Proculus ... basilicam iussit fabricari" (*Vita Juniani* 9: *MGH SRM* 3.379). St. Andrew: J. Arbellot, *Chronique de Maleu* (1848), p.25. It may have been dedicated to St. Andrew.

[45] Greg.Tur. *HF* 3.36, "Franci cum Parthenium in odio magno haberent..." See discussion of *Epist.* 2.37 below.

[46] Duchesne, *Fastes* 2.27: he succeeded Tetradius, who had attended the councils of Agde (506) and Orléans (511).

[47] Unless it was Sidonius himself.

[48] Of course, it is possible that Ruricius had family ties there of his own: see Settipani, "Ruricius," p.196.

[49] Akin to the difference between the French *tu* and *vous*.

to Ruricius own family circle; perhaps Celsus was a brother and Albinus a cousin. Ruricius also wrote to a "frater" Leontius (*Epist.* 2.42), who at an earlier time had been described by Faustus of Riez (*Epist.* "Propitia divinitate") as "individuum filium nostrum Leontium" ("our inseparable son Leontius"). This would seem not to be Ruricius' son Leontius, who may not even have been born at that time, and who would not have been called Faustus' "frater." But he probably is the Leontius who by the mid 480s was old enough to borrow books from Sidonius, at which time he seems to have been living near Ruricius (*Epist.* 1.8). This elder Leontius, after whom one of Ruricius' sons apparently was named, may have been Ruricius' younger brother. And if Leontius was a younger brother of Ruricius, one might hazard a guess that he drew his name from his mother's side of the family.

Additional suggestions regarding Ruricius' family and antecedents also might be made on the basis of nomenclature. The name Ruricius is not common,[50] nor is it known otherwise to have been used by any Gallic aristocratic families, although it is possible that homonyms are concealed in variants of Ruricius' name. For example, the name Agroecius, borne by several distinguished Gauls,[51] would have been a Greek rendition of the Latin Ruricius, in much the same way that the names "Ausonius" and "Hesperius" were used in the family of Ausonius.[52] The name "Rusticus," too, could be seen as a alternate of "Ruricius."[53] But, again, no firm conclusions can be based upon such observations.

The preceding discussion of the known and suggested family ties of Ruricius may be summarized as follows:

---

[50] The only other Ruricius cited in either of the first two volumes of *PLRE* is a *praeses* of Tripolitania in the mid 360s (*PLRE I*, p.786); in Gaul, note also Ruricius, bishop of Bourges in the sixth century (discussed above).

[51] Note, e.g., Agroecius, apparently from the Auvergne, who served as the *primicerius notariorum* ("Chief of Notaries") of the usurper Jovinus (411-413) (Greg.Tur. *HF* 2.9; *PLRE II*, pp.38-39); and Agroecius, author of a *De orthographia* ("On Orthography") and later bishop of Sens ca. 470, who may have been a descendent of the Aquitanian Censorius Atticus Agricius (ibid. p.39). Another variant of this name is "Agricius" (Agroecius, *De orthographia* praef.: H. Keil, *Gram.lat.* 7.114); and yet another would be "Agrestius"; see R. Mathisen, "Agrestius of Lugo, Eparchius Avitus, and a Curious Fifth-Century Statement of Faith," *Journal of Early Christian Studies* 2 (1994) pp.71-102.

[52] See the appropriate entries in *PLRE I*.

[53] As in Sulpicius Severus, *Vita Martini* 9 (*CSEL* 1 p.ix); see also the episcopal catalogue of Limoges, discussed below.

A FANCIFUL *STEMMA* OF RURICIUS' FAMILY

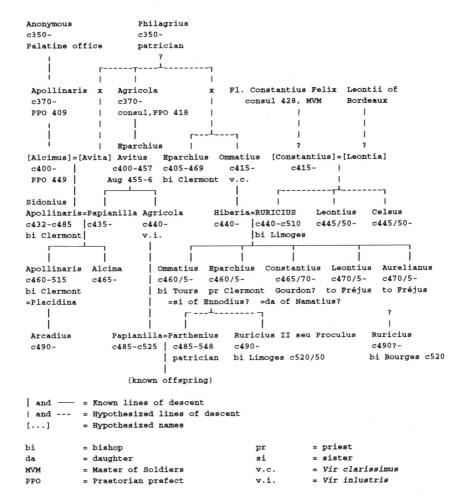

```
Anonymous                Philagrius
c350-                    c350-
Palatine office          patrician
      |                      ?
      |          r------T----L---------┐
      |          |      |              |
Apollinaris  x  Agricola    x   Fl. Constantius Felix  Leontii of
c370-        |  c370-        |        consul 428, MVM    Bordeaux
PPO 409      |  consul,PPO 418 |            |                |
      |      |      |          |            |                |
      |      |      |      r---L----┐       |                |
      |      |  Eparchius   |       |       ?                ?
[Alcimus]=[Avita] Avitus  Eparchius Ommatius [Constantius]=[Leontia]
c400-    |    c400-457   c405-469   c415-     c415-       |
PPO 449  |    Aug 455-6  bi Clermont v.c.                 |
      |  |                            r----------T--------┐
Sidonius |   r----L----┐              |          |        |      |
Apollinaris=Papianilla Agricola  Hiberia=RURICIUS Leontius  Celsus
c432-c485 |c435-     c440-       c440- |c440-c510 c445/50-  c445/50-
bi Clermont|          v.i.             |bi Limoges
      |    |                           |
      |  r-L---┐      |   r----T--------T----------T---------T-----------┐
      |  |     |      |   |    |        |          |         |           |
Apollinaris Alcima   | Ommatius Eparchius Constantius Leontius Aurelianus
c460-515  c465-      | c460/5- c460/5-  c465/70-  c470/5-   c470/5-
bi Clermont          | bi Tours pr Clermont Gourdon? to Fréjus to Fréjus
=Placidina           | =si of Ennodius? =da of Namatius?
      |              |   r---L--------┐                            ?
      |              |   |            |
Arcadius             | Papianilla=Parthenius Ruricius II seu Proculus Ruricius
c490-                | c485-c525 | c485-548  c490-                   c490?-
                     |           | patrician bi Limoges c520/50      bi Bourges c520
                     |
              (known offspring)
```

```
|  and   ——  = Known lines of descent
|  and   ---  = Hypothesized lines of descent
[...]        = Hypothesized names

bi   = bishop                    pr    = priest
da   = daughter                  si    = sister
MVM  = Master of Soldiers        v.c.  = Vir clarissimus
PPO  = Praetorian prefect        v.i.  = Vir inlustris
```

Ruricius' Personality

Ruricius' letters reveal several things about his background and personality. He presumably received the standard secular classical literary education of the day, as evidenced by his use of classical allusions, his early literary interaction with Sidonius, and his provision for the education of his own sons in the same manner (*Epist.* 1.3-4). His use of legal terminology in several letters suggests not only that he had legal training, but also, perhaps, that he may have served as an *advocatus* ("advocate"), a position often held by young aristocrats beginning a secular career.[54] Otherwise, his youth may have been spent in enjoyment of typical aristocratic *otium* ("leisure"). By the early 470s he had embarked upon the pursuit of religion. At some point between 477 and 485 he gave refuge to the exiled bishop Faustus of Riez and seems to have come rather under his influence (*Epist.*1.1-2). His introduction to Faustus may have been brokered by his friend Sidonius Apollinaris, who himself had been baptized by Faustus.[55]

Ruricius participated fully in the literary society of his day, exchanging both books and compositions with his confrères. He was familiar with biblical commonplaces and quoted liberally from scripture. But, save for some conventional references to fasts and vigils, there seems to have been little of the ascetic about him; several mentions of exchanges of delicacies suggest that Ruricius was fond of the "good life." With his friends, moreover, Ruricius was something of a joker. He liked portraying them in other identities (*Epist.* 1.10, 16), and a series of letters about a borrowed horse is especially amusing.

Toward his children Ruricius was a devoted, and rather indulgent, father. As already seen, Eparchius and Constantius appear to have been somewhat wayward. In both cases, Ruricius attempted to bring them to heel. Eparchius was apparently restored to the good graces of Euphrasius, his bishop, whereas Constantius may have eventually taken up his responsibilities and married the short-lived daughter of Namatius and Ceraunia.

The many references in Ruricius' correspondence to illnesses, infirmities, and maladies, of himself and others, suggest that he was either an incurable hypochondriac or beset by a multitude of afflictions. He intensely disliked hot weather, and his love of good food might have resulted in additional complaints. He also seems to have been something of a stay-at-home. Although he did travel, he was not nearly as peripatetic, for example, as his friend Sidonius. His letters attest to single trips to Arles and Bordeaux, both, it seems, on official business, along with several visits to Clermont. His most extensive travelling seems to have involved commuting between a presumed (although undocumented) city residence at Limoges and sojourns in the countryside to the south, at Decaniacum and perhaps elsewhere. Otherwise, Ruricius seems to have been more inclined to encourage his friends to visit him, and he even went so far, on at least two occasions (*Epist.* 1.14, 2.35), as to offer to provide transportation.

Like any late Roman aristocrat, Ruricius was sensitive to slights, real and imagined. When he got his back up, he could be quite sharp with even the most distinguished Gallic ecclesiastics: when Caesarius of Arles rebuked him for

---

[54] Note Germanus of Auxerre: "he adorned the tribunal of the prefect by means of the occupation of advocate": *Vita Germani* ("Life of Germanus") 1.

[55] See J. Harries, *Sidonius Apollinaris and the Fall of Rome* (Oxford 1994).

his failure to attend the Council of Agde in 506, Ruricius penned a decidedly trenchant response (*Epist.* 2.33). Ruricius also quarreled with bishop Chronopius of Périgueux over the parish of Gemiliacum (St-Jumilhac-le-Grand) (*Epist.* 2.6). Because Gemiliacum was under the jurisdiction of the bishop of Limoges in the seventh century, Ruricius apparently was victorious.

Ruricius and His Social Circle

The exchange of letters was one of the primary means by which Gallic aristocrats, including bishops, maintained contact with each other. It was viewed as a grave fault if someone missed the chance to send a letter when the opportunity arose. The roads clearly were not maintained as well as during imperial times, and there was a tendency to renew friendly ties in the spring, after a winter hiatus, when the roads were in better condition (e.g. *Epist.* 2.64).

Much of Ruricius' correspondence was directed to nearby bishops, who are cited only by name, which sometimes makes it a challenge to identify their cities.[56] Some are fairly easy to place, such as Aprunculus and Euphrasius of Clermont (*Epist.* 2.55-58; 2.22,29); and Chronopius of Périgueux, Heraclianus of Toulouse, Petrus of Saintes, and Clarus of Eauze (*Epist.* 2.6, 2.30, 2.38, 2.64 respectively). Bassulus (*Epist.* 1.7) and Ambrosius (*Epist.* 2.44) also seem to have come from nearby cities, the former probably from Cahors, and the latter perhaps from Rodez. Moreover, several secular correspondents resided south and southwest of Limoges, where, as seen above, Ruricius seems to have concentrated his interests. Two sent him fish from this area, Hispanus from the Duranius (Dordogne river) (*Epist.* 2.45), and Rusticus from the Visera (Vézère river) (*Epist.* 2.54), a tributary of the Dordogne. To the southwest, Freda, apparently a Goth, dwelt in the Cebennae (Cevennes) mountains (*Epist.* 1.11).

Further to the southwest, in Provence, Ruricius had additional ecclesiastical correspondents, such as bishop Sedatus of Nîmes (*Epist.* 2.18-19, 34-35), who at one point proposed to make a special trip to visit him; bishop Victorinus of Fréjus (*Epist.* 2.40), who sheltered two of his sons; and two priests of Arles, Julianus Pomerius (*Epist.* 1.17, 2.10-11), whom he had hoped to lure to Limoges, and Capillutus (*Epist.* 2.21, 31), who not only served as his letter carrier, but also received two extant letters. Ruricius also was acquainted with three bishops of Arles, Leontius (ca. 460-490), a possible relative; Aeonius (ca. 490-502), whom he visited; and Caesarius (502-540), to whom he commended his granddaughter Papianilla and her husband Parthenius.

All, or nearly all, of Ruricius' correspondents resided in the Visigothic kingdom. Only Censurius of Auxerre (*Epist.* 2.51) might have come from out-

---

[56] See the appropriate entries in Duchesne, *Fastes*, vols. 1-2; and discussion of the respective letters below.

side,[57] and only one other letter, that to Volusianus of Tours (*Epist.* 2.64), had a destination north of Limoges.[58] The reasons for this distribution pattern are not clear. They may have been political, a result of communications difficulties between the different kingdoms, or merely coincidental, a result of where Ruricius' friends, family, and professional associates resided. Or the selection may, to some degree, have been a result of an editing process.[59]

Even though Ruricius' letters have a very "local" flavor, he did share several correspondents with the better known Gallic epistolographers of this period, Sidonius Apollinaris; Avitus of Vienne; and Ennodius of Pavia. The shared correspondents, and respective letters, are shown in following table:

CORRESPONDENTS SHARED BY RURICIUS WITH OTHERS

Correspondent	Letters of Sidonius	Collection of Ruricius
Agricola	*Epist.*1.2	*Epist.*2.32
Hesperius	*Epist.*2.10	*Epist.*1.3-5
Rusticus	*Epist.*2.11	*Epist.*2.20
Apollinaris	*Epist.*3.13	*Epist.*2.26-7,41
Elaphius	*Epist.*4.15	*Epist.*2.7
Graecus of Marseille	*Epist.*6.6;7.2,7,10;9.4	Graecus,"Gratias domino"[60]
Censurius of Auxerre	*Epist.*6.10	*Epist.*2.51
Namatius*	*Epist.*8.6	*Epist.*2.1-5,62
Lupus	*Epist.*8.11	*Epist.*1.10
Faustus of Riez	*Epist.*9.3,9.9;*Carm.*16	*Epist.*1.1-2
Ambrosius	*Epist.*9.6	*Epist.*2.44
Aprunculus of Clermont	*Epist.*9.10	*Epist.*2.55-8

---

[57] And this on the presumption that the Visigoths had not in fact occupied Auxerre. The Stephanus who received *Epist.* 2.52 (q.v.) does not seem to have been Stephanus, bishop of Lyon.
[58] Even if the Verus who received *Epist.* 2.23 was the later bishop of Tours, he probably was not resident there at the time.
[59] Any of these factors might explain why Ruricius' collection does not include correspondence with other known Gallic epistolographers of the day, such as Avitus of Vienne or Ennodius of Pavia, both of whom would have been related, in some degree, to Ruricius.
[60] A letter from Graecus to Ruricius survives in Ruricius' corpus, but none from Ruricius to Graecus.

Correspondent	Letters of Avitus	Collection of Ruricius
Caesarius of Arles	Epist.11	Epist.2.33,36;
		Caesarius, "Dum nimium"
Apollinaris	Epist.24,36,51-52	Epist.2.26-7,41
Euphrasius of Clermont	Epist.43	Epist.2.22,29

Correspondent	Letters of Ennodius	Collection of Ruricius
Julianus Pomerius	Epist.2.6	Epist.1.17,2.10
Parthenius	Epist.6.23	Epist.2.37
Caesarius of Arles	Epist.9.33	Epist.2.33,36;
		Caesarius, "Dum nimium"

*It is unclear whether these are the same person.

As can be seen, there was a significant amount of overlap between the circles of Sidonius and Ruricius. Ruricius and Avitus, however, shared only three correspondents, two of them from the equidistant Auvergne, and the overlap with Ennodius was limited only to correspondents at Arles. These observations might indicate that the barbarian kingdoms created a kind of social regionalization that had not existed in the days of Sidonius.

Ruricius the Bishop

The exact date of Ruricius' entry into the clergy is uncertain. He does seem to have adopted the religious life before he became bishop.[61] In one early letter ("Propitia divinitate"), Faustus of Riez praised Ruricius' adoption of the religious life and also called him *frater*, without referring to him as a bishop. By the time of Faustus' letter "Gratias ad vos", however, Ruricius had obtained the episcopate (*summum sacerdotium*). This event would have occurred soon after the death of Euric on 28 December 484, when the vacant sees in Aquitania were filled.[62] Now, as seen above, both Limoges and Clermont lay in the province of Aquitania Prima, for which Bourges served as metropolitan city. Its bishop during the 470s was Simplicius, a *vir spectabilis* who had been chosen and consecrated, *ex laicis* ("from the laity"), by Sidonius himself.[63] If he was still in office,[64] Simplicius then should have presided over the election at Limoges; if

---

[61] It has been suggested that he was ordained in some lesser office in the late 470s under the auspices of Faustus of Riez; see Engelbrecht, CSEL 21.lxvi; and Demeulenaere, CCL 64.305.

[62] Listed in Sid.Apoll. Epist. 7.6. Hagendahl, Ruricius, p.6, wrongly places Euric's death in 485.

[63] Sid.Apoll. Epist. 7.8-9.

[64] The next bishop, Tetradius, is not attested until 506 (Duchesne, Fastes 2.27).

so, it would not be surprising if he supported Ruricius, another aristocrat with a distinguished pedigree and another protégé of Sidonius.

After his ordination, Ruricius undertook to fulfil the responsibilities of a late Roman bishop. His letters provide ample evidence of his local ministry. Eudomius and Melanthia of Limoges, for example, received a lengthy letter of condolence (*Epist.* 2.39, cf. 2.46), and his in-laws Namatius and Ceraunia received two (*Epist.* 2.2-3). On several occasions Ruricius interceded on behalf of less-privileged parishoners (*Epist.* 2.7, 12, 20, 47-48, 53), and he also assisted other bishops who were performing similar tasks (Faustus, *Epist.* "Tanta mihi", "Gratias ad vos"; Victorinus, *Epist.* "Cum beatitudinem"): he seems to have had a particular concern for the tribulations of displaced persons. On a more formal level, he acted in a judicial capacity (*Epist.* 2.51) and was consulted regarding the selection of other bishops (*Epist.* 2.31). In addition, several matters that apparently were too sensitive for mention in a letter were dealt with verbally (*Epist.* 2.29-30, 56).[65]

In other instances Ruricius referred to to the performance of his liturgical duties. He mentions the observance of a *quarta feria* ("fourth celebration") at Briva (*Epist.* 2.24), and of a *tertia feria*, apparently at the same place (*Epist.* 2.62). Now, in the generic weekly ecclesiastical calendar, the *dies dominica*, Sunday, was the first day of the week, followed by six *feriae* (daily celebrations). The third and fourth, therefore, would have taken place on Wednesday and Thursday respectively. But, more specifically, the six *feriae* following Easter had a special place in the liturgy, as seen in two early Gallic liturgical catalogues, the so-called *Missale Gallicanum vetus* ("Ancient Gallic Missal" = *MGall*), and the *Missale Gothicum* ("Gothic Missal" = *MGoth*).[66] In their current forms, they date to circa the eighth century, but both are much older; the *MGoth*, for example, is thought to have originated as early as the fifth century, in the area of Septimania.[67] The possibility that Ruricius' *feriae* are those of Easter week would seem to be supported by his two mentions of the celebration of Easter (*Pascha*) (*Epist.* 2.45, 2.64).

The only other church festival that Ruricius mentions is a *solemnitas sanctorum* ("festival of the saints") at Gurdo (*Epist.* 1.7, 1.14). Both the *MGall* and *MGoth* cite only one "festum sanctorum," that of Peter and Paul, on 29 June,[68]

---

[65] For Ruricius' use of verbal messages, see Hagendahl, *Ruricius*, pp.9-10.

[66] *MGall*: Ms. *Vaticanus palatinus latinus* 493; *PL* 71.171-216, at pp.199-200; L.C. Mohlberg ed., *Missale Gallicanum vetus* (Rome, 1958). *MGoth*: Ms. *Vaticanus reginensis latinus* 317; *PL*.71.225-318, at pp.280-281; L.C. Mohlberg, *Missale Gothicum* (Rome, 1961). For discussion, see Hen, *Culture*, pp.43-48.

[67] As suggested by its chauvinistic description (ch.16) of Toulouse as "Roma Garonnae", and by a condemnation of Arianism: "Digne [Martinus] Arrianorum non subiacuit feritati" (ch.74).

[68] *PL* 72.208,295.

and this may be the one that Ruricius meant. The devotion of Ruricius' family to St. Peter was attested later, as seen above, when Ruricius II Proculus constructed a church in his honor. Other local festivals that would have been of special significance at Limoges can be found in the so-called *Antiquum martyrologium gallicanum* ("Ancient Gallic Martyrology"), which notes under 30 June, the very next day: "On the day before the Kalends of July, at Limoges, the interment of the bishop St. Martial,"[69] who, as already seen, was the saintly founder of the church of Limoges. For Ruricius, therefore, late June would have been an especially important time of the liturgical year.

The only other festival of Limoges to appear in the Gallic martyrology is that of St. Martin of Brive-la-Gaillarde on 11 August.[70] Given the stature of this other St. Martin, Ruricius must have felt quite privileged to have had his cult under his jurisdiction, especially given the propinquity of Briva to his own property at Gurdo/Decaniacum. Both considerations could explain Ruricius' performance of services there (*Epist.* 2.24, 62).

Additional insight into how the local liturgical seasons were manifested in the neighborhood of Limoges might be inferred from a series of fasts and vigils instituted at Tours by bishop Perpetuus ca. 480/490.[71] For example, fasts were held as follows:

Regarding Fasts[72]

After Quinquagesima,[73] the fourth and sixth day of the week until the festival of St. John [the Evangelist] [14 June].

From the First of September until the First of October, two fasts per week.

From the First of October until the interment of the Lord Martin [of Tours] [11 November], two fasts per week.

From the interment of the Lord Martin until the birth of the Lord [25 December], three fasts per week.

From the festival of St. Hilary [of Poitiers] [13 January] until the middle of February, two fasts per week.

Coupled with, and often parallel to, this calendar of fasts was a catalogue of *vigilia* ("nightly vigils),"[1] which were held in connection with the festivals of

---

[69] "Pridie Kalendas Julii, Lemovicas, depositio sancti Martialis episcopi" (*PL* 71.616).

[70] "Lemovicas, sancti Martini Brivensis" (ibid.).

[71] As reported by Gregory of Tours (*HF* 10.31) as being still in use in his own time.

[72] Greg.Tur. *HF* 10.31.

[73] The *quinquagesima* was the fifty days after Easter. It ended on Pentecost, on the seventh Sunday after Easter. This period, along with the *quadragesima* of Lent before Easter, had its own separate calendar, and hence was not included in this catalogue.

[1] Greg.Tur. *HF* 10.31. For the dates, see *PL* 71.621-623; and V. Schauber, H.-M. Schindler

Christmas (25 December), Epiphany (6 January), St. John the Evangelist (27 December), St. Peter (22 February); Easter (27 March),[2] the Ascension (5 May), the "Fiftieth Day" (Pentecost: 15 May), John the Baptist (24 June), Sts. Peter and Paul (29 June), St. Martin of Tours (4 July), St. Symphorianus of Autun (22 August), St. Litorius of Tours (13 September), St. Martin of Tours (again) (11 November), St. Brictius of Tours (13 November), and St. Hilary of Poitiers (13 January).[3] Especially interesting is the special status of the Festival of Peter and Paul, which also was mentioned by Ruricius. Their local popularity also was reflected in the medieval *Prosarium Lemovicense* ("Hymn-Text of Limoges"), which contained four hymns to Peter and Paul, and four to Peter alone.[4]

The Church of St. Augustine

Aside from his letter collection, Ruricius' only known physical legacy was a church.[5] Late in the sixth century, Venantius Fortunatus noted in an epitaph for Ruricius and his grandson Ruricius, "Each in his own time built dutiful churches for a patron, the one (*iste*) for Augustine, and the other (*ille*) for Peter."[6] There has been some debate over which Ruricius the *iste* and *ille* refer to, although there seems no reason to doubt that they appear in chronological order.[7] This conclusion is supported by a fuller account found in the late *Translatio Asclepii* ("Translation [of the Remains] of Asclepius"), which noted,

> Priests living communally have overseen the present place all the way back to the times of the most blessed Ruricius, the first of that name. Indeed, at the present place this Ruricius was the first to institute regular canons, whom he established in honor of St. Augustine; from their time all the way to the present the same monastery has retained the name of St. Augustine...[8]

---

eds., *Heilige und Namenspatrone im Jahreslauf* (Augsburg, 1998).
[2] Easter fell on 27 March in the years 464, 470, 481, and 487, one of which, presumably, would be the year in which Perpetuus composed this catalogue. The date of Easter allows the dates of the Ascension and the *Quinquagesima* to be calculated for this particular sequence.
[3] The placement of this festival is curious: the others are in chronological order, but this one occurs before those that precede it. Perhaps it was added to parallel the list of vigils.
[4] See G. Maria Dreves ed., *Prosarium Lemovicense. Die Prosen der Abtei St. Martial zu Limoges aus Troparien des 10., 11. und 12 Jahrhunderts* (Leipzig, 1889), pp.199-207.
[5] See Engelbrecht, *CSEL* 21.lxviii; Krusch, *MGH AA* 8.lxv.
[6] "Tempore quisque suo fundans pia templa patroni / iste Augustini, condidit ille Petri" (*Carm.*6.5). For this epitaph, see Appendix II below.
[7] For the elder Ruricius as the builder, see Aubrun, *Limoges*, p.89; J. Becquet, "L'évêque Asclèpe à Saint-Augustin de Limoges (VIe siècle)," *BSAHL* 122 (1994) pp.12-22 at p.17; Krusch, *MGH AA* 8.lxvi; and Demeulenaere, *CCL* 64.306, who also suggests that such a dedication seems rather unlikely at this time; for Ruricius II Proculus, see *CAG* p.119; and Becquet, "Asclèpe," p.13.
[8] "presbyteros communiter viventes ... qui usque ad tempora beatissimi Roricii illius nominis

Moreover, the fourteenth-century writer Bernardus Guido noted in his *De ordinibus* ("On the Orders"), "St. Ruricius, the twenty-fourth bishop after St. Martial, is believed to have dedicated in honor of St. Augustine a place above the Vienne river where there was a common cemetery and to have instituted there canons regular and larger choirs under the rule of St. Augustine."[9] This account has a number of anachronisms[10] — for example, this rule and the *canones regulares* were not instituted until much later — but it nevertheless might embody a tradition connecting the elder Ruricius to Augustine.

The cult of Augustine at Limoges continued in the Middle Ages. For it also was said that a later bishop of Limoges, Turpio (ca. 897-944), after the ravages of the Normans, refounded the monastery after having obtained five teeth of Augustine, either at Pavia or from king Liutprand in 721 or 722.[11] In modern times, the ruins of the monastery of St. Augustine were destroyed by the construction of the Avenue Jean-Gagnant.

One might imagine that building this church was not a step that Ruricius took lightly, especially if he intended to be buried there. And Ruricius' attachment to Augustine could seem curious, given the controversial nature of some of Augustine's theological teachings in fifth-century Gaul. In particular, his concept of predestination was viewed as heretical.[12] The *Gallic Chronicle of 452* noted under the year 418, "The heresy of the predestinarians, which is said to have received its impetus from Augustine, once having arisen, creeps along."[13] In 431, Pope Celestine complained to a group of Gallic bishops, "We always have held Augustine ... in our communion, nor has even the rumor of perverse suspicion tainted him... For what reason is he opposed?"[14] And in the 490s, Gennadius of Marseille summed up the prevalent Gallic attitude toward Augus-

---

prima, Lemovicensis episcopi ... locum praesentem rexerunt. qui quidem Roricius canonicos regulares in praesenti loco primus instituit, quos in honorem sancti Augustini fundavit, a quibus nomen sancti Augustini usque ad praesens monasterium ipsum retinuit": Becquet, "Acelèpe," pp.19-21. See Appendix III for a fuller translation. Another late tradition has a Sebastianus as abbot of the monastery at Vosia (Vigeois) during time of Ruricius (see *Gallia Christiana* 2.593), although this monastery is not first attested until the late sixth century (*Testamentum Aridii*, "monachis nostris Vosidensibus").
[9] "Sanctus Roricius xxiv episcopus a s. Martiale creditur locum supra Vigennam fluvium, ubi commune coemeterium erat, in honore s. Augustini episcopi dedicasse et instituisse ibidem sub s. Augustini regula canonicos regulares et plures capellas": Labbé, *Nova bibliotheca* 2.277.
[10] See Krusch, *MGH AA* 8.xv.
[11] T. Soulard, "Reliques et reliquaires de l'abbaye Saint-Augustin-les-Limoges" *BSAHL* 116 (1989) pp.85-93 at p.87.
[12] In general, see R. Mathisen, "For Specialists Only: The Reception of Augustine and His Teachings in Fifth-Century Gaul," in J.T. Lienhard et al. eds., *Augustine. Presbyter factus sum* (Peter Lang, 1994) pp.29-41.
[13] "praedestinatorum haeresis quae ab Augustino accepisse initium dicitur his temporibus serpere exorsa": *Chronica gallica a.452*, no.81 (*MGH AA* 9.656).
[14] Celestine, *Epist.* "Apostolici verba": *PL* 50.528-537.

tine. He began by describing Augustine as "a man brilliant in divine and human learning, complete in faith and pure in his life...", but then went on to say, "whence, that which the Holy Spirit said through Solomon, 'In verbosity you shall not escape sin', also happened to him, who said a great deal... Error was incurred by his excessive speaking, was enlarged by the attack of his enemies, and not yet has escaped the accusation of heresy."[15]

By and large, however, it was only predestination that the Gauls condemned; in most other regards Augustine was respected. Prosper of Aquitaine, for example, wrote to Augustine, "Your Beatitude should know that [Helladius of Arles] is an admirer and follower of your teaching in all other things, and with regard to that which he calls into question [i.e. predestination], he already wished to convey his own thoughts to Your Sanctity through correspondence..."[16] Vincentius of Lérins, who on the one hand condemned predestination as "novelty,"[17] on the other published a extensive collection of *Excerpta* ("Excerpts") from Augustine on the Trinity and the Incarnation.[18]

The most outspoken Gallic opponent of Augustine, however, was none other than Ruricius' early mentor, Faustus of Riez. Regarding predestination, he called Augustine a "destroyer of free will."[19] He also opposed the Augustinian view of the incorporeal nature of the soul.[20] But elsewhere he defended Augustine against the deacon Graecus, later bishop of Marseille, who had presumed to challenge Augustine on a Christological point. Faustus wrote, "Even if some part of the works of the blessed bishop Augustine is thought to be suspect by the most learned men, you should know that there is nothing reprehensible in those sections that you thought should be condemned."[21] Faustus' attitude toward Augustine, therefore, was ambivalent at best, and one might wonder whether he would have encouraged Ruricius' devotion.

A more likely partisan of Augustine would have been Julianus Pomerius, the aforementined priest of Arles who, like Augustine, was both a former rhetor and a North African. In his *On the Contemplative Life*, Julianus described Augustine as "sharp in intelligence, sophisticated in eloquence, knowledgeable in secular literature, active in ecclesiastical duties, brilliant in daily discussions, organized in his every activity, orthodox in his expression of our faith, acute in answering questions, watchful in overcoming heretics, and conscientious in explicating the canonical scriptures."[22] Later in his life, Ruricius fell under

---

[15] *De viris inlustribus* 39: *PL* 58.1080.
[16] apud Augustine, *Epistulae* 225.9: *CSEL* 57.467.
[17] "novitas": Vincentius, *Commonitorium* 25 (*PL* 50.672).
[18] *CCL* 64.199-231.
[19] *De gratia* 1.10: *CSEL* 21.33.
[20] See his letter "Quaeris a me" in Appendix I below.
[21] Faust. *Epist.* 7: *CSEL* 21.201.
[22] *De vita contemplativa* 3.31.

Pomerius' spell and even attempted to attract him to Limoges (*Epist.* 1.17, 2.10-11). So perhaps Pomerius, to some degree, was behind Ruricius' devotion to the African doctor.

An Aquitanian cult of Augustine during Late Antiquity also might be attested by the presence in the "Gothic Missal" of an otherwise unknown "Benediction of the Candles," attributed to "the blessed bishop Augustine, which he wrote and chanted when he was yet a deacon."[23] Likewise, the aforementioned *Prosarium Lemovicense* contained a hymn "De sancto Augustino" ("On St. Augustine").[24] And Ruricius' personal interest in Augustine is attested by his borrowing and copying of Augustine's *De civitate dei*; in a reply to Taurentius, the lender, he even included a brief précis of the contents.[25]

Ruricius and the Visigoths

In comparison with epistolographers such as Sidonius Apollinaris, Avitus of Vienne, and Ennodius of Pavia, Ruricius is remarkably silent on contemporary historical events, and especially on developments such as the Frankish incursions into the Visigothic kingdom, which surely must have been of great concern. One finds several vague references to "temporal worries."[26] In a few instances Ruricius relates such cares a bit more specifically to his own time, as when in a letter to Apollinaris of Clermont he refers to the "tumults and necessities of this time, whether drawn out into perpetuity or suppressed for a while,"[27] an apt description of the on-again, off-again hostilities between the Visigoths and Franks.

Moreover, in spite of the great impact that the presence of the Visigoths must have had on Ruricius' life, there is not a single mention of them in his corpus. Indeed, he never refers to any barbarian people by name, nor does he ever use the word "barbarian." Even the Visigothic officials he corresponded with were Romans, and his discussion of the Visigothic-sponsored Council of Agde in 506 provides no indication that the Visigoths were involved. Ruricius' two uses of the word *hostis* (*Epist.* 2.8, 2.65) seem to be allusions to the Franks.

---

[23] "Benedictio cerae beati Augustini episcopi, quam adhuc diaconus cum esset, edidit et cecinit" (*MGoth* 32: *PL* 72.268). Another *Benedictio cerei*, by Ennodius of Pavia, also is extant (*Opusc.* 10: *MGH AA* 7.109-110).

[24] *Pros.Lem.* no.127, pp. 140-141.

[25] Ruric. *Epist.* 2.17. The aristocrat Tonantius Ferreolus also had Augustine in his library (Sid.Apoll. *Epist.* 2.9.4).

[26] "sollicitudines saeculi" (*Epist.* 1.6); cf. "in saeculi turbinibus" (ibid. 1.13); "vitae istius turbidines ac procellas" (ibid. 2.52)

[27] "tumultibus temporis huius vel necessitatibus aut dilatis in perpetuum aut parumper oppressis" (*Epist.* 2.41); cf. "deputandum tempori... turbinum procella" (ibid. 1.12); "necessitate temporis" (ibid. 2.65). Hagendahl, *Ruricius*, pp.7-8, however, dismisses such references and asserts that the letters lack "même d'allusions à l'état actuel des choses."

Ruricius' low-key approach to the Goths does not, however, appear to have been the result of any antipathy that he felt toward them or fear of reprisals. Indeed, he seems to have been on quite good terms with them. Not only was he allowed to shelter Faustus when the latter was in exile, but several of his correspondents appear to have been either Visigoths themselves (e.g. Freda and Vittamerus), or Visigothic officials (e.g. Elaphius, Praesidius, and Eudomius). His good relations with the Visigoths may in fact have been one of the factors in his election. It would appear, moreover, that the Visigoths had little direct impact upon Ruricius' localized world. His letters omit reflect political affairs because, unlike Sidonius, Avitus, or Ennodius, he was not a statesman.[28] As a result, his correspondence probably is more representative of typical late Roman aristocratic interchange, and as such provides a valuable corrective to the evidence of politically active epistolographers such as Ambrose, Symmachus, Jerome, Paulinus of Nola, Augustine, Sidonius, Avitus, Ennodius, and Cassiodorus.

The Meeting at Arles

In *Epist.* 2.8 to Aeonius of Arles, Ruricius recalled that he had never met Aeonius' predecessor Leontius, suggesting that he had not visited Arles between his ordination in 485, if not earlier, and Leontius' death ca. 485/490. In *Epist.* 2.9, also to Aeonius, Ruricius mentioned having met the former during "a few days." An occasion that would have merited such a visit to a distant metropolitan city would have been a church council. This might have been the so-called "Second Council of Arles," the name given to a collection of canons that appears in manuscripts of church councils between the Council of Vaison (442) and the Council of Agde (506).[29] If, as has been suggested, the council met ca. 500, it could have been the reason that Ruricius visited Arles.[30]

The council reaffirmed many canons of some of the most significant councils of the Gallic past, in particular, the Councils of Arles (312), Riez (439), Orange (441), and Vaison (442), not to mention the first ecumenical Council at Nicaea (325). At the same time, it also issued a number of new canons, dealing with, for example, girls in clerics' chambers (can.4); penitents who married after their husbands were dead (can.12); and worshipers of stones, trees, fountains (can.23). Canon 55, which decreed that persons in secular life could chose a cleric with whom to study, could have been influenced by Ruricius' own experience, for he had chosen to study with Faustus of Riez, even though they belonged to different dioceses. This council would have provided the first oppor-

---

[28] Hagendahl, *Ruricius*, p.8, however, faults Ruricius' "manque d'intérêt historique."
[29] *CCL* 148.111-130.
[30] See R. Mathisen, "The 'Second Council of Arles' and the Spirit of Compilation and Codification in Late Roman Gaul," *Journal of Early Christian Studies* 5 (1997) pp.511-554.

tunity in nearly a hundred years for the bishops of the Visigothic kingdom to assemble. Their endorsement of a fixed group of previous conciliar canons would have provided an ecclesiastical parallel to, and precedent for, the secular "Breviary of Alaric," which likewise granted recognition to a collection of previous Roman statutes.

The Meeting at Bordeaux

In *Epist.* 2.33 to Caesarius of Arles, Ruricius mentioned meeting him at Bordeaux in late 505. Ruricius said nothing about the circumstances of this encounter except that it occurred during the winter. Caesarius himself had been sent there earlier in the year, "as if in exile," after being charged with conniving to turn Arles over to the Burgundians.[31] As for Ruricius, one might infer from his repetitious complaints about his health at this time, and his reluctance to travel under other circumstances, that some pressing business had drawn him there. And what this was might be sought in the historical context. For, as seen above, at this time Alaric II and the Visigoths, threatened by the Franks, were attempting to reinforce their Gallo-Roman support. These efforts culminated, in 506, in the issuance of the "Breviary of Alaric" and the convening of the Council of Agde. But such initiatives surely did not arise *ex nihilo*. Several preliminary gatherings probably laid the groundwork.

The "Breviary" would have required a great deal of preparation. Its prologue proclaimed that it had been issued "So that all the obscurity of Roman laws and ancient jurisprudence might be made clear... with the assistance of bishops and the nobility...," and it asserted that "the assent of the venerable bishops and chosen provincials has strengthened" it.[32] The meeting at Bordeaux, a sometime Visigothic royal residence,[33] may have been part of this process, and Ruricius would have been one of the bishops who assisted. As an individual who, it seems, had legal training, enjoyed friendly ties with the Goths, and was an intimate of Alaric's *consiliarius* ("Counsellor") Eudomius (*Epist.* 2.39), Ruricius would have been an ideal person to ease the proceedings along. Indeed, Caesarius' release from exile may have been partly Ruricius' doing.

---

[31] "in Burdigalensem civitatem est quasi in exilio relegatus" (*Vita Caesarii* 1.21); see W. Klingshirn, *Caesarius of Arles. The Making of a Christian Community in Late Antique Gaul* (Cambridge, 1994) pp.93-94.

[32] "ut omnis legum Romanarum et antiqui iuris obscuritas adhibitis sacerdotibus ac nobilibus viris ... resplendeat.... venerabilium episcoporum vel electorum provincialium nostrorum roboravit adsensus" (Mommsen ed., *CTh* 1.xxxiii-xxxv).

[33] See Sidonius Apollinaris, *Epist.* 8.9.

The Meeting at Toulouse

As discussed above, the Council of Agde met on 10 September 506, and reflects the increasingly close ties between the Visigothic government and the Gallo-Roman ecclesiastical establishment. In Caesarius' letter "Dum nimium," written in the fall of 506 after the council had adjourned, he rebuked Ruricius for failing to attend or even to send a representative. His pique may have been exacerbated because Ruricius was not there to exercise his good offices with Eudomius. Caesarius also advised Ruricius that Eudomius was planning to organize a council to be held in Toulouse the following year that would unite both the Gallic and the Spanish bishops. This would have reflected a Visigothic desire to unify the Gallic and Spanish parts of their kingdom, a strategy in which the Nicene church clearly was intended to play a significant role.

Caesarius' remark about the plan to hold a council in Toulouse often has been connected to a passage in Sedatus of Nîmes' letter "Satis credidi," apparently sent from Toulouse, in which Sedatus expressed his disappointment at Ruricius' failure to attend an undefined "necessity that has brought us here." In the past, this has been taken to be an allusion to the council scheduled for Toulouse in 507.[34] But this is most unlikely, for the convening of such a council almost certainly would have been forestalled by Clovis' invasion of Aquitania and defeat of the Visigoths at Vouillé in the spring of 507. Furthermore, at this time regularly scheduled southern councils almost invariably met in the fall,[35] and the desire to convene the Spanish bishops certainly would have required more than a few months lead-time.

One therefore might look elsewhere for an identification of the "necessity" that brought Sedatus to Toulouse. Sedatus' wording, "ad necessitatam istam," could suggest that the secular authorities were involved; the fifth-century "Concilium septem provinciarum" (Council of the Seven Provinces), an annual assembly at Arles that did include bishops, for example, met "propter privatas ac publicas necessitates" ("on account of private and public necessities").[36]

Further elucidation might be sought in Caesarius' letter to Ruricius. Caesarius noted that "the bishop Verus deigned to mention to me that he had sent your letter with his deacon on to me at Agde." Now, Verus, who ca. 498 had succeeded Volusianus as bishop of Tours, was another no-show at Agde, but he

---

[34] As by Engelbrecht, *CSEL* 21.lxvii-lxviii; Hagendahl, *Ruricius*, p.7; Krusch, *MGH AA* 8.lxv; Loyen, *L'esprit*, p.69.

[35] E.g., the Councils of Riez (439), Orange (441), Vaison (442), Angers (453), Tours (461), Agde (506), Epaon (517), Carpentras (527), Vaison (529), and Clermont (534). Qq.vv. in *CCL* 148-148A.

[36] *Constitutio* "Saluberrima" (17 April 418): *MGH Epist.* 3.13. See J. Zeller, "Das concilium der Septem Provinciae in Arelate," *Westdeutsche Zeitschrift* 24(1905) pp.1-19.

at least had sent his deacon Leo to represent him.[37] The reason for Verus' absence is not difficult to find. Like his predecessor Volusianus, he was suspected of having Frankish sympathies. Gregory of Tours reported, "He, because of his enthusiasm for the same cause, was considered suspect by the Goths, and having been carried off into exile, he died."[38]

Verus presumably already was in exile at the time that he sent Leo to Agde, for if he had remained at Tours, he hardly could have instructed his deacon to pass on Ruricius' letter to Caesarius.[39] But Caesarius also noted that Verus subsequently had assured him verbally[40] that he had in fact forwarded Ruricius' letter. The inescapable conclusion, given that Verus surely did not speak to Caesarius at Agde because he was not there, is that Caesarius must have met with Verus after the council at some other place. And this may well have been Toulouse, where Volusianus previously had served at least part of his exile.[41]

The sequence of events now might be reconstructed as follows. Verus' deacon picked up Ruricius' letter of apology when he passed through Limoges — as he surely would have done, assuming that he followed the main road — on a journey south from Tours. He then stopped at Toulouse to visit his exiled bishop, who instructed him to represent him at Agde and to deliver Ruricius' letter to Caesarius. Then, after the council had concluded, several bishops, including Caesarius and Sedatus, travelled on to Toulouse to deal with some unfinished business: Verus' exile. Such a task would be consistent with Sedatus' words to Ruricius. His fear of "laborem, qui incubuit" ("the work that was looming ahead") sounds more like a description of some unpleasant task than of a church council, and his complaint about a protracted "absence from home" likewise would seem to be more appropriate for something other that a church council, which would have lasted only a day or two.

If, as suggested above, Ruricius had been involved in negotiations at Bordeaux for the release of Caesarius from exile, his presence at Toulouse on this occasion would have been all the more desirable. But Ruricius, pleading his infirmities, respectfully declined Sedatus' invitation to a "mutual rendezvous" (*Epist.* 2.35), and instead sent the horse that Sedatus parodied in his reply (*Epist.* "Equum quem"). And as for Verus, there is no indication that his release was secured. For this, Ruricius would have had to bear his share of the blame.

---

[37] *CCL* 148.214-219.

[38] "et ipse pro memoratae causae zelo suspectus habitus a Gothis in exilio deductus vitam finivit" (*HF* 10.31).

[39] Klingshirn, *Letters*, p.83 n.19, however, assumes that Verus was not exiled until later.

[40] "dignatus est dicere."

[41] Greg.Tur. *HF* 2.26, 2.29, 10.31. He eventually was transferred to Spain, where he died.

Ruricius' Posterity

The year of Ruricius' death is shrouded in obscurity. His latest dated letter is from the end of 506, and this has been taken to mean that he died soon afterward, perhaps in 507,[42] the year of the climactic battle of Vouillé. But he may in fact have lived longer. For one thing, the *vita* of Firminus, bishop of Uzès ca. 540-555, mentions as his relative an octogenarian bishop and "patrician" Ruricius:[43] if this is Ruricius of Limoges, then his relationship to Firminus could have been through his grandson Parthenius, for the father of Parthenius' uncle, Ennodius of Pavia, also was named Firminus.[44] Moreover, the father and son of Firminus both had the unusual name Ferreolus, as did a late sixth-century bishop of Limoges,[45] a coincidence that not only gives some credence to the existence of a tie between the family of Firminus and Limoges, but also would suggest some degree of family relationship between Ruricius and his late-sixth-century successor. Ferreolus the son of Firminus, moreover, succeeded his father as bishop at Uzès, and was the author of both a monastic rule and, like his putative relative Ruricius, a collection of letters, said by Gregory of Tours to have been written "in the style of Sidonius."[46]

If this elderly Ruricius is identified as Ruricius of Limoges, it also could suggest that the latter was still alive ca. 510 or even later.[47] Moreover, the Council of Orléans of 511 was attended by bishops from Bourges, Tours, Poitiers, Saintes, Angoulême, Périgueux, Cahors, Rodez, and Clermont, who represented cities on all sides of Limoges.[48] Only the bishop of Limoges was not present, suggesting, it would seem, that he either was incapacitated or was blatantly boycotting the council.[49] The former is perhaps the more likely case.

As to the day of Ruricius' death, an *Obituarium s. Martialis* ("Obituary-List of St. Martial"), written ca. 1300, notes, "On 18 October, bishop Ruricius,"[50] but it is unclear which Ruricius is referred to. And there are other indications

---

[42] As in *PLRE II*, p.960, which presents this as a given; Demeulenaere, *CCL* 64.306, suggests that "without doubt" he died soon after 507.

[43] *Vita Firmini* 1-2: *AASS* October V, p.641.

[44] *PLRE II*, pp.393-394, 471, and discussion above; see Arator, *Epistula ad Parthenium* 93: *PL* 68.252.

[45] See J. Arbellot, "Saint Ferréol, évêque de Limoges au VIᵉ siècle," *Seminaire religieuse de Limoges* (1869) pp.475-479, and discussion below.

[46] The *Regula monastica* survive (*PL* 66.959ff), but the letters (Greg.Tur. *HF* 6.7) are lost.

[47] Indeed, assuming a birthdate of ca. 440, he could have lived until ca. 520.

[48] *CCL* 148A.13-19.

[49] This council unfortunately does not preserve the list of representatives of bishops who could not attend.

[50] "Roricio episcopus XV kal. Nov.": see Krusch, *MGH AA* 8.lxvi; and A. Leroux, E. Molinier, A. Thomas, *Documents historiques bas-latins, provençaux et Français concernant principalement la Marche et le Limousin* vol.1 (Limoges, 1883) p.77; reprinted in *Bulletin du Limousin* 30 (1882) pp.117-300, and 32 (1885) pp.147-307.

that the elder Ruricius was commemorated on July 21 or 24,[51] which would mean that he died during the dreaded summer season. So even the day of Ruricius' death, so commonly recorded for others, is not completely clear.

Ruricius was interred in the church of St. Augustine that he had built.[52] The *Translatio Asclepii* noted, "In fact, the aforementioned Ruricius was the twenty-third bishop of the see of the church of Limoges after the blessed Martial; his body was interred in the aforementioned monastery and, elevated above the greater altar, he rests in peace along with the blessed Flavia."[53] And Bernardus Guido went on to say, "Twenty eight bishops are said to be buried [there], of whom the tombs of twelve are visible, and the bodies of the two bishops and saints Ruricius and Asclepius are in a reliquary over the greater altar along with the virgin martyr St. Flavia."[54] In the Roman martyrology, the virgin Flavia of Messina and her brother, the monk Placidus, were martyred by the pagan pirate Manuches on 5 October. Her relics may have been obtained by bishop Turpio at the same time as those of Augustine discussed above.

As already noted, Limoges itself also recedes into the mist after Ruricius' death. Even the identity of Ruricius' successor is uncertain. The confused *fasti* (episcopal catalogues) are not much help, as seen in the following excerpts from the two earliest ones, those of Adémar of Chabannes from the eleventh century and Bernard Itier from the thirteenth, accompanied by a list of bishops who are independently attested:[55]

THE BISHOPS OF LIMOGES, CA. 450-700

Limoges catalogue	*Independently Attested Bishops*
Astidius	
Rusticus	Ruricius I (ca. 485-510)
item Rusticus	Ruricius II (ca. 535-549)
Exochius	Exocius (ca. 550-565)

---

[51] Demeulenaere, *CCL* 64.306; see *AASS* Oct. VIII, pp.59-69; P. Viard, *Bibliotheca sanctorum* vol.11 (Rome, 1968) pp.508-509.

[52] See Soulard, "Reliques," p.86, for a suggestion that Ruricius was initially interred in the church of St. Paul.

[53] "erat enim dictus Roricius post beatum Martialem sedis ecclesiae Lemovicensis XXIII episcopus, cuius corpus post vitam beatam in praefato monasterio sepultum et in capsa maioris altaris elevatum cum beata Flavia in pace quiescit...": Becquet, "Asclèpe," pp.19-21.

[54] "in eo monasterio viginti octo episcopi tumulati dicuntur, quorum tumuli duodecim discernuntur, et duorum sanctorum episcoporum Roricii et Asclepii corpora in capsa supra maius altare cum s. Flavia virgine et martyre" (Labbe, *Nova bibliotheca*, p.277). See also Aubrun, *Limoges*, p.89; and R. Crozet, "Lieux de sepulture des évêques de Limoges, des origines chrétiennes à la fin du XIIe siècle," *BSAHL* 98 (1971) pp.149-152.

[55] See Aubrun, *Limoges*, pp.87-101; and Duchesne, *Fastes* 2.48-49.

Ferriolus	Ferreolus (ca. 565-591)
Asclepiodotus	
Asclepius	
Simplicius	Simplicius (ca. 640)
Felix	Felix (ca. 650)
item Adelfius	
Lupus	Lupus (ca. 625/635)
Erchenobertus	
Caesarius	
Roricius	Rusticus (ca. 670/675)
item Roricius	
Ermenmarus	Emenus (ca. 695/700)
Ermenus	
Salutaris	
Agericus	(see below)
Sacerdos	(see below)
Autsindus	Autsindus (ca. 680/685)

The *fasti* have some serious problems. For one thing, there is a confusion between the names Ruricius and Rusticus: the names are switched, and a second Rusticus/Ruricius seems to have been added in the second group. There also appear to be several doublets, viz. Asclepiodotus/Asclepius and Ermenmarus/Ermenus. And there are some serious chronological inconsistencies: a number of known seventh-century bishops are out of sequence, and the bishops Salutaris, Agericus, and Sacerdos, if they are in their proper places, must have been very short lived. All these observations suggest that the *fasti* stand in need of some pruning and re-arranging.

First, the Ruricii. The younger Ruricius is given as Ruricius' immediate successor, but, if one accepts ca. 507 as the date of the latter's death, this is virtually impossible. For it would mean that Ruricius II became bishop when he was no more than 17 years old, a most-uncanonical age, for bishops were expected to be at least 30 years of age. It may be, therefore, either that the elder Ruricius survived later than has been thought, or that there there was at least one intervening bishop between him and his grandson, if not both. One possible scenario can be found in a *Vita Sacerdotis* ("Life of Sacerdos") written by Hugo Floriacensis in the twelfth century but based, it seems, upon a ninth-century version from Périgueux.[56] Sacerdos was said to have been the son of Laban and Mundana, two aristocrats of Bordeaux. Early in his life, the "most Chris-

---

[56] See *AASS* May I, pp.12-18; *PL* 163.985ff: see also Appendix III.

tian king Anticius" arrived at the *vicus Calabrum* ("hamlet of Calabrum"), located between Périgueux and Cahors, and was asked by Laban to serve as Sacerdos' god-parent. Anticius agreed, and even granted Calabrum to Sacerdos, to be possessed "by hereditary right." As a boy, Sacerdos was educated in "literature and Christian teaching" by Capuanus, bishop of Cahors, "lest he be enveloped by heretical depravity, of which there was a great abundance in that region at that time." This suggests that Calabrum lay in this ecclesiastical jurisdiction, and this is confirmed by the *Prosarium Lemovicense*, which described Sacerdos as "born in the homeland of Aquitania, of a family of Cahors."[57] After being ordained deacon, he entered the monastery at Calabrum, and after seven years was made abbot. Only later did he become a priest (perhaps at thirty, the canonical age).[58] Subsequently, at the death of bishop Aggericus of Limoges, Sacerdos was confirmed as bishop by "the king of the Franks, Clovis the Elder, ruler of that province." At the end of his life, Sacerdos withdrew to Argentacum (Argentat) and there he died on 7 May.

If "the elder Clovis" is Clovis I,[59] it would mean that Aggericus' death and Sacerdos' ordination must have occurred after the Frankish occupation of Limoges in 507/508 and before Clovis' death in 511. This chronology would be consistent with an identification of the "heretical depravity" as Arianism and of "king Anticius" as Ecdicius, the son of Eparchius Avitus, who in the years ca. 471-474 led the Arvernian resistance against the Visigoths and in 474 was made Patrician and Master of Soldiers. This would place Sacerdos' birth in the early 470s, his entry into the monastery in the 490s, and his ordination as priest in the early 500s, all of which is consistent with his being a near successor of Ruricius. As for bishop Capuanus of Cahors, he is otherwise unknown, but the *fasti* for the city are empty for nearly the entire fifth century.[60]

If this reconstruction is correct, then it might seem that at least two bishops — Aggericus and Sacerdos — intervened between Ruricius and his grandson. The only other appearance of "Aggericus", moreover, is as the predecessor of Sacerdos in the *fasti* of Limoges, with both falling just before Autsindus, who is attested in 683.[61] This date, of course, could vitiate the chronology of the *vita* were it not for the questionable reliability of the *fasti* at this very point.[62]

---

[57] "...Aquitanica / ortus patria / Cadurcensis / stirpis": *Pros.Lem.* no.190, pp.209-210.

[58] Council of Agde, canon 17 (*CCL* 148.201).

[59] The only other one being Clovis II, king of Neustria and Burgundy from 638 to 657.

[60] See Duchesne, *Fastes* 2.41-42: the only known fifth-century bishop of Cahors is Alethius, at the very beginning of the century. Note the suggestion made at *Epist.* 1.7 below that Ruricius' correspondent Bassulus also was bishop of Cahors.

[61] Duchesne, *Fastes* 2.52.

[62] Indeed, the presence of Aggericus and Sacerdos in the *fasti* could be an interpolation from the *vita*.

In a further attempt to place Aggericus and Sacerdos, one might note a number of coincidences between the lives of Ruricius and Sacerdos: both, it seems, had connections to Bordeaux (Ruricius perhaps through the Leontii, Sacerdos though his parents);[63] they lived not far from each other (Ruricius at Gurdo/Decaniacum and Sacerdos at Calabrum); both had other connections south of Limoges (Ruricius at Briva and Userca, Sacerdos at Argenta); both had ties to Cahors (Ruricius' property was in its territory, and Sacerdos was a native); and both were connected to the family of Eparchius Avitus (Ruricius through Avitus' son Agricola, and Sacerdos to Avitus' son Ecdicius). On such grounds one might suggest not only that Ruricius and Sacerdos were related, but even that the name Aggericus conceals the name of Ruricius, for "Aggericus" is but one step removed from "Agricius" and "Agroecius," which already have been conjectured to have been alternate forms of "Ruricius."[64] If this identification is correct, not only does Sacerdos belong in the *fasti* between the two Ruricii,[65] but Ruricius' family also established something of an hereditary hold upon the see of Limoges, which could have been perpetuated by Ferreolus, who was suggested above to have been another potential relative. If such were the case, it would have been even more appropriate for Ferreolus to have commissioned Venantius Fortunatus to compose the epitaph for the two Ruricii.[66]

Finally, the preceding discussion permits the construction of revised episcopal *fasti* for Limoges ca. 450-700:

---

[63] A connection made stronger if, given the *vita*'s apparent penchant for mangling names, the name "Laban" conceals the name "Leontius."

[64] Indeed, it may even be that Ruricius had a nickname such as "Agroecius," and that he was more properly known as "Ruricius qui et Agroecius."

[65] And another late source, the *Prosarium Lemovicense*, has Sacerdos as "the successor to the virtues of Germanus of Auxerre (418-446)" (*Pros.Lem.* no.190, p.210), placing him, again, not long after the middle of the fifth century.

[66] See Appendix II. Given that Venantius seems to have ceased his poetic activities after becoming bishop of Poitiers ca. 593 (Duchesne, *Fastes* 2.83), and that Ferreolus was bishop of Limoges until ca. 591, Ferreolus, again, would seem the most likely one to have requested the epitaphs. The only other possibility would be Ferreolus' successor, Asclepius, who, as seen above, also had a connection, at least in death, to Ruricius.

THE BISHOPS OF LIMOGES CA. 450-700 (RECONSTRUCTED CATALOGUE)

Astidius (ca. 470)
[Interregnum, ordinations forbidden by Visigoths] (ca. 470-485)
Ruricius I = "Aggericus" (ca. 485-510)
Sacerdos (ca. 510-520)
Ruricius II (ca. 520-550)
Exocius (ca. 550-565)
Ferreolus (ca. 565-591)
Asclepius/"Asclepiodotus" (ca. 591-625)
Lupus (ca. 625/635)
Simplicius (ca. 640)
Felix (ca. 650)
Adelfius (ca. 650/670)
Erchenobertus (ca. 650/670)
Caesarius (ca. 650/670)
Rusticus (ca. 670/675)
Autsindus (ca. 680/685)
Ermenmarus/Ermenus/Emenus (ca. 695/700)
Salutaris (ca. 700)

THE CORRESPONDENCE:

CONTENTS, STYLE, AND ORGANIZATION

The Collection

The letters written by and to Ruricius survive in only a single manuscript (an "unica"), the *Codex Sangallensis* 190.[1] They have been edited and published several times, beginning in the early seventeenth century with Canisius, whose text and commentary appears in volume 58 of the *Patrologia latina*.[2] Subsequent editions were published by Krusch in 1887;[3] Engelbrecht in 1891;[4] and, most recently, Demeulenaere in 1985.[5] Three letters of the collection also were edited individually by Morin.[6] In addition, a proposed early eighteenth-century edition by J. Danton, based upon the text of Canisius, survives only in the pre-publication manuscript.[7] The translation below has benefited from the textual criticism of all these editors.[8]

In the manuscript, the letters written by Ruricius himself are divided into two books of very unequal length. The first has 18 letters and, depending on how they are enumerated, the second has 63, 64, or 65: the variations were caused because *Epist.* 2.12 is repeated as 2.53; and *Epist.* 2.9 lacks a heading and is therefore sometimes merged with *Epist.* 2.8. The Canisius edition retains both

---

[1] See below for discussion of the manuscript itself.

[2] H. Canisius, *Antiquae lectiones*, vol.5 (Ingolstadt, 1604) pp. 461-523; reprinted in the *Maxima bibliotheca veterum patrum* (Lyon, 1677) vol.8, p.524ff; and reprinted and renumbered in *PL* 58.67-124, with the letters to Ruricius, and other letters of Faustus included, on col.837-871.

[3] B. Krusch ed., *Fausti aliorumque epistulae ad Ruricium aliosque*, *MGH AA* 8 (Berlin, 1887) pp.265-298; and *Ruricii epistulae*, ibid. pp.299-350.

[4] A. Engelbrecht ed., *Fausti Reiensis et Ruricii opera*, *CSEL* 21 (Vienna, 1891): *Fausti epistulae*, pp.161-219; *Ruricii epistularum libri duo*, pp.349-450; *Epistulae ad Ruricium scriptae*, p.443ff.

[5] R. Demeulenaere ed., *Foebadius, Victricius, Leporius, Vincentius Lerinensis, Evagrius, Ruricius*, *CCL* 64 (Turnholt, 1985): *Ruricii Lemovicensis epistularum libri duo*, pp.312-394; *Epistulae ad Ruricium scriptae*, pp.397-405; *Epistulae Fausti ad Ruricium*, pp.406-415.

[6] G. Morin, *Sancti Caesarii episcopi Arelatensis. Opera omnia. Vol. II. Opera varia* (Maretioli, 1942) pp.7-8 (*Epist.* "Dum nimium" of Caesarius to Ruricius, and Ruricius, *Epist.* 2.33, 36 only).

[7] *Codex Parisinus latinus* 11,378, dated 1732, with the title, "Anicii Ruricii Aquitani Lemovicensis episcopi ac quorumdam virorum illustrium ad ipsum epistolae omnes quae exstant... studio et labore Joannis Dantonii J.C." Danton reorganized the letters into what he considered to be chronological order: see, A. Engelbrecht, "Eine handschriftliche Ausgabe der Briefe des Ruricius," in *Idem, Patristische Analecten* (Vienna, 1892) pp.20-47. Stephanus Baluzius also may have done a manuscript edition in the mid seventeenth century (Engelbrecht, *CSEL* 21.lxxiv).

[8] In addition, Hagendahl, *Ruricius*, pp.101-108, also has suggested a number of emendations (cited below simply as "Hagendahl"), and the edition of Krusch in *MGH AA* 8 adds additional conjectures by Lütjohann and Mommsen.

letters to Praesidius and combines *Epist.* 2.8 and 2.9 into a single letter, resulting in 64 letters in book II. The more recent editions of Krusch, Engelbrecht, and Demeulenaere, however, rightly separate *Epist.* 2.8 and 2.9. Krusch suppresses the second copy of the letter to Praesidius, and therefore also has 64 letters in book II.[9] Engelbrecht and Demeulenaere retain both copies of the Praesidius letter, and have 65 letters in book II. This last enumeration that is used below, giving a total of 83 letters written by Ruricius.

One noteworthy aspect of the Ruricius collection is that it also contains thirteen letters, by seven different persons, that were addressed to Ruricius.[10] And even though the letters by and to Ruricius appear in the manuscript in two separate groups, it is clear that nearly all of the letters to Ruricius, not to mention three additional letters to Ruricius from Sidonius' collection, either resulted in extant replies from Ruricius or were replies to extant letters of his.[11] For this reason, in the translations below the letters written to Ruricius are presented either before or after the appropriate letter written by Ruricius. These sequences of letters provide a rare opportunity to see series of letters in an exchange, and they show how Gallo-Roman writers tailored their correspondence to each others' individual needs, expectations, and personalities.

All of the letters in the collection are personal letters;[12] none was written on behalf of any secular authority (as were some of the letters, for example, of Avitus of Vienne). The writers and their subjects appear as real people, with cares and concerns often very much like our own.[13] They experience personal problems, such as illnesses, deaths, or difficulties with wayward children. They get into trouble; they apologize for minor offenses, real or imagined; they become angry if they feel slighted; they sometimes fail to carry out their responsibilities; they become ill; they joke; and they grieve.

Ruricius' collection can tell us much about how the Gallo-Roman aristocracy responded to the disappearance of Roman authority and the "barbarization" of Gaul. For epistolography was a literary genre that was admirably suited to its

---

[9] As do H.W.G. Peter, "Ruricius (und Faustus)," in H.W.G. Peter, W.G. Hermann, *Der Brief in der römischen Literatur* (Leipzig, 1901) pp.158-162 at p.158; A. Loyen, *Sidoine Apollinaire et l'esprit précieux en Gaule aux derniers jours de l'empire* (Paris, 1943) p.68; and M. Schanz ed., *Die römische Litteratur von Constantin bis zum Gesetzgebungswerk Justinians*, in M. Schanz, C. Hosius eds., *Geschichte der römischen Litteratur bis zum Gesetzgebunswerk Justinians* vol.4.2 (Munich, 1920) p.551.

[10] At one point it was suggested by that these letters all had been written by Faustus of Riez "sub variorum nominibus" ("using various names") (Canisius, *PL* 58.865).

[11] Compare the corpus of Sidonius, which includes a single letter written by someone else, *Epist.* 4.2, by Claudianus Mamertus of Vienne, which is followed (*Epist.* 4.3) by Sidonius' response.

[12] See Hagendahl, *Ruricius*, p.11, "Ses lettres sont de vraies lettres privées."

[13] Contrary to the unsympathetic views of Loyen, *L'esprit*, p.169, who suggests that Ruricius' letters have only "un intérêt très médiocre"; and Hagendahl, *Ruricius*, p.4, who asserts that they are not "spontané et plein de vie," and, in general, are "dénuées d'intérêt réel" (p.10).

times. It permitted the preservation, even if only of the form, of the old ways of doing things, and gave Gauls a medium in which they could continue "business as usual" regardless of their personal circumstances. It provided for the day-to-day maintenance of friendships and social intercourse at a time when Gallic aristocrats, living in the secluded splendor of their estates, increasingly felt cut off from each other. Gauls who were isolated by geographical distance and political boundaries, not to mention the occasional outbreaks of warfare, and who generally had little, or no, opportunity to meet, or who had never met at all, could interact, by means of their letters, in the same manner as in the past.

A number of repetitious themes appear in the letters, and can provide some insight into what their writers had on their minds. In particular, there was a great concern for maintaining ties of friendship, and letter writing even was viewed as a duty. Friends expected each other to write, even if only a brief pro forma letter, whenever a carrier happened to be available, and they peevishly complained when a friend passed up the opportunity to do so. They expressed desires to visit each other even when it was fairly clear that such visits would never occur. Friendly ties were reinforced with various kinds of favors, including the loaning of books, gifts of edibles, and the furnishing of building materials and artisans. For bishops, letters provided a venue for the fulfilment of one's episcopal duties, as seen in letters of intercession, condolence, and, in particular, exhortation to lead a better life or to undertake or maintain a life of penitence. In all of these regards, Ruricius' correspondence provides examples of the kinds of material and spiritual interchange that late Roman aristocrats sought and provided in their attempts to preserve their familiar world.

Composition, Style, Vocabulary, and Thought

Ruricius' letters exhibit many idiosyncracies of composition, style, and vocabulary. For example, Ruricius often cited other works. In particular, he enjoyed quoting himself, and recycling what he must have considered to be good passages. Indeed, Ruricius' love of his own boiler plate might lead one to wonder whether some passages of an "all-purpose" nature also were used elsewhere, perhaps in his sermons.[14] Ruricius also was fond of reprising the words of distinguished correspondents, such as Sidonius and Faustus, in letters either to the original writer or to other correspondents. The latter practice would presume, of course, that the recipient would be conversant with the words or style of the person quoted. Nor should this technique be dismissed as mere imitation

---

[14] For example, the sermon "On the Natal day of the Apostles Peter and Paul" in the Eusebian corpus, which dates to Gaul circa the late fifth and early sixth centuries (*CCL* 101.377-380). It contains several Rurician elements, such as extensive alliteration (e.g. "clamat utique christianorum cordibus sanguis piorum, sanguis spiritalium bellatorum"), and references to ill health.

or the result of a lack of creativity on the part of Ruricius or his correspondents.[15] It was meant rather as a sincere form of compliment, and it gave Ruricius and his friends a shared sense of elitism and mutual understanding when, for example, they quoted to each other works of other friends.[16]

Ruricius also quoted from famous writers of the classical past. He cited not only Cassian, and in particular the *De incarnatione contra Nestorium* ("On the Incarnation against Nestorius") (*Epist.* 1.3-4,9,11, 2.3,11,18,41); but also Eucherius of Lyon (*Epist.* 1.1), Paulinus of Nola (*Epist.* 1.1,16, 2.3,17,34,52), Prudentius (*Epist.* 1.3), Jerome (*Epist.*1.3,5,8, 2.11,30), perhaps Cicero (*Epist.* 2.1), and, of course, Vergil (*Epist.* 1.17, 2.4,10). There also are several citations (*Epist.* 1.16,18, 2.41,64) from the *Epistula ad Claudiam sororem suam de ultimo iudicio* ("Letter to his Sister Claudia on the Last Judgment"), which is attributed to Sulpicius Severus but whose author is in fact unknown.[17]

Like all ecclesiastical authors of his day, Ruricius quoted extensively from scripture, sometimes in a rather cavalier fashion: on one occasion (*Epist.* 2.23), for example, he concluded a string of biblical citations with the rather flippant words, "et reliqua" ("and so on"). His quotations seem often to have been from memory and sometimes seem rather heavy-handed, as if he knew that he was expected to work them in, but was not quite sure how to do so effectively. Any awkwardness in this regard might have been, in part, the result not only of his unfamiliarity with the material (not having studied it during his schooling) but also because of his desire to tailor his letters to their recipients. He made particular use of the Bible in letters to intellectuals such as Faustus of Riez (*Epist.* 1.1-2) and Julianus Pomerius (*Epist.* 1.17).

The predilection to use literary tags implies the ownership of a rather extensive library, and like many Roman aristocrats of his day, Ruricius was a dedicated bibliophile. For example, Sidonius Apollinaris assisted him in obtaining up-to-date copies of scripture (Sid.Apoll. *Epist.* 5.15). Ruricius regularly exchanged books with his confrères to be read, copied, and cited. Along with works of his friends Faustus of Riez and Sidonius (*Epist.* 1.1, 2.26),[18] he mentions having in his library volumes of Cyprian of Carthage, Hilary of Poitiers, Ambrose of Milan, and Augustine of Hippo (*Epist.* 1.6, 2.17; Taurentius, *Epist.* "Litterae sanctitatis"). Cyprian, however, is the only one of these authors actually cited in Ruricius' extant correspondence (*Epist.* 1.5, 2.1,4).

---

[15] See J. Basnagius (*PL* 58.68): "He seems guilty of theft (*plagii*) because he appropriated words and phrases so often"; and Hagendahl, "Ruricius plagiare" (*Ruricius*, pp.12-31), who presumes (p.26) that it was always Ruricius who mimicked others, and never vice versa.

[16] As when Ruricius quotes Sidonius to Hesperius (*Epist.* 1.4)

[17] *CSEL* 1.219-223. Ruricius' citations suggest that the letter may have originated in the context of Ruricius' own literary circle.

[18] G. Bardy, "Copies et éditions au Ve siècle, " *Revue des sciences religieuses* 23 (1949) pp.38-52, however, assumes (p.50) that Ruricius did not have a copy of Sidonius.

Ruricius was well acquainted with all the stylistic tricks of the trade, and used them with gay abandon.[19] He loved *traductio*, the use of different forms of the same word, and he also made much use of alliteration, chiasmus, and antithesis. He tried to live up to Sidonius' literary model, but he confessed (*Epist.* 2.26) that he himself had a hard time following Sidonius' rhetoric.[20] Ruricius had certain favorite metaphors, such as the prodigal son, the irrigation of parched soil, the seeking of subterranean channels, and the assaying of gold. He used agricultural terminology to refer to literary works, such as "blossoms from that twig" (*Epist.* 1.5), or "shoots from my fir trees" (*Epist.* 1.11). Ruricius also made repeated references to aspects of judgment, such as judicial verity and upright judges, which may reflect his legal training. And some particularly Rurician usages include the phrase "habeo tanti," meaning to "consider important"; and use of "unde" ("for this reason") at the beginning of a sentence.

In matters of social etiquette, Ruricius was sensitive to the proper way to address his correspondents.[21] In both his texts and his salutations he used several different kinds of elaborate honorifics, modified by either *vester*/*vestra* (plural "your") or, for his intimates, *tuus*/*tua* (singular "your"). Some honorifics reflected a family tie, such as *vestra* or *tua germanitas* ("brotherhood"). Others referred specifically to an individual's aristocratic status, such as *vestra dignatio* ("worthiness"), *vestra nobilitas* ("nobility"), *vestra potestas* ("authority"), or *vestra sublimitas* ("exaltedness"). Other titles were reserved for ecclesiastics, whether bishops (*vester apostolatus*[22] ["apostlehood"], *vestra sanctitas* ["sanctity"],[23] *vestra sanctimonia* ["holiness"]); clerics in general (*vestra* or *tua beatitudo* ["blessedness"], *vestra gratia* ["grace"]); or clerics and penitents (*vestra* or *tua veneratio* ["veneration"], *vestra fraternitas* ["fraternity"]). For a more intimate touch, personal characteristics could be personified in honorifics such as *vestra* or *tua caritas* ("charity"), *vestra dignatio* ("worthiness"), *vestra divinctio* ("steadfastness"), *vestra dulcedo* ("sweetness"), *vestra* or *tua magnanimitas* ("magnanimity"), *vestra* or *tua pietas* ("piety") (used for both laypersons and ecclesiastics), and *vestra* or *tua unanimitas* ("single-mindedness").

---

[19] In general, see Loyen, *L'esprit*, pp.169-173, "La préciosité de Ruricius"; and Hagendahl, *Ruricius*, for use of *clausulae* (prose rhythms) (pp.32-50); rhyme and various kinds of parallel structure (pp.51-66); and figures such as antithesis, plays on words, and metaphor (pp.67-89).

[20] For conventional professions of lack of skill and affectations of modesty, see Hagendahl, *Ruricius*, pp.94-98.

[21] See, in general, E. Jerg, *Vir venerabilis. Untersuchungen zur Titulatur der Bischöfe in den ausserkirchlichen Texten der spätantike als Beitrag zur Deutung ihrer öffentlichen Stellung* (Vienna, 1970); and M.B. O'Brien, *Titles of Address in Christian Latin Epistolography* (Washington, 1930); and, in particular, A. Engelbrecht, "Titel und Titulaturen in den Briefen des Ruricius und seiner Genossen," *Patristische Analecten* (Vienna, 1892) pp.48-83.

[22] A rare honorific of masculine gender.

[23] Used fifteen times, all bishops except for *Epist.* 1.6, to the priest Nepotianus.

In general, Ruricius' manner of presentation and use of rhetorical tropes and figures sometimes may seem a bit overdone, but one must remember that he was manifesting the preferred style of his age. Ruricius in fact developed an artful, subtle, and often unappreciated independence of expression even as he wrote within the context of the conventional rhetorical principles that he had learned so well. Even when repeating commonplaces, he shows a surprisingly modern sensitivity to how people interact, and to how human society functions. In one instance, for example, he suggested (*Epist.* 2.18), "In no way can we assess better the secrets of the hearts of others than by the contemplation of our own hidden thoughts." And in a passage that many modern teachers could take to heart he noted (*Epist.* 2.26) that one "ought to learn before teaching, because one too quickly adopts the haughtiness of the scholar unless one has initially endured the servitude of the student."

Assembly and Organization

At first glance, it appears that Ruricius' letters, and particularly those in the mammoth second book, lack any organizational structure. Careful investigation, however, can identify some patterns that unify different sections of the corpus.

The 18 letters of Book I include only correspondence written between ca. 470 and ca. 485/490. It has elements of homogeneity not only topically, but also with regard to the clustering of letters sent to the same person, viz.:

1-2	Two letters to Faustus of Riez
3-10	Letters relating to literature and learning:
3-5	Three letters to Hesperius on teaching and literature
6-8	Book borrowing
8-9	Two letters to Sidonius regarding literature and learning
10	Mythological topics
12-14	Three letters to Celsus, a childhood friend and likely relative
15-17	To distinguished persons (Aeonius, Sidonius, Julianus Pomerius), the first and third of them being from Arles
18	To his son Ommatius, another family member

These letters seem to be in rough chronological order, beginning with the letters to Faustus, which date perhaps to the early 470s, and concluding with four written in the mid to late 480s.[24] Moreover, the final letter provides a kind of

---

[24] If these last letters are indeed all of similar date, it would suggest that Aeonius became bishop of Arles in the mid to late 480s and not in the early 490s, as generally assumed (see Duchesne, *Fastes* 1.257; Peter, "Ruricius," p.159). His predecessor Leontius is last attested in 474 (Sid. Apoll. *Epist.* 7.6), and his own first dated appearance is in 494 (Gelasius, *Epist.* "Inter difficultates" = *Epist.Arel.* 22: *MGH Epist.* 3.33). *Epist.* 1.16-18 also refer or allude to Ruricius' new episcopal status. Peter, ibid., suggests that the first fourteen letters are in chronological order, and notes that none of the addressees received any of the letters in Book II.

"book-end" vis-à-vis the initial ones: just as Ruricius adopted the religious life in the first few letters, his son Ommatius did so in the last one. The letters in this book also are quite homogeneous in length, with none being over 50 lines (as measured in the *CSEL* edition) long. Furthermore, the 18 letters in book I are what one might consider to be a "normal" number: Sidonius' nine books of letters, for example, contained anywhere from 11 to 25 letters each.

All of these considerations suggest that the first book of letters was carefully organized as a unit in its own right; it may even have circulated as such before ca. 490. Furthermore, the organizational structure of the first book also seems to have been mirrored, to some extent, in the organization of the letters written to Ruricius, for in the manuscript the five letters from Faustus to Ruricius appear at the beginning of their group, just as Ruricius' own corpus begins with two letters to Faustus. This must have been done consciously, either by Ruricius himself or by whomever assembled the collection in its present form.

Book II is more difficult to assess. As a whole, the letters clearly are not in chronological order: many of *Epist.* 2.49-64, for example, had to be written before 496,[25] but *Epist.* 2.33-36 date to 506. As seen already, moreover, the book contains some 65 letters, enough for approximately four conventional books. But even though there are no indications of divisions in the manuscript, there are some organizational patterns suggesting that this book is not merely a farrago of letters lumped together into a single elephantine unit.[26]

Someone, it seems, attempted to organize some of the letters into internally consistent "dossiers", including, for example, 1) Groups of letters to the same individuals, such as *Epist.*2.1-5, to Namatius and Ceraunia, and *Epist.* 2.55-58, to Aprunculus of Clermont; not to mention *Epist.* 2.8-9 to Aeonius of Arles; 2.10-11 to Julianus Pomerius; *Epist.* 2.18-19 and 2.34-35 to Sedatus of Nîmes; *Epist.* 2.24-25 to Constantius; *Epist.* 2.26-27 to Apollinaris; and even *Epist.* 2.61 and 2.63 to Vittamerus; and 2) Groups of letters dealing with related issues or circumstances, such as *Epist.* 2.26-28, sent together to Clermont; and *Epist.* 2. 33-40, all dated to ca. 506, nearly all addressed to or relating to bishops of Provence, and paralleled by four of the extant letters to Ruricius.

Other indications of organizational structure can be found in patterns of salutations and farewells. Some salutations are simple, such as, "Bishop Ruricius to Bishop Euphrasius" (*Epist.* 2.22), whereas others are very fulsome, for example, "Bishop Ruricius to the Lord of his Spirit and a Lord to be Cultivated with his Innards in Christ, Pomerius" (*Epist.* 2.10). Now, in Book I the

---

[25] See Krusch, *MGH AA* 8.lxviii.
[26] E.g, Peter, "Ruricius," p.159, divides book II into two groups: 1) Epist. 2.1-40, ordered chronologically (with the first five written before 485), with elaborate titulature, and with extensive citations from scripture; and 2) *Epist.* 2.41-64, described as not chronologically ordered, "briefer and more friendly," with shorter titulature and essentially without biblical citations.

salutations are very consistent in form; the first sixteen letters begin with words addressing and describing the recipient in the dative, followed simply by "Ruricius"; the final two add "episcopus" ("bishop"), reflecting Ruricius' new status.

The first twenty letters of Book II follow the same pattern, with rather elaborate salutations in the dative followed by "Ruricius," "Ruricius episcopus," or "episcopus Ruricius." But beginning with *Epist.* 2.21, a new form appears, with Ruricius' name at the beginning, followed by the recipient in the dative: thirty of the remaining forty-four letters use this formula. *Epist.* 2.21-40, moreover, not only have a tendency to use a salutation formula that ends in "salutem" ("greetings") or "suo salutem" ("greetings to his own...") (*Epist.* 2.21, 26-31, 41), but also are the only letters in the corpus to have farewell salutations.

Farewell salutations were written in the hand of the sender to give a personal touch to the missive, especially if the body of the letter had been written by a secretary.[27] Only the copy of a letter that was actually sent (or an exact transcript of it) would contain these parting words. For example, of the twelve complete letters in the *Sangallensis* sent to Ruricius, eight have farewell salutations.[28] Farewells occurred in both long and short forms. The former often began with a subjunctive reference to the divinity and concluded with the recipient being directly addressed in the vocative. For example, Faustus' letters to Ruricius conclude with the words such as, "May our Lord God multiply his blessings in you through a longevity happy and pleasing to him, most pious lord and a son to be esteemed by me with the greatest honor in Christ the Lord." This type can be so long as to virtually constitute a separate paragraph.[29]

The letters written by Ruricius, however, only make use of the short form, including variants such as "Vale" ("Farewell") (*Epist.* 2.28, 30); "Ora pro me" ("Pray for me") (*Epist.* 2.22, 29, 34-36, 38, 40); or "Opto bene agas" ("I hope you are doing well") (*Epist.* 2.32, 37, 39).[30] And it would seem that in later copies of the correspondence an effort was made to show that Ruricius' farewell salutations originally had been written in "another hand", that is, Ruricius' own, for rather than being copied in the usual miniscule script, they are written partly or wholly in uncial or semi-uncial, early forms of display script (Figs.8-9).[31]

---

[27] At the end of his longest letter, *Epist.* 2.4, for example, Ruricius writes, "I have dictated ... these words," indicating his own use of a secretary. For discussion of farewell salutations, see R.W. Mathisen, "*Et manu papae*: Papal Subscriptions written *sua manu* in Late Antiquity," in G. Schmeling ed., *Festschrift for Paul Lachlan MacKendrick* (Chicago, 1997).

[28] The letter of Faustus to Paulinus, "Admiranda mihi," also has one.

[29] Of the letters with farewell salutations written to Ruricius, six use the long form, and two, those of Taurentius and Caesarius of Arles, use a short form, "Ora pro me."

[30] *Epist.* 1.16 also includes an anomalous form of farewell, "Pax, pax, pax."

[31] For the use of a different type of script for the farewell salutation, see E.A. Lowe, "The Script of the Farewell and Date Formulae in Early Papal Documents," *Revue bénédictine* 69 (1959) pp.22-31.

As for why the other letters do not have farewell salutations, it is possible, of course, that they were edited out by the *Sangallensis* copyist. But, if this was the case, why were they retained only for letters in this particular group? It might be better, perhaps, to adopt a working hypothesis that they do not appear in the other letters because they were not present in the exemplar (the manuscript from which the *Sangallensis* was copied). And this may be because *Epist.* 2.21-40 were for some reason treated differently by Ruricius, or his secretary, when they were written or copied. Such a suggestion gains some support from the observation that this group includes the latest of Ruricius' letters; indeed, many, and perhaps all, of them seem to be dated to after ca. 495. They therefore would represent Ruricius' epistolography, and perhaps his archive as well, in their most developed and up-to-date forms.

Furthermore, if the first book of letters covers the years ca. 470-485/490 and *Epist.* 2.21-40 date to after ca. 495, it does not seem untoward to suggest that *Epist.* 2.1-20 tend to deal with the intervening years: ca. 485-500, a hypothesis that is corroborated, for example, by the letters, such as those to Aeonius of Arles, that can be dated. *Epist.* 2.1-20 and 2.21-40, therefore, form two relatively homogeneous groups, of 20 and 19 letters respectively, with regard to both their form of presentation and their date, and one therefore might speculate that they formed the kernel of proposed second and third books in the collection.

If the preceding reconstruction is valid, it would mean that the remaining letters, *Epist.* 2.41-65, were in some sense "left-overs" from the initial organizational effort.[32] And several considerations do suggest that these letters did comprise something of the remnants of the selection process. For example, the letters in Book I average about 30 lines each, those in "pseudo-Book II" (*Epist.* 2.1-20) some 44 lines each,[33] and those in "pseudo-Book III" (*Epist.* 2.21-40) about 28 lines. But the average length of the remaining letters plummets to 16 lines, with 8 being 10 or fewer lines long.

Which is not to say, however, that suggestions of selection and grouping cannot be found even in this final section. For example, several of the letters in this group (*Epist.* 2.41-42, 45-46, 48, 54-55, 62, 65), have at the end the notation "finit" (Fig.10). The only other place this notation occurs is at the end of *Epist.* 1.1. It is not immediately clear whether this was a contemporary scribal addition, made at the time the manuscript was created, or part of the exemplar. A possible argument in support of the former suggestion is that most of the notations are in a distinctive cursive script, which may mark an attempt, as in the case of the farewell salutations, to distinguish between different usages in

---

[32] In the same way, perhaps, that Sidonius did not include all of the letters that he had preserved in his earliest books of letters.

[33] Note that two giant letters, of 129 and 132 lines, somewhat skew the average.

the exemplar.[34] These observations do not, however, deal with the question of why only certain letters had these notations, and why, after beginning with the very first letter, they are lacking until *Epist.* 2.42. One possibility could be that a "finit" that occurred in Ruricius' original drafts was deleted when the pseudo-books "II" and "III" were created.

Analysis of their salutations, moreover, suggests that at least some of these concluding letters were organized into dossiers on this basis also. For example, the salutations of *Epist.* 2.43-47 are the only ones to cite the addressee using *ad* ("to") plus the accusative and Ruricius in the genitive, for example, "Of Ruricius to so-and-so." And the salutations of *Epist.* 2.50-61 all are of the form "Bishop Ruricius to so-and-so, Greetings," whereas in the final four letters, *Epist.* 2.62-65, the salutation begins "Bishop Ruricius" followed by the addressee in the dative. One wonders whether the brevity of the salutations beginning with *Epist.* 2.43 reflects actual variations in Ruricius' epistulary style, or is the result of abbreviations introduced either by the original compiler or by a later copyist as the end of the task approached. In favor of the former hypothesis, perhaps, is Ruricius' known tendency to mimic the style of others, and Sidonius, his early model, used these brief forms of salutation in his own published letters,[35] whereas the letters Ruricius received after Sidonius' death used the longer style. So perhaps the variations of salutation forms merely represent different stylistic choices made by Ruricius.

In general, one cannot know whether the groups with similar salutations resulted from letters that were written at the same time and filed together, or from a later organizational attempt to group letters that had a similar appearance. There clearly was some degree of editorial intervention at some point with regard to the salutations, as seen where the actual salutations were replaced by phrases such as "item alia" ("Another, likewise"). But, once again, it is unclear just when these substitutions were made. Are they artifacts of Ruricius' own filing system? If so, then one might suppose that Ruricius preserved copies of letters to the same individual on separate pages, and declined to recopy the salutation for successive entries. Otherwise, one must conclude that the substitutions were made by later copyists, who observed that the addressee remained the same and, in order to save a bit of space, did not repeat the salutations.

Potentially instructive in this regard are *Epist.* 2.12 and 2.53, which might appear simply to be copies of the same letter; indeed, in this belief Krusch

---

[34] Alternatively, however, it could be an indication of a scribal addition made when the manuscript was created.
[35] Letters of Sidonius to secular friends commence,"Sidonius to His Friend So-and-so, Greetings"; letters to bishops are headed, "Sidonius to the Lord Bishop So-and-so, Greetings." This style also was used in the published letters of earlier epistolographers, such as Pliny the Younger.

deleted *Epist.* 2.53 from his edition. But there are some variations that could suggest that Ruricius in fact preserved two separate drafts of the same letter. For example, in *Epist.* 2.12 one of the appellants is named Lupicinus, but in *Epist.* 2.53 he is called Lupus. More significantly, the salutations are very different: *Epist.* 2.12 reads "Domino sublimi semperque magnifico fratri Praesidio Ruricius episcopus," but *Epist.* 2.53 merely, "Ruricius episcopus Praesidio filio salutem." So, either Ruricius used two formats in two different drafts of the letter, or a later copyist for some unfathomable reason substituted a totally different salutation when *Epist.* 2.12 was mistakenly recopied as *Epist.* 2.53. And if these two copies do in fact represent slightly different versions of the same letter, it may be that other letters in the collection likewise were not verbatim transcripts, but rather drafts of letters that were somewhat different from the versions that were actually sent.

The preceding analysis also might suggest that there were in fact two different sets of salutation formulae that were used for different purposes: a very flowery form that was used in copies that were actually sent, and an abbreviated, more standardized, form that was used in file copies, and perhaps in rough drafts. Such a thesis could explain, for example, the high level of standardization, and even monotony, in the salutations of letters in the collection of Sidonius, especially if in this regard Sidonius was himself mimicking the published letters of his model Pliny. This hypothesis also could explain the duplication of *Epist.* 2.12 and 2.53: perhaps Ruricius had made a fair copy to send (*Epist.* 2.12, with the long salutation), and then realized that it had the wrong name, Lupicinus rather than Lupus. This could have necessitated the creation of yet another master copy, leaving two copies in Ruricius' bookcase.

The organizational elements discussed above suggest that the letters in Book II were not randomly thrown together. The group seems rather to preserve, at the beginning, traces of plans to create two additional books, and, toward the end, elements of a rudimentary filing system. Nor should the latter be surprising, given that Ruricius kept copies of some letters, such as those to or from Faustus or Sidonius, for thirty years of more.[36] Ultimately, it may be that the mammoth second book was assembled after Ruricius' death, with the compiler bringing together several small dossiers that were found in Ruricius' desk. Even if Ruricius did not live to complete any plans to create or circulate books of letters, his organizational efforts may have been one of the factors that led to the preservation and survival of his collection.

---

[36] Sidonius likewise tells of finding, "at the very bottom of my bookcase, about twenty years later, trifles nibbled by mice" (*Epist.* 9.13.6).

THE MANUSCRIPT TRADITION

The *Codex Sangallensis* 190[1] consists of 178 parchment folia, in octavo format, numbered as 357[2] pages and bound in sections (or "quaternions") of 16 pages each.[3] The manuscript in fact has two sets of quaternions, the first numbered I-III (pp.1-49), and the second I-XVII (pp.50-317).[4] It has been in the Stiftsbibliothek at the monastery of St. Gallen in Switzerland at least since 1461, when it appeared in a library catalogue.[5] But it does not seem to have been written there. For even though its script, a form of early Caroline miniscule, dates it to the late eighth or early ninth century,[6] it is not found in any of the ninth-century catalogues of St. Gallen.[7] Nevertheless, based upon idiosyncracies of its script, it may well have been written somewhere in south-eastern Germany.

---

[1] For the manuscript and its contents, see Demeulenaere, *CCL* 64.307-308; Engelbrecht, *CSEL* 21.xlvi; Krusch, *MGH AA* 8.lxix-lxxiv; and G. Scherer, *Verzeichniss der Handschriften der Stiftsbibliothek von St. Gallen* (Halle, 1875; repr. Olms, 1975) pp.68-69; also H. Canisius, *PL* 58.869-870 (first published 1604); E. Ewald, "Der S. Galler Bienensegen," *Neues Archiv* 8 (1883) p.356-357; C. Leutjohann, *MGH AA* 8 (Berlin, 1887) p.lxxv; W. Arndt, *MGH Epist.* 3.191-192; L. Armbruster, "Vom St. Galler Bienensegen," *Archiv für Bienenkunde* 32 (1955) pp.30-32; and G. Morin, "Pages inédites de l'écrivain espagnon Bachiarius," *Bulletin d'ancienne littérature et d'archéologie chrétiennes* 4 (1914) pp.117-126; and *Idem*, "Pages inédites de deux pseudo-Jérômes des environs de l'an 400," *Revue bénédictine* 40 (1928) pp.289-318. Notes of Stephanus Baluzius (1630-1718) are glued inside the front cover.

[2] There actually are 356 pages, but when the pages were numbered, number 11 was omitted.

[3] That is, each large parchment sheet made from the skin of a sheep was cut in half twice to form four smaller sheets. These small "bifolia" were folded in half and bound together to create a quaternion (or "gathering") consisting of eight small folia (hence "octavo" format) and sixteen pages.

[4] The sequence numbers appear at the bottom of the last page of each quaternion; the remaining quaternions in the manuscript (pp.318-357) do not have them.

[5] See J. Duft, "Die Handschriften-Katalogisierung in der Stiftsbibliothek St. Gallen vom 9. bis zum 19. Jahrhundert," in B. Matthias von Scarpatetti, *Die Handschriften der Stiftsbibliothek St. Gallen, Beschreibendes Verzeichnis Codices 1726-1984 (14.-19. Jahrhundert)* (St. Gallen, 1983) p.9 ff; and F. Weidmann, *Geschichte der Bibliothek von St. Gallen seit ihrer Gründung um das Jahr 830 bis auf 1841* (St Gallen, 1841) p.412: it has the catalogue number "Z 10" and the notation, "Codex de assumptione s. Johannis Evangelist[a]e. Relevatio Ysidori de eodem, Ep[ist-u]l[a]e diversorum ut in primo folio" ("A codex about the Assumption of St. John the Evangelist. [Also] the Revelation of Isidore regarding the same person and letters of diverse individuals, as in the first folio").

[6] For the "ninth century": see Gundlach, *MGH Epist.* 3.716; Krusch, pp.lxix, lxxii; Schanz, *Geschichte*, p.551; Ewald, "Bienensegen," p.356; and Morin, "Pages," p.293. See Goldbacher, *CSEL* 34.158, 57.176, and 58.xxxvii, for a suggestion of the eighth/ninth century.

[7] See Duft, "Stiftsbibliothek," pp.11-16; and Weidmann, *Bibliothek*, pp. 360-400.

The *Sangallensis* 190 contains several works, many originating in southern Gaul, that are known from no other source. These include not only the correspondence of Ruricius and Faustus, but also letters to and from Desiderius of Cahors (ca. 620-655); two letters written to women ca. AD 400; a curious bee benediction; and a letter written by the abbot Evantius about the mid seventh century. Also found in the manuscript are an apocryphal "Assumption" of John the Evangelist; an extract from the mid-seventh-century "On the Death and Life of the Fathers" of Isidore of Seville; the earliest surviving copy of the "Confession" of the priests Marcellinus and Faustinus of ca. 390; and the earliest extant sections of Augustine's "On Marriages and Concupiscence" and two of his letters.

The manuscript has been described as written "most negligently."[8]   At times, the copyists omitted words or even sentences; put word and sentence breaks in the wrong places; added false words; and read words wrongly.   There also was a tendency to replace less common words with more common ones, such as "notos" ("well-known") for "nothos" ("illegitimate").   But on the other hand, the manuscript was copied from an exemplar of the highest quality, and it contains many readings that are more correct than those in the few of its works that appear in other manuscripts and can be checked against it, such as some of the letters of Faustus.

The index that appears on the second and third pages begins with a dedication to an otherwise unknown abbot "Lando Vedeleobus" and is rather problematical: several items that appear in the index do not appear in the manuscript itself, and a few items in the text are not in the index.   The following summary of the manuscript's contents cites not only the index entries as they appear in the manuscript, but also works found in the manuscript that are not listed in the index.   Works in **bold** appear in both the index and the manuscript text; works in ***italicized bold*** are listed in the index but are not in the text; and works in normal type appear in the manuscript but not in the index.   Note that the orthography of the manuscript is reproduced as much as possible; the copyist, for example, often linked prepositions such as *ad* and *de* with the following word, and many words were abbreviated.   Letters omitted as a result of abbreviation are indicated by [...], letters omitted by error by (...), and letters mistakenly included by <...>.   The manuscript page numbers are cited at the left.   The index begins, "This codex, for abbot Lando Vedeleobus, contains the Assumption of St. John the Evangelist; a narrative of St. Isidore [of Seville] regarding the the same evangelist..."

---

[8] Englebrecht, *CSEL* 21.xlviii-xlix.

Contents of the *Codex Sangallensis* 190

Ms. page nos. *Index Entry or Description of Contents*

(The first group of quaternions, numbered I-III)

1	Excerpt from Augustine, "On Marriages and Concupiscence"[9]
1	*"Benedictio apium"* ("Bee benediction")
2	**HICCODEX.LANdONI uede**
4-25	**leobo abbat[i] contin& adsumptio**
	nem s[an]c[t]i iohannis evangelistae
25- 27	**Relationem s[an]c[t]i esydori deeodem evangelista**

(The following left-indented entries are in the manuscript margin)

27- 48	**epistulas**	(Three letters
	tres Fausti	of bishop Faustus
	ep[iscop]i ad Felice[m]	to Felix
	& ad Gr(a)ecu[m]	and to Graecus
	diacone[m]. &	the deacon and
	ad Lucid<i>u[m]	to Lucidus
	p[res]b[yte]r[u]m	the priest)
37	*"Benedictio apium"* (A second version of the one on p.1)	
49	Excerpt from Baudonivia's "Life of St. Radegund"	
49	Excerpt from the preface to Jerome's "Commentary on Ephesians"	

(The second group of quaternions, numbered I-XVII)

50- 66	**Epistulas**	(Two letters
	ieronimi	of Jerome
	p[res]b[yte]ri duas	the priest)[10]
50- 55	Anonymous letter, "Nisi tantum"	
55- 66	Anonymous letter, "Quamlibet sciam"	
66- 83	**Epistulas quinqu<a>e Fausti ep**	(Five letters of bishop
	[iscopi].adRuricium.ep[iscopu]m	Faustus to bishop Ruricius)
84	**Epistula(m) gr(a)eci adruricium**	(Graecus to Ruricius)
85- 86	**Epistula(m) victorini.adruricium**	(Victorinus to Ruricius)
86- 89	**Epistula(m) taurencii.adruricium**	(Taurentius to Ruricius)
89- 91	**Epistulas sedati.adruricium duas**	(Sedatus to Ruricius, two)
91- 92	**Epistula(m) eufrasii adruricium**	(Euphrasius to Ruricius)
92-111	Letter of Faustus, "Quaeris a me" (addressee unknown)	
111-126	**Epistula(m) fausti.adpaulinum**	(Faustus to Paulinus)
126-128	**Epistula(m) caesarii.adruricium**	(Caesarius to Ruricius)

---

[9] Omitted from all lists of the manuscript contents; see Scherer, *Verzeichnis*, pp.68-69; and Krusch, *MGH AA* 8.lxix.

[10] The following two letters to two women are not in fact by Jerome.

128-130   **Epistula(m) sedati.adruricium**   (Sedatus to Ruricius)
130-132   Letter of Sidonius to Ecdicius[11]   [2.1]
    Epistula(m) sidoni.adconstantium   (letter to Constantius)   [3.2]
    Alia(m)sidonii.adeuc(h)erium   (another, to Eucherius)   [3.8]
    alia(m)sidonii.adtetradium   (another, to Tetradius)   [3.10]
    alia(m) sidonii.ada\<s\>perum   (another, to Aper)   [4.21]
    al[ia](m) sidonii.adp[ro]culum   (another, to Proculus)   [4.23]
    al[ia](m) sidonii.addomnolum   (another, to Domnolus)   [4.25]
    al[ia](m) sidonii.adnym phidium   (another, to Nymphidius)   [5.2]
    al[ia](m) sidonii.adsimplicium   (another, to Simplicius)   [5.4]
    al[ia](m) sidonii.adt(h)aumastum   (another, to Thaumastus)   [5.7]
(The second page of the index begins here)
    al[ia](m) sidoniiadruricium   (another, to Ruricius)   [5.15]
    al[ia](m) sidonii.adpa pianillam   (another, to Papianilla)   [5.16]
    alias sidonii.adlupum ep[iscopu]m, ii (others to Lupus, two)   [6.1,4]
    alia(m)sidonii.adcensorium   (another, to Censorius)   [6.10]
    Al[ia](m)sidonii.adpacientem   (another, to Patiens)   [6.12]
    alia(m)sidonii.admamertum   (another, to Mamertus)   [7.1]
    Alia(m)sidonii.adagroecium.ep[iscopu]m (to bishop Graecus)   [7.5]
    Alia(m) sidonii.adsulpicium   (another, to Sulpicius)   [7.13]
    Alia(m) sidon ii.adruricium   (another, to Ruricius)   [8.10]
    alia(m) sidonii.adgothum[12]   (another, to "Gothus")   [8.12]
    al[ia](m)sidonii.adprincipium.ep[iscopu]m (bishop Principius) [8.14]
    alia(m) sidonii.adremegium.ep[iscopu]m   (bishop Remigius)   [9.7]
    alia(m) sidonii.adfaustum.ep[iscopu]m (to bishop Faustus)   [9.9]
    alia(m) sidonii.ad\<he\>(O)resium   (another, to Oresius)   [9.12]
132-277   **hab& insequenti.epistularum**   (Next it has two books of let-
    libros ii.domni rurici ep[iscop]i   ters of the lord bishop Ruricius)
278-300   **deinde epistularum librum unum** (Then one book of letters
    domni desiderii ep[iscop]i   of the lord bishop Desiderius)
300-328   **ite[m] epistulas diverso[rum]**   (Likewise, letters of various per-
    adeundem domnum desiderium   sons to the same lord Desiderius]
(After some erasures, there appear entries in another hand)
328-332   **Exemplar[em] ep(is)t(ula)e Lucidi p[res]b[yte]ri co[m]mun[ion]is**
    (Copy of a letter of the priest Lucidus ... communion)[13]

---

[11] The book and sequence numbers of the letters in Sidonius' corpus are on the right.
[12] This is probably Trygetius, a friend of Sidonius who fought on the side of the Goths; the sub-
stitution of "Gothus" might be another example of Ruricius' use of nicknames.
[13] The word *communis* actually belongs at the end of the next line.

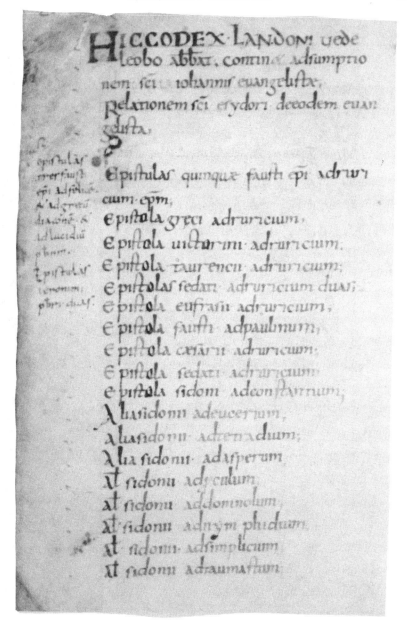

Figs.1-2: The *Codex Sangallensis* 190, pp.2-3. The index of contents. Reproduced by permission of the Stiftsbibliothek, St. Gallen.

It sidoniiadruricium;
It sidonii adpapiamllam·
Alias sidonii adlupum epm, ii
Alia sidonii adcensorium,
It sidonii adpacientem;
Alia sidonii admamertum,
Alia sidonii adagroecium epm;
Alia sidonii adsulpicium;
Alia sidonii adruricium;
Alia sidonii adgothum·
It sidonii adprincipium epm,
Alia sidonii adremegium epm
Alia sidonii adfaustum epm;
Alia sidonia· adhererium;
haba insequenti epistularum libros
ii domni ruricii epi,
deinde epistularum librum unum;
domni desiderii epi;
Ite epistulas diuersos adeundem
domnum desiderium;

Exemplar epte lucidi pbri·   comanis
De confessione uere fidei et ostentatione facer
Ipsa eauinis abbatis contra eos qui sanguine redunt
Ipsa augustini adianuarium·

332-347	**De confessione vere fidei & ostentatione sacr[a]e**
	(On the confession of the true faith and demonstration of holy[14]...)
348-353	**Ep[is]t[ul]a(m) Evantis abbatis c[on]tra eos qui sanguine[m] n[on] edunt**
	(Letter of the abbot Evantius against those who do not eat blood)
354	**Ep[is]t[ul]a(m) Augustini adIanuarium**
	(Letter of Augustine to Januarius) (Aug. *Epist.* 54)
353,355-7	Letter of Augustine, *Epist.* 194

The "Ruricius Collection"

Of particular interest here are not only the letters to and from Ruricius, but also the letters to and from Faustus of Riez and the letters of Sidonius, both of whom were two of Ruricius' most noteworthy correspondents. The letters of Faustus appear in two sections. Those to Felix, Graecus, and Lucidus are found on pp.27-48, whereas the five to Ruricius, as well as others to Paulinus and to an unnamed correspondent, appear on pp.66-130, along with the other letters written to Ruricius, and just before Ruricius' own letters. Appended on p.328, finally, is Faustus' subscription to the letter to Lucidus on p.48, followed by Lucidus' reply.

The first three Faustus letters seem to be separate from those in the Ruricius group for several reasons. For one thing, none is addressed to Ruricius. Furthermore, in the index, they are cited only in the margin, implying they were in some way not part of the original collection.[15] And finally, not only do they appear in a different part of the manuscript, but they also are in the first series of quaternions, whereas the other letters are in the second. It may be, therefore, that this little group of letters, all of which deal with Faustus' views on heresies, viz. Arianism, Nestorianism, and Pelagianism-cum-predestination, were added at some time after the Ruricius collection was compiled, perhaps because the compiler encountered these additional letters of Faustus, which did in fact circulate independently,[16] and decided to include them in the manuscript to accompany the Faustus letters that were preserved in the Ruricius collection.

Another idiosyncracy of the index concerns the 27 letters of Sidonius that are painstakingly listed individually. None of them actually appears in the manuscript. At some point after the creation of the index, therefore, all of the

---

[14] Add the word "communion" from the end of the previous line.

[15] It may be that the marginal entries originally were at the end of the index, in the erasures after the entry for Desiderius and just before that for Lucidus, but were moved to match the location of the documents in the text.

[16] See Appendix I.

letters to Sidonius dropped out of the body of the manuscript. Curiously, however, the last section of Sidonius' *Epistula* 2.1, which is not cited in the index,
is in the manuscript, merged with a letter of Sedatus of Nîmes whose end is
missing.[17] It would appear that an earlier copy of collection lost a section that
began in the midst of Sedatus' letter and ended in the midst of Sidonius' *Epist.*
2.1. And because *Epist.* 2.1 does not appear in the index, this loss must have
occurred even before the index was created.

The 27 Sidonian letters in the index form only a small selection from Sidonius' nine books of 180 letters. Based on the names of the addressees, moreover, book and sequence numbers can be assigned to them (as done in the table
above), and a striking pattern emerges: the letters appear in the index in the
same order as in the full corpus.[18] This would suggest either that a compiler
had a complete collection available and used some selection process to pick out
letters exactly in sequence, or that a collection of loose letters was purposely
organized into the proper order. There also is an additional pattern to the selection, for, with the exception of books V (five letters) and VI (four letters), three
letters were chosen from each book. Furthermore, some of the triads are numeri-
cally close, and are comprised of alternating (or nearly so) letters; e.g. letters
21, 23, and 25 from book IV; 2, 4, and 7 from book V; 10, 12, and 14 from
book VIII; and 7, 9, and 12 from book IX.

It seems clear, therefore, that some selection process was at work here. And
if this is the case, then one might infer that letters from books I and II also were
originally included, but for some reason now are missing from the list. This
suggestion would seem to be confirmed by the presence of part of *Epist.* 2.1 in
the manuscript. But any other letters from Books I and II disappeared before
the composition of the index. And if this reconstruction is correct, then it
would mean that not just a single folio or two were lost, but perhaps an entire
quaternion of sixteen pages, and that, along with the letters of Sidonius, other
letters to Ruricius that followed the partial letter of Sedatus also also dropped
out of one of the predecessors of the *Sangallensis*.

It would appear, moreover, that just as the inclusion of the letters by Sidonius was the result of some unknown selection process, their subsequent omission
from the *Sangallensis*, unless one attributes it to some curious chance that affected only them and nothing else, may have been because they failed to meet
some equally unknown selection criteria when the *Sangallensis* was created.

---

[17] It is a curious coincidence that one of the few passages of Sidonius cited verbatim by Gregory
of Tours comes from the very section included in the *Sangallensis*: "ut Sollius noster ait, nec
'dabat pretia contemnens nec accipiebat instrumenta desperans'" (*HF* 4.12). The standard text of
Sidonius reads "accipit"; the *Sangallensis* has "accepit."
[18] This pattern allows exact book and sequence numbers to be assigned to letters in cases where
an individual received more than one letter.

Perhaps the library already had a complete copy of Sidonius, and the letters, an incomplete selection at that, were omitted to save space. Or perhaps the manuscript was intended only to include rare works, and the Sidonius letters were considered to be too well-known. Presumably, the fragment from *Epist.* 2.1 survived only because it lacked a heading and was assumed to be part of Sedatus' letter; otherwise, it too would have been deleted.

The letters of Ruricius are by far the largest single work in the manuscript, 177½ of the 356 pages. All were copied by the same hand, which also entered the last few letters to Ruricius and the Sidonius fragment. Moreover, the great bulk of the material in the *Sangallensis* — 39 of the 48 index entries and 235 pages, or approximately two-thirds of the total contents — is that associated with Faustus, Ruricius, and Sidonius. Ruricius also provides an external unifying element. He was an intimate of both Faustus and Sidonius, and his collection includes multiple letters to each of them.[19] And Sidonius' own corpus contains no less than three letters to Ruricius, two of which (*Epist.* 5.15, 8.10) are cited in the *Sangallensis* index.[20] Moreover, Faustus spent part of his period of exile ca. 477-485 with Ruricius, which could account for Ruricius' possession of letters that Faustus wrote to, or even received from, others, such as Faustus' letter "Quaeris a me," and Faustus' letter to Paulinus of Bordeaux. Ruricius also must, of course, have been in possession of the letters written to him included in the *Sangallensis*. On such grounds, one might suggest that the Ruricius-Faustus-Sidonius material incorporated into the *Sangallensis* between pages 66 and 277 represents some of the contents of Ruricius' personal archives, and might be dubbed the "Ruricius Collection." But Ruricius' collection does not seem to have been preserved at Limoges,[21] so how, one now might ask, did it eventually resurface centuries later in the *Sangallensis* 190?

The Archives of Desiderius of Cahors

In an attempt to approach this question, our attention now can turn to the next two entries in the original index: the letters to and from Desiderius, a na-

---

[19] Ruric. *Epist.* 1.1-2 (to Faustus), 8-9, 16 (to Sidonius).

[20] As for the lack of *Epist.* 4.16, which Ruricius in fact quoted in his own *Epist.* 1.4, one simply does not know how the group of Sidonius letters preserved in the index was assembled.

[21] Several twelfth- and thirteenth-century versions of the library catalogue of the monastery of St. Martial at Limoges show that the monastery preserved many late Roman texts, including works of Hilary of Poitiers, Ambrose, Jerome, Orosius, Augustine, Sidonius, Isidore of Seville, and Venantius Fortunatus; not to mention a *De vita contemplativa* ("On the Contemplative Life") attributed to Prosper (but probably of Julianus Pomerius), the *De Agricultura* ("On Agricultural Matters") of Palladius, the *De re militari* ("On Military Matters") of Vegetius, a *liber vetus* ("old book") of Fulgentius, and many saints' lives, but there is no mention of anything by Ruricius or Faustus, or of any of the other material (save the letters of Sidonius) in the *Sangallensis*: see H. Duplès-Agier ed., *Chroniques de Saint-Martial de Limoges* (Paris, 1874) pp.323-355.

tive of Albi[22] who served as bishop of Cahors ca. 620-655, a century and a
half after the times of Sidonius and Ruricius.[23] Several circumstantial considerations, besides the geographical proximity of Cahors to Limoges and Clermont, suggest that Desiderius had a family connection to Sidonius, and thence
to Ruricius, which could provide a link between Desiderius' letters and the "Ruricius Collection." For example, in the 530s, Sidonius' daughter and daughter-
in-law, Alcima and Placidina, went into exile from Clermont to Cahors.[24] And
a sister of Desiderius was named Avita, suggesting a tie to the Aviti of Clermont.[25]

   Like Ruricius and Sidonius, moreover, Desiderius belonged to an aristocratic
and literary circle of some repute. His correspondent bishop Sulpicius II (c.620-
640) of Bourges, for example, would have been a relative of the sixth-century
bishop Sulpicius I of Bourges, who was praised thus by Gregory of Tours: "He
is in fact a man very noble and from the first-ranking senators of Gaul, well
educated in rhetorical learning and, truly, in the metric arts second to none."[26]

   After Desiderius' death, a collection of documents relating to himself and
his family was preserved, apparently at the monastery of St. Amatius at Cahors,
which Desiderius had founded and where he was buried.[27] And there is reason
to believe that this archive also contained the letters of Desiderius' putative
forebear Ruricius, for eight possible citations from Ruricius' letters have been
identified in Desiderius' letters, and several others in letters written to him.[28]
This could suggest that Ruricius' letter collection was available not only to
Desiderius himself, but also to those with whom he corresponded.

   If so, one might propose that the letters to and from Ruricius, the letters of
Sidonius, and the letters to and from Desiderius formed part of an epistolographic collection preserved by the family and literary circles of first Ruricius and

---

[22] *Vita Desiderii* 1.1.1, 6.11.20, 9.17.30, 11.19.35-36: for the *vita*, see R. Poupardin, *La vie de
saint Didier, évêque de Cahors (630-655)* (Paris, 1900); and W. Arndt in *MGH SRM* 4.455ff.
[23] For editions of Desiderius' letters, see W. Arndt, *MGH Epist.* (Berlin, 1892) 3.191-214; and
D. Norberg, *Epistulae S. Desiderii Cadurcensis* (Stockholm, 1961).
[24] Gregory of Tours, *HF* 3.12.
[25] For all these relationships, see Mathisen, *Ecclesiastical Aristocracy*, passim, and *Idem*, "Epistolography," passim.
[26] "est enim vir valde nobilis et de primis senatoribus Galliarum, in litteris bene eruditus rheto-
ricis, in metricis vero artibus nulli secundus" (*HF* 6.39). On this occasion, circa 584, the earlier
Sulpicius had presided over a council that confirmed that certain parishes belonged to Cahors.
[27] *Vita Desiderii* 20, 30-31, 38; see Arndt, *MGH SRM* 4.552, 557; and Poupardin, *Vie*, pp.vii-viii.
For a thorough discussion of manuscript copying during this period, see R. McKitterick, "The
scriptoria of Merovingian Gaul: A Survey of the Evidence," in H. Clark, M. Brennan eds.,
Columbanus and Medieval Monasticism (Oxford, 1981) pp.173-207.
[28] See Norberg, *Epistulae*, passim: in Desiderius, *Epist.* 1.1 (Ruric. *Epist.* 2.8, 2.35, 2.49), 1.2
(2.40), 1.4 (2.58), 1.5 (2.15), 1.7 (2.40), and 1.10 (1.12); in letters to Desiderius from Sulpicius
of Bourges (Desiderius, *Epist.* 2.1, cf. Ruricius, *Epist.* 2.18, 22, 33, 51), Paulus of Verdun (2.12,
cf. 2.63), and Verus of Rodez (2.19, cf. 2.49).

then Desiderius. Indeed, several considerations regarding the manner in which Desiderius' letters are presented in the *Sangallensis* suggest that their compiler had access to Ruricius' collection. For one thing, both collections include letters from and to the person in question. Moreover, the letters to Ruricius begin with those from Faustus of Riez, and Ruricius' own corpus begins with letters to Faustus; the letters of Desiderius, on the other hand, end with a letter to bishop Felix of Marseille, and the collection of letters to him ends with one from him.

As of the mid seventh century, therefore, it would seem that much of the raw material that later appeared in the *Sangallensis* collection, that is, the epistolographic collections of Ruricius and Desiderius, was present in or near Cahors, quite likely at Desiderius' monastery. And it may have been at this point that a master copy was made that incorporated Desiderius' letter collection into the "Ruricius Collection." This copy, which one now might call the "Desiderius Collection,"[29] also would have included a new master index[29] which could have propagated any errors and omissions (such as those involving the letters of Sidonius) that had occurred while the materials in it consisted of separate dossiers, perhaps with their own indices, and this could help to account for some of the inconsistencies between the index and contents that are found in the *Sangallensis*. The "Desiderius Collection," therefore, formed the original core of the epistulary material preserved in the *Sangallensis*.

The preceding reconstruction accounts not only for nearly 75% of the material in the *Sangallensis* 190, but also, in particular, for everything in the original index except for the two initial entries on John the Evangelist. One might suggest that after these two hagiographical works had been entered into the mysterious Lando's[30] manuscript, the "Desiderius Collection", beginning with its own index, then was appended *in toto* to form the "Lando Collection," which represented everything in the original index. What still remains unclear, however, is whether the "Lando Collection" is the *Sangallensis* 190 itself, or whether the *Sangallensis* merely incorporated it. If the former, then one must explain the inconsistencies between the original index and the contents: why were so many works included that were not covered by the original index at all, and why were some of them inserted into the midst of the text without being reflected in the index?

---

[29] Note the developmental cited in the index: "in sequenti... deinde... item."

[30] Lando has proven difficult to place. An abbot Lando appears, for example, in the mid ninth century at the monastery of Gengenbach, located northwest of St. Gallen (*MGH LC*, p.214). Equally intriguing is the aforementioned "Obituarium" of Limoges, which notes, for 15 June, "XVII kal. Lando abbas. Amblardus abbas" ("17 days before the Kalends. Lando the abbot. Amblardus the abbot") (Leroux et al., *Documents*, p.73). There is no indication of when or where this abbot Lando lived; he may even be identical to the abbot Lando of Gengenbach. His appearance in this catalogue of Limoges does provide a potential connection between an abbot Lando and the "Ruricius Collection."

So perhaps the latter suggestion is to be preferred: the *Sangallensis* 190 was a copy, created ca. 800, of several groups of material, by far the largest of which was the "Lando Collection." Rather than representing an attempt to create a "master index," the index at the beginning of the manuscript is merely a verbatim transcript of the index of the "Lando Collection," updated after the manuscript had been completed to reflect the inclusion of additional material. This would mean that there were at least three stages of compilation: the creation of the "Desiderius" and "Lando" collections, followed by the copying of the *Sangallensis* 190 itself, a conclusion that would in fact help to explain how the inconsistencies noted above could have crept in.

The Correspondence of Ruricius and Ninth-Century Literary Culture

It is by no means clear how the *Sangallensis* 190 itself, wherever it was written, eventually fetched up at St. Gallen. No known monks of Limoges or Cahors appear, for example, in the St. Gallen *Liber confraternitatum* ("Book of Shared Brotherhoods"), which listed monks from other monasteries who had "exchange privileges" with St. Gallen: the only Gallic monasteries represented were at Tours, Lyon, Vienne, and Besançon.[31] On the other hand, however, the monks of St. Gallen did acquire manuscripts from other places in central Gaul, including Tours,[32] Auxerre,[33] and Vienne[34] during the ninth century, the very time of the composition of the *Sangallensis* 190. So it may be that the exemplar or exemplars of this manuscript, too, came to the area of St. Gallen in the course of one of what must have been many literary exchanges.

As one final question one might ask whether there is any evidence that the material in the *Sangallensis* 190, and in particular the letters of Ruricius, were ever used in the neighborhood of St. Gallen. And a curious literary reminiscence does suggest that the *Sangallensis* may have been there not long after it was written. The *Formulae Sangallenses* ("Formulae of St. Gallen"), which include several personal letters of the late ninth century from a local literary circle, contain a letter written in 878 by bishop Salomo II of Constance to an unidentified recipient. The letter describes a horse that Salomo had sent to his friend, and the relevant section reads,[35]

---

[31] See *MGH LC*, passim.
[32] Lesne, *Livres*, p.163 n.4.
[33] The *Codex Sangallensis* 177, which was created for bishop Heribaldus of Auxerre (829-857).
[34] The *Codex Sangallensis* 566, sent from bishop Ado in 870, and the *Codex Sangallensis* 454, a copy of Ado's martyrology.
[35] *Formulae Sangallenses miscellaneae* no.40: K. Zeumer ed., *MGH Leges V. Formulae Merowingici et Karolini aevi* (Hanover, 1886) pp.421-422).

De caballo, quem me expostulastis, scitote, quia *praestantissimum* vobis *mitto, illorum de gente, "patri quos daedala Circe / Supposita de matre nothos furata creavit"* [Vergil, *Aeneid* 7.282-3] quod ne fabulosum existimetis, aerius ei *color* innatus hoc verum esse comprobat. qui montes oppositos laetus et alacris exsuperat, et fluvios rapaces innatet et latissimos lacus *transvadet...* et ... cognoscat, quomodo sub quolibet homine se gerere debeat, hoc est sub iuvenibus et indisciplinatis transversus et supinus, sub senioribus vere et gravibus humilis et rectus incedere norit... vos autem vobis ipsis aut ministris de eius *vilitate,* non mihi fideli vestro succensete.

Regarding the horse that you requested from me, know that I send to you a most excellent one, of the same sort as those
> whom ingenious Circe bred as bastards
> from the mare she had mated,

for, lest you think that this description is fanciful, its airy inborn color proves that this is true... It happily and swiftly surmounts opposing mountains, and it swims racing rivers and traverses the most enormous lakes... And one might recognize how it ought to conduct itself under each type of person: that is, it is cross-ways and supine under the young and undisciplined, but under the elderly and serious it knows how to advance humbly and properly... As for you, be displeased with yourself or your domestics regarding its vileness, but not with me, your faithful servant.

This passage has some striking similarities to a series of letters that were exchanged, using the same vocabulary, among Ruricius of Limoges and his friends describing a horse that Ruricius proposed to lend to Celsus (*Epist.* 1.14) and Sedatus of Nîmes (*Epist.* 2.35). Sedatus' reply, a parody of Ruricius' characterization of the horse, is particularly similar in both sense and wording to Salomo's letter, the most striking parallel between these two horse stories being the use of the same Vergilian tag (Sedatus, *Epist* "Equum quem"):

Equum, quem per fratrem nostrum presbyterum transmisistis, accepi... in via *vilem* ... *colore vilissimum...* quem priusquem viderem... *illorum de gente,* esse credidi, *"...quos daedala Circe / Supposita de matre nothos furata creavit"* [Vergil, *Aeneid* 7.282-3]. putabam illum ... celeritate ventos et flumina praecursurum... credebam etiam, quod ... duo fortiores viri, ne *evaderet,* retinerent. nec me fefellit, nam trahebunt eum aliquot, impingebant alii et plures caedebant. quem ut sic exhibitum vidi, optavi, ut talia qualia erant. non qualia epistula mea continet, semper caris vestris munera *mitteretis...*

I received the horse that you sent... vile on the hoof... most vile in color... before I saw it I believed it to be of the same sort as those
>whom ingenious Circe bred as bastards
>from the stolen mare she had mated.

I thought then that ... it would be an outstripper of the winds and rivers in speed... I believed then that two very strong men, lest it escape, would restrain it... And it did not disappoint me, for several pulled it, others pushed it, and even more pummelled it. When I saw it displayed thus, I wished that you always would send to those who are dear to you gifts just as they were, not such as my letter contains...

The verbal parallels are accompanied by some clear parallels in the development of the theme. Following the quotation from Vergil, both letters then depicted the horse's abilities and the way it responded to its handlers, and concluded with a note on how it was thought the gift would be received. One can only wonder whether Salomo had heard of, or even seen, the letters in Ruricius' collection in the *Sangallensis*.

TRANSLATION NOTES

Because nearly all of the letters translated below survive in only one manuscript, there is no concern for manuscript collation.[36] But, as noted already, even though the manuscript is based on a first-rate exemplar, the quality of the copying often left much to be desired. In many instances, the manuscript has readings that clearly need correction, and editors from Canisius thorugh Demeulenaere have suggested many alternate readings, which often differ among themselves. In the translations below, variant readings will sometimes be noted, not only to indicate alternate interpretations, but also to draw attention to passages whose meaning may not be entirely clear, to allow the reader to postulate alternate translations, and simply to give a flavor of what the manuscript is like. In general, the reading used in the translation is given first in a list of variants. The manuscript reading is referred to as "S". In cases where the manuscript has been corrected by what seems to be a contemporary hand, the original reading is called "S¹" and the correcting hand "S²". Readings without attribution are those of the translator.

Usually left unnoted are variants of single letters (i for e, or e for ae); emendations of verb tenses (e.g. *portaret* for *portare*); quibbles regarding the division of words in the manuscript; and cases where one or the other of two manuscript readings is accepted as correct. In the translated text, <...> indicates a restoration to the text, and [....] indicates a word not in the text inserted for the sake of readability or clarity. Letters of compounds are not assimilated, e.g. *subfarcinatus* rather than *suffarcinatus*.

In some instances, words that have essentially the same meaning have been translated differently for the purposes of consistency and differentiation. For example, of words that could be translated "love," only *amor* is consistently translated thus, whereas *affectio* is generally rendered as "affection," *caritas* sometimes as "charity," and *dilectio* often as "esteem."

Translations of scripture are not taken from any particular English translation; both the King James Version and Revised Standard Version have been used, as has been the translator's own, depending on the sense of the translation in context. In cases where numbering of biblical books, chapters, and verses differs between the Vulgate (Latin) and, for example, the Revised Standard Version (English), as in the Psalms, that of the former is cited.

---

[36] Occasionally, the manuscript readings can be checked against those of a few works that appear in other mss., including the partial letter of Sidonius, and four of the letters of Faustus, as discussed in Appendix I below.

Latin names of both persons and places are generally left in their Latin forms throughout, except in cases where a placename is used repetitiously (for example, "Limoges") or where a personal name is so familiar in its Anglicized form that use of the Latin would seem overly pedantic (for example, "Augustine" rather than "Augustinus"). Wherever possible, Latin place names are given their modern equivalent upon their first appearance.

In general, moreover, titles of ancient works are given an Anglicized title in the text, but left in their Latin forms in the notes, as they are also in the bibliography of primary sources. In bibliographical citations in the notes, usually the full citation is given in the first reference, with an abbreviated form being used in subsequent references. Full citations of nearly all the primary and secondary sources cited to in the text are given in the Bibliographies.

Along with the translation of the letters in the "Ruricius Collection," there also are included in the appendix full or partial translations of other works that are especially germane to a study of Ruricius and his literary circle, including not only letters to and from Faustus of Riez, but also several hagiographical works relating to Ruricius or to Limoges.

POEMS OF SIDONIUS APOLLINARIS[1]

RELATING TO RURICIUS AND HIS FAMILY

Sidonius Apollinaris, *Carmina* 10 [ca. 463/467]

The works of Sidonius Apollinaris include three poems germane to Ruricius' family. The first two were written on the occasion of Ruricius' marriage to Hiberia, and the third to Hiberia's father Ommatius. If Ruricius was born ca. 445, the marriage could have taken place just before ca. 465 at the earliest. On the other hand, all the poems must have been written before 469, when Sidonius became bishop and claimed to have given up the writing of secular poetry. And given that Sidonius was in Rome from late 467 until late 468, it may be that the marriage poems were written ca. 463/467. The translation is from Anderson, *Sidonius*, 1.198-201, reprinted by permission of the publishers and the Loeb Classical Library.

PREFACE OF THE EPITHALAMIUM RECITED TO RURICIUS AND HIBERIA[1]

When Pelion displayed the marriage-feast of the sea-maiden in a Pagasaean cave beneath an Emathian crag, the stately pageantry of the gods taxed the ground to hold it; on this side the sky, on that the sea vied one with the other in their treasures, and the song and dance were led by the bride's father almost hidden in his green robe and himself of the same hue as his sea-coloured mantle. The nymph also, coming naked from the waves to her marriage, was seized with fear of the bridegroom's draped form. Then every god that was present laid aside his dreadfulness and exhibited a playful version of his special power. Jupiter hurled a thunderbolt that had neither heat not force, and said, "At this time it is more fitting for our lady of Cythera to show warmth." Pollux then won praise with the boxing glove, Castor with reins, Pallas with her plumed helm, the Delian goddess with her arrows; Hercules frolicked with his club, Mars with his spear, the Arcadian god with his wand, Bromius with the fawn-skin. At this moment the Muses also had been introduced by the incomparable Orpheus with strings, voice, hand, songs, and reeds. Hymen, eager to show off,

---

[1] The works of Sidonius have been edited by A. Loyen ed., *Sidoine Apollinaire: Poèmes* (Budé, 1960) and vols.2-3, *Sidoine Apollinaire: Lettres* (Budé, 1970); W.B. Anderson, *Sidonius Apollinaris: Poems and Letters*, vols. 1-2 (Loeb, 1936-1965); P. Mohr, *C. Sollius Apollinaris Sidonius* (Teubner, 1895); and C. Lütjohann, *Gai Sollii Apollinaris Sidonii epistulae et carmina, MGH AA* 8 (Berlin, 1887).

Sidonius Apollinaris, *Carmina* 10

[1] An "epithalamium" was a marriage poem, and, like this one, usually was in elegaic couplets.

mustered there all arts, and he who did not give pleasure by his merit gave pleasure belike by his spirit. But Fescennine jests were not admitted until our Apollo[2] had made his song ring forth on the familiar lyre.

Sidonius Apollinaris, *Carmina* 11 [ca. 465/467]

> Sidonius' *epithalamium* actually has very little to say about the couple at all, and
> consists almost exclusively of mythological commonplaces. The translation is
> from Anderson, *Sidonius*, 1.200-211, reprinted by permission of the publishers
> and the Loeb Classical Library.

EPITHALAMIUM[1]

Between the Dark-blue Rocks, Ephyra's peaks, where the summit of a sea-
worn mountain raises Orithyion above Idalium to the sky, in which place, as it
chanced, the wandering Symplegades were fixed fast by the trembling Tiphys
even as he fled from them there emerges into the sea of the Isthmus a bay enclosed by wings of piled rocks jutting from the cliff; in which retreat, just as if
the whole radiance of the sky were concentrated there, the daylight is gathered
together into a narrow space, and penetrating the quivering waters it searches
out the secluded depths, and so the ripples pass on, bathed in deep-shining
brightness, and, wondrous to tell, the water drinks in the sun and the light,
pushed into the limpid stream, bores unwetted through the wet with arid ray.

This site favored a labor of love; for there the Lemnian god amused himself
by building a mimic temple for Venus, and swarthy Pyragmon, abandoning the
thunderbolt, raised his smoke in the place many a time. Here is stone from five
regions, giving forth five hues, Aethiopian, Phrygian, Parian, Punic, Spartan —
purple, green, mottled, ivory, white. The yellow glow of topaz flashes through
the doorpost; porcelain, sardonyx, Caucasian amethyst, Indian jasper, Chalcidian
and Scythian stones, beryl and agate, form the double doors that rise upon silver
pivots, and through these doors the shadowy recess beyond pours out the sheen
of the emeralds that are within. Onyx thickly encrusts the threshold, and hard
by the blue color of amethyst casts upon the lagoon a harmonious hue. Outside
is no dressed stone, but towering walls of rock that has been roughened by the
constant lashing of the waters. In the inner part Mulciber mimicked in gold the

---

[2] That is, Sidonius himself, who was known among his friends as "Phoebus," a nickname derived from both his name, "Apollinaris," and his poetic skill: see R. Mathisen, "Phoebus, Orpheus, and Dionysus: Nicknames and Some Difficult Passages in Sidonius," in *Idem, Studies in
the History, Literature, and Society of Late Antiquity* (Amsterdam, 1991) pp.29-44.
Sidonius Apollinaris, *Carmina* 11
[1] In epic hexameters.

crags that rise up far and wide, and with his skill to guide him counterfeited with mighty art the artless creations of Nature, plying his work diligently — for not yet did he know of that deception which afterward he punished with his Lemnian chains. Hither scaly Triton with heart aflame bore amid the waters Venus, seated where the boundaries of his double back meet above the windings of his writhing belly. But Galatea has brought up close to him her weighty, glittering shell, and presses his side, which she pinches with inserted thumb, promising by that stealthy touch connubial bliss; whereupon the lover, rejoicing in that torturing jest, smiles at the wound and anon lashes his beloved with a gentle stroke of his fishy tail. Behind them comes a column of Loves in ardent squadrons; one controls a dolphin with reins of roses, another rides on a green sea-calf, despising bridle's aid and clinging to the horns; others are on foot, swaying with the motion, slipping on their dripping soles and steadying their steps with their wings.

Venus had let her soft cheek rest upon her bended arm; the violets about her grew languid and her neck had begun to sink, ever heavier with slumber as the flowers pressed against her. Of all the troop of brothers one alone was missing, the love-god, the fairest of them all; for he was contriving a glorious marriage-feast for the Gauls, a feast that the bride's father Ommatius,[2] scion of a patrician race[3] and the greatest of his great line, was gracing with splendor for his daughter and her bridegroom amid happy auguries. But when in due course the great day dawned, then the god with swift flight sought his mother, with torch, bow, and quiver slung upon him. Stooping down and resting on the edge of his left hand, with his wings he lashed his feet, as they hung poised in the air, and thus he snatched kisses from his mother; and as she floated back into wakefulness he began to graze her half-slumbering eyes with the light touch of a feather. Then before she could speak he briskly addressed her thus: "I bring you a new joy, Mother, the joy of a happy capture. That proud Ruricius is set aflame by our torch; he has caught the sweet poison and heaves sighs of welcome pain. If those olden times were now, the maid of Lemnos would have lavished on him her sovereignty, the Cretan maid the thread for the labyrinth, Alcestis her life, Circe her magic herbs, Calypso her apples, Scylla the fatal hair, Atalanta her swift feet, Medea her mad passions, Hippodrome her wax, Jupiter's swan-daughter her crown; for him Dido would have rushed upon the sword, Phyllis to the

---

[2] The father of Hiberia.

[3] His patrician descent probably was through Philagrius, the ancestor of a number of Gallic families, including that of another Arvernian, Eparchius Avitus (*PLRE II*, p.693). He is not known to have held any office, and is known only from these poems. He was the namesake of one of Ruricius' sons. Sidonius also invited him to a birthday party; see *Carm.* 16 below, which indicates that he was a native of the Auvergne.

halter, Evadne into the flames, the maid of Sestos into the waves."

His mother answered: "I rejoice, my son, that thou dost both vanquish and praise that stubborn resister. But the maid's beauty is such that if the hero whom Sthenoboea loved in bygone days had beheld her he would not have had to overcome the dread Chimaera through slighting her charms; he who, arrogantly proud of his Amazon mother, spurned the reckless prayers of his Cretan stepmother, would, if he had seen the maid, have been doomed indeed, but on a true charge; nay, if she had chanced to contend with me as a fourth competitor in the trial of beauty, then the shepherd on Rhoetean Ida would have given his verdict even against me. "Lose the contest," he would have said to me, "or, if thou choosest (and this I prefer), give the girl to me;" and I should have given him all that beauty in return for the prize of beauty. Such are the charm and comeliness of her cheeks that compared with their radiance the purple pales that encircle her neck is dimmed to darkness by the light of her countenance. Her also would men have wooed by all manner of exploits, Pelops attesting his prowess by his chariot, Hippomenes by running, Achelous by wrestling, Aeneas by wars, Perseus by the Gorgon. Yea, hers is the beauty for whose sake Jupiter would so oft have become the Delian goddess, a bull, a swan, a satyr, a serpent, thunder, or gold. So let them be straightaway united, for they are alike in wealth and beauty and lineage; there is naught that is ill-matched in these victims of thy shaft.[4] But why am I thus delaying their marriage?"

Thus she spake and called for her chariot. Its yoke was of crystal, which in early winter, when the ice of the young world began to increase, the bulk of Caucasus, was compacted of a piece of the Tanais by dint of the northern frosts, assuming the nature of a gem because it lost the nature of water. The car was pierced by a pole of the yellow metal, metal which had been sent by the river beneath whose waters the nymphs fondled Mygdonian Midas, who, poor in the midst of gold, enriched Pactolus' stream when his prayers had been turned against him. Brightly gleamed the wheels, encircling the spokes with translucent rims; they were got from the jaws of the Libyan beast, while the monster bewailed the disarming of his mouth with the tusks wrenched away. This also was a gift, sent by the Indian, a man like the Ethiopian in hue and with the grease of unguent on his hair, who troubles warm Erythrae as he roams about naked in his fragrant hunting. Her swans, wont to feed in Cyprus, Venus held firmly with reins of beribboned myrtle; the rest of their bodies was tense and taut, but their milk-white necks were bent by a circlet of red coral.

So they begin their journey: the poised wheel cleaves the empty air, leaving in the clear expanse no rut to be smoothed out. Here the three Graces attend her, linked in a single embrace; here Plenty casts fragrance from Fortune's open

---

[4] Such concerns were of great importance in aristocratic marriages; cf. Ruricius, *Epist.* 2.1-2.

horn; here Flora scatters flowers from baskets, flowers ever blooming; here Egyptian Osiris accompanies Sicilian Ceres; here Pomona carries the folds of her robe loaded with the fruits of the season; here Pallas comes with oil-mills that are oozing between the presses; here the Bacchanal, her side mottled with a dappled fawnskin, plies the whirling Indian revelry of Bromius with the Theban thyrsus; here the Corybant too, who represents the rites of Dindyma in the caves of Sigeum, unmanned though he now is, feels the old glow return, and from that hoarse throat the hollowed box-wood groans out through its double pipe the fire that is within him.

Thus they come to the bridal; incense, nard, balm, and myrrh are here; here Phoenix presents the cinnamon of his living pyre. Nay, even the winter so near at hand[5] has felt the warm breath of the festival and has grown less cold, and the wedding preserves a suggestion of spring and gives to that spot a boon which the seasons do not give to the world. Then the goddess of Paphos, clasping the right hands of man and maid, chanted the hallowed blessing in but few words, unwilling that even words should bring delay: "Pass your lives in happiness and concord; may ye have children and grandchildren; and may your great-grandchildren see in their great-grandparents[6] the bliss which they themselves would fain enjoy!"

Sidonius Apollinaris, *Carmina* 17 [ca. 467/469]

> For Ommatius, see the previous poem. The poem is in elegaic couplets. The translation is from Anderson, *Sidonius*, 1.252-255, reprinted by permission of the publishers and the Loeb Classical Library.

To THE *VIR CLARISSIMUS*[1] OMMATIUS

Four days before the first dawn of August raises above the earth its corn-wreathed head there will be celebrated by my family a sixteenth birthday,[2] which craves to be made lucky by your coming. You shall not have a meal set for you on jeweled tables, nor shall Assyrian purple provide your dining-couch. I shall not bury in the manifold recesses of a glittering side-board masses of dark old silver;[3] nor shall there be offered here a cup whose twisted handles

---

[5] The marriage, therefore, took place near the end of the year, perhaps in November.

[6] A prophecy that came to pass: see Ruricius, *Epist.* 2.32.

Sidonius Apollinaris, *Carmina* 17

[1] A formal designation of rank indicating the most junior senatorial status.

[2] Like the previous poem, this one should date to before 469. On the other hand, Sidonius was married no earlier than ca. 450; if he had a sixteen-year old child, the poem therefore must have been written ca. 467 or later.

[3] Anderson's translation of "silver-plate" minimizes Sidonius' wealth; for the disposition of

clasp sides overlaid with ruddy gold. Our salvers are of moderate size, and not
so made that their artistry atones for their lack of bulk. The rustic table of your
Gallic friend will not receive loaves that were wont to make the fields yellow
by the Libyan Syrtes. As for wines, I have none of Gaza, no Chian or Falerni-
an, none sent by the vines of Sarepta for you to drink. There are here no cups
distinguished by the name of that canton which the triumvir himself established
in our land.[4] Nevertheless, we beg you to come; Christ will provide all things,
by whose grace this has been made a real homeland[5] for me through your love.

Sidonius' family silver service to the poor after he became bishop, see Greg.Tur. *HF* 2.22.

[4] Anderson, *Sidonius* 1.255 n.4, explains this as a reference to the founding of Lyon by the soon-
to-be triumvir M. Aemilius Lepidus in 43 BC. Some of the inhabitants came from Vienne,
which was known for its wine.

[5] Sidonius calls himself "Gallic" above because he was a native of Lyon, located in Gallia
Lugdunensis in the diocese of "Gallia," whereas Clermont was in Aquitania, in the diocese of
"Septem Provinciarum." Clermont became his new *patria* through his marriage to Papianilla, the
daughter of the emperor Eparchius Avitus (455-456), a native of the Auvergne.

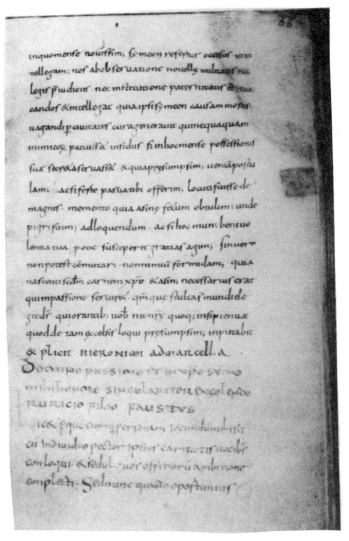

Fig.3: The *Codex Sangallensis* 190, p.66. The letter "Licet per" of Faustus of Riez to Ruricius at the bottom of this page marks the beginning of the "Ruricius Collection." It is addressed "Domino piissimo et in xp[ist]o sum[m]o I mihi honore singulariter excolendo I Ruricio filio Faustus." It follows immediately upon the second of two letters falsely attributed in the manuscript to Jerome, whose colophon reads "Explicit Hieronimi ad Marcella" ("The [letter] of Jerome to Marcella ends"). The change in the script and the color of the ink demonstrates that these two letters are parts of different corpora. See p.92 below. Reproduced by permission of the Stiftsbibliothek, St. Gallen.

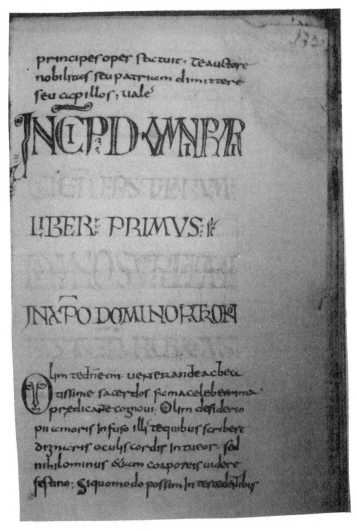

Fig.4: The *Codex Sangallensis* 190, p.132. The elaborate heading of Ruricius' first book of letters. It reads, "Incip[it] domni Ruri I cii ep[iscop]i epistularum I liber primus." It then continues with the salutation of the first letter, "Domino suo peculiari I in Xp[ist]o domino patrono I Fausto ep[iscop]o Ruricius." The use of complex ligatures, the enclosure of some letters within others, and the diamond-shaped "O" are typical of insular techniques, and could suggest that that the manuscript was written where there was British or Irish influence. Each letter begins with an ornate capital letter. See p.87. Reproduced by permission of the Stiftsbibliothek, St. Gallen.

The Correspondence To and From

Ruricius of Limoges

The First Book
of Letters of the
Lord Ruricius Begins[1]

1.1 [ca. 475/477]

The corpus of letters written by Ruricius begins with two letters to Faustus, bishop of Riez ca. 460-490, in the place of honor.[1] On the other hand, the set of letters written to Ruricius begins with no less than five letters by Faustus. Both considerations attest the importance that Ruricius attributed to this correspondence, which documents his spiritual journey from pious layman to bishop. Faustus was a native of either Britain or Brittany. In the 420s he withdrew to the monastery on the island of Lérins off the coast of southern Gaul, where in the early 430s he became abbot in succession to Maximus, whom he also succeeded as bishop of Riez ca. 460. He was one of the most distinguished bishops and theologians of fifth-century Gaul, and the author, in the early 470s, of extant works including the *De spiritu sancto* ("On the Holy Spirit") and the *De gratia* ("On Grace"). In the latter work he crafted the definitive Gallic interpretation of divine grace, which rejected strict Augustinian predestination and recognized the need for human labor if salvation was to be obtained. He also was a close friend of Sidonius Apollinaris, whose *Epist.* 9.3 and 9.9 are addressed to him. Indeed, it may have been Sidonius who put Ruricius in touch with Faustus when Ruricius was becoming seriously interested in adopting the religious life, probably in the early to mid 470s. During the years ca. 477-485 Faustus was exiled by the Visigothic king Euric (466-484), and he spent part of this period with Ruricius, who then would have come even more under his influence. In this letter, one of the earliest in the collection, Ruricius indicates that he and Faustus have never met. He asks for Faustus' advice and guidance as he embarks upon the religious life; Faustus' letter "Propitia divinitate," which follows below, makes several allusions to this letter, and may be a direct reply to it.

---

[1] The large ornate heading (see the book cover and Fig.4), in three lines with red highlighting, reads, "Incip[it] domni Ruri | cii ep[iscop]i epistularum | liber primus."

1.1

[1] On the importance attributed to the first letter in a book, note Sidonius Apollinaris, *Epist.* 9.11.5, to Lupus of Troyes, "sicut tu antistitum ceterorum cathedris prior est tuus in libro titulus" ("Just as you are first among the ranks of other bishops, your superscription is first in the book").

RURICIUS TO BISHOP FAUSTUS, HIS OWN PERSONAL LORD PATRON IN CHRIST
THE LORD

For a long time, my reverend lord and most blessed prelate,[2] I have known
you through the report of your far-flung fame;[3] for a long time, with the longing of pious love imparted to those words that you deign to write, I have gazed
upon you with the eyes of my heart. But I am no less eager to see you with my
corporeal eyes as well, should there be any way that, through your intercession,
I could shatter the chains of my sins and, having received the wings of that
dove,[4] evade the nets of the fowlers and, settled with you, find peace in the
Lord's law. I then might extinguish the thirst that I have acquired by reading
your treatises,[5] gulping more greedily in your very presence, whence they gush
forth. As a result, an enduring flame might magnify the flicker of charity that
you aroused with blazing sparks in the lukewarm embers of a sleeping spirit,[6]
with fuel provided from the succinctness of the scriptures. A flame which, ig-
nited by the eloquence of your blessed tongue, in its accustomed manner displays in the breast of a sinner the force of its potent nature by warming what is
chilled, by illuminating obscurities, and by incinerating the thorns of transgressions. "My soul," excellent teacher, "clings to thee."[7] Your discourses help me
to spurn terrestrial concerns and to crave the celestial, because "the body, which
is corruptible, weighs down the soul,"[8] so that it cannot bend its ear to the divine prophecies, so that forgetting the home of the father and obeying the command of a caller it departs from its homeland and family[9] and lusts rather for
what is described to it.

---

[2] *sacerdos*, a word used of both bishops and priests.

[3] Repeated in *Epist.* 1.16 to Sidonius.

[4] Cf. Psalms 54.7, "O that I had wings like a dove." Peter, "Ruricius," p.159, asserts that Ruricius does not make any biblical citations in these two letters to Faustus, or in *Epist.* 1.7 to Bassulus, when he in fact does so quite artfully.

[5] References, perhaps, to Faustus' *De gratia* and *De spiritu sancto*, which were written in the
early 470s; and given that Faustus had not yet suffered his exile of 477, and that Ruricius and
Faustus had not yet met, which they did during Faustus' exile, this letter would seem to date to
the early-to-mid 470s.

[6] The text reads "in tepidis ... favillis ferventibus," but by analogy with *Epist.* 2.26, *scintillis* is
restored after *favillis*. The theme of embers kindling is a repeated one in Ruricius' letters: see
Epist. 2.26, 55, 62, 64.

[7] Psalms 62.9.

[8] Wisdom 9.15.

[9] "de terra sua et cognatione discedat": cf. Hilary of Arles, *Sermo de vita Honorati* ("Sermon on
the Life of Honoratus") 12, "exeunt de terra sua et de domo et de cognatione sua" ("they depart
from their homeland and their home and their family"), and note the use of the traditional image
of the prodigal son (Luke 15.11-32).

At this point, in fact, my puniness[10] has not even the strength to expel the dread of this blameworthy condition and to open a cleansed heart to perfected charity, so that abandoning temporal things I might seek the eternal, and with the legacy of the bondswoman cast aside,[11] I might be able freely to secure my paternal inheritance.[12] For this reason, my lord, I hope that you will pray for me ceaselessly and that, however many times you deign to drench the dryness of my soil with the showers of your eloquence, you will not, as you now do, ignorant of my infirmity, lay before me tempting and delightful dishes, but those which are more austere[13] and appropriate to my illness, because temptations convey no benefit to a simpleton. Afterwards you may extend a censorious[14] approval to those who betrayed me,[15] who, in the manner of human nature, shackled by excessive affection and avoiding judicial verity, embrace falsity for the sake of love.[16] Nor, certainly, should Your Sanctity fear that the right hand of a caresser will be more welcome to my wounds than that of a surgeon, because I know that I cannot cure them myself and, in addition, by the gift of God, I now feel that they have become gravely putrescent.[17] I therefore prefer, moreover, to have a just man reprove me with the rebuke of pity, rather than to have "the oil of a sinner anoint my head."[18] I beg, therefore, with a prayer of supplication, that, like the most skilled physicians, you who, helped by the grace of God, daily heal the innumerable and varied illnesses of the sick, likewise send from that treasury of your innermost recesses, whence you customarily

---

[10] "pusillitas nostra": cf. the end of Faustus, *Epist.* "Propitia divinitate", "pusillos cum maioribus," a reference to Ruricius' household.

[11] *eiectoque ancillae hereditatem*: S. There seems to be a missing masculine or neuter word after *ancillae*: Engelbrecht and Demeulenaere suggest *heredem*, and Lütjohann *filio*; Canisius offers *eiectaque ancilla hereditatem*; and Krusch has a lacuna after *ancillae*. See Genesis 21.10, "Whereupon [Sarah] said unto Abraham, 'Cast out this bondswoman...'" In Faustus' correspondence with Ruricius (*Epist.* "Propitia divinitate" and "Gratias domino"), Ruricius' wife Hiberia is referred to as "Sarah."

[12] Such sentiments suggest that Ruricius had not yet adopted the religious life.

[13] "austeriores"; cf. Faustus, *Epist.* "Propitia divinitate", "austerius."

[14] Two Censors were appointed every five years. In Republican times, one of their responsibilities was to inquire into the moral uprightness of members of the Senate.

[15] "meis proditoribus"; cf. Faustus, *Epist.* "Propitia divinitate": "proditoribus tuis." Ruricius uses this loaded word facetiously, apparently referring to those who had encouraged Faustus to write. Sidonius Apollinaris would have been such a one, for Faustus had been his own spiritual mentor: see J. Harries, *Sidonius Apollinaris and the Fall of Rome* (Oxford, 1994) pp. 103-124, 169-186. For Sidonius' own role in Ruricius' Christian education, note his *Epist.* 5.15, translated below.

[16] That is, they supposedly spoke too highly of Ruricius' moral probity.

[17] The theme of "putrescence" is reprised in the next letter.

[18] Cf. Psalms 140.5.

bring forth new and old cures,[19] medications that you know to be appropriate for my malaise.

IT IS FINISHED[20]

1.2 [ca. 475/477]

In this letter, written at about the same time as the previous one, Ruricius continues to seek Faustus' guidance in his pursuit of the religious life. Ruricius, as indicated by his reference to Faustus as "pater," had not yet become a bishop. The legal terminology reflects Ruricius' forensic training, and the medical imagery of the previous letter continues.

RURICIUS TO BISHOP FAUSTUS, HIS OWN PERSONAL LORD PATRON IN CHRIST THE LORD

Until now, my lord, impious negligence and negligent impiety[1] have possessed me to such an extent that I do not know what in myself I should especially accuse,[2] and I cannot find anything that I should primarily excuse.[3] Indeed, should I attempt to present any defense "to busy myself with wicked deeds,"[4] I would be adding another sin to my sin without the proceedings of a trial;[5] I myself would be implicating myself in a double and greater transgression, so that I who am guilty of hesitancy would begin to be guilty of falsity

---

[19] Cf. Matthew 13.52.

[20] "Finit." It is not immediately clear whether Ruricius himself used this word to indicate the conclusion of the letter, or whether it was a later scribal addition. A special effort seems to have been made to retain an idiosyncratic script, with a distinctive cursive "F" and a "t" which has a sharply diagonal cross-bar with a curl on the bottom end and a looped flourish on the top (see Fig.10). This could be an indication that this concluding word had been written "alia manu," that is, in Ruricius' own hand. The word also appears at the ends of *Epist.* 2.41-42, 45-46, 48, 54-55, 65. For further discussion, see Introduction.

1.2

[1] "impia neglegentia et neglegens impietas": note the use of chiasmus, a favored Rurician figure.

[2] "quid ... accusem"; cf. Faustus, *Epist.* "Propitia divinitate", "Iustus ... sui est accusator."

[3] "quid, domine mi, in me potissimum accusem, nesciam, et, quid in me primum excusem, non inveniam": copied virtually verbatim from Cassian, *De incarnatione* ("On the Incarnation") 1.5.2 (*CSEL* 17.1.242), itself a direct quote from Leporius, *Libellus emendationis* ("Notice of Correction") 1. Perhaps Ruricius was being clever here: Leporius had been accused of Pelagianism shortly after 410, and Faustus' own *De gratia* was largely a refutation of Pelagianism; see R. Mathisen, *Ecclesiastical Factionalism and Religious Controversy in Fifth-Century Gaul* (Washington, 1989) pp.126-129.

[4] Psalms 140.4. Ruricius quoted the immediately subsequent verse in the previous letter, which could suggest that these two letters were written at about the same time.

[5] "sine recordatione iudicii": more legal metaphors.

and I would extend my guilt completely beyond the human ability to punish it; awaiting now only a paternal sentence for the fault of torpor I would become liable, truly, to a divine judgment for the avenging of falsehood, in particular because a true confession merits forgiveness but a false excuse opprobrium. I prefer, therefore, to seek pardon by a confession as simple as it is suppliant, rather than to double my transgressions.

Thus, you, best father, chosen shepherd, have me as a spontaneous confessor of my iniquity. You have both in the error of your disciple that which you can correct, and in the weakness of your lamb that which you can cure. And it is up to your power and judgment whether you choose to rip open the putrescence of my sore with the severity of steel, or to heal it with the mildness of your medications. Regardless, I will unflinchingly embrace whichever cure you choose. Neither will I avoid the slap of a fatherly right hand, provided that I obtain a portion of the promised inheritance, nor will I pay heed to what punishment there is for me in the whip, but to what portion[6] I might have in the will. It is better for me, indeed, to weep because of the father than, condemned by the father, to be disinherited, because the piety of parents does not persevere as a punishment but disrupts so that it may correct, nor does the arrogance of a prideful person bring as much grief to them as the humility of a confessor brings joy. Thus, that most indulgent father in the evangelist received his son, the squanderer of his anticipated substance, with a joyful embrace, more ready to rejoice in his return than to find fault with his error.[7]

In sum, his misdeeds are not denounced, nor his luxury, nor his poverty; the reappearance of the convert alone repays all the losses, because, for the father, the value of the return no doubt was greater than the value of the property. Thus, he whom departure had made guilty, return made innocent, and, for the heir, forgiveness was sufficient. But in fact, the pardon of paternal clemency alone is not sufficient, insofar as it it cherishes with embraces, insofar as it soothes with kindness, unless it also generates bountiful gifts. The father gives a ring, lest, led astray by perfidy, the son depart again from his father. The father gives shoes for his feet, whereby the son may disdain more easily the harshness and roughness of the journey.[8] The father also gives the very best cloak, which the son had lost, so that he might endow with his intrinsic immortality the one whom he had regained from the dead. The same calf is offered

---

[6] "quem habeam in testamento." Several editors postulate that a word has dropped out. Lütjohann suggests *locum* before *habeam*; Engelbrecht *patrem* after *habeam*; Canisius assumed a repetition of *poena* and emended *quem* to *quam*. But perhaps there is no lacuna at all, and a repetition of *portionem* is to be understood.

[7] The prodigal son again; cf. *Epist.* 1.1, and Luke 15.11-32.

[8] Presumably the journey home, equivalent to the difficult journey to heaven.

up for the returned younger son which, as a lamb, had been offered up for the
elder son who was about to depart from Egypt, because the Father himself was
the leader out of Egypt.[9]

So, re-creating the faith of a parent, grant succor to sinners, furnish remission to those who are struggling, bestow intercession, and not only allot pardon
yourself to a confessing son, but also pray yourself for pardon for him, so that
he whom you call free in a foreign land you may see freed in his very own
land,[10] and so that he who through himself has lost the generosity of the Lord,
through you may deserve to obtain freedom, and so that he who is sequestered
from the reward will not be separated[11] from your succor.

Faustus, *Epistula* "Licet per" (*SG*[1] no.1) [ca. 475/477]

> The five letters from Faustus to Ruricius are presented at least in rough chronolo-
> gical order. The first and third address Ruricius as *filius* and either *piissimus* or
> *devinctissimus*, indicating that he had not yet become a bishop; the fourth and
> fifth address him as *beatissimus*, *frater* and *episcopus*, and therefore must have
> been written after the "filius" letters, that is, ca. 485 or later. The second calls
> Ruricius *frater*, but because it also uses the more secular *devinctissimus* (cf. Ru-
> ricius, *Epist.* 1.3-5, 2.1-5, 23, 42) and does not describe him as either *beatissimus*
> or *episcopus*, he almost certainly was still a layman. In the first letter in the se-
> quence, Ruricius, still a layman, has sent a letter, not extant, which was delivered
> by a bearer who had recently become a religious. Apparently in reply to some
> ideas that Ruricius had presented, Faustus advised him on how to manage one's
> property when adopting the religious life, recommending that it be turned over to
> a monastery — preferably that at Lérins — and, failing that, that it not be alienated.
> Given that this letter seems to have been written before Faustus' exile in 477, but
> that Faustus wrote the next one from exile, this letter might be dated to just
> before 477. Text: *CCL* 64.406-408; *CSEL* 21.406-408; *MGH AA* 8.274-275.

---

[9] Cf. Exodus 12.3-4, where the Israelites were to slaughter a lamb and place its blood on their
doorposts so their eldest sons would be spared. Ruricius' analogy is a little strained: the calf is
parallel to the lamb, just as the father of the prodigal son is parallel to God the father. The elder
son, having followed the guidance of his father, has already reached the "promised land."

[10] Gaul (the "foreign land") is contrasted with the city of God.

[11] *qui sequestrat praemio*: S; *qui sequestratur <a> praemio*: Krusch; cf. Cassiodorus, *Variae*
1.3.1, "quae sequestrata a praemio."

Faustus, "Licet per"

[1] Whereas the letters written by Ruricius are presented in the translations in the order in which
they appear in the manuscript, the letters written to Ruricius are included as they relate to Ruricius' own letters. Their sequence in the manuscript is indicated by the "*SG*" numbers.

FAUSTUS TO HIS SON RURICIUS, A LORD MOST PIOUS AND TO BE CULTIVATED
SINGULARLY BY ME WITH THE HIGHEST HONOR IN CHRIST

Although it would be pleasant for me to converse with your inseparable
heart through the voices of charity itself by means of any person at all, and for
you to be embraced through our sedulous pursuit of our duties,[2] yet I now received, as much opportunely as eagerly, the pledge of your spirit through the
ministry of your domestic bearer; your missive[3] revealed less about his merit
than his appearance verified. And I moreover am overjoyed that, to your profit,
he has been reborn, that in him a better life has abolished the condition of his
initial birth, and that in him the manumission of religion has banished the blemish of his origin, that, through faith, by the adoption of Christ he has freed and
transferred his servile status.[4] Regarding the manner in which we ought to act
in the presence of the milky-white sincerity of him or of the other brothers,[5]
moreover, you described the apostle's most wide-ranging commission[6] in your
ready address, and because your most learned page liberates those who are less
learned, in the cleansed character of these persons we also enjoyed an abundance of reading through the gift of your gentleness and humility.

In fact, the endowment of grace overwhelms the principles of teaching. For
in only a short time a gleaming purity and an unclouded simplicity of perception,[7] through which the mirror of the divine image shines in the glow of the
interior man, introduced itself within their shining breasts and transparent innards. Of the divine image, I say, for we read thus about the Lord: pure, simple, precise. But that divine purity provides a very different example, inasmuch
as in us there is a two-fold substance, in the spirit and in the flesh. We have

---

[2] That is, their letter-writing, an indication that Faustus and Ruricius had been corresponding for
some time.

[3] This letter of Ruricius does not survive.

[4] "manumissio ... personam mancipii fide emancipavit et transcripsit": Faustus uses the secular
technical legal terminology associated with the freeing of a slave. Perhaps also an allusion to St.
Paul's "Letter to Philemon," discussing the case of a slave who was freed through Christ.

[5] "apud reliquorum fratrum": the identity of these "brothers" is unclear. It may be that Ruricius
had established his own monastery, much as Sacerdos, in the *Vita Sacerdotis* translated in Appendix III, while still a layman built a church and a monastery. If so, then Ruricius would have
been following the advice that Faustus gave him in the previous letter.

[6] "dispensationem": In the *Vulgate*, this word is only used in the letters of the apostle Paul, and
Faustus may have had in mind 1 Corinthians 9.17, referring to the preaching of the Gospel: "si
enim volens hoc ago mercedem habeo si autem invitus dispensatio mihi credita est" ("For if I do
this of my own will, I have a reward, but if not of my own will, I am entrusted with a commission").

[7] Faustus contrasts Ruricius' *doctrina* ("learning") with the divine *simplicitas* ("simplicity").

what we have received, for the different spiritual gifts[8] of virtues are appended, they are not inborn; and, without doubt, that which can be withdrawn is proffered. We share in the goodness of our author, with the result that we become good. Indeed, it is through Him that we live, but we are not life, as He is. We have the ability to be just, but not to be justice. Therefore, He is "simple" because nothing is bestowed upon Him from an external benevolence. He exists from Himself, he appropriates nothing from elsewhere. God is equally living and life, good and goodness, pitying and pity. In the glory of His virtues He Himself is that which He manifests. Man, so to speak, is gold-plated, God is gold.[9] That which in man is grace, in God is nature; and moreover, because nothing is added to Him from outside, nothing can be removed from Him. He does not suffer any loss because He knows no augmentation. He Himself is the creator of both Himself and the Son, because there is a single source for the fountain and the river. Among things that exist without a beginning there is a commonality, not a transference.

And because we read regarding the Son, "His is the splendor of the brightness of God,"[10] just as God is never without splendor, likewise the Father was never without the majesty of the Son.[11] And just as the names of both are coeval — indeed, the one could not be said to be the Father unless the other had been born — thus the antiquity of the paternity of the one contains them both without separation. He came from Him, but He is not after Him, just as the face has its origin from its head but is not, nevertheless, considered to be younger than its head. And thus our God is neither mixed nor divided in His own persons;[12] a single virtue is divided in neither power nor time, just as He is three-fold in His existence,[13] because whoever exists in Himself is thus "simple" in substance, because one substance, not knowing how to precede itself, accepts itself as neither following or preceding. Thence, we also share in this simplicity if in us there is nothing dissonant, nothing dissimilar, nothing disparate, if, with commendable devotion and our sentiments grounded in Christ, we always struggle to be the same, so that, unchangeable in goodness, we be changed only through new advancement every day.

---

[8] *charismata*, a rare word.

[9] "hoc est ipse, quod possidet ... homo deauratus est, deus aurum est": reprised from Faustus, *Epist*. "Admiranda mihi" to Paulinus of Bordeaux (*CSEL* 21.193) (see Appendix I), which apparently was written earlier.

[10] Hebrews 1.3.

[11] Such assertions were used to counter the Arian teaching that the three persons of the Trinity were not of the same substance, and that God had preceded Christ.

[12] *personis*: a references to the three "persons" of the Trinity.

[13] *subsistentia*: Engelbrecht, Demeulenaere; *substantia*: S, Krusch. A scribal "correction" to *substantia* is understandable, but *subsistentia* is parallel to *subsistit* later in the line.

Moreover, regarding a point that a certain person has raised out of love of provocation,[14] it is a salvific and perfected practice,[15] after the management[16] of terrestrial property has been distributed among a greater mumber of persons,[17] to lighten the cares of the spirit, and afterwards, in a three-fold deliberation, to consider this: whether it is better to endow[18] or to administer or to disperse one's own property. Verily, the first would be good, so that as a servant of Christ one might hasten to embark, in every regard a pauper, upon the path of a pauper, should it be possible to seek out the perfected company[19] of some great monastery or, certainly, the insular service[20] of an angelic congregation.[21] For it is as difficult as it is valiant for a monastic society to be established in the midst of the secular world.

Or, for the sake of a lightening of the spirit, in place of one's self one can impose the second weight upon one's family,[22] but this factor must be considered, whether any of one's sons can cope with such a difficulty,[23] so that the authority of a paternal command[24] does not, perhaps, <compel> submission to the father <...>[25] [In such a case] it is best to endure the second choice, under an administrator indebted because of your benefactions, either if there is the will to do so or if the amount of the annual income fills the need.[26]

The third [option] is to oversee an amount of property that has been retained under one's own but lesser sollicitude by means of the discriminating care of

---

[14] *provocationis*: or, legally, "appeal." This would seem to be a response to a point that Ruricius himself, the "certain person," had raised in his own letter.

[15] *meditatio*.

[16] *regimen*: S², edd.; *regione*: S¹.

[17] "per plures"; apparently sons.

[18] *locare*; that is, to turn it over to a monastery.

[19] *schola*; a word also used for units of the imperial bodyguard, and hence having a military flavor.

[20] *militiam*; another word with military connotations.

[21] A pointed reference to the island monastery at Lérins, where Faustus himself had retreated ca. 420 and had served as abbot from about 432 until his own ordination as bishop of Riez ca. 460. Faustus seems to be trying to "recruit" Ruricius. The several elements of "normality" in this letter, ranging from Faustus' reception of Ruricius' messengers to the freedom to deal as one wished with one's property to the continued possibility of a stay at Lérins, all seem to suggest that the letter was written prior to Faustus' exile in 477.

[22] *suis*: that is, the *plures* referred to above, i.e., one's children.

[23] *tam arduo*: edd.; *iam acduo*: S. Engelrecht and Demeulenaere add *officio*, "for such a difficult duty."

[24] *paternae iussionis*: edd.; *paterna eius sonis*: S.

[25] *in patrem <...> optimum est*: There is a lacuna here; perhaps a whole line has dropped out.

[26] Faustus clearly does not approve of this approach, perhaps because he knew Ruricius' sons and was well aware at least of Constantius' and Eparchius' irresponsible ways (see *Epist.* 2.24-25,57).

faithful servants, [who have been] assigned the duty of an imposed oversight, and to direct a path[27] straight along the middle of the royal road.[28]   When I urge this,[29] I think that I being mindful of both our own best interest and that of the poor.   In this regard, the revenue is not insufficient if the property is distributed with its use retained.[30]   Therefore, indicating briefly what the first, second, and third options might be, let me reserve the choice to the judgment or the decision of the one making the deliberation.   Let him deign to indicate anything more that he might seek that can be readily provided; this encouragement is itself organized for the sake of his apprehension[31] and love.

May our Lord God multiply His blessings in you through a longevity happy and pleasing to Him, most pious lord and a son to be esteemed by me with the greatest honor in Christ the Lord.[32]

Faustus, *Epistula* "Propítia divinitate" *(SG* no.2) [ca. 477]

> In this lengthy letter Faustus congratulates Ruricius on his adoption of the religious life.   Even though, in his salutation, he calls Ruricius *frater* rather than *filius*, the use of the honorific *devinctissimus* (rather than *beatissimus*) and the failure to call him *episcopus* suggest that the *frater* was intended as a way of saying "welcome to the club," and that Ruricius was still a layman, albeit a very pious one.   This conclusion is consistent with Faustus' references to being in exile, which began ca. 477, although unless the letter is an affectation, it does not seem that Faustus was yet residing with Ruricius.   Faustus picks up on the theme of "property" from the previous letter, which suggests, again, that it was not written long after, and this letter contains a number of verbal reminiscences of Ruricius' *Epist.* 1.1 and 2.   Much of this letter also is repeated in Faustus' letter "Magnum pondus" to Felix (see Appendix I), which likewise was written during his exile.   Text: *CCL* 64.408-412; *CSEL* 21.408-412; *MGH AA* 8.274-275.

FAUSTUS TO HIS BROTHER RURICIUS, A LORD MOST STEADFAST AND TO BE CULTIVATED SINGULARLY WITH THE FULL FORCE OF DUTIFULNESS

With the favor of the divinity, in a suitable and most peaceful refuge of religion, situated in silence, in which the Lord moves His file[1] of salvific castiga-

---

[27] *cursum*: Engelbrecht, Demeulenaere; *cum*: S; *tamquam*: Mommsen, Krusch.

[28] "per viam regiam": cf. Faustus, *Epist.* "Quod pro sollicitudine" to Leontius of Arles (*CSEL* 21.4), "ne ... omissa via regia in dexteram cadens in sinistram declinare nos crederet..." (see Appendix I).

[29] Only grudgingly.

[30] Faustus here represents the traditional aristocratic view that property should not be alienated.

[31] *timor*: as he approaches the reality of adopting the religious life.

[32] The farewell salutations of all Faustus' letters have several similarities, including references to longevity and eternity and his practice of essentially repeating his introductory greeting.
Faustus, "Propitia divinitate"

tion over the rust produced by a long indifference, amidst this great peaceful-ness, I say, if we acknowledge [it], endowed with leisure, as we acquire new citizens through the commerce of charity, as we rejoice over the salvation of those acquired, positioned among these benefits we scoff at our present exile, and we recognize that we have not lost our homeland but transformed it.[2] For as long as faithful servants of God exercise the goodness of their devotion on behalf of our needs, we are landlords lacking estates, and prosperous without possessions; rather, we enrich those who receive the comfort of our revenue. In a marvelous manner, our comforters[3] do business with petty paupers and obtain everlasting riches from the needy.

I, moreover, observe first of all this munificence granted by God, that my most dutiful Ruricius, after the tempests[4] of this life, guided by the hand of the exalted salvation, has turned his prow to the port of religion,[5] and that after the shadows of seductive vanities and the illusions of fleeting dreams, he has craved what is enduring and solid, and with the world finally disdained, he has spurned its great unhappiness; he has obtained happiness and riches of his own from a perishing world. Behold! Passing along with a faithful <...>[6] and an avoidance of ephemeral things, in this way he treated with contempt the riches that now can offer nothing for his own use. Therefore, let us now serve the Lord with the same zeal with which we pursued[7] secular interests.

And because Your Piety constrains me to speak to you more austerely[8] re-garding the curing of sins, and does not embody the resentment of that saying, which says, "Initially, the just man accuses himself,"[9] therefore, in the first place, let us avoid lapses of the mouth and heart. But because we speak of the mouth, if you attempt to impose guardianship on the heart you will not need to

---

[1] *limam ... admovit*: edd.; *elima ... admonuit*: S.

[2] That is, Faustus is now in exile, in the same way that Sidonius Apollinaris was exiled to the fortress of Livia by the Visigothic king Euric at the same time (Sid.Apoll. *Epist.* 8.11.1).

[3] *consolatores*: S[2], edd.; *consolatoris*: S[1].

[4] *iactationes*: edd.; *iactationis*: S.

[5] "ad portum religionis proram salutis excelsi manu gubernante"; cf. *Epist.* 2.13, "ratem ad portum salutis ... domino gubernante."

[6] The manuscript reads "ecce fideli atque conlabentium rerum fuga praeteriens." Engelbrecht and Demeulenaere emend *ecce fideli* to *aeque fideliter*, and Krusch suggests *pace fideli*. But in the manuscript "ecce" is preceded by a colon and begins with a large capital letter. The copyist, therefore, clearly intended it to start a new sentence, and as just seen, it also is difficult to suggest a suitable emendation. It may be that a word has fallen out next to "fideli."

[7] *militavimus*.

[8] "austerius": cf. Ruricius, *Epist.* 1.1, "austeriores."

[9] "Iustus ... sui est accusator" (Proverbs 18.17): cf. Ruricius, *Epist.* 1.2, "quid ... accusem." That is, Ruricius does not arrogantly assume that he can cure himself, but humbly asks for Faustus' guidance.

labor to impose discipline on the mouth. One can "place a watch upon the door of one's lips"[10] without difficulty[11] insofar as one produces with one's voice what one first designed in the workshop[12] of one's conscience. The exterior presents what the interior dictates. The mind exercises authority, the tongue obedience, and furthermore we are taught by the celestial eloquence, "The mouth speaks from the fullness of the heart".[13] What appears to be begotten from speaking was first conceived in thought, with the result that the spirit ordains just things so that the sound of the mouth does not put forth unworthy things.

Also, the fact that there are two kinds of fasting.[14] One is to force the desire of incontinence away from the wickedly alluring charms of delicacies, so that the exterior, earthly man, leveled by the plowshare of the cross, crumbles into comfortable infirmity.[15] Another kind of abstinence is much more exalted, much more precious. No infirmity can challenge it;[16] it controls the vagaries of the mind and irrational agitations; and it restrains, with an internal judgment, the tumults of thoughts that conflict among themselves; and it joins battle, so to speak, against secret ambushes as if[17] against domestic enemies[18] with the authority of a furious faith; and through benevolence, kindness, endurance, and tranquility it cultivates on the face of its inner self the image of God, whose glory makes its imprint[19] not in the figure of the body, but, by the skill of the Maker, in the form of the spirit.

Malignancy and sadness will not shatter one pondering upon what is spiritual and divine; happiness will not enervate him; the magnanimity of evenness will display a heart secure in the fear of God, so that the eminent beginning of

---

[10] Psalms 140.3.

[11] Engelbrecht and Demeulenaere add to the text here the words "qui cautus fuerit in sensibus suis" ("who was cautious in his thoughts"), drawn from a similar section in a Eusebian sermon in the *Codex Parisinus* 1547.

[12] *officina*: this letter is full of commercial terminology.

[13] Matthew 12.34.

[14] Faustus now turns to a second method for "curing sins"; in fact, he largely cribbed this entire section, down to "by a second death," from his letter "Magnum pietatis" to Felix (*CSEL* 21.195-200) (see Appendix I), which itself appears in an earlier section of the *Sangallensis* 190. Clearly, Ruricius was not the only writer given to recycling what he considered to be good passages.

[15] Even though this theme is developed at rather greater length in the letter to Felix, Faustus adds to the letter to Ruricius two references to *infirmitas* that are lacking in the letter to Felix; it is difficult not to see here a sensitivity to Ruricius' concern with his own physical ailments.

[16] Faustus now argues that this kind of spiritual strength gives one a means of overcoming one's infirmities, an argument sure to appeal to the hypochondriac Ruricius.

[17] *velut*: Faustus, *Epist.* "Magnum pietatis"; *vel*: S.

[18] That is, as in a civil war.

[19] *inpressit*; an unusual word; one would expect *inprimit*.

that book[20] also can be adapted to us, where that magnificent individual Helcana, whose name is interpreted as "the possession of God," one man named by a mystical expression,[21] said, "There was one man."[22] He is always steadfast, because in him there appears nothing unsure, nothing devious, nothing inconstant, nothing irresolute; adversities do not affect one who remains in a state of virtue with its order unperturbed; changeable circumstances do not change him, nor, as is characteristic of ocean billows, do the fickle buffets of the winds blow him in different directions. Thus, also, the apprehensive servant of God, settled upon a vast mound of faith, is changed only to this extent, so that with Christ operating within him he always is clothed in new graces; useful things are planted in the field of the heart, and harmful things are mowed down. And for this reason the divine instruction commands its soldiers, "When you go forth to war and you seek among the captives a maiden, you shall shave her head and pare her nails and thus you will join with her in marriage."[23] Likewise, girded in the fear of Christ, let us make ourselves subject to the blessed prudence of the world, a captive of spiritual wisdom, which God made simple, uncorrupted, and untainted, and, by shearing away our sins, let us cut off what is unncessary to her and let us join her to our heart in a chaste union.

Before all, to whatever extent we are able, with the help of God, let us take care[24] to overcome those five passions of the senses within us. Whatever, indeed, is pleasing to see, whatever is alluring to smell, whatever is titillating to touch, whatever is sweet to taste, whatever corrupts with its sound,[25] all these things, if we abuse them, divert the attention of the mind from spiritual to earthly things. And, therefore, just as the father of our faith,[26] in the midst of his three-hundred and eighteen dependents, whose hidden significance is concealed within the letter,[27] overcame those five kings, likewise, with the help of the Lord and through His cross, let us strive to overcome the allurements of these five principal sins (indeed, among the Greeks the result of two[28] calculations is determined by means of the sign of the cross and the blessed name of Jesus).[29]

---

[20] That is, the beginning of the first book of Samuel (or Kings, in the *Vulgate*).

[21] See Jerome, *Liber interpretationis hebraicorum nominum* ("Book of the Interpretation of Hebrew Names"): *CCL* 72.75, 103.

[22] 1 Kings 1.1 = 1 Samuel 1.1, referring to Elkanah, the father of the prophet Samuel.

[23] Deuteronomy 20.10-13.

[24] *curemus*: Engelbrecht, Demeulenaere; *curremus*: S, Krusch.

[25] This section clearly struck Ruricius' fancy, as he reused it in *Epist.* 1.18 and 2.13.

[26] That is, Abraham, whose name is given in the letter to Felix. See Genesis 14.14, "He led forth his trained men, born in his house, three hundred and eighteen of them..."

[27] "intra litteram latente": Faustus will explain this shortly.

[28] *utriusque*: edd.; *utrius*: S.

[29] The numerological significance of the number 318 is explained more fully by Faustus in the

Those who overcome carnal delights with these weapons will deserve to say, "I will give the crown of life to the conqueror," and "The one who conquers will not be stricken by a second death."[30]

For this reason you easily despise terrestrial things and you dispose of them as if you were making a profit while you think upon that time when sinners will be burned like straw,[31] when, scorched by the perpetual fury of Gehenna whose "smoke rises into the age of ages,"[32] those who ignored what was offered to them, about to die in life and about to be vanquished in a death without end, will be punished by such a death that they are not allowed to die in grief, as long as, I say, with a mind anticipating the future[33] you keep before your eyes that time regarding which we say, "I will enter into your house with burnt offerings,"[34] that is, when, stuffed with the fruit of good works and wreathed with the adornments of justice, you will enter the door of life in triumph over your conquered flesh, regarding which we read, "The daughters of Tyre will worship him with gifts,"[35] that is, souls acquired for Christ from the nations offer gifts to our Lord, about to declare with a speech of thanks,[36] "Behold, I have multiplied the talent that you gave; receive, with interest, your profit."[37] For there will be a certain commerce of giving[38] and receiving between man and God. Man offers the labor that he has done, and God provides what He promised.[39] At the time when, along with your Sarah,[40] you are to be rewarded like for like, about to be bedecked with a double crown for the sake of your

---

De spiritu sancto 1.1, "ideo sacer numerus diximus, quia trecenti in aera vel supputatione Graeca signum crucis, decem et octo vero Iesu adorandum nomen ostendunt" ("Therefore we speak of this number as sacred because in the Greek calculation or number, three-hundred signifies the sign of the cross and eighteen, indeed, the blessed name of Jesus"). The five kings, moreover, would have represented the five senses.

[30] Revelations 2.10-17.

[31] There is a play on words between *fenerantis* (one making a profit, that is, "making hay") and *fenum* (straw).

[32] Revelations 19.3.

[33] "provida in futurum mente disponis"; cf. Faustus, *Epist.* "Gratias domino", "provida in futurum cogitatione disponit."

[34] Psalms 65.13.

[35] Psalms 44.12-13.

[36] "cum gratiarum actione": an *actio gratiarum* was a formal speech of thanks delivered on ceremonial occasions.

[37] Cf. Matthew 25.14-30. In the parable, the master merely told the servant who had buried his talent that he at least could have left it with the moneylenders and received the interest; in Faustus' version, the talent actually does bear interest.

[38] *dandi*: edd.; *dandandi*: S.

[39] Faustus here reprises his concept of the significance of human labor, in implied contrast to Augustine's idea of unconditional predestination.

[40] That is, Hiberia, Ruricius' wife, with the metaphor of Ruricius as Abraham continuing.

shared salvation, you will deserve to hear, "Rejoice, good and faithful servant: because you have been faithful in a little I will place you over much; enter into the joy of your Lord."[41] Then you will marvel at how your use of the present has been transformed into your possession of the eternal, and, about to be extolled by those who have betrayed you,[42] you will rejoice that you have been made into their[43] debtor by a pleasant metamorphosis of things.

I greet, with dutiful courtesy, our inseparable son Leontius[44] and your entire household, the lesser along with the greater.[45] May our Lord God multiply His benefits in you with a longevity[46] happy and pleasing to Him, most steadfast lord and to be esteemed singularly with the complete virtue of dutifulness.

Faustus, *Epistula* "Gratias domino" (*SG* no.3) [ca. 477/480]

> In this letter, perhaps written not long after the preceding one, Ruricius and Hiberia continue to pursue the religious life, and Faustus continues to advise them on how to manage their property. Ruricius has not yet become a bishop, as seen in Faustus' reference to him as *filius*, and this letter may have been written before Faustus took refuge with Ruricius. Text: *CCL* 64.412-413; *CSEL* 21.412-413; *MGH AA* 8.274-275.

FAUSTUS TO HIS SON RURICIUS, A LORD MOST STEADFAST AND TO BE CULTIVATED SPECIALLY WITH PARTICULAR HONOR

Thanks be to God, who granted this, in a general dispensation, that among those whom distances of spaces separate, a spirit free and restrained by no restrictions of absence might wander about, and that nothing should be so inpenetrable that it is not open to the surveillance of the mind, but that rather through the mediation of grace those who are dear see each other reciprocally through the gaze of the heart, where charity itself resides.[1] Inasmuch as our interior

---

[41] Matthew 25.21-23.

[42] "proditoribus tuis"; apparently an allusion back to Ruricius, *Epist.* 1.1, "meis proditoribus," referring to those like Faustus who had pointed out to Ruricius the errors of his ways and encouraged him to adopt the religious life. Krusch's suggested emendation to *creditoribus* is certainly wrong. Cf. also Faustus, *Epist.* "Gratias domino."

[43] *eis*: Engelbrecht, Demeulenaere; *ei*: S; *dei*: Krusch.

[44] This would appear to be Ruricius' brother, or brother-in-law (*Epist.* 2.42), rather than his son (see *Epist.* 2.40) of the same name, who may not even have been born yet.

[45] "pusillos cum maioribus": cf. Ruricius, *Epist.* 1.1, where he referred to himself as "pusillitas nostra."

[46] *longaevitate*: edd.; *longe vitae*: S.

Faustus, "Gratias domino"

[1] This entire introductory section is copied virtually verbatim in Ruricius' *Epist.* 2.10 to the abbot Julianus Pomerius, and rather more freely in *Epist.* 2.52 to Stephanus.

also has its own eyes, with which, as a witness to its perceptiveness, it inspects itself; with which, turned in upon itself, it considers what to regret and what to celebrate; with which it surveys the final day; with which, anticipating the future, it displays in thought,[2] before its own mind's eye, the story of its entire life, whether disordered[3] or, by the grace of God, praiseworthy, anticipates in the present period of frightening anxiety[4] the time when an account must be rendered, and depicts in the secret pages of its heart, with hope creating the image, the things "that God has prepared for those who love Him."[5]

You yourself, so I think, always lift up these eyes to the verdict of this fearful judge, so that that prophetic saying could deservedly be said about you, "The eyes of a wise man are in his head".[6]   Thus it is, my son, that I have there, in fact, your own betrayers;[7] thus it is, I say, that, like a greedy profiteer,[8] through your redemption of captives,[9] in the manner of a sower you commend into the lap of the remunerator the reliance upon present things, which must be relinquished; you create property by using it up and you convert what is going to perish into everlasting treasures.   Thus it is that with your most faithful Sarah, under a single yoke of Christ, stretching out for your shared crown,[10] a despiser of terrestrial things and a seeker of the celestial, a pilgrim in this world and a candidate for paradise, as a reclusive soldier of Christ you scorn this world, which no longer has anything that can deceive or seduce you. With your ally in the endless kingdom, the two of you, in a pious conspiracy, beat upon the door of life with fasts and prayers and with a hand, so to speak, of faith, so that you might seize the double palm of a shared salvation.

But in the midst of all this, whatever is done is too little for the unhealable causes to be healed here, for the the inextinguishable fires to be extinguished here, for the insuperable necessities to be overcome here, for the arrows of sins to be plucked from the innards of the soul here, for the wounds pressed into

---

[2] "provida in futurum cogitatione disponit"; cf. Faustus, *Epist.* "Propitia divinitate", "provida in futurum mente disponis."

[3] *confusibilem.*

[4] "in praesentiam trepidae sollicitudinis": perhaps an allusion to the uncertainties associated with Faustus' exile.

[5] 1 Corinthians 2.9.

[6] Ecclesiasticus 2.14; cf. Ruricius, *Epist.* 2.34.

[7] "tuos proditores": by now this has become a commonplace between them; cf. Faustus, Epist. "Propitia divinitate", and Ruricius, *Epist.* 1.1.

[8] *faenerator*: from *faenus*, "hay," which is consistent with the "sowing" imagery in the preceding letter and to follow.

[9] See Faustus' subsequent letters, "Tanta mihi" and "Gratias ad vos," which deal with specific manifestations of this very issue.

[10] "cum fidelissima Sarra tua ... communem tendens coronam"; a reference to Ruricius' wife Hiberia, an image reprised from the previous letter: "cum Sarra tua ... corona duplici."

one's very marrow to be cured here, for invisible blemishes to be cleansed here, for eternal joys to be provided by the labor of faithful efforts here. Certainly, that kind of life will be the reward of this life, but it is necessary that this life be the price of that one.

Therefore, having offered my dutiful compliance,[11] I beg that, when an opportune chance presents itself, you allow me to rejoice regarding your health and character. On behalf of my sons and deacons[12] I offer abundant thanks, and I salute my lady daughter,[13] having admired her, with suitable respect, as an example of piety and a reflection of religion. May our Lord God fill your goodness, to be magnified by me, with good things in the present and may He render it worthy of eternal things, most steadfast lord and a son to be specially esteemed by me with particular honor.

Faustus, *Epistula* "Tanta mihi" (*SG* no.4) [ca. 485/486]

> The following two letters, written ca. 485 or just afterwards, allude to how Ruricius, before he became bishop, sheltered Faustus during the latter's exile. It is not known how long Faustus remained with Ruricius, but he presumably did not arrive until after the composition of the preceding three letters. He could not have returned to Riez until after the death of Euric at the end of 484, at which time Ruricius himself became bishop of Limoges. The chronological gap between these letters and Faustus' earlier ones is reflected in a changed tone that portrays Ruricius much more as an equal. Text: *CCL* 64.413-414; *CSEL* 21.413-414; *MGH AA* 8.274-275.

FAUSTUS TO BISHOP RURICIUS, A MOST BLESSED LORD AND A BROTHER TO BE ESTEEMED SINGULARLY BY ME BEFORE ALL OTHERS WITH THE GREATEST HONOR

I have such great faith in the kindness of your spirit that no longer am I content to gulp alone from its most pure waters, but I also invite others, who might be revived along with me through its use; especially because its extended largess redounds to the profit of the bestower, and the recipient is so enriched by its goodness that the one imparting is not lessened but is augmented, as if with profit, through his expenditures,[1] my lord most blessed and to be cultivat-

---

[11] That is, his letter.

[12] "pro filiis et diaconibus meis": given the immediately subsequent mention of deacons, the *filii* would seem to be priests. If this letter was indeed written while Faustus was in exile, and it is hard to believe otherwise, he apparently was accompanied by something of a retinue, as also suggested by the reference to Memorius in the following letter.

[13] "domnam filiam meam": Hiberia; for the terminology, cf. *Epist.* 2.32.

Faustus, "Tanta mihi"

ed singularly by me before all others with the greatest honor.[2]

Therefore, with this letter I exhibit the irrepayable payment of charity, by which the property of the bestower is further enriched, and I presume to offer the opportunity for a good deed through my commendation of those in trouble, because I have faith that my intercession pertains to your profit, and therefore I was unable to deny pity, which ecclesiastical humanity is accustomed to offer to the miserable, to the bearer of this letter, who has suffered captivity in Lugdunensis. Would that the largess of the faithful could be as prompt as the need of this individual is all too obvious. And because, having gained freedom to an extent with regard to his own person, he is yet held captive through the servitude of his wife and children, having extended my good offices I beg you to adhere to your customary kindness even in the consolation of this one and to pursue through letters what he has requested with regard to those concerned.[3]

My fellow servants, especially your admirer, my brother, the priest Memorius,[4] give their blessing most reverently with me.

May our Lord God keep your pious beatitude mindful of me through happy longevity to the profit of His church, my brother, a lord most blessed and to be cultivated singularly by me with the highest honor before all others.

Faustus, *Epistula* "Gratias ad vos" (*SG* no.5) [ca. 485/486]

> This letter seems to have been written shortly after Faustus' return to Riez and Ruricius' consecration as bishop. It may predate the preceding letter, "Tanta mihi," by a bit. Text: *CCL* 64.414-415; *CSEL* 21.414-415; *MGH AA* 8.274-275.

FAUSTUS TO BISHOP RURICIUS, A MOST BLESSED LORD, AND A BROTHER TO BE RECEIVED WITH FITTING PIETY AND MOST WORTHY OF AN APOSTOLIC SEE

Thanks be to you, while we[1] write from our homeland, you who made a homeland for us amid our wandering, you who tempered our desire for home with untiring liberality, conferring through successive benefactions something like the force of divine justice, so that whatever pertained to castigation it converted to honor, it adapted to consolation, it changed to peace; it neglected our deserts so that it might magnify yours, forgiving our debts and multiplying your

---

[1] Cf. Graecus of Marseille's letter "Gratias domino" to Ruricius below.

[2] "domine beatissime et summo mihi honore ante omnes singulariter excolende": Faustus must have been nodding, for these same words are repeated in the salutation and in the farewell.

[3] "apud antepositos": the only "aforementioned persons" are the wife and children, but Faustus seems to be asking Ruricius to pursue the case with some other individuals, i.e. "the authorities."

[4] Memorius, otherwise unknown, seems to have accompanied Faustus in exile and thus also to have enjoyed Ruricius' hospitality; he may be one of the retinue alluded to in "Gratias domino."

[1] If these are true plurals, then Faustus went into exile accompanied by some of his clergy.

wealth, exercising the magnitude of its goodness on both sides, it enriched us with your indulgence while it enriched you with our exile.[2] For this reason, it turns out that already, at the present, impatient of the future, it dispenses a benediction and lifts its most faithful servant atop the candelstick of its house[3] with the cooperation of pity, justice, sincerity, continence, and kindness, that is, with domestic supporters. Behold, at what price has my Ruricius procured the highest priesthood![4] What he purchased it with is itself the thing that he purchased, and with his own supporters shouting their approval,[5] as a fugitive[6] from office he revealed in himself reasons for office. Therefore, one who knows how to acquire such a great burden also knows how, in the name of Christ, to administer it.

I commend to you the bearer of this letter, the holy priest Florentius — known to me for a long time now and adorned both with the model of his master[7] and with the blossoms of his character — because he is traveling for the sake of the freeing of his sister; as a welcome intercessor[8] he has offered this opportunity to me.

We bless your entire house, the seniors along with the juniors, with a paternal affection. My fellow servants, your debtors and admirers, give their blessing most reverently with me.

May our Lord preserve Your Beatitude, to be magnified by me, to the profit of his church, and with a long life made perfect by our joy, my most blessed lord, and a brother to be received with fitting piety and most worthy of an apostolic see.

Graecus, *Epistula* "Gratias domino" (*SG* no.6) [ca. 472/475]

> Graecus was a distinguished bishop of Marseille in the 470s and 480s (Duchesne, *Fastes* 1.274) who debated the Arian theologian Modaharius and in 475 (along with Faustus) was one of four episcopal ambassadors to Euric who surrendered the Auvergne to the Visigoths. Faustus corresponded with Graecus when the latter was a deacon (*Epist.* "Honoratus officio tuo": *MGH AA* 8.284-288; see Ap-

---

Faustus, "Gratias ad vos"

[2] The metaphors reprise those at the beginning of the previous letter.

[3] Cf. Mark 4.21

[4] "summum sacerdotium," that is, the episcopate. Faustus discusses Ruricius' election.

[5] "testibus propriis adclamantibus": it was customary for officials, from emperors and bishops on down, to be greeted with "acclamations" shouted by the people.

[6] The manuscript reads *refuga*, which seems preferable to the *refugia* suggested by Engelbrecht and Demeulenaere. The allusion here is to the tradition of "nolo episcopari," the affected unwillingness of episcopal candidates to hold the office.

[7] "exemplis magistri": perhaps a reference to Florentius' unnamed bishop.

[8] Presumably on behalf of his sister. *mediator*: edd.; *mediatur*: S.

pendix I), rebuking him for misunderstanding Augustine: see R. Mathisen, "For Specialists Only: The Reception of Augustine and His Theology in Fifth-Century Gaul," in J.T. Lienhard et al. eds., *Augustine. Presbyter factus sum* (New York, 1994) pp.29-41. In the manuscript, Graecus' very conventional letter to Ruricius follows those written by Faustus, a indication (along with Graecus' reference to Ruricius as his "son"), that this is an early letter, likely written at the time of Faustus' early letters to Ruricius. Sidonius Apollinaris, a close friend of Graecus (*Epist.* 6.8, 7.7, 7.10, 9.4), may have encouraged him to write to Ruricius in the same way it was suggested above that he motivated Faustus to do so. Of those who sent extant letters to Ruricius, Graecus is the only one who does not have a letter from Ruricius in the collection. It must have meant much to Ruricius for him to have preserved it so long. Text: *CCL* 64.397; *MGH AA* 8. 274-275.

GRAECUS TO A LORD EXALTED[1] BY HONOR OF RELIGION AND ESTEEMED BY MERITS OF FAITH, HIS SON[2] RURICIUS

Thanks be to the Lord that the merit of your faith profits from devotion just as it also grows by deeds. You anticipate the needs of those in trouble through your solicitude, you cherish them with kindness, you sustain them with humanity. Indeed, in these matters, according to the apostle, "Burning with spirit, serving the Lord, rejoicing with hope,"[3] you acquire for yourself the divine recompense of eternal <life>.[4] But such things are not new for Your Exaltedness, because just as your spirit is full of the fear of God, it is similarly full of charity: with charity, I say, which is the only thing that gains profit through use and increases through largess, recognizing the expenditure but not sensing the loss.[5] Indeed, while it is spent it is not expended, but it is further augmented while it is outstretched; and thus its grace, which grants, in the likeness of divinity, what it has and retains what it has given, is rewarded, perceiving that by endowing it is not lessened.

1.3 [ca. 475/480]

The first of three successive letters, which seem to have been written at about the same time, to Hesperius, a rhetor who educated some of Ruricius' sons. Hesperius (*PLRE II*, p.552) was a protégé of Sidonius Apollinaris (Sid.Apoll. *Epist.* 2.10,

---

Graecus

[1] *sublimi*: a reference to Ruricius' high aristocratic rank; cf. the reference to Ruricius as *vestra sublimitas* below.

[2] Ruricius has not yet become a bishop, hence this letter must have been written before ca. 485.

[3] Romans 12.11.

[4] The manuscript reads only *aeternae*, and there seems to be a noun missing. Engelbrecht and Demeulenaere suggest *vitae*.

[5] Cf. the beginning of Faustus' letter "Tanta mihi" above.

4.22.1), and probably came from Clermont. Because Ruricius does not yet seem
to be bishop, the letter must pre-date 485, and for him to have sons who required
a rhetor, it probably was not written before ca. 475. And given that Hesperius
seems to have been from Clermont, and that Ommatius and Eparchius were living
there by ca. 485/490, these may be the sons to whom Ruricius is referring.

RURICIUS, TO A MOST STEADFAST[1] AND ALWAYS MAGNIFICENT[2] SON, HESPE-
RIUS

Affection has opened to me the opportunity, which my ignorance had obstructed, of writing to Your Single-Mindedness. And piety, the governess[3] of
all, through whom rigid things are bent, stony are softened, swollen are collapsed, harsh are refined, gentle are excited, savage are mellowed, mellow are
made savage, dull are sharpened, barbarous are tamed, and monstrous are placat-
ed, fulfilling her work even in me, has unbarred my inarticulate mouth,[4] drawing me forth from the safest retreat of silence to public and frightening judgment, and compels me, in a life already old,[5] to undergo something new.[6] I, of
course, as one who hitherto followed the ancient sentiment[7] by which it is said
that it is generally preferable to be silent rather than to speak,[8] would prefer to
conceal[9] my ignorance in the taciturnity of modesty rather than to display it
impudently in awkward speech. But now, as much[10] negligent of my own habit as forgetful of my rusticity, as if changed suddenly from Arion into Orpheus,[11] with a garrulous tongue I would appear to your most learned ears not so

---

1.3

[1] Ruricius uses the honorific *devinctissimus* elsewhere only for Hesperius (*Epist.* 1.1-3), Namatius and Ceraunia (*Epist.* 2.1-5), Verus (*Epist.* 2.23), and Leontius (*Epist.* 2.42). And Faustus
used it for Ruricius.

[2] The title *magnificus* probably is gratuitously applied by Ruricius and not a formal designation
of aristocratic rank (*pace PLRE II*, p.552).

[3] *dominatrix.*

[4] "os elingue reservavit"; cf. *Epist.* 1.12, "os elingue reserare," and Prudentius, *Peristephanon* 10:
CCL 126.330.2.

[5] *veteri*: Engelbrecht, Demeulenaere; *v[est]ri*: S.

[6] That is, invitations to write or publish something. Virtually repeated from Cassian, *De incarnatione* praef.1: *CSEL* 17.1.235.9-13: "producens me ex ... silentii recessu in [Ruricius: *ad*]
publicum formidandumque iudicium et ... nova subire cogit [Ruricius: *compellit*]." Apparently
the requested material (see *Epist.* 1.5) was enclosed with this letter.

[7] An ancient commonplace.

[8] A commonplace.

[9] *tegere*: edd.; *legere*: S.

[10] *tam*: edd., *iam*: S.

[11] Arion, a mythical minstrel from Lesbos, invented the dithyramb, a hymn to Dionysus. He
jumped from a ship to escape pirates and was carried to shore by dolphins. Orpheus was an
equally mythical poet who invented music after being given a lyre by Apollo. He was torn to

much dutiful as injurious, as I both attempt the unknown and undertake the unaccustomed.

But you, I presume, will grant pardon to one approaching from the necessity of a necessary need,[12] because a breast aware of a shared passion[13] recognizes that which affection in the minds of mortals appropriates for itself through the power of nature. Therefore, lest by delaying any longer in excuses I extend my page to such an extent that my rather inelegant language not only does not produce <...>[14] in you, but even [produces] disgust through its inordinate length, I now burst forth in the voice of devotion and blurt out words of desire, commending to you my security,[15] your deposit,[16] through the receipt of whom you have grasped hold of me. To you, indeed, to you alone, I have entrusted all my prayers, my hope in the present life and my consolation, if the divinity assents, for the future. I have chosen you as the stimulator and shaper of my noble jewels,[17] you as the assayer of gold, you as the discoverer of hidden[18] springs,[19] you, who know how to restore the gems concealed in stones[20] to their unique excellence: amid such worldly confusion they would indeed lose their nobility if they did not have you as an example.[21] Similarly, gold, mixed in with the vilest sands, unless it is washed in water and smelted in fire[22] with the skill[23] of the craftsman, can retain neither its splendor nor its worth. Likewise, unless the industry of the seeker most diligently excavates the enclosed channels[24] of running water and the cavity for the flow covered by

---

pieces by Thracian women and his head went singing down the Hebrus river. In general, Dionysus represented the senses and Apollo the intellect, and this contrast may lie behind Ruricius' comparison. "Orpheus," "Phoebus" (sc. Apollo), and "Dionysus" also were nicknames used in the literary circle of Sidonius Apollinaris, see Mathisen, "Phoebus," passim; note also Vergil, *Eclogues* 8.55-56, "let Tityrus be Orpheus / Orpheus in the forests, Arion among the dolphins."

[12] "veniam venienti ex necessitudine necessariae necessitis", a rather heavy-handed use of the rhetorical figure *traductio*. The allusion to *necessitudo*, family relationship, is a bit more clever.

[13] Cf. Jerome, *Epist.* 14.1.1.

[14] At least one word apparently has dropped out here; Engelbrecht suggests *gaudium* ("joy").

[15] That is, his sons. Krusch, *MGH AA* 8.lxii, supposes that only a single son was involved.

[16] "depositum tuum"; cf. *Epist.* 1.8, where "depositum vestrum" is a book loaned by Sidonius.

[17] Once again, Ruricius' sons.

[18] *latentis*: edd.; *lantis*: S[1]; *lentis*: S[2]; *laticis*: Mommsen.

[19] A repeated Rurician theme; see *Epist.* 1.5.

[20] It was commonly believed in antiquity that cut jewels were concealed in raw gemstones.

[21] A striking affirmation of the perceived value of a classical education: see R. Mathisen, *Roman Aristocrats in Barbarian Gaul* (Austin, 1993), p.109. *iudicem*: S, Canisius; *indicem*: edd.

[22] Cf. *Epist.* 1.12.

[23] *sollertia eluatur*: edd.; *sollertiae lu*tur*: S[1]; *sollertiae laetur*: S[2].

[24] Cf. *Epist.* 1.5, also to Hesperius. For water-dowsing near Limoges in the sixth century, see Gregory of Tours, *Glor.mart.* 36.

the land, the ripples of the liquid will not flow. Thus also, the perspicuity of the youthful senses, until now hemmed in by the murk of ignorance as if by the density of rough blight, unless it is brightened by the ceaseless polishing of the teacher, cannot shine of its own will.[25] Therefore, it now is up to you yourself to answer equally to your own expectation and to my judgment, lest either you appear to have presumed falsely or I to have chosen thoughtlessly.[26]

1.4 [ca. 475/485]

Here Hesperius apparently has edited a work by Ruricius, referred to as an *epistula* and a *volumen*, and proposes to circulate it. This work does not survive, unless it is one of the letters included in Ruricius' surviving corpus. Ruricius' connection to Sidonius is emphasized by three direct quotations with which Hesperius presumably would have been very familiar.

RURICIUS, TO A MOST STEADFAST AND ALWAYS MAGNIFICENT SON, HESPERIUS

I have received the words of Your Single-Mindedness, sprinkled as much with grace as with eloquence, as much with love as with congeniality, as much with salt as with honey,[1] in which there is no lack of either sweetness or refinement. Although they excel in every skill of speaking and reasoning, they nevertheless seem to contradict themselves only with regard to their judgment, for when, following either the path of rhetoric or the feeling of affection, you hasten to attribute greatness in merit to my little pages,[2] which are unsuitable for praise but suited for vituperation on account of their rusticity, you have departed from the standard of an upright judge. In this regard, I think that your[3] perfection has lapsed not through the fault of ignorance but because of a willful plan with a threefold purpose: so that in this trivial matter you could display the acumen of your talent, the eloquence of your tongue, and the lavishness of your speech. Just as the farmer's stamina appears greater when, faced with dry and fallow terrain, he either overcomes the defiance of the tenacious clods with the oft-repeated furrowing of his plow or enriches the excessive infertility by the spreading of manure,[4] in order to produce through his industry an abundant har-

---

[25] "rubiginis ... lima"; cf. Faustus, *Epist.* "Propitia divinitate", "rubiginem ... limam".

[26] Perhaps a veiled threat to Hesperius' continued employment.

1.4

[1] "recepi apices ... tam sale quam melle respersos"; cf. Sidonius Apollinaris, *Epist.* 4.16.1, "accepi .. paginam vestram, quae plus mellis an salis habeat..."

[2] *paginulae*: presumably those that Hesperius had requested in the previous letter. It is unclear whether they are copies of some of Ruricius' letters, or treatises of some other sort; see Mathisen, *Aristocrats*, p.113.

[3] Engelbrecht adds *tuam*, although the sense remains clear without it.

[4] "ingenii... sicuti in ieiuno atque otioso caespite magis strenuitas cultoris apparet, cum aut

vest that nature denied to the soil, thus you likewise have enriched the poverty of my letter[5] by means of the richness of your eloquence, so that if you suppress it, it can be praiseworthy through your declaration; but if[6] you rather make it public, it will generate shame both in me on account of the false praise and in you on account of your error in judgment. And therefore, because you have desired my ignorance to be the fruit of your decency,[7] beware lest, through my not living up to your praise, your endorsement be endangered. Therefore, if you have any belief in me, if you have any concern for us both, conceal that volume[8] unworthy of memory, most worthy of oblivion, if you desire both that I obtain fame as an orator through your judgment and that you obtain a reputation as an upright judge.[9]

1.5 [ca. 475/485]

Ruricius here proposes to turn the tables and reminds Hesperius that the latter had promised to send some of his own literary efforts.

RURICIUS, TO A MOST STEADFAST AND ALWAYS MAGNIFICENT SON, HESPERIUS

You promised, dearest son, that you would send me some blossoms from the twig that you appropriated to be changed and transmuted from bitterness into domestic delectableness, by whose fragrance I would recognize what hope of hope I ought to have: whether the flowers themselves promise seeds or the

---

rebellionem glaebarum tenacium repetita saepius inpressione vomeris domat aut ariditatem nimiam stercoris aspersione fecundat..."; cf. Sidonius Apollinaris, *Epist.* 8.10.2, "ingeniorum ... quasi quendam fecundi pectoris vomere figere, ubi materia sterilis argumentum velut arida caespiti macri glaeba ieiuna."

[5] "epistulae meae": Ruricius seems to be referring to a single letter that Hesperius has edited and proposes to circulate. For an extant letter of Ruricius that was reworked, perhaps in a similar fashion, see Sedatus of Nîmes, *Epist.* "Equum quem," translated below.

[6] *si*: added by editors.

[7] "imperitiam meam tui pudoris opus esse voluisti, cave, ne praeconio tuo nobis not respondentibus tua periclitetur electio..."; cf. Cassian, *De incarnatione, praef.* 5, "tui pudoris opus est, ora et obsecra ne imperitia mea periclitetur electio tua, et opinioni tantae nobis non respondentibus..."

[8] *volumen*: the work of Ruricius that Hesperius proposed to circulate.

[9] Note also *Epist.* 1.10; and a letter of Mamertus Claudianus of Vienne to Sidonius: "tu modo faxis uti memineris non absque cura tui prodi oportere, quod publicari iubes... proinde consilium tuum adserito et defensitato, quoniam, se in his secus aliquid, ego conscriptionis periclitabor, sed tu editionis..." ("Now see to it that you remember that you share the responsibility for the production of the work that you order to be published... Accordingly, protect and defend your position, for if I run any risk by being the author of this work, you do so by being the editor") (*CSEL* 21.20). See T. Janson, *Latin Prose Prefaces. Studies in Literary Conventions* (Stockholm, 1964), pp.141-144; and, for this letter, Mathisen, *Aristocrats*, pp.106-107.

seeds themselves, on the other hand, fruits of their own quality; and again likewise, whether the fruits can become softened by your simmering and satisfy the hearts of listeners with the sweet nourishment of eloquence. Because you have delayed[1] doing this for some unaccountable reason, I have discovered a suitable occasion for admonishing you, wherein, in the universal harmony of the world, animate brutes, and likewise the speechless, walking,[2] flying and reptilian, each in their own ways, with their own hisses, each with their own voices, even if with a discordant sound or with a dissimilar mouth, nevertheless with equal feeling, as if in unified concord, burst forth in praise of their creator, and reveal that they can sense the power that they are unable to express.

For, indeed, at this time the restored appearance of the whole world is renewed,[3] and whatever in it hitherto was dingy with dirt, congealed with chill, hardened with ice, disfigured by barrenness, or prematurely dead through dryness emerges in the image of resurrection, so that human weakness might learn to recognize the invisible in the visible and the future in the present, and, putting aside despair, comprehend the hope of the coming better age. Now, indeed, the earth, having conceived after being mated as if by a virile seed in hidden channels,[4] in this way in the springtime opens for birth the veins that had been enclosed by sterile stiffness. And hence it produces everything, whatever is sweet with delights, whatever is pleasant to eat, whatever is useful to use, whatever is necessary for sustenance, whatever is pleasurable to behold, whatever is pleasing to smell, whatever is alluring to touch. As if this is that temperateness that nursed the matter of the newborn world, soft as if still, so to speak, in its cradle, as if in the lap of the mildest nurse, lest either the summer heat burn up[5] this substance, untoughened by any labor, or the winter chill extinguish it, or the gusts of the winds bear it off. Therefore, your endeavor has a most appropriate[6] season, during which the apathy of the spirit, at last deterred,[7] whets the dullness of the heart;[8] and, if it is unable to declaim among men, at least let it rush to bellow among the cattle or to chatter among the birds.

1.5

[1] *distulisti*: edd.; *detulisti*: S.

[2] *incedentia*: edd.; *incendentia*: S.

[3] That is, Ruricius was writing in the spring, when, perhaps, the roads again were more passable.

[4] Cf. *Epist.* 1.3.

[5] *exureret*: edd.; *exuretur et*: S.

[6] *convenientissimum*: edd.; *conventissimum*: S.

[7] *detestata*: S²; *depstata*: S¹; *deposita*: Krusch.

[8] Cf. Jerome, *Epist.* 147.3.1: *CSEL* 56.316.15.2.

1.6 [ca. 475/485]

This letter is the first of three dealing with the exchange of books, a regular aristocratic practice (see Mathisen, *Aristocrats*, pp.111-112). By addressing the otherwise unknown priest Nepotianus as *pater*, rather than as *filius*, Ruricius shows that he has not yet become a bishop, and that this letter must have been written before ca. 485. Another Nepotianus was a Master of Soldiers (general) of the Visigothic king Theoderic II (453-466) ca. 459-461 (*PLRE II*, p.778). But a more likely relative of this one is the Nepotianus who was bishop of Clermont ca. 385-390 (Gregory of Tours, *HF* 1.45-46, *Glor.conf.* 35; Duchesne, *Fastes* 2.33), so perhaps this Nepotianus, too, came from the Auvergne.

RURICIUS, TO THE MOST BLESSED LORD AND MOST PIOUS FATHER, THE PRIEST NEPOTIANUS

I received the books that Your Sanctity sent, which are radiant with eloquence, perfected in wisdom, upright in doctrine, and translucent with purity of faith. Enriched by a wealth of sacred testimonies, outstanding in authority, and blazing with light, they easily both illuminate the minds of the faithful, and expose and overcome the errors of the unfaithful. Tantalized rather than refreshed by an excessively slight taste of them, I was unable to become satiated because of the worries of our age.[1] Indeed, just as the stomach, when it is burning with the heat of fevers, neither accepts previously pleasant foods when they are proffered nor desires them after they have been removed,[2] thus the spirit also, exhausted by worldly cares and anxieties, neither desires spiritual feasts that are lacking nor seizes those that are served or notices those that have been digested.

Even though these circumstances have this effect upon me, you nevertheless have exhibited both the affection of a dutiful parent and the responsibility of a solicitous teacher. You also have fulfilled the duty of a diligent physician by sending to a sick man medication that is suited to such weariness. Even if[3] I am unable to regain my health through it on account of my own negligence, you nevertheless will reap a reward from a just paymaster, who customarily returns benevolent gratitude in exchange even for ingratitude. Therefore, I have retained, as you instructed, one of the aforementioned books; I have returned the other, which you will find is that of Saint Hilary, bishop of the city of Poitiers.[4]

1.6

[1] "sollicitudines saeculi": it is unclear whether Ruricius is referring to some particular event, to the general uncertainties of the times, or just to the nature of life in this world.

[2] *oblatos recipit nec requirit*: edd.; *oblatus recepit nec requiret*: S.

[3] *etsi*: edd.; *et*: S.

[4] Hilary, bishop of Poitiers ca. 353-367, was a leading opponent of Arianism in the mid fourth century, and the author of works including the *De trinitate*, a chronicle, and the oldest surviving

I have been careful to point this out because these were your instructions. I have decided, in fact, to copy the book I retained, with your permission,[5] so that whatever I cannot commit to memory at least I can entrust to the written page.[6]

1.7 [ca. 475/485]

Ruricius invites bishop Bassulus to a "festival of the saints" at Gurdo, a place with a rather "backwoods" reputation: Gallus, a character in the *Dialogues* of Sulpicius Severus, apologetically commented: "As a Gaul about to speak among Aquitanians, I fear that my somewhat rustic speech will offend your too-urbane ears. You shall hear me as a man from Gurdo (*Gurdonicum hominem*) who speaks without ornament or drama" (*Dial*.1-27: *CSEL* 1.179). Gurdo presumably is to be identified as one of the modern places named Gourdon. Krusch, *MGH AA* 8.lxiii, and most others suggest the one in the département of Lot near Cahors, which in the Middle Ages, as Gordonium, was the site of a Cistercian abbey. Ruricius' mentions of other places south of Limoges would tend to corroborate this hypothesis. This, in turn, would suggest that Bassulus was the bishop of Cahors, in whose ecclesiastical jurisdiction Gurdo lay (the only attested bishops of Cahors at this time are Alethius in the early fifth century and Boethius in AD 506: Duchesne, *Fastes* 1.44-45). It would have been a breach of ecclesiastical etiquette for Ruricius to invite a bishop from another city. A possible relative of Bassulus who also had literary interests is the Aquitanian Bassula, who was instrumental in the publication of some of her son-in-law Sulpicius Severus' works ca. 400 (*PLRE II*, p.1006); in 614 another Bassulus was bishop of the neighboring see of Angoulême (Duchesne, *Fastes* 2.69). Bassulus' letter-writing and literary interests foreshadow those of his seventh-century successor Desiderius (ca. 620-650), whose letter collection, like that of Ruricius, survives only in the *Codex Sangallensis* 190.

RURICIUS, TO HIS OWN PERSONAL PATRON IN CHRIST, THE LORD BISHOP BASSULUS[1]

You demonstrate with manifold affection how your blessed piety and your pious blessedness[2] deigns to esteem me. As long as you send material to be

---

Latin hymns. He is not cited in any of Ruricius' letters.

[5] The manuscript reads only *permittitur*; Engelbrecht prefaces *dum*, Krusch *si*, and Mommsen *ut*.

[6] *paginis*: the copying of borrowed books was a common practice and, indeed, the primary means of expanding one's library. It was customary to ask the permission of the owner of the borrowed book before doing so. Perhaps it was felt that not only the physical copy but also the contents in a sense "belonged" to the book's owner: see *Epist*. 1.8 for a similar example.

1.7

[1] Wrongly called "Bassula" by G. Bardy, "Copies et éditions au Ve siècle, " *Revue des sciences religieuses* 23 (1949) pp.38-52 at p.50.

[2] The rhetorical figure of *chiasmus*.

read and you correct what has been neglected, you arouse esteem by esteeming, and whatever you proclaim with words you demonstrate with examples. But because your seed cannot thrive in my sterile and brushy ground, inasmuch as it is suffocated by overgrowing brambles, and lest the vine-master decide to prune me, whom he oversees in vain so continually, like that unfruitful little fig tree,[3] fend off a harsher sentence by praying, until my fruitless bitterness is enriched, as if with manure,[4] by the fertility of your teaching. But because there are in me more sins than words, and I cannot atone for my deeds with speeches, I dispense at least an epistulary compliance, and I note that I have returned the book that you lent, and I hope that in the future you will order[5] another of yours to be sent through the bearer of this letter, if you then have no need of it, and, at the same time, let me know in your reply if you are planning to attend, God willing, the festival of the saints[6] at Gurdo.

Sidonius Apollinaris, *Epistulae* 8.10 [ca. 470]

Ruricius' most distinguished correspondent was Sidonius Apollinaris (ca. 432-485) (*PLRE II*, pp.115-118), one of the most blue-blooded aristocrats of late Roman Gaul. Sidonius was a native of Lyon and the grandson of the Apollinaris who was Praetorian Prefect of Gaul ca. 411-413, and he married Papianilla, the daughter of the short-lived emperor Eparchius Avitus (455-456), who came from the Auvergne. In 468, while on a diplomatic mission to the emperor Anthemius (467-472), Sidonius was named Urban Prefect of Rome, and after returning to Gaul he was chosen bishop of Clermont ca. 469. His surviving collections of poems and letters, including several addressed to Ruricius and his family, provide invaluable insights into life in late Roman Gaul. This, the last of three letters to Ruricius in Sidonius' corpus, may be the earliest one. It also is one of the letters of Sidonius listed, but not included, in the index of the *Sangallensis* 190. It dates to a period when Ruricius seems to have been concerned primarily if not exclu-

---

[3] Matthew 21.19.

[4] *pinguedine ... stercore*: edd.; *pinguine ... stere*: S; for *stercor*, and other agricultural imagery, see also *Epist.* 1.4.

[5] *iubeatis*: S; *valeatis*: Krusch.

[6] "solemnitatem sanctorum"; cf. *Epist.* 1.14. Except for generic "masses of the sainted martyrs", the *Missale Gallicanum vetus* and *Missale Gothicum* (see Introduction) both cite only a single "Festum sanctorum," that of Peter and Paul, celebrated on 29 June: "Legenda in festo sanctorum Petri et Pauli" (*PL* 72.208); and "Missa sanctorum Petri et Pauli" (ibid.p.295). These may well have been the saints involved. For one thing, Ruricius' grandson Ruricius II Proculus construct- ed a church for St. Peter (see Introduction), attesting some special local devotion to him. Fur- thermore, the so-called *Antiquum martyrologium Gallicanum* cites for the very next day, "Pridie Kalendas Julii, Lemovicas, depositio sancti Martialis episcopi..." ("On the day before the Ka- lends of June, at Limoges, the death of St. Martial the bishop") (*PL* 71.615). For Ruricius, then, the end of June was an especially important time of the liturgical year.

sively with secular literature, and when Sidonius seems recently to have become bishop. The translation is based upon Dalton, *Sidonius* 2.157-158, reprinted by permission of Oxford University Press.

TO HIS FRIEND RURICIUS

I am indeed delighted that you derive from letters at once a benefit and a pleasure. But I should be freer to extol the fire and fluency of your style, were it not that while assiduously praising me yourself you forbid me to return the compliment with interest. Your letter had all the sweetness of affection, all the grace of natural eloquence, all the mastery of style; it failed only in one respect — the choice of subject, and even there you have the credit of good intention, an error of judgment forms its own fault. You cover me with immense laudation. But you should have spared my blushes, and recalled betimes the saying of Symmachus: "True praise adorns, false praise scorns." But unless I misjudge your genius you have not only shown sincere affection, but also remarkable dexterity. The really eloquent love to show the stuff they are made of by choosing a subject full of difficulty; they drive the accomplished pen as if it were the plough of fertile speech through matter sterile as dry and barren soil. Life abounds with examples of skill similarly applied. The hopeless case proves the great doctor, the tempest proves the steersman; for both, the perils traversed enhance reputation; their talent wastes unseen until it finds a proper scope. In the same manner the great orator proves his ample genius most effectively in strait places. Thus Marcus Tullius, who always surpassed his rivals, in his speech for Aulus Cluentius surpassed even himself. Marcus Fronto stood head and shoulders above others in all his pleadings, but in that against Pelops he rose above his own high level. Gaius Plinius won greater fame for his defense of Attia Viriola from the centumvirs' tribune than for the panegyric which almost matched the timeless Trajan. You have followed these great examples; confident in your powers, you have not feared to take so miserable a subject as myself. But let me rather have the succor of your prayers in my weakness;[1] do not lure me with a cozening eloquence, or crush my frail and ailing soul by the weight of an illusory renown. Your diction indeed is fine, but your life finer; and I think you will serve me better by your orisions than by your perorations.[2] Farewell.

1.8 [ca. 470/475]

In the first of Ruricius' three surviving letters to Sidonius, which may be the earliest one in the collection, there is no indication that Ruricius has yet begun to

---

[1] "languoribus": Dalton's "depression" has rather a pathological connotation.

[2] Sidonius' concluding words suggest that he has just become bishop.

approach the adoption of the religious life. Ruricius here returns a book borrowed from Sidonius, and one again encounters, as in *Epist*.1.6, the practice of
receiving permission from a book's owner before making a copy.

RURICIUS, TO HIS OWN PERSONAL LORD IN CHRIST, THE LORD PATRON BISHOP SIDONIUS

I recall that I have heard very often when you are preaching[1] that in no
way can we be cleansed of iniquities unless we confess our sins with a contrite
conscience. Indeed, who is able I would not say to obtain but even to seek pardon, unless he joins to his moans a confession of error, because error requires
pardon, not pardon error?[2] I, recognizing this to be very valid, have not hesi-
tated to report to Your Piety my recently committed crime, lest that which now,
if I speak out, has a chance of pardon, might later, if I am silent, produce
blame. But now I bring forth into the open my precise mischief. I affirm to
you that I am guilty of a theft, and I proclaim that, with you unaware, I have
illegally taken advantage of your loan. But in order that I might commit this
act, you yourself, either putting my greed to the test or desiring to educate one
who is unlearned, provided the opportunity for perpetrating the deed. For I confess that I have copied the book[3] that you asked me to recover from my brother
Leontius.[4] If you approve this, then grant pardon; if you condemn it, then recognize[5] that excuses are linked with my confession. For my will first of all
impelled me to read the book, and it then compelled me to copy it. For, because until now I had tasted few morsels from the feast of this work, so much
did it tempt me with the tempting taste of its flavor, that as an imitator, in some
way, of the first parent,[6] having precipitately ignored the Lord, I desired to
attain satiety, and I heeded more the cajoling of a tempter[7] than the authority of
a master. For, and I make manifest all the secrets of my heart, I seemed to hear
the words of the book itself exhorting me,[8] "Why do you hesitate, ingrate, why
do you dither? You know the feelings of our shared lord toward you, how on

---

1.8

[1] Ca. 469 or later, presumably at Clermont, attesting, again, Ruricius' connections there.

[2] The rhetorical figure of antistrophe, or *conversio*.

[3] It is unclear what *codex* this is. Ruricius' failure to compliment Sidonius suggests that it was
not one of his works; for a copy of something by Sidonius, see *Epist*. 2.26 to Apollinaris.

[4] "de fratre meo Leontio"; apparently a biological brother of Ruricius. See *PLRE II*, p.670; also
Epist. 2.42; and Faustus, *Epist*. "Propitia divinitate."

[5] The manuscript reads *ignoscite ... agnoscite*, as translated here and followed by Canisius and
Engelbrecht. Krusch and Demeulenaere transpose the two words.

[6] That is, Adam, who also disobeyed, and gave in to temptation.

[7] *consilium suadentis*, cf. *Epist*. 1.1, *vocantis imperio*.

[8] The rhetorical figure of apostrophe.

various occasions he hastens to perfect you,[9] how this good shepherd customarily dishes out spiritual nourishments to you even when you are unwilling. Believe me, there will be more fault in you if you delay than if you duplicate, because it is customary for those desirous of learning to be supportive, not envious."[10] Compelled equally by these and similar words of the silent book, and voluntarily of my own will,[11] I threw myself into its shackles; I hurriedly undertook to copy it, and it now hangs in your judgment whether I ought to return the original or, such as it is, the transcribed version.[12] I, in any event, will freely accept the penalty that you impose, because I believe that your judgment is my remedy, and I consider your sentence to be a cure,[13] not a punishment.

Sidonius Apollinaris, *Epistulae* 4.16 [ca. 470/475]

> This is Sidonius' reply to the previous letter; both letters concern secular literary topics. If we did not have the previous letter, we never would have guessed from this one that Sidonius was a bishop. This letter does not appear among those listed in the index of the *Sangallensis* 190. The translation is based upon Dalton, *Sidonius* 2.29-30, reprinted by permission of Oxford University Press.

TO HIS FRIEND RURICIUS

Paternius[1] has given me your letter; I can hardly say whether it pleases most by wit or charm.[2] It presents such eloquence, such fragrant flowers of diction, that your progress is clearly due to something more than an acknowledged study: you must be working in secret as well. The abstraction of a book of mine to copy, for which you so apologize, I regard as an act redounding to your credit, and requiring no excuse. What can you do really wrong, when even your faults are laudable? I am not the least vexed at being played this little

---

[9] Cf. Jerome, *Epist.* 96.1.2: *CSEL* 55.2.159.13.

[10] A theme also used by Sidonius, e.g., in his *Epist.* 3.14.4, 9.7.5, 9.14.9.

[11] The text reads, "voluntarius pariter et coactus sponte"; Demeulenaere and Hagendahl (p.101) transpose *voluntarius* and *coactus*, an emendation that is used here, even though one might not put it past Ruricius to use *sponte* with *coactus*.

[12] Personal copies like this one could be written in a quite nasty cursive script, as attested by sixth-century papyrus fragments of sermons of Avitus of Vienne; see A. Audin, "Alcimi Ecdicii Aviti Viennensis episcopi homilia dicta in dedicatione superioris basilicae: Ms. sur papyrus, Paris, Bibl. nat. 8913+8914," *Studi in onore de Aristidi Calderini e Roberto Paribeni*, vol.2 (Milan, 1957) pp.433-51, so perhaps Sidonius prefered the return of his original which, if created by a professional scribe, might have been in the more readable uncial or semi-uncial script.

[13] *medella*.

Sidonius Apollinaris, *Epist.* 4.16

[1] An otherwise unknown letter carrier.

[2] Cf. the beginning of Ruric. *Epist.* 1.4.

trick in my absence; it is no loss at all, but really a signal privilege. The volume you appropriated to your use has not therefore ceased to be my property; your knowledge has not been increased at the cost of other people's. On the contrary, you shall have full credit for your action, and rightly; for your nature has the quality of flame,[3] which communicates itself entirely and yet remains entire; it is proper that you should act like your own element. Be no more uneasy, then; that were to betray a little too much uncertainty of your friend, who would only deserve the wound of blame were he vulnerable to the dart of envy. Farewell.

1.9 [ca. 472/476]

> In this letter to Sidonius, Ruricius seems to be turning in the direction of the religious life. It may have been written at about the time Ruricius initiated his correspondence with Faustus of Riez (*Epist.* 1.1-2).

RURICIUS, TO HIS PERSONAL LORD IN CHRIST, THE LORD PATRON SIDONIUS

Your recent pronouncement[1] and the longstanding affection of Your Piety has allured me so much that, desiring to partake in your learning, as much as my sterile little talent can, I dare to cause injury yet again to your ears with my ineptitudes. Even if it is glorious and laborious to attain such learning, it is nonetheless exquisite and exhilarating to pursue it, because not only the acquisition, but even the imitation itself of the highest things ought to be praised, because hardly anyone ever totally lacks a portion of something that he struggles to surmount and attain.[2] I desire, therefore, My Lord, I desire, I say, to be replenished by your nourishment, to drink at your fountain, to be satiated by your feasts, to be fattened at your banquets: if any guest at your table, with you serving, did not taste this fare with the tip of his tongue, but gulped it down, craving it with the innermost parts of his spirit, and departed in order to ponder it later in the privacy of his heart, he would begin to burst forth with incessant belches

---

[3] Reprising Sidonius' reference to Ruricius in his *epithalamium* as "set aflame by our torch."

1.9

[1] Apparently a letter of Sidonius, perhaps even the preceding one.

[2] "quam etsi adsequi grande est atque difficile, sequi tamen pulchrum est atque sublime, quoniam summarum rerum non adeptio tantum, sed etiam imitatio ipsa laudanda est, quia numquam fere aliquis eius rei portione ad integrum caret, ad quam scandere ac pervenire contenderit"; cf. Cassian, *De incarnatione* 7.31.5: *CSEL* 17.1.390.21-26, "quod etsi adsequi grande est ac difficile, sequi tamen pulchrum atque sublime. quoniam in summa rerum non adeptio tantum sed etiam imitatio ipsa laudanda est, quia numquam fere aliquis eius rei portione ad plenum caret, ad quam scandere ac pervenire contenderit."

in praise of the omnipotent lord,[3] replenished in his heart although starving in his mouth, while satiated he is hungry and being hungry he is satiated, to be satiated yet more in rebirth. Nor can nourishment be lacking whose fodder[4] is in your word. Therefore, through your patronage, provide that I shall merit being a partaker in these delicacies, and summon supporters[5] for me as I struggle beyond the limit of my abilities, and likewise pray that I will not be found separated from the sheepfold entrusted to you. Restore this errant sheep from the pastures of the world to the folds of the Lord, for I have faith that by your intercessions it is possible for one who merits being your disciple to become a lamb.

Sidonius Apollinaris, *Epistulae* 5.15 [ca. 472/476]

Although it is not clear whether this is the immediate response to Ruricius' previous letter, Sidonius' forwarding of scripture suggests that this letter was written at a time when Ruricius was engaged in serious religious study. The Biblical texts the Sidonius sent presumably are some of those that Ruricius cited in his subsequent letters. A reference to this letter appears in the index of the *Sangallensis* 190. The translation is based upon Dalton, *Sidonius* 2.68, reprinted by permission of Oxford University Press.

To HIS FRIEND RURICIUS

The usual salutations over, I at once urge upon your notice the claims of our bookseller,[1] because I have made discriminating and unbiased trial of the man, proving him to my complete satisfaction at once loyal in sentiment and alert in service to our common master — yourself. He brings in person the manuscript of the Heptateuch[2] all written out by his own hand with the utmost neatness and rapidity,[3] although I read it through myself, and made corrections. He also brings a volume of the Prophets;[4] this was edited by him in my absence, and with his own hand purged of corrupt additions, nor did he always have the help of the proof-reader[5] who had promised him assistance; I fancy illness prevented

---

[3] For similar imagery, see *Epist.* 2.34.

[4] *pastus*: edd.; *partus*: S, which may yet be correct.

[5] "auxiliatores": these may be persons like Faustus and Graecus, whose letters Ruricius preserved and are included above, who encouraged Ruricius to undertake the religious life.

Sidonius Apollinaris, *Epist.* 5.15

[1] *bybliopolam*; a professional copyist.

[2] The first seven books of the Old Testament.

[3] This could imply that the copy was made in cursive rather than the more ornate, time-consuming, and presumably expensive uncial or semi-uncial text.

[4] Also from the Old Testament, and including, it seems, the Psalms. The Old Testament was so long that it was usually broken up, and rarely incorporated into a single volume.

[5] "illo contra legente": copies often were made from dictation.

him from carrying out his undertaking. It remains for you by encouragement or promise of your influence[6] to show appropriate recognition of a servant who has done his best to satisfy, and deserves to succeed; and if this is in proportion to his arduous task, he will soon begin to look for his reward. All that I ask for the moment is your benevolence toward him; it is for you to decide what he deserves, although indeed I think the good opinion of his master is far nearer to his heart than any recompense. Farewell.

1.10 [ca. 470/480]

Lupus probably is to be identified with Lupus of Périgueux, an orator and poet who was a friend of Sidonius Apollinaris (Sid.Apoll. *Epist.* 8.11); see *PLRE II*, p.694. Périgueux bordered on the territory of Limoges to the south-west, and Lupus therefore may have lived close to Ruricius' estate at Gurdo/Decaniacum.

RURICIUS, TO THE LORD OF HIS OWN HEART, LUPUS[1]

I received the letter of Your Magnanimity, in which you deign to make the excuse that it is for lack of a carrier that you rarely sprinkle me with the dew of your eloquence. Indeed, you declare at the same time that you wonder why, when I have available an abundance of carriers and have no lack of an elegant multitude of words, I hesitate to write to you more often. I have no doubt that you utter this in irony,[2] such is the eloquence of your wit, for not only are you awash with letter-carriers but you also know that, just as the course of a drying channel[3] in the summer months trickles rather than flows, I suffer from a poverty of speech and the sterility of a meager talent. You add, moreover, that just as Patroclus is with Achilles,[4] or Theseus with Hercules,[5] or Pirithous with Theseus,[6] you likewise ought to be associated with me. In these tales and exploits of our ancestors we ought to embrace not the preeminence of the indi-

---

[6] E.g., by recommending him to others.

1.10

[1] "Domino pectoris sui Lupo Ruricius," a form of address otherwise used only for the three letters to Celsus (*Epist.* 1.12-14), with "Domno" used for "Domino."

[2] *ironiam*: edd.; *hiruinam*: S.

[3] Cf. *Epist.* 1.3, 1.5.

[4] Patroclus was the comrade of Achilles, the son of Zeus, in the *Iliad*. Of the five heroes mentioned here, Patroclus is the only one who was not the son of an Olympian god.

[5] The legendary hero Theseus, the son of Poseidon, was commonly seen as the comrade of Hercules, the son of Zeus, whom he accompanied on his expedition against the Amazons.

[6] Peirithous, a Lapith of Thessaly, was the son of Zeus, and a close friend of Theseus, whom he assisted in the abduction of the young Helen.

viduals but the pattern of their affection, so that recalling the names of friends[7]
we follow their examples. And transferring their names to ourselves[8] we endow ourselves with their merits, and seizing upon anything splendid and upright
in their actions, we apply it usefully to our own life, and we preserve ourselves
in unsullied charity rather than in tainted adulation. And let us take care that
whatever the fantasy of those poets concocted regarding friendships the verity of
our spirits shall accomplish in us, so that when we appear to be imitating ancient examples we leave behind what should be imitated, and so that by praising
the deeds of our elders we may be praised by our descendents.[9] Therefore, My
Lord, flame of my heart, because the bearer is in a hurry, I have dictated[10] this
letter quickly and abbreviatedly, trusting more to your knowledge of me than to
mine of myself. If you have any consideration for the modesty of your friend,
your experience and your uprightness either will be obliged to conceal it or will
take care to emend it.[11]

1.11 [ca. 475/485]

Freda is otherwise unknown, although his name suggests a Germanic, in this case
Visigothic, origin: see *PLRE II*, p.483. *Fredae* is an emendation from the manuscript reading *Fredar*. He provides a rare example of a Goth possessing an estate
in the Aquitanian countryside. The letter probably was written before Ruricius
became bishop: he does not refer to himself as such, and had he been one he
probably would not have addressed Freda, a *saecularis*, as *frater* ("brother").

RURICIUS, TO HIS EXALTED[1] LORD AND ALWAYS MAGNIFICENT BROTHER,
FREDA

Because you desired to graft the ineptitudes of my barrenness to the charm
of your grove, I have sent, as you enjoined, shoots from my fir trees, which are
sure to please not by their beauty but by their length, admirable not for their
fruits but for their peregrination, unfitted for use but delightful in charm, be-

---

[7] *amicorum*: S; Krusch suggests *antiquorum*, i.e., "recalling the names of the ancients."
[8] For the use of such nicknames by Sidonius, Ruricius, and others, see Mathisen, "Phoebus"; and
note Faustus' allusions to Hiberia as "Sarah" (*Epist.* "Propitia divinitate" and "Gratias tibi").
[9] Like Sidonius, and unlike some fifth-century Gallic ecclesiastical writers, Ruricius had no
qualms about drawing moral paradigms from the classical pagan past.
[10] Like most Gallo-Roman aristocrats, Ruricius had a personal secretary to take care of the me-
chanics of his correspondence.
[11] Cf. *Epist.* 1.4.
1.11
[1] *Domino sublimi*. The designation *vestra sublimitas* ("Your Exaltedness") was used for secular
officials, suggesting that Freda held, or had held, some kind of office.

cause, when they have taken root, they will provide, in the thickness of your Cevennian[2] shadows, an oceanic[3] coolness in the summer heat. And this transpires among those most lustrous trees of a different kind,[4] which excel as much by beauty as by utility: abundant with produce, distinctive in bloom, fragrant[5] in smell. Indeed, your industry endows them[6] with what the nature of the soil did not produce. For, as I shall pass over[7] the redness of roses, the whiteness of lilies, the perpetual greenness[8] of the laurel, and other similar sights[9] of this sort, because through repetition precious things often become cheapened and because an everyday abundance causes disdain, there with you, indeed, the errant charms of meadows, buds, and bushes are combined, blossoming for both visibility and utility.[10]

But what should be praised or admired there first, where even the intemperateness of the season is tempered? In fact, there the heat of a torrid summer is averted by the chill as much of the shadiness as of the springs; even the harshness of winter is not felt to such a great extent, because the warmth of the air and the song of the birds create the image of spring for those situated indoors.[11] But why, my lord, do I, forgetful of my lack of sophistication, with meager words venture to describe or recount the riches, the delights of your fields in the praise of which even greater talents would succumb?[12] Therefore, pardon my impudence, which you have extorted; my respect for you compelled me to appear garrulous to your ears. I trust that a rather lengthy letter to you, my lords,[13] if it is displeasing in its discourse will be pleasing in its devotion,

---

[2] Freda, therefore, lived in the area of the Cevennes mountains, located in southwesternmost Aquitania, between Rodez and Nîmes. See Ausonius, *Ordo urbium nobilium* 19.8, "Cebennae, Aquitanica rura." Ruricius may have travelled this way, and perhaps stayed with Freda, on trips to Provence. This would put Freda's estate perhaps between Rodez and Lodève.

[3] *oceani sint*: edd.; *oceanis in*: S. Unless the contrast is merely conventional, it could suggest that Ruricius is writing from someplace near the coast, perhaps from the home of Ceraunia and Namatius.

[4] Ruricius now turns from metaphorical vegetation to the real thing.

[5] *fragrantes*: Krusch; *flagrantes*: S; *fraglantes*: Engelbrecht.

[6] *illic*: S, edd.; *illis*: Canisius.

[7] The rhetorical figure of *praetereo* (claiming to "pass by" things).

[8] *virorum*, from *vireo*.

[9] *similia visibus*: S²; *[fa?]milia visibus*: S; *vilia visibus*: Krusch, Mommsen; *similia vilibus*: Canisius.

[10] The language suggests that this letter was written in the spring. Ruricius compares his own literary accomplishments to Freda's agricultural pursuits; it may be that Ruricius could find little positive to say about Freda's own literary endeavors, if any.

[11] *intra aedem*: Krusch, Lütjohann; *intra eadem*: S.

[12] "ingenia maiora succumberent": cf. Ruricius, *Epist.* 1.12, with *succumbere* instead.

[13] Ruricius momentarily switches to plural addressees.

because you should realize that it abounds not with the charm of eloquence but with love for you; and, likewise, because I recall that Your Exaltedness rebukes in your friends taciturn modesty more than the audacious outspokenness of familiarity.[14]

1.12 [ca. 475/485]

Ruricius presents three consecutive letters, all apparently written before he became bishop, to Celsus, a relative — perhaps a brother (see Introduction) — who is otherwise unknown; see *PLRE II*, pp.279-280. Other Aquitanians of this name include a saint at Limoges, whose head was at the church of St. Stephen (*AASS* August II, p.191), and a *consularis* ("consular") who visited Sulpicius Severus at Primuliacum circa 404/405 (Sulp.Sev. *Dialogues* 3.1.7; *PLRE II*, pp.279-280).

RURICIUS, TO THE LORD OF HIS HEART, CELSUS

I tremble to unbar an inarticulate mouth in praise of you, to whom I know even greater talents rightly succumb.[1] What indeed should I recall first in praise of your affection or of your regard? You conveyed to me all the pleasures of the countryside, of character,[2] and, what is greater than all these, of charity. Or, certainly, if any of these was missing, it must be attributed to the times,[3] it must not be imputed to you. For I have found in you everything that a heart considers dear or the world noteworthy. You have defrauded me of no joy whatsoever. Nay, by your proximity[4] you rather have made even the loneliness[5] of my little homestead[6] desirable to me. And therefore I rejoice that I am nearer to you, because one who associates with good men[7] cannot be wholly bad.

---

[14] "inmemor inperitiae meae paupero sermone .. taciturnitatis verecundiam, quam loquacem familiaritatis audaciam"; cf. Cassian, *De incarnatione* praef. 1: *CSEL* 17.1.235.2-6, "sermo nostrae imperitiae ... per taciturnitatis verecundiam loquacitatis audaciam."

1.12

[1] Cf. *Epist.* 1.11.

[2] *moris*: S; *oris*: Engelbrecht; *nemoris*: Krusch.

[3] *deputandum tempori*: a typically vague Rurician reference to the political situation.

[4] "vestra vicinitate": Celsus, therefore, lived not far from Ruricius' estate.

[5] "desertum": a suggestion, perhaps, that Hiberia was away at Clermont.

[6] "hospitioli mei": probably Ruricius' estate at Gurdo/Decaniacum, especially if the festival to which Ruricius invited Celsus in *Epist.* 1.14 is that mentioned in *Epist.* 1.7. Celsus presumably lived in the area.

[7] An aristocratic commonplace: for the *boni* ("good people"), see Mathisen, *Aristocrats*, pp.10-13, 90-91

But, lest a longer speech by its <very>[8] ineptitude arouse your disdain, I extend my very best regards, and I confirm that I have sent the glassworker[9] as you requested. His work ought to be imitated for its brilliance, not for its fragility, so that the affection that has been left to us by our parents, passed on by our teacher,[10] and strengthened by our shared experiences, might in good times be perfected and in bad ruptured not at all by any storm of whirlwinds.[11] For just as the precious pureness of gold and silver, if it has been corrupted by the mixing of copper, or of lead, or of any other worthless material, unless it is cleansed by the heat of fires,[12] can have neither its natural splendor nor its natural sound, and renders neither its brightness to the eye nor its ring to the ear, and resounds more raucously and stridently if it is struck <...>[13]

Therefore, my best brother, equally guarding and following this sentiment, not mine but the Lord's, let us steer our lives along the middle channel, with the Lord Himself as our helmsman,[14] in such a way that, although[15] serenity smiles,[16] a favorable wind beckons, and a calm sea coaxes, knowing nonetheless that the flatness of that calm surface can rise suddenly into the shape of mountains, let us not permit ourselves to drive our ship onto the deep, where either a storm may destroy it or a wave submerge it.

1.13 [ca. 475/485]

Ruricius here pretends that Celsus was offended by his previous letter.

RURICIUS, TO THE LORD OF HIS HEART, CELSUS

I received the words of Your Brotherliness,[1] which rendered me not a little uneasy. Indeed, I fear that you feel[2] otherwise than I had intended concerning

---

[8] The manuscript reads *esse*, which makes no sense and seems to have been mistakenly recopied from a preceding line. Canisius suggests *ipsa*, and Krusch *seu*; Engelbrecht deletes it.

[9] *vitrarium*.

[10] The use of the singular suggests that Ruricius is speaking of a particular individual, and that he and Celsus had studied together.

[11] "turbinum procella": i.e. secular misfortunes; cf. *Epist.* 1.13.

[12] See *Epist.* 1.3 for a similar analogy.

[13] There seems to be a lacuna here, for the analogy is left incomplete.

[14] "gubernatore ipso domino"; cf. *Epist.* 1.13 and 2.13, "domino gubernatore."

[15] *quamquam*: Engelbrecht; *quam*: S; *cum*: Canisius; *quamvis*: Krusch.

[16] *adrideat*: edd.; *adreddat*: S.

1.13

[1] The word *germanitas* generally refers to a blood relationship, as already suggested on the basis of the previous letter.

[2] *senseritis*: edd.; *inseritis*: S.

the little letter I sent,[3] and as a result you appear to reprove me, as it were, for rash presumption, while you demand that I pray for and advise you more often. Would I dare, my best brother, to castigate you, I who am incapable of castigating myself? Would I castigate you, when already, from a more exalted summit or a higher hill, so to speak, you observe me presently wavering[4] amid the whirlwinds of the world[5] as if on a shaky skiff amid oceanic tempests? Would I castigate you, who, with the Lord as a helmsman,[6] <have come>[7] to the port of pardon through the privilege of penitence?[8] I wrote in such a manner, my esteemed brother, neither so that, flattering myself in some way, I might gnaw at you with a merciless tooth[9] nor in order to offend you, but so that I might bind[10] you to myself by the familiarity of my letter. For if you consider well, those were words regarding prayers, not deeds, of one wishing rather than warning, because I have suggested not what we should do, but how I believe that we should live. But if you censure the deeds of my past and present life, with your most intimate and most special brother as a witness, you will be ashamed to bear the things that you were not ashamed to promise with God as a witness.[11] For the sake of these transgressions of mine I hope that you instead will pray to the Lord that those whom in the present life He desires to be partakers of friendships and family ties[12] in the future He decree to be sharers of all good things.

1.14 [ca. 475/485]

This may be an invitation to the same "festival of the saints" at Gurdo to which Bassulus was invited in *Epist.* 1.11. Ruricius reused the horse joke in *Epist.* 2.35 to Sedatus of Nîmes.

---

[3] Apparently the previous letter; Ruricius purports to think that Celsus found his commonplaces objectionable.

[4] *fluctuantem*: edd.; *fructuantem*: S.

[5] "in saeculi turbinibus": cf. *Epist.* 1.12.

[6] "domino gubernatore"; cf. *Epist.* 1.12, 2.13.

[7] There seems to be a word missing; Hagendahl (pp.88,108), following *Epist.* 2.12 and 2.53, and Demeulenaere suggest *venistis*; Krusch proposes *iam appulistis.*

[8] If Ruricius is taken literally, Celsus, by becoming a penitent, has taken up the religious life.

[9] "inprobo dente morderem," cf. *Epist.* 2.40, and Sidonius Apollinaris, *Epist.* 4.22.6.

[10] *vincirem*: edd.; *vincerem*: S.

[11] That is, Celsus should follow his own advice.

[12] *propinquitatis*: another indication of a blood relationship.

RURICIUS, TO THE LORD OF HIS HEART, CELSUS

I have sent the sort of horse you requested,[1] placid in gentleness, strong in limbs, hardy in strength, excelling in appearance, well-proportioned in form, temperate in spirit, neither, of course, excessively quick in speed nor lazy in <slowness>:[2] the use of the bit and goad is at the will of the rider, and in the carrying of burdens it is both willing and able, with the result that it neither succumbs to the one superposed atop nor drops what has been imposed.[3] Having made this known, therefore, as is fitting, having extended my greetings, and having fulfilled my promise, we[4] demand what you have promised, and that, God willing, you deign to come to us for the festival of the saints,[5] together with our[6] sister,[7] in order to demonstrate regard for your patrons,[8] affection for the brothers,[9] and consideration for the people.

1.15 [ca. 485/490]

Bishop Aeonius of Arles received letters from popes Gelasius (23 August 494) and Symmachus (29 September 500), and was a relative of Caesarius, who became bishop of Arles in 502 (Duchesne, *Fastes* 1.257). The bishops of Arles laid claim to pre-eminent status in Gaul based on the pious fiction that the church had been founded by St. Trophimus, who had been sent from Rome in the second century.[1] This letter is a reply to a letter from Aeonius. He generally is thought to have succeeded Leontius as bishop ca. 490 (Duchesne, ibid.), but given the dates of the other letters in Book I, Aeonius' ordination may have occurred rather

---

1.14

[1] Another indication that Celsus lived nearby, and perhaps a sign that he was of slim means.

[2] *tarditate*, omitted from the manuscript, but restored from *Epist*. 2.35.

[3] This entire section was reprised, virtually verbatim, in *Epist*. 2.35 to Sedatus of Nîmes, who, in his reply, "Equum quem," parodied Ruricius' description.

[4] Perhaps Ruricius and Hiberia.

[5] "solemnitatem sanctorum"; perhaps the same "solemnitatem sanctorum" at Gurdo mentioned in *Epist*. 1.7.

[6] *nostra*: S, Krusch; *vestra*: Engelbrecht, Demeulenaere. If Celsus was Ruricius' blood relative, as suggested above, then the manuscript reading is correct.

[7] Krusch, *MGH AA* 8.lxiii, suggests that this is a reference to Celsus' wife, who, once Celsus adopted a religious lifestyle, would have become his "sister" in a religious sense. For similar references to Ceraunia, note *Epist*. 2.4 and 2.15.

[8] Perhaps the saints, whose festival this was, are meant.

[9] "affectum fratribus": Krusch, *MGH AA* 8.lxiii, suggests that these were monks from a nearby monastery; if so, perhaps they are to be identified as the "other brothers" of Faustus' *Epist*. "Licet per." This might suggest, again, that Ruricius had established his own monastery.

1.15

[1] For Trophimus, see Mathisen, *Factionalism*, pp.49,53,176-177, q.v. passim for the status of the church of Arles.

earlier; indeed, Aeonius' letter may have congratulated Ruricius on the latter's election. Ruricius had ties of his own in Arles, and even may have been a relative of Leontius (see Introduction). He and Aeonius subsequently maintained a cordial correspondence (*Epist.* 2.8-9, 16).

RURICIUS, TO HIS PERSONAL LORD IN CHRIST, THE LORD PATRON BISHOP AEONIUS

When I learned of the passing of my lord, your predecessor, Leontius,[2] of blessed and revered memory for me, I was distressed in spirit and mind for a long time, and greatly saddened, both because, hindered by my own sins, I had not deserved to meet so great a bishop,[3] and also because I had been deprived of so great a parent.[4] Even if I never enjoyed the sight of the exterior man, I nonetheless delighted in the grace of the interior.[5] I clung constantly to the acumen of his mind, through which and in which, in some way, he was present, discerned by my gaze, heard in conversation,[6] felt by my touch, and held in my embrace, because, indeed, those who are dear see each other in no place better than in the heart, the seat of charity itself. I therefore desired all the more to see him also with my physical eyes,[7] he whom I was accustomed to look upon thus with the spiritual. But these merits of his which in the past granted consolation now give solace to my grief, because I have faith that I am one whom he esteemed with a paternal piety and now watches over with constant intercession.

But I deliver[8] these words at the dictate of love, speaking to Your Sanctity as if I were with you, and seeking from you a lightening of this very grief. Now, truly, as I had begun to say, having learned[9] of the summoning[10] of my lord himself and of the ordination of Your Apostleship, it occurred to me to write as a courtesy to you. But you have anticipated the compliance of my humility with your own kindnesses,[11] which endow me with an even greater confidence as I write because I presume that he whom you deem worthy of your

---

[2] Bishop of Arles (ca. 460-ca. 485) (Duchesne, *Fastes* 1.257); this letter apparently was written shortly after Leontius' death, and is the only evidence that Aeonius was his direct successor.

[3] This would suggest that Ruricius did not visit Arles during Leontius' episcopate.

[4] "tali ... parente": wording that is not inconsistent with Leontius being a relative, albeit, perhaps, a rather distant one.

[5] "hominis ... interioris"; cf. *Epist.* 1.16, "interioris hominis".

[6] *affatu*: edd.; *affectu*: S.

[7] "oculis ... carnalibus", repeated in *Epist.* 1.16.

[8] *retulerim*: S; *rettuleram*: Hagendahl (p.33); *retuleram*: Engelbrecht; *rettulerim*: Krusch.

[9] Ruricius, therefore, already had learned (perhaps through Capillutus, see *Epist.* 2.21, 31) of Leontius' death and Aeonius' election, but did not write until after the arrival of Aeonius' letter.

[10] *arcessione*: cf. *Epist.* 2.4; *arcersione*: S; *accersione*: edd.; from *arcesso*, "summon to a court of justice." Referring to the death of Leontius.

[11] Ruricius, therefore, had received news of events in Arles even before Aeonius' letter arrived.

liberality you would not regard as estranged from your spirit. And therefore, seeing that you let it be understood that you deign to consider it important,[12] I extend a profuse salutation to Your Beatitude through my letter. And I likewise earnestly request with a personal prayer on this account, that you consider it important[13] to treat me with affection, so that I might recognize that the lord Leontius was a foreshadowing, and has been transformed rather than lost.[14]

1.16 [ca. 485]

> This letter provides one of the best illustrations of Ruricius the prankster. The salutation reads: "Domino venerabili admirabili et sanctis omnibus aequiperando fratri Sidonio Videnti Ruricius". The word *videnti*, from *videns*, is to be interpreted in light of 1 Samuel 9.9, "Come let us go to the seer (*videntem*), for he who is now called a prophet was formerly called a seer (*videns*)." The salutation as *frater* signifies that Ruricius, too, was a bishop, and indicates that Sidonius lived at least until 485.[1]

RURICIUS, TO THE VENERABLE LORD, ADMIRABLE AND COMPARABLE TO ALL THE SAINTS, BROTHER SIDONIUS THE SEER

For a long time I have known you, my dearest brother, through reports of your far-flung fame,[2] and in the abode of affection I have beheld you with the eyes of the mind,[3] with which you yourself more effectively gaze down upon terrestrial things and consider celestial and divine matters; for this reason I ascribed to you the name[4] of the very one with whose gifts I see[5] that you

---

[12] "tanti habere": a favorite Rurician construction.

[13] "tanti habeatis."

[14] Ruricius is concerned to establish his status vis-à-vis Aeonius, and may have felt that Aeonius, in his insistence upon a reply, was just a bit too presumptuous; for an even more touchy response to Caesarius, see *Epist.* 2.33.

1.16

[1] Consistent with Gennadius, *De viris inlustribus* 102, who dates Sidonius' death to the reign of Zeno (474-491). Peter, "Ruricius," p.159, however, dates this letter to before 480. Hagendahl, *Ruricius*, p.6, dates Sidonius' death to 479, but for the more suitable date of ca. 486, see A. Loyen, *Recherches historiques sur les panégyriques de Sidoine Apollinaire* (Paris, 1942) p.11.

[2] "fama celeberrima praedicante cognovi": apparently repeated from the beginning of *Epist.* 1.1 to Faustus, which was written before Ruricius became bishop. Indeed, many of the sentiments in these two letters are parallel, and may reflect Ruricius' knowledge of the close tie between Sidonius and Faustus.

[3] *mentis aspexi*; cf. Faustus, *Epist.* "Gratias domino," *mentis aspectibus*.

[4] For the "transferring of names," see also *Epist.* 1.10 above. This makes it clear that "Videns" was a nickname.

[5] A pun: *vidi* ("I see") as opposed to *videns* ("seer"). Note other verbs of "seeing" in this letter, viz. *consideras ... aspexi ...[intueor] ... admiror ... contemplor.*

have been endowed. And therefore, as I gaze upon[6] you diligently in the mirror of my heart, and earnestly admire the beauty of your interior self, you have aroused to longing the innards of my mind, which have been excited to such great affection for you by the most unadulterated esteem that he whom I contemplate with spiritual eyes I crave to observe with the physical.[7] Therefore, offering my best regards in Christ the Lord, I particularly beseech that, together with my lord the bishop,[8] who, I trust, intends to come to us for the sake of the respect in which he is held, you might do yourself the injury of visiting Our Humility,[9] so that, situated together,[10] we might be able to gain profit from our mutual presence,[11] as long as the exertion of the questioner suits the erudition of the responder, and a shared profit results in some way for both the student and the teacher.[12] Peace, peace, peace![13]

1.17 [ca. 485/490]

Julianus Pomerius was an African rhetor who, fleeing the Vandals in the late fifth century, settled in Arles, where he became a priest: see Gennadius, *De viris illustribus* 99; Isidore of Seville, *De viris illustribus* 12; and Mathisen, *Factionalism*, pp.242-244. Caesarius of Arles was among his pupils (*Vita Caesarii* 1.8-9). He authored the extant *De vita contemplativa* ("On the Contemplative Life") (*PL* 59.415-520); lost works include a *De virginibus* ("On Virgins"); a *De contemptu mundi* ("On the Contempt of the World"); and a *De natura animae et qualitate eius* ("On the Nature of the Soul and Its Character") and *De resurrectione* ("On the Resurrection"). In the *De natura animae* Pomerius supported the view of Faustus of Riez that the soul was corporeal. After initially being under the influence of Faustus, Ruricius later in life came under the spell of Pomerius, who may have strengthened Ruricius' devotion to Augustine. This letter, which provides the only evidence that Pomerius was an abbot, was written when Ruricius was bishop and may have been sent at the same time as *Epist.* 1.7 to Aeonius.

---

[6] Mommsen posits a verb such as *intueor* to go here, and other editors suggest a lacuna. The *admiror* goes with the second clause.

[7] Cf. the previous letter.

[8] Another part of the joke, for the bishop is Sidonius himself, as opposed to "Videns," the purported addressee.

[9] For the *humilitas* of Ruricius' city, see *Epist.* 2.33.

[10] "in unum positi": cf. "vobiscum positum" in *Epist.* 1.1 to Faustus.

[11] "fructum de nostra ... capere praesentia"; repeated in *Epist.* 2.41; cf. pseudo-Sulpicius Severus, *Epistula ad Claudiam sororem*: *CSEL* 1.219, "de nostra nos fructum faciat capere praesentia." The latter is another "fake" letter, although Ruricius may not have known this.

[12] For the student-teacher antithesis, see also *Epist.* 2.26 to Sidonius' son Apollinaris.

[13] "Pax pax pax": this is the only one of Ruricius' letters that ends in such a way, and provides another indication that it is not the normally stuffy Gallo-Roman missive. These words also could serve as a means of begging Sidonius' indulgence for his joke, akin to his similar request at the end of another humorous letter, *Epist.* 2.35 to Sedatus.

BISHOP[1] RURICIUS, TO THE LORD OF HIS SPIRIT TO BE ESTEEMED WITH ALL
THE VISCERA OF LOVE IN CHRIST THE LORD, THE ABBOT POMERIUS

It is written, as you yourself know well, "'Vengeance is mine, I will repay,'
says the Lord."[2] Thus, if you find any fault in me, grant forgiveness, because
you can assume that the Lord has taken vengeance.[3] You know that I have
been led into such hidden solitudes on such trackless journeys that the spirit
shudders to recount them, the mind flees from doing so,[4] the tongue is unable
to do so. For I tread upon a path obstructed by brush, restricted in width, bris-
tling with thorns, enveloped by bushes, blocked by brambles, rugged in terrain,
impeded by heaps of rocks, strewn with entangled roots, submerged in mud, so
that amid such varied and manifold difficulties there is no single type of danger.
While the strength of the roots impedes the hooves of the horses, and the foul-
ness of the soil fails to support them, the road truly seems both to extend into
the heights and lie submerged in the depths of ravines to such an extent that I
believe that I am on a journey through a wavy sea that is aroused by the blasts
of savage winds, with the daylight snatched from my eyes by mists and clouds.
Because even if a ray of the sun did shine on the world, its splendor and
warmth was not strong enough to penetrate to me because of the thickness of
the forest, whereas the height of the inauspicious foliage oppressed me thus
during the journey and the inundations of rain spattered in such a way that, stif-
fened or compelled by the chill, I sought[5] the sunniness of a greater fire in the
days of the dog-day heat.

But when, enveloped in water and drenched with thirst, I arrived at the
place toward which my desire was straining, I began to waste away, because, although there was, as I said, frigidity in the air, there was nevertheless warmth in
the fountain, pungency in the stream, sweltering in the field,[6] scorching in the
encampment. And, so that I might conclude all this in a few words, know that I
have traced a path along such a road upon which, I say, no one would desire to
go to Paradise, let alone to exile.[7] For this reason, because Our Lord directed

---

1.17

[1] The first time in the corpus that Ruricius refers to himself as *episcopus* in a salutation.

[2] Romans 12.19.

[3] "si quid imputatis, ignoscite, quia..."; cf. Cassiodorus, *Variae* praef.12, "ignoscite.. et si qua.. imputate..."

[4] "animus horreat, mens refugiat"; cf. Vergil, *Aeneid* 2.12, "quamquam animus meminisse horret luctuque refugit incipiam." Was Ruricius trying to impress the ex-rhetoric professor by dropping Vergilian tags?

[5] *quaerimus*: edd.; *querimus*: S.

[6] *in campo*: S[2], edd.; *in comite*: S.

[7] Not a physical exile (see Krusch, *MGH AA* 8.lxiii, and Engelbrecht, *CSEL* 21.lxvi-lxvii), but a metaphorical "exile from the world," as in *Epist.* 1.2.

me to encounter all this and you to evade it, distinguishing my sins from your merits even upon this visible journey, so that[8] you, who advance spiritually along a narrow and laborious route, do not encounter[9] adversity upon it,[10] whereas I, who travel a more broad and spacious road,[11] always looking backwards, incur injuries upon it, beseech the Lord, for whom we confess that all things are possible, that, even if by a different path, He might nevertheless cause us to meet in the same city,[12] to which mercy can bring me, and merits you.[13]

1.18 [ca. 480/490]

Ommatius, who was born ca. 460 at the earliest, was the most distinguished son of Ruricius and Hiberia, the name of whose father he bore. He became a priest at Clermont (Ruricius, *Epist.* 2.28, 2.57-58) before 490, and later served as bishop of Tours ca. 522-526 (see *PLRE II*, p.805). Gregory of Tours had a high opinion of Ommatius' maternal family, describing him (*HF* 10.31) as "coming from the senators and citizens of Clermont, and particularly wealthy in landed property." Because he is addressed as an adult and is living on his own away from Ruricius, the letter would date to ca. 480 or later, and because he seems not yet to have become a priest, it would have been written before ca. 485/490.

BISHOP RURICIUS, TO HIS SWEETEST AND SINGLE-MINDED SON, OMMATIUS[1]

Know that it was because of business, not because of negligence or of any grievance, that I failed to write to Your Sweetness through Venerius.[2] I therefore have sent these words through Amelius,[3] whereby I extend my most fervent greeting, and I admonish you always to be mindful of your objective. And may not either a more appealing sight lure your spirit, already dedicated to God, from its undertaken journey,[4] or a more soothing sound corrupt it, or a more delectable taste defile it, or a more gentle touch tempt it, or a more pleasant fragrance entice it,[5] and[6] let not death be admitted to your soul through the win-

---

[8] *ut*: Engelbrecht; *et*: S.
[9] *inceditis*: Krusch; *incederitis*: S; *incedere debitis*: Mommsen.
[10] That is, the journey.
[11] Cf. Matthew 7.14.
[12] That is, the City of God.
[13] Repeated nearly verbatim at the end of *Epist.* 2.52.
1.18
[1] *Ommatio*: edd.; *Omacio*: S.
[2] An otherwise unknown letter carrier, presumably from either Limoges or Clermont.
[3] Another otherwise unknown letter-carrier.
[4] Indicating that Ommatius had just entered the religious life at Clermont.
[5] "blandior visus ... corrumpat auditus aut dulcior gestus ... tactus aut suavior odoratus"; cf. Faustus, *Epist.* "Propitia divinitate", "pulchrescit visu, quidquid blanditur odoratu, quicquid

dows of the body. But, holding the plow handle, you should not look back,[7] contrary to the will of the Lord, and cause the furrow to lose its linear straightness.[8] No, rather, with all your senses you should yearn after Him and, dedicated in your heart, you should cling to Him, to the one to whom, at His own inspiration, you have vowed yourself, to such an extent that, when even one forbidden form of the aforementioned evils assaults you,[9] it will be unable to enter a breast fortified by firm faith and divine meditation. And however much you may seem to be placed in confusion, entering the retreat of your heart, with your door closed, you should not cease to beseech the Lord[10] so that He, who sees you in your place of concealment, may say to you, just as He said to blessed Moses, who was crying out to Him not with his voice but with his heart, "Why do you cry to me?"[11] And I hope that in such prayers you will deign to remember even me, and that, even if our[12] affection does not bring you quickly back to us, the desire for sweet and salubrious rest will lead you here.[13]

THE FIRST BOOK OF LETTERS OF THE LORD RURICIUS ENDS[14]

---

lenocinatur adtactu, quicquid dulcescit gestu, quicquid corrumpit auditu..."

[6] *et*: S, edd; *ut*: Krusch.

[7] Cf. *Epist.* 2.13.

[8] "retro respicias... sulcus amittat"; cf. pseudo-Sulpicius Severus, *Epist. ad Claudiam* (*CSEL* 1.220), "retrorsum conversa respicias... sulcus amittat", and also Luke 9.62.

[9] As were experienced by Ruricius' son Constantius (*Epist.* 2.24-25).

[10] Cf. Matthew 6.6

[11] Exodus 14.15.

[12] Presumably Ruricius, Hiberia, and other family members.

[13] Ommatius had chosen, therefore, to pursue his career among his maternal relatives at Clermont, where he soon became a priest. Ruricius asks him here, in essence, to take a vacation.

[14] "Expl[icit] domni Ruricii epistolaru[m] lib[er] primus"; in large capitals.

Book II Begins[1]

2.1 [ca. 485/495]

Ruricius' corpus contains eight letters to Namatius and/or Ceraunia. Five of them occur in the form of a small dossier at the beginning of the second book; the other three, *Epist.* 2.15, 2.50, and 2.62 may have been incorporated after this group of five already had been compiled. It generally has been assumed (e.g. Krusch, *MGH AA* 8.lxii) that the two came from Clermont because ca. 435-450 a Namatius was bishop there (Duchesne, *Fastes* 2.34; Gregory of Tours, *HF* 2.16, 21). But Ruricius' statement that their daughter, who had married one of his sons, had given him another "homeland" (*Epist.* 2.4) would seem to belie this suggestion, as Ruricius already would have claimed Clermont as a *patria* through his wife. Another possibility would be the Namatius who, in the 470s, had property at Oléron in Novempopulana and commanded Visigothic naval forces in the area of Saintes (*PLRE II*, p.771; Sid.Apoll. *Epist.* 8.6). Ruricius had ties of friendship in both areas (see *Epist.* 2.38, 2.64), and the latter Namatius perhaps is Ruricius' friend. As for Ceraunia, one notes a bishop Ceraunius of Nantes in the late fifth century (Duchesne, *Fastes* 2.366). In this letter, Ruricius has just returned from a visit, and plans are underway for a marriage between their children.

RURICIUS, TO HIS SUBLIME LORDS AND MOST STEADFAST BRETHREN IN CHRIST THE LORD, NAMATIUS AND CERAUNIA

Ancient savants have said that two friends have a single soul,[1] which I claim and affirm is especially true, for after my departure from Your Brotherhood I feel that I have been divided and I realize that part of me has remained behind with you; in your absence I seem to myself[2] not to be whole. And because I cannot find myself in myself, I return[3] to you and seek myself in your presence, and there I realize that however much of myself I have left with you,[4] this much of you I have taken with me. And thus, before the prayed-for union of our offspring, the Lord willing, could occur, a rupture of our own spirits already transpired. This rupture[5] must be embraced rather than avoided by those who esteem each other, for through it there occurs in their hearts a sincere outpouring of complete charity, by whose fetters I rejoice that I have been bound

---

[1] "Incip[it] liber II." See the Introduction for the suggestion that *Epist.* 2.1-20 date to ca. 485-500 and *Epist.* 21-40 to ca. 495 and later.

2.1

[1] "Antiqui sapientes amicos duos unam animam habere dixerunt." For this commonplace, see Cicero, *Laelius* 81; and cf. *Epist.* 2.10 to Julianus Pomerius, "Sapientes saeculi amicos duos unam animam habere dixerunt," which goes on to repeat the entire first section of this letter, down to "I had taken with me," virtually verbatim.

[2] *mi*: Hagendahl, Demeulenaere; *me*: S.

[3] *reversus*, cf. *Epist.*2.10, *regressus*.

[4] *mei vobis*: Engelbrecht; *me iubes*: S; *me vobis*: Krusch. Cf. *Epist.* 2.10.

[5] *quae divisio*: Canisius; *quae divino*: S.

by you, and shackled by such chains I exult, and I desire to be constrained by,
rather than loosened from, their bindings, which I trust secure you as well.
Therefore, I extend my best regards through your[6] returning messengers, and,
giving thanks for all things, I omit what pertains to your praise: I note that I
have been silent in this regard because it is said that "boasting in praise of one-
self is hateful".[7] In fact, praise of you is praise of me, and therefore, as I said,
I thought it better to be silent about Your Magnanimity because whatever I
might say about you I seem to have conferred upon myself.

2.2 [ca. 485/495]

In this letter the marriage contract is being drawn up.

RURICIUS TO HIS SUBLIME LORDS AND MOST STEADFAST BRETHREN IN CHRIST
THE LORD, NAMATIUS AND CERAUNIA

Among the thanks that rightly remain to be rendered to you by me, I give
great thanks[1] <for>[2] the presence and appearance[3] of our mutual patron, the
lord Postuminus,[4] because you have caused our[5] little abode[6] to be made illustrious[7] by his prayers, for as he displays faith to you he grants benediction to
us. And although he was a most watchful inspector, a most demanding exactor,
and a most strict collector,[8] nevertheless, we estimate all this to be negligible
because of your grace and the weight of his holiness, because, as it is written,

---

[6] *vestris*: S; *vobis*: Engelbrecht.

[7] "in propriis laudibus, sicut dicitur, est odiosa iactatio": cf. Cyprian, *Ad Donatum* 1.4, "in pro-
prias laudes odiosa iactatio est," for whom see Taurentius, "Litterae sanctitatis" below.

2.2

[1] *grates* (thanks rendered to the gods) ... *gratiae* (thanks rendered to persons).

[2] *pro*: Lütjohann; Krusch suggests a lacuna.

[3] *visione*; *usione*: S; *visitatione*: edd.

[4] Otherwise unknown, Postuminus served as a go-between in arranging the marriage of Ruricius'
son and Namatius' and Ceraunia's daughter. Ruricius' terminology suggests that Postuminus
was a priest, perhaps of Namatius' and Ceraunia's personal chapel. Note also the Aquitanian
Postumianus who participated in the *Dialogues* of Sulpicius Severus.

[5] *nostrum*: Krusch; *vestrum*: S; an indication that Hiberia was there as well.

[6] *hospitiolum*: probably at Gurdo/Decaniacum, see *Epist.* 1.12 above.

[7] *inlustrari*: a loaded word in the world of late Roman aristocrats, for the *inlustres* were at the
top of the aristocratic hierarchy.

[8] "inspector ... exactor ... exsecutor": technical legal terms, qq.vv. in H.E. Dirksen, *Manuale latinitatis fontium iuris civilis romanorum* (Berlin, 1837). An *inspector*, for example, examined
goods to be sold (p.480). *Exactores* oversaw income and expenditures, cf. *CTh* 11.7.15, *De
exactionibus* (p.336). *Exsecutores* were responsible for collecting debts, and were dispatched in
cases of fraud, see *CTh* 8.8.7, *De exsecutoribus* (p.354).

"Charity bears all things, charity never ends,"[9] especially because whatever he appeared to exact we believe that he has instead conferred[10] upon us through the kindness of God. Therefore, I have given these words to him as he returns with the favor of the divinity,[11] not because they were necessary but because he himself wished it, with which I, in your absence, proclaim a profuse greeting to Your Inseparable Brotherhood. And I mentally anticipate my journey and the sight of you, and I emphasize that, as you requested and was fitting and proper, everything has been examined, passed along, and confirmed.[12] Nor have I any fear, which might trouble your spirits even a little, that a single syllable would appear to have been subtracted from the dowry contract,[13] because you should realize that whatever is lacking in the amount is not only reimbursed but even augmented in the husband.[14]

2.3 [ca. 485/495]

Ruricius consoles Namatius and Ceraunia after the death of a son.

RURICIUS TO HIS SUBLIME LORDS AND MOST STEADFAST BRETHREN IN CHRIST THE LORD, NAMATIUS AND CERAUNIA

How gravely I was stricken by the cruel news of your grief you can imagine more readily on the basis of our mutual love than I can express in words,[1] be-

---

[9] 1 Corinthians 13.7.8.

[10] *contulisse*, the last word of the previous letter.

[11] *propitia divinitate*: Lütjohann, cf. *Epist.* 2.63; *propria divinitate*: S[1]; *propria civitate*: S[2]. Cf. Faustus' letter "Propitia divinitate" above.

[12] "inspecta, tradita, firmata": more legal terminology, parallel to the three occupations noted at the beginning of the letter.

[13] "de libello dotis." A dowry remained the property of the wife, to revert back to her in case of divorce or if her husband predeceased her, and its amount had to be guaranteed by the husband. See K. Kagan, "The Nature of Dowry in Roman Law: Rights of Husband and Wife," *Tulane Law Review* 20 (1944-1945) p.55ff. Here, however, it seems that a bride-price, technically a "donatio nuptialis" ("marital contribution"), the contribution of the groom's family, that is being referred to, although the contract specifying the contributions of both families probably still was called a "libellum dotis." Indeed, by this period the terms were interchangeable; see *Codex Justinianus* 6.20.20 (6 August 529), "ante nuptias donatio vel dos a patre data vel matre vel aliis parentibus pro filio vel filia" ("before the marriage, a contribution or dowry [is given] by the father or mother or other relatives for a son or daughter").

[14] *marito*: Krusch; *merito*: S. Even if Krusch is mistaken, the word *merito* ("deserved"), in this context, would have called *marito* to mind. Ruricius' wordplay may be an attempt to soft-pedal the fact that his contribution fell short of expectations.

2.3

[1] Many of these sentiments are repeated in *Epist.* 2.39.

cause a spirit afflicted by excessive grief refuses to express what it shudders to recollect. I grieve, most steadfast brethren, at your so harsh misfortune <and>[2] I sympathize with my whole heart. For even if at the present I am separated[3] from you physically, I am nevertheless always joined to you emotionally,[4] and as long as I do not depart from you in spirit, I believe that I will be present in your grief, because according to the divine words, "If one member suffers all suffer together"[5] in the body. We, indeed, not only are part of the same body through our faith in Christ, but we also are joined by the union of our children.[6] For this reason, indeed, if such a great intemperateness of the weather permitted, I would come to console you myself, in place of this letter.[7]

But what are we doing,[8] my finest brethren? Just as we cannot resist the divine command by means of our own strength, we likewise ought not to do so by our will, and we ought to exercise all our vigilance[9] not to be found blasphemous or in some way injurious to the Lord by bemoaning our sweet offspring with excessive sorrow, lest the author of this very death,[10] having found an opportunity, afflict our spirit more direly than He smote it by the taking of our dear ones. Therefore, in all sorrow and grief we must flee to Him and all our misfortunes must be rendered wholeheartedly to Him, who heals the wounded, who unburdens the troubled, who consoles the afflicted. And that observation of the sanctified Job must be uttered universally, "The Lord gave, the Lord has taken away, just as it is pleasing to the Lord, thus also is it done: blessed be the name of the Lord."[11] I have presumed therefore, lords of my heart, to write to you thus, so that even with the divine eloquence I might assuage somehow our common grief, which I know that[12] I could not mitigate[13] with my own words. Truly, you can take solace not least from the will of Christ, because, whereas the death itself remains premature, He deigned to accept him as

---

[2] *et*: added by Engelbrecht.

[3] *disparatus*: S[1]; *separatus*: S[2]; cf. *Epist.* 2.36, *disparati corpore*.

[4] "etsi ad praesens a vobis disparatus sum corpore, tamen semper mente coniungor": cf. Cassian, *De incarnatione* 7.31, "etsi corpore absum ... etsi nunc praesentia non admisceor, tamen mente coniungor"; also Paulinus of Nola, *Epist.* 18.1.

[5] 1 Corinthians 12.16.

[6] So, the marriage discussed in *Epist.* 2.1-1 by now has taken place.

[7] This would suggest that Ruricius was living some distance away from them at this time.

[8] The section from here to the end is repeated or paraphrased in *Epist.* 2.39 to Eudomius and Melanthia, who also had lost a son.

[9] *advigilantia*: S; *sollicitudine*: *Epist.* 2.39.

[10] *mortis*: *Epist.* 2.39; *meritis*: S.

[11] Job 1.21. Repeated in the next letter.

[12] *sciebam quod*: edd.; *sciebam quo*: S; ommited in *Epist.* 2.39.

[13] *moderarer vere*: Krusch; *moderare vere*: S1; *moderarem et vere*: S2; *moderarer et vere*: Engelbrecht; *moderare revere*: *Epist.* 2.39.

such a one of the sort who, He said, possess the kingdom of heaven,[14] so that in your son you may have a patron, and may grieve less for the one you have lost, whom you see to have been received by the Lord.

2.4 [ca. 485/495]

This letter, written on the occasion of the death of Namatius' and Ceraunia's daughter, Ruricius' daughter-in-law, is, at 132 lines in the *CSEL* text, the longest in the collection; *Epist.* 2.15 — also to Ceraunia — is just a few lines shorter, with the next longest letter, *Epist.* 2.11, being some 50 lines shorter. Loyen asserts (*L'esprit*, p.169) that only this letter exhibits "une émotion vraie et profonde." Sections of this letter recur in *Epist.* 2.46 to Eudomius and Melanthia.

RURICIUS TO HIS SUBLIME LORDS AND MOST STEADFAST BRETHREN IN CHRIST THE LORD, NAMATIUS AND CERAUNIA

Very often, dearest brethren, I have resolved, because of the most bitter misfortune of our common grief, to write to you or to come to you, but always has my bodily infirmity[1] restrained me from setting out on the journey,[2] and the excessive grief of my heart detained me from my epistulary duty. For whenever I attempted to direct my mind to writing, immediately my senses shuddered, my mind cringed, and so much weeping came to me in place of words that I deluged my page with a storm of tears before I spotted it with my pen, just as the poet said, showing paternal piety over the loss of a son:

Twice he attempted to depict his misfortunes in gold,
Twice the paternal hands dropped...[3]

Or rather, as I say, because "my spirit refuses to be consoled."[4] Not without cause. Indeed, I have lost a daughter,[5] whom I rejoiced that I had nurtured and you had begotten, I have lost the solace of my life, the hope of my posterity, the delight of my family, the joy of my heart, the light of my eyes. Nor am I stricken by a solitary loss. For along with a daughter I also have lost my brethren, to whose affection I was accustomed, in whose closeness I exulted. The bond of our brotherhood, dearest brethren, has been shattered, the pledge of our mutu-

---

[14] Cf. Matthew 19.14: "Suffer little children ... to come unto me, for of such is the kingdom of heaven."
2.4
[1] Another reference to Ruricius' maladies.
[2] A suggestion, again, that the two did not live in Ruricius' immediate neighborhood.
[3] Vergil, *Aeneid* 6.32-33: "bis conatus erat casus effingere in auro / bis patriae cecidere manus."
[4] Psalms 76.3.
[5] A daughter of Namatius and Ceraunia, who had married one of Ruricius' sons (see *Epist.* 2.2).

al regard has been torn away. Woe to me, my finest brethren. With the loss of
your deposit,[6] by the surrender of whom you had captured me, I have simulta-
neously lost you, and therefore I lament the solace of a great many family ties
that have been lost to me by means of this single family tie.

I will not, in fact, lose the homeland[7] that was only acquired for me
through her, for I will especially regard as my homeland the land that she occupied corporeally. But, why, forgetful of duty yet mindful of obligation, under
the impulse of grief do I go forth and, with renewed recollection as if with a
new incision, reopen the wound that for a time had been somewhat healed over,
and why do I, who wish you in turn to be consoled by the divine promise, not
find[8] consolation myself? I will, in fact, explain to you the reasons for this return of grief. Somehow, indeed, a spirit afflicted with sorrow already began to
receive consolation from the apostolic exhortation that says, "I do not want you
to be ignorant of those who sleep, brethren, lest[9] we grieve like those others
who have no hope."[10]   But when her husband,[11] our communal unfortunate,
arrived and I spied him without that jewel with which he had previously glit-
tered, through which he made himself both more acceptable[12] and more pleasing to me, he seemed to me to be both unbecoming and, so to speak, despoiled
of his proper ornamentation. But, dearest brethren, he who searches out the hidden feelings of our hearts knows that my grief was suddenly doubled to such an
extent that my emotion and grief were duplicated from day to day, because of
the great excellence of the one and the desolation of the other to such an extent
that I can neither behold him <nor>[13] recollect her without tears, and I often
repeat that saying of the prophet, "Who will provide water for my head and a
fountain of tears for my eyes?"[14]   But he bemoaned the sins of his people, I rather my own, which oppress both of us by their quantity and weight, so that I
grieve for her death and for my life, for her decease and for my own survival.

Far different for you, venerable sister, as you once presumed regarding my
merits, because you raised so many expectations for yourself, deceived, against

---

[6] Ruricius' uses legal terminology (*vinculum, pignus, depositum*) to describe the nature of the
bond between the two families: see H.E. Dirksen, *Manuale latinitatis fontium iuris civilis Romanorum* (Berlin, 1837) pp.269-270, 716-717, 1003..

[7] For discussion of the *patria* that Ruricius would have acquired through Namatius' and Cerauni-
a's daughter, see *Epist.* 2.1.

[8] *capio*: Engelbrecht; *cupio*: S.

[9] *ne*: edd.; *nec*: S.

[10] 1 Thessalonians 4.13.

[11] Ruricius' son.

[12] *acceptior esse solebat*: edd.; *acceptiores se solebant*: S.

[13] *nec*: added by editors.

[14] Jeremiah 9.1.

my protests, by too much charity for my prayers, so that you believed not only that your household would be healed through my intercession but also that your daughter would be made not mortal, if I may say so, through me.[15] But my merits quickly became evident, and they both wounded me with an irreparable injury and smote you, who believed in a sinner rather than as you ought, with the loss of so great a pledge. Indeed, now, venerable sister in Christ the Lord, you will recognize that you believed falsely and that I spoke truly. But, too long forgetful of the heavenly precepts, we accede to human grief. We must return to divine precepts, lest we grieve so much for those dead in their bodies that we ourselves die in our hearts.[16] Putting aside for a moment our present concerns, therefore, let us think rather of the future, so that those whom the present weakens, the future may strengthen. Dearest brethren, we ought to bear that condition of human fragility, which the prophets and the apostles and the saints and all the just and, what is greater, our Lord of all thought it appropriate to accept. It is fitting for us to grieve, but even more so to give thanks to God and to rejoice because we had our daughter, as we desired her to be, for as long as He, who gave her, permitted, and because we have not lost her, as we desired her to be, but have sent her ahead to Christ, at His own request. It is a common privilege to have children, but it is a special reward to have good children, just as living is common to all, but to live well and depart[17] well from this life is granted to few, and is not, moreover, a condition of nature but of human culpability, nor is it by divine prescription but by our own will.

And therefore "let not our heart be distressed,"[18] nor should we grieve for our daughter because of her loss but because of our desire to be with her, lest we appear to be disbelieving of the master's promises or resistant[19] to his precepts. Let those mourn for their children who[20] are unable to have hope in the resurrection, which they lost by their own perfidy, not by divine verdict. Let those who are dead[21] mourn for their own dead,[22] whom they believe to have died forever, let them have no[23] respite from their sorrow, those who do not believe that there is respite for the dead. But for us, for whom Christ is both our hope and our allotment, there is hope in the land of the dead, an allotment

---

[15] This seems to suggest that the deceased had gone through a period of illness, and that Ruricius' prayers had gone for nought.

[16] Cf. *Epist.* 2.46.

[17] *discedere*: edd.; *discendere*: S.

[18] John 14.1, 27.

[19] *obnisi*: edd.; *obtimi*: S.

[20] *quos*: cf. *Epist.* 2.46; *quod*: S.

[21] "Spiritually" dead, that is.

[22] Cf. *Epist.* 2.46.

[23] *nullam*: edd.; *nulla*: S.

in the territory of the living: for us for whom that kind of death is the end not of our nature but of the present life, because we believe that it[24] must be renewed for the better, according to the saying of the apostle, "For this corruption puts on incorruption,"[25] because the prophet must be cited, "The Lord gives, the Lord taketh away, just as it seems best to the Lord, thus it is done. Blessed be the name of the Lord,"[26] because in times of temptation one must grasp at penitence, lest one be compelled to lapse by word[27] or intent.

Therefore, let ready faith wipe away our[28] tears, because we believe that our dear ones do not so much lose[29] their lives as transform them; that they relinquish the world, full of misfortunes and miseries, and hasten to a realm of joy; that they withdraw from an arduous peregrination and arrive at the homeland of peace, whence the prophet also says, "Lead my spirit from prison to the confession of your name."[30]

Believe me, dearest brethren, she is already secure in her peace and concerned about our safety.[31] If she were able to engage in dialogue with us, she would speak thus:[32] "Devoted parents, do not long to grieve for me, do not appear to be ungrateful to such a kind Lord with the wailings of excessive affection. Let it be; your devotion partook[33] in this sorrow at the time of my summoning,[34] now, with time, faith should temper your grief, because even if I am dead to you, I live in God. Or do you think that you can love me more than the Lord, who made me as <He wished>,[35] who redeemed me because He wished, and who received me in accordance with His own devotion when He wished?[36] Or what greater solace can you have for your grief than that our Lord deigned to sacrifice His only Son on our behalf? And because the Son of God was will-

---

[24] *eam*: S[2]; *enim*: S[1].

[25] 1 Corinthians 15.53-54.

[26] Job 1.21. See previous letter.

[27] *aut ore*: edd.; *auctore*: S.

[28] *nostros*: edd.; *nostro*: S.

[29] *perdere*: edd.; *perdedere*: S.

[30] Psalms 141.8.

[31] "de sua quiete secura de nostra est salute sollicita"; Cf. Cyprian, *De mortalitate* 26, "de sua incolumitate secura adhuc de nostra salute sollicita."

[32] The rhetorical figure of apostrophe.

[33] *habuerit*: edd.; *habueret*: S.

[34] *arcessitionis*: edd.; *arcisitionis*: S; cf. *Epist.* 1.15.

[35] The manuscript reads *quomodo novi* at the end of one page ant *tremit redimit* at the beginning of the next. Clearly something has dropped out. Engelbrecht has missing letters between "novi" and "tremit"; Krusch fails to note the reading at all. Canisius emended the phrase to "qui me donavit vita, emit, redimit," but subsequent editors suggested "quomodo voluit redemit."

[36] "Dominus ... quia voluit et quando voluit"; cf. *Epist.* 2.46, "Dominus ... quando voluit et quod voluit."

ing to die in the flesh, should man endure the nature of the human condition so bitterly? For this reason, most pious parents, lament[37] rather your own sins and contemplate the retribution for your own iniquities, so that if you esteem me in Christ, because you cannot truly esteem me unless you esteem me in the Lord, then you may deserve to arrive in the lap of the patriarch, where the Lord placed me[38] because of the purity of my innocence and because of His own devotion, "because His mercy is better than life,"[39] so that there we can exult equally in joys that are true not false, eternal not temporal."

With such and similar precepts and pledges of the Lord, best of brethren, we should console ourselves, because, just as the future already has been realized in the Lord, thus the faithful catholic, in some way, ought already to possess the heavenly promises that he trusts will be fulfilled in due time: to anticipate them in hope, possess them in faith, obtain them by works.[40] Indeed, these are the things that furnish us with solace in the midst of grief, confidence in the midst of hardships, and self-restraint in the midst of prosperity, lest we be made overconfident by good fortune, or yield to adversity, or be consumed by sorrows.

I therefore have dictated these words to be sent to you, dearest brethren, as a form of mutual consolation, not at all[41] without great sorrow of spirit. Nor did an abundance of words compel me to draw out my discussion a little more extensively, but rather the agitation of my spirit, so that[42] this prolonged repeated[43] commemoration might soften the longing that recollection rekindled.[44] And in this regard let us indeed acknowledge an equal gratitude toward our common daughter and, just as her death has bound[45] us together, her memory likewise will preserve in us the same affection as before.

2.5 [ca. 485/495]

If this pro forma letter was written, as it seems to have been, after the marriage of Namatius' daughter and Ruricius' son (*Epist.* 2.1-2), it is unclear why it is not addressed to Ceraunia as well. Perhaps it was sent when Namatius was away

---

[37] *deflete*: S[2]; *deflere*: S[1].

[38] *me meae*: Mommsen; *meae*: S.

[39] Psalms 62.4.

[40] Ruricius makes his contribution to the theological debate over the interplay among predestination, grace, and good works.

[41] *haud*: Lütjohann, edd.; *ut*: S.

[42] *ut*: edd.; *et*: S.

[43] *crebra*: Canisius, Engelbrecht, Demeulenaere; *cebra*: S; *acerba*: Mommsen, Krusch.

[44] A favorite Rurician metaphor.

[45] *devinxerat*: edd.; *devixerat*: S.

from home on naval duty (see *Epist.* 2.1). The entire letter is repeated in the first paragraph of *Epist.* 2.36 to Caesarius of Arles.

RURICIUS TO HIS MOST SUBLIME LORD AND MOST STEADFAST BROTHER IN CHRIST THE LORD, NAMATIUS

We who seek out an opportunity for writing by right of our family tie[1] ought not to disregard one when it is offered,[2] so that our correspondence, as a mediator,[3] might render us a kind of shared presence; it is sent forth and not lost,[4] it is bestowed[5] and yet retained, it seems to depart[6] and yet does not withdraw, it is sent by me and received by you, written by me and read by you, and it is not detached when, as if detached, it is kept whole in each of our hearts, because, like the divine word, it is relinquished and does not depart, it is conferred upon the needy and is not taken from the author, as profit for the recipient without loss to the donor, enriching[7] the pauper without impoverishing[8] the landlord.

2.6 [ca. 485/506]

Chronopius, bishop of Périgueux, was a prelate of some standing: his father and maternal grandfather had been bishops, he attended councils at Agde (506) and Orléans (511, 533), and his epitaph was later composed by Venantius Fortunatus (*Carm.* 4.8); see Duchesne, *Fastes* 2.87-88. Ruricius also corresponded with another inhabitant of Périgueux, Lupus (*Epist.* 1.10).

BISHOP RURICIUS TO HIS OWN LORD AND PERSONAL PATRON IN CHRIST THE LORD, BISHOP CHRONOPIUS

In the regulation and rule of the Lord's flock it is fitting that among the auditors and overseers there be not presumption but purpose, and concern for custody not contention over expansion, lest[1] they suffer being stigmatized[2] as

---

2.5

[1] *necessitudinis.*

[2] "occasionem scribendi"" cf. *Epist.* 2.27, "scribendi opportunitatem.... occasionem scribendi."

[3] *mediator*: *Epist.*2.36; *meditatur*: S.

[4] *amititur*: edd.; *admittitur*: S.

[5] "non amittitur, tribuitur": cf. *Epist.* 2.27, "quod tribuitis, non amittitis."

[6] *discedere*: edd.; *discendere*: S.

[7] *ditans*: edd.; *dictans*: S, *Epist.* 2.36.

[8] *nec adtenuans*: *Epist.*2.36; *negat tenuans*: S.

2.6

[1] *ne*: edd.; *non*: S.

[2] *notam*: edd.; *notandum*: S.

hired thugs[3] when they do not abide by the discipline of shepherds, and lest, as the apostle says,[4] they be discovered pursuing not the glory of Christ but their own, as long as they prefer to acquire praise from men rather than to await a recompense from the Lord, seekers of gain in the present and scorners of the eternal reward. Whence, just as the same apostle teaches,[5] if we are harmonious within a congregation peaceful in its blessed work, if we are diligent without dissension, if we minister with compassion, if we are the limbs of a single head, then we ought to be like-thinking custodians of the body, because the sheepfolds of the Lord's flock may be many in number, but they are not disparate in the nature of their faith, so that, just as the Lord himself deigned to foretell, a manifold schism ought not to develop among us, with us disagreeing because of jealousy and dismembering the Lord's flock because of dissension. But rather, with us gathering the Lord's flocks through the unity of a single doctrine, let there be among us "a single flock and a single shepherd,"[6] who, just as He is King of Kings and Lord of Lords,[7] priest of priests and prelate of prelates, let Him likewise be perceived as shepherd of shepherds. For this reason, in my desire for charity rather than cupidity, I have sent these words to Your Sanctity <through>[8] my priest in regard to the diocese[9] of Gemiliacum[10] (regarding which[11] I already had written to you previously),[12] lest, if I were silent, it be attributed to negligence rather than to a desire for harmony, and lest I seem to have yielded to an irrational purpose[13] rather than to peace,[14] so

---

[3] *mercennariorum.*
[4] John 7.18; cf. 1 Thessalonians 2.6.
[5] Cf. Romans 12.9.
[6] John 10.16.
[7] Revelation 19.16.
[8] *per*: added by editors.
[9] *dioecesi*: the equivalent of a modern parish.
[10] Modern Jumilhac-le-Grand (Dordogne). In 591 it appeared in the will of abbot Aredius of Limoges: "basilicae sancti domni Martini ... dono Gemiliacum cum aedificiis, pratis, silvis et pascuis ... sancto Martiali..." ("to the basilica of the lord Martin ... I bequeath Jumilhac-le-Grand, along with the buildings, fields, forests, and pastures") (*Testamentum Aredii*: Aubrun, *Limoges*, pp.413-417). Given that Gemiliacum seems here to be under the administration of an abbot of Limoges, it would appear that Ruricius was the victor in his quarrel with Chronopius. It is not to be identified with Genouillac (Creuse), called Genuliacum in 833, which was the site of gold mines, but which was in the the opposite direction from Périgueux: see *CAG* 23, p.168; and *Bilan Scientifique, Aquitaine* (1992) pp.27-28.
[11] Ruricius often uses *unde* in this sense.
[12] This letter does not survive.
[13] "rationi irrationabili"; that is, Chronopius' attempt to appropriate Gemiliacum. Ruricius' cleverly repeats the use of *ratio*, contrasted with *praesumptio*, at the beginning of the letter.
[14] *rationi irrationabili viderer cessisse non paci*: Engelbrecht; *rationi inrationabilis vider cessisse non pauci*: S; *rationi irrationabili viderer cessisse non paci*: Krusch; *rationi irrationabili. sua-*

that, if you recognize that what I say is true, or that what I seek is just, you will no longer allow me to suffer injury[15] or yourself apprehension.

2.7 [ca. 485/486]

> In this letter Ruricius speaks as if he had only recently become bishop. The recipient probably is the Elaphius with whom Sidonius Apollinaris corresponded circa the 470s (Sid.Apoll. *Epist.* 4.15; *PLRE II*, p.387); he lived near Rodez and owned a *castellum* ("fortified estate") for which he had built a baptistery. In Ruricius' letter, he seems to be in Visigothic service, perhaps as the governor of Aquitania Prima. Elaphius apparently belonged to a family that continued to be important in this area. In the early sixth century an Elaphius was bishop of Poitiers (Duchesne, *Fastes*, 2.83); and another served Bourges in the sixth century (ibid. 2.72, 83). More significant might be the Elaphius who was described as "born of a noble family in the city of Limoges" ca. 510/520 (*Vita Elaphii: AASS* August III, p.747). He became bishop of Châlons-sur-Marne and died in 580 (Gregory of Tours, *HF* 5.40; Duchesne, *Fastes* 3.96). A Merovingian gold tremissis with the reverse legend ELAFIVS MONETAR[ius] found at Brive-la-Gaillarde (see *CAG* 19, p.75; and *Epist.* 2.24) likewise could reflect the continuing status of Elaphius' family.

BISHOP RURICIUS TO HIS SUBLIME LORD AND ALWAYS MAGNIFICENT BROTHER, ELAPHIUS

With the favor of God, the fame of your achievements has become so widespread that all those engaged in labors insist, with all the imploring of their pleas, on being commended to Your Brotherhood[1] because they have no doubt that their persistence will have an effect upon you. That is why, in fact, the bearer of these words, Ulfila[2] by name, whom the priest Fraretrius[3] commended in his own letter to me, has requested a letter of attestation[4] to you, which I

---

dent cessisse non pauci: Mommsen.

[15] *iniuriam*: edd.; *iuriam*: S.

2.7

[1] The term *germanitas* suggests that Elaphius was a relative of Ruricius by blood or marriage, and the subsequent reference to their "affectio germana" strengthens this inference.

[2] Perhaps a Visigoth: Ulfila was the name of the Arian bishop of the Goths, ca. AD 337-383, who devised a Gothic alphabet and translated the Bible into Gothic.

[3] *Fraretrius*: S, Canisius; *Pharetrius*: edd.; *vel Frasetrius*: Canisius. A priest of Limoges, it would seem, for it would be quite irregular for a priest to bypass his own bishop and write directly to another bishop in such a case.

[4] *commendaticias*: see the Council of Agde (AD 506), can. 38 (*CCL* 148.208-209), which required clerics and monks to receive *commendaticiae epistolae* ("letters of recommendation") from their bishop before going on a journey; see also the next letter. The term also was used in a more general sense for letters of reference, as here. For *commendaticiae* being directed to

have freely granted to him, both because of the divine command and because of our shared purpose.[5] With it I particularly extend my best regards to Your Inseparable Charity, and I presume to commend the aforementioned individual in virtue of our kindred affection rather than of my pontifical authority, because rank loses its rank in a sinner, for whom undeserved honor is a burden rather than an honor. Although I trust that my office gratifies you because of our attachment, nevertheless, if you bestow upon me any sincere or shared love, I hope that you will sympathize rather than rejoice because such an important position does not uplift me, unworthy and totally undeserving, but depresses me.[6]

2.8 [ca. 490/502]

> In this letter to bishop Aeonius of Arles, Ruricius writes on behalf of another refugee, this one having arrived from the area of Nantes. For other letters to Aeonius, see *Epist.* 1.15, 2.9, and 2.16.

BISHOP RURICIUS TO A SANCTIFIED AND APOSTOLIC LORD, AND A PATRON FOR ME BEFORE OTHERS TO BE ESTEEMED PERSONALLY BY WORSHIP AND AFFECTION IN CHRIST THE LORD, BISHOP AEONIUS

However often[1] any individuals, depressed by the mass of their troubles, are compelled to seek out sanctified and apostolic men, whose good deeds of compassion, services of good deeds, and life of services commend them, and who are made known by the fame of all their virtues, these individuals, when they seek solace for their distress in correspondence, confer a favor upon us, and although their distress troubles us, nevertheless, through our conferring of service, their need becomes in some way our expression of kindness, by which, when we acquiesce to their petition we satisfy our own desire, and it thus turns out that the poverty of the petitioner benefits the bestower.

Therefore, when he requested letters of attestation[2] to Your Apostlehood I readily indulged our brother and fellow-priest, Possessor by name, unfortunately, rather than by property,[3] because that which he had, he lavished[4] upon the redemption of his brother; he became a possessor of Paradise when he ceased to be a possessor of secular property. If Your Sanctity should deign to compre-

---

secular officials, see also *Epist.* 2.12, 2.20, 2.48, and 2.53 [a repetition of 2.12].

[5] *iussione*: S; *visione*: Demeulenaere, Krusch, Hagendahl, pp.79, 108; *missione*?

[6] Ruricius' wording suggests that this letter was written relatively soon his ordination.

2.8

[1] *quotiensque*: S, Krusch; *quotienscumque*: edd.

[2] *commendaticias*: see *Epist.* 2.7 for discussion.

[3] Ruricius cannot resist making a pun: the word "possessor" meant "landowner."

[4] *profudit*: edd., *profuit*: S.

hend his need more fully, you may consider it sufficiently important to review the letter that our brother, bishop Eumerius,[5] sent through him to My Humility, and you may recognize there how fitting it is to counsel him in the customary manner and to sympathize with him for the sake of our mutual esteem. In order that he render his brother free of the enemy[6] he prefers himself to be a captive of creditors,[7] and in order that he not lose his life through a most cruel death, he himself has been made an exile from his home.[8]

2.9 [ca. 490/502]

> This letter was sent to Arles, along with *Epist.* 2.10, following a visit there by Ruricius, possibly on the occasion of a church council which may have been held ca. 500: see Introduction, and Mathisen, "Second Council." After many conventional pleasantries, Ruricius requests Aeonius to permit Julianus Pomerius to visit him. Much of the phrasing was repeated in the letter "Cum beatitudinem" that Ruricius received from Victorinus of Fréjus (see below).

---

[5] Bishop of Angers, in office between Thalassius (last attested in 461) and Eustochius (first seen in 511) (Duchesne, *Fastes* 2.366).

[6] "ab hostibus": a rare Rurician reference to political events. The identity of the *hostes* who were holding Possessor's brother for ransom is not clear. They seem not to have been the Visigoths, who at this time administered both Limoges and Arles. One could suspect the Bretons (cf. Sid.Apoll. *Epist.* 3.9), or freebooting bandits, such as the Vargi, who engaged in selling captives into slavery (ibid. 6.4.1); indeed, there seems to have been something of a tradition of hostage-taking in this area: Gregory of Tours reports that in the mid 460s a certain Adovacrius "took hostages from Angers and elsewhere" (*HF* 2.18). But *hostes* seems too strong a word for mere bandits, so perhaps the Franks were meant: for Frankish captive-holding at about this time, see Avitus of Vienne, *Epist.* 46 (discussed in Introduction above).

[7] Apparently Possessor had gone south to attempt to raise money for his brother's ransom; for the role of the bishops of Arles in this regard, see W. Klingshirn, "Charity and Power: Caesarius of Arles and the Ransoming of Captives in Sub-Roman Gaul," *Journal of Roman Studies* 75 (1985) pp.185-203.

[8] Here, Krusch, Engelbrecht, and Demeulenaere all have a lacuna, which, they suggest, has swallowed the salutation, and perhaps even part of the text, of the following letter. But a lacuna is unnecessary. *Epist.* 2.8 does end rather awkwardly, but Ruricius has made his points, and any apparent abruptness may have resulted from haste. As for *Epist.* 2.9 and its missing salutation, none of the editors notes that, in the manuscript, its first line begins with the large capital letter reserved for the beginning of letters. It is clear, therefore, that the copyist meant to indicate that a new letter began here. Moreover, the last line of *Epist.* 2.8 consists only of the words "e patria," and enough space remained to squeeze in the salutation of the next letter, as was done elsewhere in the manuscript. It would seem, therefore, that the copyist simply neglected to add the heading for *Epist.* 2.9 which, given that it also was to Aeonius, probably consisted of words like "Eiusdem alia" ("Another of the same person") (cf. *Epist.* 2.25).

<ANOTHER OF THE SAME PERSON[1]>

[Bishop Ruricius to a Sanctified and Apostolic Lord, and a Patron for Me Before Others to be Esteemed Personally by Worship and Affection in Christ the Lord, Bishop Aeonius][2]

Emulating[3] the saying of the apostle Saint Paul, wherein, writing to the Romans, he says, "I do not wish you to be unaware, brethren, that I often have proposed to come to you, but until now I have been prevented,"[4] I also, motivated by shame, am compelled to say, "I have repeatedly wished to send a letter to Your Most Sincere Piety, but until now have been prevented, prevented certainly by what customarily stands in the way of good intentions, impeding, that is to say, my profit and your affection, my affection and your profit. My profit and your affection because your teaching is my learning and my letter is the conveyance of your desire, and, on the other hand, your profit and my affection because my learning is your recompense and the timely[5] conveying of my longing for you is embodied in the affection of my words."

Thus, indeed, during those few days,[6] which your affection made for me truly both few and most fleeting, when my gaze not only was unable to be satiated through contemplating you but even was aroused more by the sight because I longed for you even when you were present and sought you even[7] when we were together,[8] you watered my senses with the purest spring of a kind heart, with the result that to whatever extent I am unable subsequently to receive the precious gifts of your blessed mouth, I nevertheless possess your presence within the recesses of my mind and in the mirror of my heart I gaze upon your form, which a perfected[9] affection depicts there in such a way that it can be destroyed by no forgetfulness of old age, because it is renewed at every moment by a continuous recollection.[10]

2.9
[1] See previous note.
[2] A likely salutation is reconstructed from that of the previous letter.
[3] *contuentes*: S[1], edd.; *constituentes*: S[2].
[4] Romans 1.13.
[5] *temporaria*: Engelbrecht; *tempora*: S; *opera et*: Krusch, Mommsen.
[6] Ruricius' visit to Arles, presumably during peacetime.
[7] *adhuc*: edd.; *ad hoc*: S, Canisius.
[8] *coram positos*: edd.; *curam positus*: S.
[9] *perfecta*: S, Krusch; *perfectam*: Engelbrecht, Demeulenaere.
[10] "brevissimos... contemplatione vestra... munera pretiosa... praesentiam tamen vestram intra mentis... possideam... caritas... iugi recordatione"; cf. Victorinus, *Epist.* "Cum beatitudinem," "brevissimo... vestrae... contemplationisque... munera pretiosa ... praesentiam tamen vestram intra mentis... possideam... caritas... iugi recordatione."

There, indeed, I secretly converse with you, as is the custom of Your Piety, there indeed I deliberate upon the formulation of a better life, there I kiss you with the lips of my mind and embrace you with the arms of my heart. Whence[11] it happens that true esteem, which is nourished in my innards by the living portrayal of your aspect and is set ablaze by the spark of charity, renews for me the promise of the reciprocation of your love, and my spirit assists me as the guarantor of your spirit when I ask my heart,[12] aware as it is of our mutual esteem, how far I should presume upon your feelings toward me.

For this reason, with an opportunity to write finally, at long last, opened to me through your prayers,[13] I extend a greeting and request your intercession for my sins, begging this with a special prayer: that with ceaseless prayers you entreat the pity of our God in such a way that,[14] with all my sins[15] and <transgressions>[16] having been removed,[17] with your assistance, through his customary clemency and abundant goodness,[18] He might bid us attain, if not the same reward,[19] at least the same harbor of repose, so that, to the same extent that in this world we are unable to see each other more often with our corporeal eyes on account of the intervening extent of territory, we might indeed rejoice at our shared presence in the same place, so that, when the crown of merits is rendered to you by a just judge, pardon for my sins will not be denied to me by a most pious redeemer and most perfect advocate.[20] He himself deigns to present the case before the sinner is judged lest He apportion[21] guilt in the judgment, because He knows, being omnipotent, that neither is the severity of the judgment lost in the goodness of clemency, nor is the goodness of clemency lost in the severity[22] of the judgment. And therefore, He deigned to demonstrate to us through his ineffable employment of pity and virtue that those whom He has joined in truth here He will not separate in dwelling there.

Recollecting your promise, I personally request that Your Sanctity not only not retain brother Pomerius,[23] but also[24] that you compel him to visit us and

---

[11] *quo*: edd.; *quod*: S.

[12] "quo fit ... pectus interrogo": repeated in Victorinus, *Epist.* "Cum beatitudinem."

[13] "orationibus vestris." It may be that only now did a period of peacetime provide an opportunity for correspondence.

[14] *ut ita misericordiam*: Engelbrecht; *id a misericordiam*: S; *id a misericordia*: Krusch.

[15] *delictis*: S; *deletis*: edd.

[16] A word is missing; Hagendahl and Demeulenaere suggest *peccatis*.

[17] *deletis*: Hagendahl, Demeulenaere; *delictis*: S, edd.

[18] Cf., perhaps, Tertullian, *De pudicitia* ("On Modesty") 19.17: CCL 2.1322.

[19] *eundem praemium*: S, Krusch; *idem praemium*: Engelbrecht, Demeulenaere.

[20] That is, Christ.

[21] *ponit*: S[1]; *puniat*: S[2], edd.

[22] *severitatem*: Hagendahl, Demeulenaere; *veritatem*: S, edd.

[23] See *Epist.* 1.17, and the following two letters.

that, through him, you transmit to us an undivided part of yourself.[25]   And you should not think that he departs from you if he comes to me, because here, not only will he find you in me, but you also will come with him, we trust, in spirit, leaving your body behind.   Moreover, in this way too you will be able to have no small compensation if through his teaching my rusticity gains some increase in its fear of God.[26]

2.10 [ca. 490/502]

> A personal letter asking Pomerius to visit. This letter probably was sent with the previous one. For other letters to Pomerius, see *Epist.* 1.17 and 2.11.

BISHOP RURICIUS TO THE LORD OF HIS SPIRIT AND A LORD TO BE CULTIVATED WITH HIS INNARDS IN CHRIST, POMERIUS[1]

Secular savants have said that two friends have a single soul,[2] which I, in fact, certify to be true with ecclesiastical testimony where it says: "The spirit and heart of those who believe is one,"[3] one, that is, in charity, not in number, and in simplicity of faith, not in the soleness of person.   This, therefore, I proclaim and approve, for since the time when I departed[4] from Your Single-Mindedness I feel that I have been halved and I recognize that part of me has remained with you, nor, in your absence, do I believe that I am whole, and, when I do not find myself in myself, having returned to you I seek myself in you and there I see that however much of myself[5] I have left with you, this much of you I have taken away with me.   And I render thanks to omnipotent God for His gift, so admirable, which He deigned to grant with a general dispensation in such a way so that, among those whom distances of spaces separate, a spirit free and restrained by no restrictions of absence might wander about, and so that

---

[24] *verum etiam*: edd.; *vestrum etiam*: S.

[25] *per utriusque*: S, edds.; *per utriusque redintegrationem*: Mommsen.

[26] There is no indication that Pomerius ever made this journey; renewed secular unrest, and perhaps his preference to remain in a more cosmopolitan environment, may have forestalled it. The reference to "teaching" suggests that Ruricius saw Pomerius, a rhetor in secular life (see *Epist.* 2.11), as a teacher for his sons. Perhaps it was after the failure of this plan that Ruricius decided to send Leontius and Aurelianus south to Nîmes (*Epist.* 2.40).

2.10

[1] A curious salutation repeated in *Epist.* 1.17, also to Pomerius.

[2] *unam animam*: edd.; *unanimam*: S. Much of this section is repeated in *Epist.* 2.1 to Namatius and Ceraunia. For this commonplace, see Cicero, *Laelius* 81.

[3] Acts 4.32.

[4] The same visit as that to Aeonius in the previous letter.

[5] *mei*: Engelbrecht, Demeulenaere; *me*: S, Krusch. Cf. *Epist.* 2.1.

nothing is so unpenetrable that it is not open to the surveillance of the mind, but rather through the mediation of grace those who are dear see each other reciprocally through the the gaze of the heart, where charity itself resides.[6]

And therefore, extending a greeting to Your Piety, which, as I presume in my own mind, is most abundant[7] regarding me, I beseech you with every exertion of my entreaties, if you return an equal affection to me, if you esteem me with a similar charity, if my love[8] has any effect upon your innards, if my esteem penetrates all the way to the marrow of your heart, if[9] by the sweetness of its power it overpowers you for my sake as it overpowers me for your sake to such a degree that you are neither willing nor able to resist its authority: hasten,[10] if you desire,[11] to come as quickly as possible to your desiring brother,[12] with this objective, both to pay off the debt you incurred and to assuage our mutual affection, because positioned face-to-face I will provide for you an equal benefit, from contemplating me and speaking with me, and, if you esteem me as I esteem you, there will be as much return to Your Charity by me as you yourself bestow upon me.

Nor, assuredly, in coming need you fear fatigue, because, as the poet said, "Piety subdues a difficult journey,"[13] and according to our apostle, "Charity sustains all things," it neither "insists upon its own way,"[14] nor does it know how to end.[15] Indeed, opportunely for one desiring to travel, the temperateness of the autumnal season[16] is consistent with our charity, if, that is to say, the heat of the past summer warms it and the chill of the coming winter does not overwhelm it.

---

[6] The entire section from "which He deigned" is repeated virtually verbatim at the beginning of Faustus, *Epist.* "Gratias domino," cf. also Ruricius, *Epist.* 2.51.

[7] *plenissimae*: edd.; *plenissime*: S.

[8] *amor noster*: Engelbrecht; *amore noster*: S, Krusch.

[9] *si ita*: Engelbrecht; *sic a*: S; *si tam*: Krusch.

[10] *festina eo*: Hagendahl, Demeulenaere; *festinabo*: S; *festinato*: Engelbrecht; *festina*: Krusch.

[11] *si desideras*: Krusch; *si desiderans*: S; *desiderans*: Canisius, Engelbrecht, Demeulenaere.

[12] Technically, Pomerius, a priest and abbot, should have been addressed as Ruricius' "son," but for Ruricius' use of "brother," see the beginning of the next letter.

[13] "vicit iter durum pietas" (Vergil, *Aeneid* 6.688). It seems that Ruricius could not resist including Vergilian tags in letters to Pomerius: cf. *Epist.* 1.17. Of his two other Vergilian quotations, one was to Ceraunia (*Epist.* 2.4), and the other to another rhetor, Hesperius (*Epist.* 1.3).

[14] 1 Corinthians 5.5-8.

[15] *excedere*: S; *excidere*: Engelbrecht, Demeulenaere, cf. *Epist.* 2.11, "a qua excideramus."

[16] This letter, therefore, was written in the fall. See *Epist.* 2.33 and 2.35 for Ruricius' dislike of summer travel.

2.11 [ca. 490/502]

> This letter probably was written not long after the previous one. It is the first (although see *Epist.* 2.9) of several letters in which the original salutation is replaced by a circumlocution such as "item epistula domni Ruricii" ("Likewise, a letter of Lord Ruricius"), or "eiusdem alia" ("Another of the same person").

LIKEWISE, A LETTER OF LORD RURICIUS

[Bishop Ruricius to the Lord of His Spirit and a Lord to be Cultivated with His Innards in Christ, Pomerius][1]

After reading my letters perhaps you marvelled that I wrote to Your[2] Reverence as a brother,[3] because this is appropriate neither to our ages nor to our ranks, because just as you are greater in age, you likewise are lesser in rank. And therefore, if I had looked to your longevity, by the grace of God, or to my office-holding, I ought to have written to either a father or a son. But [I addressed you thus] because the sanctified John the apostle also writes in his letter indiscriminantly to fathers and youths and children, one and the same, saying "I write to you, fathers, because you recognized Him who existed from the beginning. I write to you, youths, because you overcame evil. I write to you, boys, because you recognized the Father."[4] By this choice of words he highlights not the age of the outer man but the quality of the inner. Doubtless we are called fathers to the extent that we profit through the understanding and esteem of God. But to the extent that we fight strongly against the adversary who "circles like a lion, seeking someone to devour,"[5] we are understood to be youths. And to the extent that we are committed to indolence and slothfulness and we fail, weak in faith, to travel the road of the commandments and, as a result of our pursuit of secular activities, we arise as if lethargic from sleep to observe and follow the divine precepts, we are most correctly evaluated as having the levity of children.

In this regard, also, the apostle Paul warned the delinquent thus: "Rise, you sleepers, and arise from the dead," and you will touch Christ or "Christ will enlighten you."[6] For the Lord also, in the Gospel, when He was addressed by those standing around him, "Behold your mother and your brothers are looking for you and wish to see you," responded thus, "Who is My mother and who are

---

2.11

[1] The salutation is reconstructed from the previous letter and *Epist.* 1.17.

[2] Ruricius here switches from the *vester* of the previous letter to the much more intimate *tua*.

[3] Cf. the previous letter and *Epist.* 2.33, describing Capillutus, also a priest of Arles.

[4] 1 John 2.13-14.

[5] 1 Peter 5.8.

[6] Ephesians 5.14.

My brothers?" And pointing out the apostles following him, He said, "Are they
not these, who carry out the will of My Father?"[7] We even can be called the
mother of Christ, when we carry Christ in our hearts. For the sanctified Mary,
who conceived as a virgin, gave birth as a virgin, and remained a virgin, conceived our Lord not by means of a virile embrace but by means of a marriage
of faith.[8] We are made His brothers when we arrange, bolster, and embellish
our lives with every kind of virtue, so that we can be "heirs of God" and "co-
heirs of Christ."[9] For whom, indeed, can there be doubt that if we are made
heirs of God we rightly can be called brothers of Christ, adopted by Him Himself, who created us as His own,[10] ransomed us as strangers, chose us as His
servants, and acknowledged us as His sons? Indeed, He creates us by His power, redeems us through His suffering, <He chooses>[11] us through His prescience, and acknowledges us through His grace. Furthermore, we are adopted
sons, He alone is a natural son, He who, so that He might recall us to the same
blessedness whence we had departed, although He did not completely cease to
be what He was, He nevertheless wished to be what He was not so that the
word might become flesh and so that, when He the Creator descended to the
humility of a human, a human might rise to the sublimity of the Creator.

It happens thus so that divine matters might be communicated to humanity
and so that human activities might share in the divinity according to those
words of the apostle:[12] "He who,[13] being in the form of God, thought it not
robbery to be equal with God, but made Himself of no reputation, and took
upon Him the form of a servant, and was made in the likeness of men, and
being found in fashion as a man, He humbled Himself, and became obedient
unto death, even the death of the cross. Wherefore God also has highly exalted
Him, and given Him a name which is above every name, that at the name of
Jesus every knee should bow, of things in heaven, and things in earth, and
things under the earth, and that every tongue should confess that Jesus Christ is
Lord, to the glory of God the Father."[14] For this reason likewise the same
doctor writing to the Corinthians: "Therefore, we regard no one from a human

---

[7] Mark 3.32-33; Matthew 12.47-50; Luke 8.20.
[8] "fide maritante": Faustus, *Epist.* "Magnum pietatis" (*CSEL* 21.205), and, perhaps, Cassian, *De
incarnatione* 7.25.
[9] Romans 8.17.
[10] *suos*: edd.; *vos*: S.
[11] There are at least a few words missing here. Several editors, including Demeulenaere and
Lütjohann suggest "eligit in," as this sentence repeats the verbs of the previous one.
[12] "humanitati divina communicent et divinitati humana participent": from Cassian, *De incarnatione* 1.5.
[13] That is, Christ.
[14] Philippians 2.6-11; this is one of Ruricius' longest biblical citations.

point of view; even though we once regarded Christ from a human point of view, we regard Him thus no longer,"[15] because when the corporeal infirmity in Him ceases to exist, He is believed to be complete in divine virtue. And therefore, according to this apostle, seeing that we are "all one in Christ,"[16] we most correctly are called brothers, both because one womb of the sacred font brought us forth and because, with the spirit giving life, the same breasts of mother church suckled us. And for this reason I likewise write to you as brother, both because I know that, with the favor of God, you have converted your spirit <from>[17] secular activities[18] to the eternal blessedness and have become an imitator of that merchant in the Gospels,[19] who sold all his possessions and procured a most precious pearl, or of he,[20] who, having discovered a treasure in a field, sold all that he had[21] and purchased the same field with praiseworthy greed, not as a vexatious coveter of the property of another, but as a provident administrator of his own resources, retaining in a perfected heart a charity that is absolutely the most sincere, not so that he might sell it more sparingly but so that he might lend it more liberally.

I rejoice at this act and I give thanks to God, because in accordance with the riches of his goodness and virtue, because of his inestimable pity, He condescended nearly to go, if I may say so, against his own conviction, because, although He himself said that it is difficult for those who have money to be able to acquire the kingdom of heaven, behold! He both glorified you with such things in the secular world[22] and hastened to propel you into his kingdom. But, nevertheless, with the moderation of His pity the same Lord continually tempered the rigor of this earlier conviction, which the apostles intensely feared, saying that what is impossible for men in themselves through nature is possible in them by God through grace. For the sake of the affection of our shared charity, I recommend this in you, that committed[23] and accepting of the costs you should you take pains for this labor, and as a strenuous builder apply yourself thus to the building of that turret which the Lord in the Gospel[24] ordered to be built, so that your adversaries might have something to lament regarding its perfection rather than something to ridicule regarding its incompletion.

---

[15] 2 Corinthians 5.16.

[16] Galatians 3.28.

[17] *a*: added by editors.

[18] "a saeculi actibus": presumably a reference to Pomerius' secular career, perhaps as a rhetor.

[19] Matthew 13.46; cf. Jerome, *Epist.* 107.5.1.

[20] Matthew 13.44.

[21] *distractis quae*: edd., *destractisque*: S.

[22] A suggestion that Pomerius' secular career had been successful.

[23] *totus*: Engelbrecht, Demeulenaere; *totis*: S; *otiis*: Mommsen.

[24] Cf. Luke 14.28-29.

2.12 [ca. 490/500]

Praesidius probably held some office under the Visigoths (see *PLRE II*, p.903). A Praesidius was bishop of St-Bertrand (Lugdunum Convenarum) rather later, ca. 533/541 (Duchesne, *Fastes* 2.98). This letter is repeated as *Epist.* 2.53. For other letters of intercession addressed to secular officials, see *Epist.* 2.7 and 2.20.

BISHOP RURICIUS TO THE SUBLIME AND ALWAYS MAGNIFICENT LORD PRAESI-
DIUS[1]

Several persons, because they are confident that I have much influence with Your Inseparable Exaltedness, not because of the merit of my life but because of the privilege of friendship, seek from me letters of attestation[2] by means of which they might be excused to you. The responsibility of my office does not allow me to deny these letters, not because of any audacity of presumption but because of the discipline of ministry, so long as I desire to provide solace in the present life for them and in the eternal for you, both so that they might be preserved for penitence through your forbearance[3] and so that you might come to pardon through pity, just as the scripture says, "For there will be judgment without pity for him who does not have pity,"[4] because He who said, "Forgive and you will be forgiven,"[5] doubtless in the future will restore what he promised to one whom he sees doing here what he orders. Indeed, for us[6] His truth is ready at hand <if>[7] our faith in Him is not lacking. For this reason, you are most manifestly able to realize that the pardon of sinners is equivalent to the absolution of your own afflictions, and that whatever you grant[8] to the prayers of others must be granted to your own, according to the saying of the same person in the Gospels, "You will be judged on the basis of the judgment you pronounce."[9] And therefore, on behalf of Ursus and Lupicinus,[10] who, as I said above, came to me as if I was on most intimate terms with you, given that I am

---

2.12

[1] "Domino sublimi semperque magnifico fratri Praesidio Ruricius episcopus"; cf. the less fulsome salutation of *Epist.* 2.53, "Ruricius episcopus Praesidio filio salutem" in which Praesidius is accorded the status of "son" rather than of "brother."

[2] *commendaticias*, but not the ecclesiastical kind; see *Epist.* 2.7.

[3] "patientiam ... paenitentiam."

[4] James 2.13.

[5] Luke 6.37.

[6] *nobis*; *Epist.* 2.53 reads *vobis*.

[7] *si*: added by editors.

[8] *praestiteritis*; *Epist.* 2.53 reads *praestatis*.

[9] Matthew 7.2.

[10] *Lupicino*; *Epist.* 2.53 reads *Lupo*.

bound by the mandate of love with respect to intercession for their crimes,[11] I approach you as a suppliant, so that you might impart and yield,[12] first to God and then to me, that which they have done, and so that you might not put me to shame[13] regarding the punishment of those who believed that they already[14] had been absolved when they were escorted[15] to My Humility.

2.13 [ca. 490/500]

> Here, Praesidius, who must have been near retirement, is encouraged to become a penitent and, as a consequence, adopt a religious lifestyle. Ruricius includes a number of reminiscences from Faustus' letter "Propitia divinitate," on very much the same topic, and may have had it before him as he wrote.

ANOTHER LIKEWISE

[Bishop Ruricius to the Sublime and Always Magnificent Lord Praesidius][1]

I rejoice that, amid the adverse and diverse storms on the sea of this age, you have guided your rocking boat, with the Lord as a helmsman,[2] to the port of safety.[3] Settled within His trustworthy and peaceful mooring-place, you now will ridicule rather than fear the billows of this same perfidious, troublesome, and bitter sea, regarding which you now can have as much joy as you have little fear, because you either look back at those left behind or, settled upon a higher peak, you look down, and you marvel that you have escaped. It remains that, placing your hand on the rudder, you keep watch, always intent upon the stars, and that you set your sail upon the voyage you have undertaken in such a manner that a stronger blast does not blow you into the deep, and nearby rocks on the shores do not shatter you. Nor, indeed, according to the saying of our Lord Savior, should you imitate Lot's wife, looking back when you have set your

---

[11] Ruricius seems positively apologetic for his intercession, twice stressing that it occurred as a result of ecclesiastical necessity.

[12] *et infieri*: omitted from *Epist.* 2.53.

[13] *confundas*, cf. *confundabatur* at the end of *Epist.* 2.34.

[14] *iam tum*: from *Epist.* 2.52.

[15] "deducti sunt": this could suggest that they had physically been brought before Ruricius' *episcopalis audientia* ("episcopal judgment"), and that he then had referred them to Praesidius.

2.13

[1] Reconstructed from the previous salutation.

[2] "domino gubernatore": cf. *Epist.* 1.12-13.

[3] "ratem ad portum salutis tandem aliquando domino gubernante": cf. Faustus, *Epist.* "Propitia divinitate", "ad portum religionis proram salutis excelsi manu gubernante."

hand to the plow,[4] struck perhaps[5] by the cries of Sodom as it falls, and, having already set out from Egypt and having passed through the waves of the Red Sea, overhanging on the left and right, which provided such great[6] succor for you and prepared such great doom for your pursuers, and undertaking the arduous wilderness journey, then remember "the flesh-pots"[7] or the onions,[8] which, in the manner of corporeal pleasures, are known to be corrupted and foul by their very nature, and are neither pleasant to use nor pleasing to smell nor enduring in durability.

Whatever in this life is soothing to hear, soft to touch, solicitous in aspect, in fact flatters so that it might capture, ministers so that it might grasp, tempts so that it might destroy.[9] For no matter what pleasure you wish to grasp, that which punishes persists, but that which gives pleasure passes away; fugitive delight is transient, but awareness, damning and to be damned, endures. For this reason, in fact, Solomon said, "The lips of the harlot drip honey, but in coming days you will find her more bitter than gall."[10] Nonetheless, he even encountered this situation himself, after he had foretold it. And therefore, observe that which is evil, dearest brother, because it is admitted even when it is despised, and when it is shunned it can scarcely be avoided. Therefore, you too, as scripture says: "Preserve your heart with every safeguard,"[11] and obliterate your awareness,[12] lest you emotionally cling to that whose physical aspect has vanished. But you should rather say to the Lord, along with the prophet, "My soul follows hard upon you, and your right hand supports me,"[13] or even this, "It is good for me to follow hard upon God, and to place my hope in God,"[14] so that you will serve God with as great labor and as great persistence as you served in the secular world,[15] with the apostle saying or advising, "I speak after the manner of men because of the infirmity of your flesh: for just as you have made

---

[4] Cf. *Epist.* 1.18.

[5] *forte*: edd; *fonte*: S.

[6] *tantum*: Engelbrecht; *tanti*: S; *aestuanti*: Krusch.

[7] *ollas carnium*: edd.; *ollae carnium*: S. Cf. Exodus 16.3, "... in the land of Egypt, when we sat by the flesh-pots..."

[8] *caepas.* See Numbers 11.5, "We remember the fish we ate in Egypt for nothing... the onions..."

[9] "quicquid ... mulcet auditu, mollescit adtactu, lenocinatur aspectu, blanditur ut capiat...": cf. Faustus, *Epist.* "Propitia divinitate": "quicquid enim pulchrescit visu, quicquid blanditur odoratu, quicquid lenocinatur adtactu..."; cf. also Ruricius, *Epist.* 1.18.

[10] Proverbs 6.3-4.

[11] Proverbs 4.23.

[12] *conscientia.*

[13] Psalms 62.9.

[14] Psalms 72.28.

[15] "militasti saeculo": an allusion to Praesidius' secular office-holding.

your members servants to uncleanness and to iniquity, likewise now make your members servants to righteousness in holiness. For, indeed, when you were the servants of sin, you were free from righteousness. What fruit, therefore, did you then have in those things of which you now are ashamed? For the end of those things is death. But, truly, you have been freed from sin, and having become servants of God you have your fruit in holiness, and the end, truly, is everlasting life."[16]

Therefore, dearest brother, penitence must be undertaken not in word but in deed. It must be performed with not the tongue but the heart. It is true that just as in both, that is, in the interior and the exterior man, we have sinned, thus we likewise must repent in both, so that just as the same apostle says, "The heart trusts in righteousness, but the mouth makes confession for salvation."[17] Thus our heart, with our awareness as a goad, produces groans and our tongue pours them forth through a confession of our disquiet. Truly, let the fiftieth Psalm,[18] which is applicable equally to penitence and to forgiveness, be sung night and day with roaring and tears, so that truly and salubriously it can be said, "I roared because of the groans of my heart,"[19] and, "I acknowledge my iniquities and my sin is always in front of me,"[20] or even this, that "I declare my iniquity and I will meditate upon my sin."[21] Indeed, our sins ought to be before us here, so that they cannot act against us in eternity, because one reads thus in the prophets, "Declare, you, your iniquities beforehand, so that you may be justified."[22] By whom will our previous sins be related or betrayed in the presence of the Lord if not, assuredly, by the devil, who is both the inciter and the divulger of our sins? Indeed, he himself instigates us to sin, he himself accuses us when we sin, and therefore in the confession of sins let us anticipate him in this world so that he will not have anything that he can produce against us in the future.

2.14 [490/500]

This letter was written after *Epist.* 2.51, in which Foedamius was implicated in the theft of some pigs belonging to the church of Auxerre. Even though Engelbrecht (*CSEL* 21.470-471); Demeulenaere (*CCL* 64.514); and Krusch, *MGH AA* 8.426, assume that a different Foedamius stole the pigs, the reference to Foedami-

---

[16] Romans 6.19-22.
[17] Romans 10.10.
[18] In fact, of the following three quotations, only one was from Psalm 50.
[19] Psalms 37.9.
[20] Psalms 50.5.
[21] Psalms 37.19.
[22] Isaiah 43.26.

us' return to grace with another bishop, presumably Censurius of Auxerre, indicates that the two are in fact the same person. Vilicus is otherwise unknown. The pig case clearly left some hard feelings, and Ruricius tried to patch things up on the one hand while scolding the two priests on the other.

BISHOP RURICIUS TO BRETHREN MOST BLESSED AND MOST VENERABLE IN CHRIST, THE PRIESTS FOEDAMIUS AND VILICUS

Although I did not receive[1] letters from Your Fraternity through the subdeacon Contemptus,[2] nevertheless, on an affectionate impulse I[3] have sent these to you, also through him, both so that I might satisfy my desire and so that I, as the first one, that is to say the earlier one, might open the doorway[4] of communication, lest at a later time any place be left for excuse-making and lest, as a conscious act, this be imputed to distrust or a sense of shame.[5] Therefore, I send my best regards in Christ the Lord to Your Beatitude, and I hope that, as befits ecclesiastical men, you will esteem me not with your lips but with your heart, and that you will undertake to speak of me with a charity that is based on sincerity rather than past history, because if it had been genuine, it would have endured; if it had been shared, it would not have shifted.[6] But on whose side it has changed, only our consciences know and a judge of consciences without a claimant[7] recognizes, whom I present as a witness to my avowal that neither was I culpable at the beginning of our feud,[8] nor did there remain in my heart anything of what was said or done later on,[9] because I know that it has been said to us by an eternal and true judge that unless we forgive our brothers in our heart, we ought not to be forgiven. You have, therefore, my promise: return your faith to me, because in my letter you will undoubtedly find whichever kind of bond you desire, either of a charity that salubriously secures and safeguards,

---

2.14

[1] *perciperem*: S, Engelbrecht; *perceperim*: edd.

[2] An otherwise unknown minor cleric.

[3] *ego*: edd., *ergo*: S.

[4] *aditum*: S²; *auditum*: S¹.

[5] That is, Ruricius took it upon himself to write even though the two priests had not done so when they had the opportunity, and in so doing saved them from the need to make excuses or be judged in the future. Cf. *Epist.* 2.6 for another difficult letter written out of a desire not to remain silent.

[6] *mutua mutuata*: edd.; *mutuata mutuata*: S.

[7] "cognitor sine adsertore": technically, a *cognitor* was a judge, an *adsertor* was one who made a claim regarding a person's free or servile status. See the *Fragmenta vaticana* ("Vatican Fragments") 324, in the section "De cognitoribus et procuratoribus."

[8] *simultatis*: edd.; *sumulatis*: S. Or, using the reading of S, "nor can you pretend that I was culpable at the beginning."

[9] *deinde*: Engelbrecht, Demeulenaere; *de*: S; *inde*: Krusch, Mommsen.

or of a perfidy that shamefully entwines and destroys.[10] Nor should you blame[11] me for any part of the judgment of an earlier time,[12] because it is my practice to preserve concord in friendship and to uphold censure in judgment. Indeed, I rejoice more personally in this, that I recognize that you have returned to full friendship with my lord and brother.[13] It remains that whatever his benevolence grants to your benefit, your striving[14] shall safeguard in the Lord.

2.15 [ca. 495/500]

> This letter, in which Ceraunia is dealing with legal matters in her own capacity, is addressed to her alone, suggesting that her husband Namatius (cf. *Epist.* 2.1-5, 2.62) was deceased. In it Ruricius provide some of his thoughts on divine grace.

BISHOP RURICIUS TO A VENERABLE MISTRESS AND MAGNIFICENT DAUGHTER IN CHRIST, CERAUNIA

I did not send the painter[1] to you previously for this reason, because I believed you to be occupied by the arrival[2] of the new governor[3] and thus discouraged from thinking about such matters. But because, with God's favor, I understand both from your letters and from the verbal reports of your people that you are carrying on and doing well according to your design,[4] I present my salutation and send the painter, although he was fully occupied here, and his apprentice,[5] because I preferred to postpone my own need in order to satisfy your request. But because both your and our purpose demands attention,[6] I pre-

---

[10] Ruricius gives them a choice of how to interpret his overture.

[11] "mihi ... inputetis": Faustus of Riez used the same words at the end of his letter ("Honoratus officio") rebuking the deacon Graecus: "mihi ... credideris inputandum."

[12] Perhaps the ruling that Foedamius had to return the pigs.

[13] That is, Censurius, bishop of Auxerre.

[14] *insequella.*

2.15

[1] *pictor.*

[2] *adventu*: technically, an *adventus* was the ceremonial arrival of a secular or ecclesiastical potentate; see S. MacCormack, "Change and Continuity in Late Antiquity: The Ceremony of Adventus," *Historia* 21 (1972) pp.721-752. Here, however, Ruricius may be using the term more loosely.

[3] "novi iudicis": the identity of this person, who would have been the governor of either Aquitania Prima or Aquitania Secunda, is unknown; he may have been one of the Visigothic officials with whom Ruricius corresponded.

[4] "ex sententia"; that is, in accordance with her choice of lifestyle. An alternative translation might be "as a result of the judgment," that is, of the new governor, perhaps relating to the disposition of her husband's estate.

[5] Evidence of a thriving industry.

[6] That is, both Ruricius and Ceraunia have taken up the religious life, Ceraunia apparently after

sumed to advise Your Reverence regarding these few matters, so that from the painter's efforts you might gain an example for undertaking penitence and the newly assumed vestments of a new person, so that in you aged Adam might perish and He who vivifies might come forth.

In the manner that he paints the walls with manifold art in varied painted colors, thus you should adorn your spirit, which is the temple of God,[7] with different kinds of virtues, so that you might be able to speak spiritually regarding your spiritual home, with the prophet, "Lord, I have loved the grandeur of Your house, and the place where Your Glory dwells"[8] because according to the saying of our Lord himself, "God does not dwell in places made by hand, nor is there pleasure for Him in the tabernacles of man,"[9] "But He takes pleasure in those who fear Him and in the one who has hope in His mercy."[10] And He Himself again deigned to instruct us through the prophet, "Heaven is My throne, and the earth is My footstool. What house can you build for Me, and where will be the place of My rest? Did not My hand make all these things? Or whom shall I look over if not over one who is humble and tranquil and who trembles at My words?"[11] And the Lord Himself proclaims in the Gospel, "Come to Me, all who labor and are heavy-laden, and I will refresh you,"[12] and the other words that follow.

And therefore, dearest sister and daughter, having put aside the fervor[13] of your initial conversion, you should assume a humility of heart in Christ the Lord, dispense compassion to the needy, procure chastity not only of the body but also of the soul. In order to gain the strength both to acquire and safeguard this, with the help of the Lord you must fast often and pray always, because Adam was appointed as the protector and tenant[14] of Paradise so that free will would have room to maneuver, and so that parsimonious abstinence might protect what an industriousness of praying obtained. But because he neglected to maintain his fasting, he lost both life and immortality on account of forbidden concupiscence.

---

the death of her husband.

[7] Perhaps the painter had been working on the church of St. Augustine (see Introduction); this would make Ruricius' analogy even more appropriate.

[8] Psalms 25.8.

[9] Acts 17.24.

[10] Psalms 146.10-11.

[11] Isaiah 66.1-2.

[12] Matthew 2.28.

[13] *ambitione*.

[14] *colonus*, a tenant farmer.

Under Hierobabel[15] those who had returned from captivity restored the walls of Jerusalem. When they became involved in a war against other peoples because of the restoration of the wall, they worked with their right hands and fought with their left, extending, of course, on the left the shield of faith against their adversaries, and building on the right a wall of good works as if of fitted stones. But these same men who built along with their prophets also worked with their loins girded up, which the Lord also commands us to do in the Gospel, saying, "Let your loins be girded about and your lamps blazing."[16] One's loins are girded whose flesh serves chastity and not pleasure, and whose mind shines forth like a blazing lamp that Christ ignites with His precepts. It is fitting for us to know that, according to the apostle, all these things "were done as warnings for us,"[17] because, for as long as we were occupied in worldly activities, taken from Judaea just like captives of the Babylonians and their king, we were slaves in enemy territory. From there, returning through penitence to our homeland, that is, to the celestial Jerusalem,[18] the mother of all the faithful, with every kind of virtue we ought to repair what has collapsed, to mend what is torn, to expunge the past, to take care for the present, to prepare for that to come, so that through the benevolence of God, freed from the captivity of our past sins, we might serve not the king of the Babylonians but the king of the heavens, Christ, in Jerusalem, which[19] is a city built by the congregation of the saints. And therefore we ought to cleanse our faces with tears rather than with washings, so that we might be able to say, along with the prophet, "For I eat ashes like bread, and mingle tears with my drink."[20]

We ought to discipline our body with ceaseless vigils and continual fasts, judging truly between the soul and the flesh, so that the flesh does not dominate the spirit, but the flesh, overcome, serves the spirit. The Lord provides us with an example of this situation when He speaks through an angel to Hagar, the maidservant of Sarah, who wished to desert her mistress rather than heed her, saying to her, "Return and be obedient to your mistress,"[21] so that dedicated to all these labors and to good works, with both perfected conversion and devoted confession, you might be able to abide in the kingdom even of Him, your Fa-

---

[15] A form of the name Zerubbabel, who was governor of Judah under the Persian king Darius (522-486 BC) (Haggai 1.1, cf. Matthew 1.12). The wall actually was built ca. 444 BC under Nehemiah at the time of Artaxerxes (464-422 BC) (2 Esdras = Nehemias, passim).

[16] Luke 12.35.

[17] 1 Corinthians 10.6.

[18] Ruricius here reprises the theme of Augustine's *City of God*, which he had borrowed from Taurentius (*Epist.* 2.17). For the celestial Jerusalem, see *De civitate dei* 17.3.

[19] *quae*; *quequae*: S; *quaequae*: edd. *quaeque*: Engelbrecht.

[20] Psalms 101.10.

[21] Genesis 16.9.

ther, about whom the Lord says in the Gospel, "Do not wish to call anyone your father on earth, for you have one Father."[22] In that crowd of the blessed you will gleam, concordant with your name, like a true Ceraunia[23] and you will stand out as an exemplar of your name, <regarding>[24] the splendor of which the Lord says, "Thus let your light shine among men, so that they might see your good works and praise" not you, but "your Father, who is in heaven."[25] It is from him that all is given, and all that is given is his, because according to the apostle, "All good that is given descends from on high from the Father of lights,"[26] by whom free will is granted and its consequence is provided.

For penitence must not only be obtained in name, but also must be pursued indeed; penitence is not a mere name that obtains the appellation[27] from the laborious nature of work. For one who perpetrates things that are to be repented cannot be said to be penitent, but rather one who renounces past sins or faults with humility of heart, subjection of the body, sedulity of good deeds, assiduity of prayer, constancy of lamentation, beating of the breast, and profusion of tears, so that one may say, with the prophet, "May you not recall our past iniquities,"[28] at least the daily ones; and again, "I labored in my lamentation, I will drench my bed every night, I will soak my mattress with my tears";[29] and again, "I roared because of the groans of my heart";[30] and, "I acknowledge my iniquities and my sin is always in front of me,"[31] Therefore, may our sins be before us here, so that they may not stand against us on the day of judgment,[32]

---

[22] Matthew 23.9.

[23] *Ceraunia* was a gemstone, perhaps a kind of onyx, mentioned by Pliny the Elder, *Historia naturalis* ("Natural History") 37.9.51, "Est inter candidas et quae ceraunia vocatur, fulgorem siderum rapiens, ipsa crystallina, splendoris caerulei, in Carmania nascens" ("There also is among shining things that which is called 'Ceraunia,' which snatches the lightning from the heavens, itself a splendid blue crystal found in Carmania [a region of Persia]"). The word came from the Greek *keraunos*, "thunderbolt."

[24] *de*: added by editors.

[25] Matthew 5.16.

[26] James 1.17.

[27] Ruricius continues, as with "Ceraunia," with the theme of the origin of names.

[28] Psalms 78.8.

[29] Psalms 31.5.

[30] Psalms 37.9. These two biblical citations are repeated in the anonymous Eusebian homily "Ad monachos X" (no.45: *CCL* 101A.535-542) in the opposite order; also cited is the quotation from Psalms 101.10 given just previously in this letter. This homily was written in Gaul circa the mid sixth century by someone familiar with canon law, for it cites the Councils of Vannes (ca. 461/491), Arles II (ca. 500), Agde (506), Orléans (511), Marseille (533), and Orléans (538). One wonders whether its author had seen Ruricius' letters.

[31] Psalms 50.5.

[32] "Sint ideo hic crimina nostra ante nos, ut contra nos in die iudicii esse non possint"; cf. *Epist.* 2.13, "Hic enim ante nos peccata nostra esse debent, ut in aeternum contra nos esse non pos-

and, even in this world, may we deserve to say with faith this: "I acknowledge my sin and I have not hidden my iniquities. I have said, 'I will testify against myself to the Lord regarding my iniquities,' and You have forgiven the impiety of my heart."[33] It is clear that to the extent that you disapprove of your earlier bahavior, so much will the Lord approve of you; and to the extent that you are pleasing to yourself, so much will you no doubt be displeasing to Him who says, "For He scatters the bones of those who are pleasing to themselves."[34]

And therefore, like the most rigorous censors[35] let us, ourselves, very strictly take responsibility for our faults; let us, ourselves, by means of varied torments of the body[36] appear in a certain manner as our own torturers and judges, so that in that time of the just inquiry the king's verdict will not have anything to condemn in us, whom the discipline of a more chastened life already has corrected in this world, for a just and pitying judge will not condemn the same thing twice,[37] that is to say, He will show himself to be merciful toward one who He finds has been cruel to himself for the sake of the satisfaction of his sins in this world. He will be kindly toward one who He recognizes has been harsh toward himself in this life, according to the Gospels, "Whoever has lost their soul for my sake shall find it,"[38] or this, "Blessed are you who grieve now because you shall laugh."[39] Indeed, everything that transpires in this world is brief, whether good or evil, just as you have demonstrated in your own experiences, as God either permitted or desired. And therefore for the sake of sustaining the constant pressures for the love of God we ought to be constant, because, if "weeping abides in the evening, in the morning happiness" follows.[40] Now, therefore, let us sow in tears what we later shall reap in joy.[41]

Let these few words serve as a solace of exhortation for strengthening your faith. Even if I do not embody them myself, I exhort you nonetheless to follow them. Indeed, I know that profit is fixed in exhortation, for we read, "Weep

---

sint," which also cites two of the previous biblical citations.

[33] Psalms 31.5. Compare the text of Ruricius, "Delictum meum ego cognosco et iniustitias meas non operui...," with that of the *Vulgate*, "Delictum meum cognitum tibi feci, et iniustitiam meam non abscondi..." One encounters such variations throughout, indicating either that Ruricius was using a text different from the *Vulgate*, or, more probably, that he was quoting from memory.

[34] Psalms 52.6.

[35] See also *Epist.* 1.1.

[36] Ruricius, who gives no indication of being a fervent ascetic, doubtless is speaking of figurative torments.

[37] Ruricius here applies his legal expertise to the Last Judgment.

[38] Matthew 10.39.

[39] Luke 6.21.

[40] Psalms 29.6.

[41] "nunc seramus in lacrimis, quod tunc metamus in gaudiis": cf. *Epist.* 2.17, "nunc seminemus in fletu, quod postmodum metamus in gaudio."

with those who weep,"[42] and, lest perhaps you say in judgment, "I looked for some to take pity, but there was none; and for comforters, but I found none."[43] Truly, you may search out counsel that is greater and more perfected in the divine scriptures, whence this has been excerpted, if you desire either to finish what you have begun or attain what has been promised. If you seek this, God will grant you the knowledge and virtue in equal measure, so that you will understand what you have read and safeguard what you have understood. For when the father of orphans and the guardian of widows has seen that you have such hope in Him, He will both grant protection to your children[44] with paternal piety and, with a judge's remuneration, lead you to your reward.

2.16 [ca. 490/502]

In this fairly conventional letter Ruricius strives to establish the proper relationship between Aeonius and himself; see also *Epist.* 1.15, 2.8-9.

BISHOP RURICIUS TO A SANCTIFIED AND APOSTOLIC LORD, AND A PATRON FOR ME BEFORE OTHERS TO BE ESTEEMED PERSONALLY BY WORSHIP AND AFFECTION IN CHRIST THE LORD, BISHOP AEONIUS

I received the letters of Your Sanctity a short time ago. In them you considered it of great importance to counsel rather affectionately regarding undutifulness, saying, "Nothing is more outstanding than charity." I especially affirm this to be true, and according to the apostle I say that that charity is perfected and sublime which "proceeds from a pure heart and a good conscience and a faith that is not contrived,"[1] and which according to the same apostle "is long suffering, is kind, is not proud, is not begrudging, does not seek that which is its own, does not rejoice over iniquity, but rejoices rather in the truth. It trusts in all things, hopes in all things, and thence it never falls."[2] "It is long suffering" because it stands immovable, fixed upon God, in the face of the temptations and tempests of this world. "It is kind" because it delights in the prosperity of its neighbors. "It is not proud" because it does not scorn the humble. "It is not begrudging" because it does not envy its equals. "It does not seek that which is

---

[42] Romans 12.15.

[43] Psalms 68.21.

[44] *pupillis*: a *pupillus* or *pupilla* was a fatherless orphan, suggesting that Ceraunia still had children to care for.

2.16

[1] 1 Timothy 1.5.

[2] 1 Corinthians 10.4-8.

its own" so long as, according to the saying of the Lord,[3] it places even the least persons before itself and to its own disdavantage purchases things advantageous to others. "It does not rejoice over iniquity" because it knows not how to be happy except through the prosperity if its brothers. "But it rejoices, rather, in the truth" because it reveres a friend with esteem that is sincere, not falsified;[4] nor does it mock[5] him with false adulation but esteems him with true honor. "It trusts in all things" because it has faith in the divine mandates and promises. "It hopes in all things" because it has no doubt that it will be repaid great things for the smallest, perpetual things for the transitory, and eternal for the temporal. "It never falls" because humility cannot fall but can only ascend, and it constantly meditates on lofty things, even though it does not presume to dwell in the heights. Although its habitat is in heaven, it itself nevertheless seems to cling to terrestrial things, possessing with a humble spirit the wherewithal that it might glory in the Lord without being exalted in this world.

I have presumed to write these words because you ordered me to do so; reliant not upon my erudition but upon your regard for me. Truly, it is your duty to instruct me and always to encourage this same regard by your own efforts, because the mutual esteem, which, through epistulary intercourse, is always initiated and nurtured among those who are apart before they have met ought to be augmented, not diminished, by corporeal vision, and what began through discourse ought to grow through visitation.[6]

2.17 [ca. 490/500]

A letter of exhortation to Ruricius' friend Taurentius (*PLRE II*, p.1055), who seems to have been middle-aged and to have lived near Limoges. Taurentius' reply to this letter follows; he also received *Epist.* 2.47.

BISHOP RURICIUS TO A SUBLIME LORD AND ALWAYS MAGNIFICIENT SON, TAURENTIUS

The affection of an attentive heart compels the speech of an unlearned mouth[1] to be put forward, nor does the opprobrium of my rusticity cause me to blush as long as it fulfills the command of love, just as the blessed apostle says:

---

[3] Cf. Matthew 25.40.

[4] *fucata*: edd.; *fugata*: S.

[5] *subsannat*.

[6] The friendship between Ruricius and Aeonius had begun through correspondence (*Epist.* 1.15), and they only subsequently had met (*Epist.* 2.9).

2.17

[1] *imperiti oris*: S, Demeulenaere; *imperitioris*: Krusch, Engelbrecht.

"Perfect love casts out fear,"[2] because it is far better to love a near one sincere-
ly than to declaim perfectly, inasmuch as many more are found in the world endowed with the charm of eloquence than are perfected in the vigor of love,
because, just as the good is rare, likewise the eternal[3] is difficult to obtain.
For, according to the saying of the Lord, it is a sloping and trodden road that
leads headlong to gehenna;[4] the one that uplifts to glory is more narrow and
difficult. Why is this, unless[5] because many travel on the former,[6] but on the
latter only a few? And therefore, with the end of the present epoch now immi-
nent[7] and with the day of old age nearby at every moment, just as even the hair
cut from our heads teaches us,[8] and as it is fitting, that in our mature years we
should not contemplate juvenile activities and that a worn-out body and an infirm heart should not be ruled by adolescent lust, regarding which at the time of
judgment in that fearful examination of the eternal evaluation (when that witness
and judge of all mortals[9] will not only weigh one's merits and deeds, but even
will assess one's words and wishes,[10] according to His own promise that He
would give to some a reward for their offering of cold water,[11] but to others a
punishment for the levity of their empty words)[12] he might find us guilty, even
if not of the pleasure of a crime that has been committed, at least of of the desire of concupiscence, because, "Everyone who looks at a woman lustfully has
already committed adultery with her in his heart."[13]

It is fitting that we likewise observe this principle concerning all other
things, so that after the individual[14] elements of eager desire of this feeble
body have been severed, we, weakened thus)by limbs such as these and[15] nevertheless whole, might enter into the kingdom rather than,[16] healthy and nevertheless eternally lost, be cast into the fire. With all these matters salubriously

---

[2] 1 John 4.18.

[3] *quod aeternum*: edd.; *quoaeternum*: S.

[4] Cf. Matthew 7.13-14.

[5] *quae nisi*: S; *qua enisi*: Krusch, Mommsen; *quae <causa> nisi*: Engelbrecht, Demeulenaere.

[6] *illa*: edd.; *ulla*: S.

[7] "imminente iam praesentis aevi termino": a typical apocalyptic sentiment of this period.

[8] "caesaries detonsa": i.e., in that it is grey.

[9] *mortalium*: edd.; *mortalis*: S.

[10] "quando ... merita ponderaturus et facta, verum etiam verba est discussurus et vota": cf. *Epist.*
2.23, "quando non solum merita ponderaturus" etc.

[11] Matthew 10.42.

[12] Cf. Matthew 12.36.

[13] Matthew 5.28. This is one of Ruricius' more lengthy and convoluted sentences.

[14] *singulis*: S, Engelbrecht; *sine ullis*: Krusch, Mommsen.

[15] *et*: edd.; *ut*: S.

[16] *quam*: edd.; *quasi*: S.

reviewed and suitably examined, as long as a truce[17] is granted, let us veer away from evil and ceaselessly do good, let us forget our pasts, despise the present, and crave the future; let our deeds be forgotten and our consciences remembered; so that each of our sins might die in this life, let them live through penitence; let us now sow in weeping what we later will reap in joy.[18] For the time of this life is a time for labor, but the day of retribution is a time for harvest, when, without doubt, that will appear for each person in the flower what they now sow in the seed, just like a certain one of the saints says, "My righteousness will answer for me tomorrow,"[19] assuredly by "tomorrow"[20] meaning the day of resurrection.

I have trustingly presumed to write these words to Your Single-Mindedness, best brother, at the instigation of love; not by pontifical authority[21] but with fraternal piety. Toward you and concerning you I demonstrate not the temperament of a dictator but the affection of a brother.[22] Therefore, offering my regards, I ask you, as you thought it proper to promise, to send me without delay through the bearer of this letter the book of Saint Augustine, *On the City of God.* By reading it you edify me upon this earth, and you prepare for yourself a habitation of this very city in heaven, where we can arrive in no other way unless we ascend by the steps of charity, because this is itself a more outstanding road which associates us who are positioned upon it with God and which, when completed, leads to God, concerning which even the prophet testified: "They walked from virtue to virtue; the God of gods will be seen in Zion."[23] Therefore, let us here make the eyes of our heart sharper with the eye-salve of good works,[24] so that there we may be able to see God, because according to the evangelist, "Blessed are the pure in heart because they will see,"[25] and thence it is fitting that the vision of the interior man be prepared here so that the gaze will not be dimmed there.

---

[17] *indutiae*; that is, the time prior to the Last Judgment.

[18] Cf. *Epist.* 2.15.

[19] Genesis 30.33.

[20] *cras.*

[21] "pontificale auctoritate": an indication that Ruricius was Taurentius' own bishop.

[22] *germani*: usually an indication of a blood relationship, but in this case Ruricius is speaking metaphorically, so perhaps it is not.

[23] Psalms 83.8.

[24] "collyrium bonorum oculos cordis acuamus"; cf. Paulinus of Nola, *Epist.* 45.1, "collyrio declarationis infuso oculis mentis meae." Cf. also Ruricius, *Epist.* 1.5, "oculis cordis"; 1.16, "oculis mentis"; 2.34, "oculos nostri cordis"; and 2.52, "oculis mentis."

[25] Engelbrecht, following the *Vulgate*, adds *deum* (but not *ipsi*), viz., "they will see God."

Taurentius, *Epistula* "Litterae sanctitatis" (*SG* no.8) [ca. 490/500]

> The reply to the preceding letter; this is the only surviving letter to Ruricius written by a person in secular life. Text: *CCL* 64.398-400; *MGH AA* 8.274-275.

TAURENTIUS TO BISHOP RURICIUS, A SANCTIFIED AND BLESSED LORD, A FA-
THER TO BE VENERATED BY ME WITH ALL WORSHIP AND HONOR, AND A LORD
PATRON IN CHRIST

The letter of Your Sanctity has aroused me, nourished by its spiritual food, to hope for the future, and your words, shining with prophetic clarity, have blazed forth with the purest light and have dispersed the clouds of errors. I recognize an affection full of charity, and I embrace the sincerity of your pious reproof. You demonstrate eloquence in your words, perfection in your deeds, grace in your counsel, diligence in your granting of kindness, constancy in truth, truth in admonition, and knowledge in your teaching.

You have returned the ancient interpreters of scriptures and exegetes[1] of the divine volumes, names that I revere, Cyprian, Augustine, Hilary, Ambrose,[2] some blooming with the flower of eloquence, some, indeed, spiritual in the re-vealing of what is hidden, some charming in their delighting of the senses of the uneducated, some striving in their assertion of faith. We enviously fault time past because our own times did not produce these men most worthy of admi-ration. But at least men of more recent times seek out the teaching <of those>[3] who taught before.

I, moreover, acknowledge that my age is the result neither of clippings of greying hair nor, as Your Beatitude derived from a secular author,[4] from the color of a whitening beard,[5] because, even if there was a mistake in their reck-oning, I would sense the years of old age from the lethargy[6] of my limbs result-ing from the progress of disease.[7] But I beg with the humility of all my entrea-ties that you will make an appeal in your holy prayers for the correction of my

---

Taurentius, "Litterae sanctitatis"

[1] *tractatores*: edd.; *tractares*: S.

[2] Ruricius, therefore, already had borrowed these books, and it would appear that Taurentius was quite a bibliophile. A retired Gallic aristocrat with an extensive library was Tonantius Ferreolus, who owned, along with Augustine, Varro, Horace, Prudentius, and a translation of Origen (Sid.Apoll. *Epist.* 2.9.4). Ruricius quoted Augustine in *Epist.* 2.34; and Cyprian in 1.5, 2.1, and 2.4; but Ambrose and Hilary of Poitiers not at all; he also borrowed Hilary from the priest Nepotianus (*Epist.* 1.6).

[3] *eorum*: added by Engelbrecht, Demeulenaere.

[4] None of the editors of this letter has been able to identify the source of this citation.

[5] Taurentius, therefore, was up in years.

[6] *de torpore*: edd.; *de corpore*: S.

[7] Yet another reference to illness in the corpus.

character, for the inspiring in me of the desire for repentance, for the favor of our Lord, so that you, who point out, in order that one might avoid descending to the road that leads to ruin, a path straight and to be traveled with labor, might achieve both the beginning of a good work and the effect of pious emendation brought about not through the lash of discipline but through the medicine of indulgence and the gentleness of pity. Confer also this reward upon yourself: you indeed owe to the Lord interest from the treasure that was entrusted to your faith and was received by you at His recommendation.[8] Win over the despairing, reprove the negligent, arouse those surrendered to the slumber of an idle security, excite those who have become complacent. It is fitting for a good shepherd to carry back the lost lamb upon his shoulders and enclose within better-protected folds those for whom the wolf lies in wait.[9]

As you directed, I have found the saint Augustine, which I had thought was in the possession of our mutual son, the priest Rusticus.[10] The cost to you is that you admire my zeal, for, because I did not in fact know until now what treatises it contains, I examined the chapter headings[11] as I was about to pass it along. It is a papyrus book[12] and insufficiently strong to bear mistreatment, because, as you know, papyrus is quickly consumed by age. Read it, if you wish, and copy it. And I hope that, after it has become familiar to you, it will be returned to me, to whom it is unknown, because I propose to correct my negligence by repeated reading of this very document.[13] Pray for me.[14]

---

[8] *commendante*: edd.; *commendam*: S.

[9] Taurentius' conveying of advice to a bishop suggests, again, that he was both distinguished and elderly.

[10] Apparently Taurentius' son by blood, Ruricius' by religion. The name was much used among the Gallic aristocracy: see *PLRE II*, pp.963-965. He is not to be identified with the influential layman Rusticus of *Epist.* 2.20 and 2.54.

[11] "capitulatim ... inspexi."

[12] *chartaceus liber*: edd.; *cartaceus liber*: S[1]; *carthacius liber*: S[2]. Papyrus was made in Egypt from the inner pith of the papyrus plant, which was cut into strips (*schedae*) that were glued together in two layers perpendicular to each other. A papyrus page was known variously as a *charta*, a *pagina*, or a *scheda*; a papyrus roll was a *volumen*. An average roll was 8-13 inches in breadth and about forty feet long. Text was written in columns about 5-10 inches wide. Taurentius was correct in his assessment of the fragility of papyrus, which did not bear up well under heavy use. His own book could not have been more than eighty years old and was already crumbling. More durable writing materials like parchment (*pergamenta*), made from sheepskin, and vellum (calfskin) were expensive, and many documents, especially shorter ones, like letters, continued to be written on papyrus.

[13] *membranae*: the word *membrana* ordinarily refers to parchment, but, given the specific reference above to papyrus, it must be rather a generic reference to a "document."

[14] "Ora pro me": a farewell salutation previously favored by Sidonius Apollinaris, and also adopted by Ruricius, cf. *Epist.* 2.22, 29, 34-36, 38, 40.

Sedatus of Nîmes, *Epistula* "Refecit me" (*SG* no.10) [ca. 495/500]

Bishop Sedatus of Nîmes attended the Council of Agde in AD 506 (Duchesne, *Fastes* 1.312). Eight extant sermons are attributed to him; see I. Machielsen ed., *Clavis patristica pseudepigraphorum medii aevi*, vol.1 pt.b (Turnhout, 1990) pp. 931-932; *PL* 39.1977-1981, 2206-8, 1863-4; *CCL* 104.786-788, 984; 103.251-4, 254-8; and *CSEL* 21.252-5, 255-9, 262-6, 267-73; P.P. Verbraken, "Sermons jumeaux de Sedatus de Nîmes pour la fête de Nöel," *Revue Bénédictine* 88 (1978) pp.81-91; and A. Wilmart, "Une homélie de Sedatus, évêque de Nîmes, pour la Nativité de Notre-Seigneur," *Revue Bénédictine* 35 (1923) pp.5-16. Another three were written either by him or by Sedatus of Béziers, who lived in the late sixth century: see Machielsen, pp.927-930; and *PL* 72.769-772. Ruricius' corpus includes four letters to Sedatus (*Epist.* 2.18-19, 34-35) and three from him. Sedatus seems to have been a friend of the family, and may have met several of Ruricius' sons. The letter here is very pro forma, probably written in haste as Ruricius' messenger, who had not carried a letter to Sedatus and probably had just been passing through Nîmes on the way to or from Provence, was about to depart. It could be the one that elicited the response of Ruricius in the following letter. Text: *CCL* 64.401; *MGH AA* 8.274-275.

SEDATUS TO A SANCTIFIED LORD AND A POPE[1] TO BE RECEIVED[2] WITH APOSTOLIC REVERENCE AND A PATRON SPECIAL TO ME IN THE PRESENCE OF THE LORD, RURICIUS

Announcing[3] your health and greeting to me, our son[4] has restored me; I have sent a letter with him even though I was not worthy to receive one [from you], thereby satisfying my desire, should this dutiful page in fact reach you. Therefore, I extend my best regards and I ask that, by means of that charity that announces your affection and respect toward me, you not find it irksome, however often there is an opportunity, to visit your servant through the kindness of letters, because I call God to witness that, next to your presence, nothing is more pleasant to me than if I should merit having conversation with Your Most Desired Piety even through the courtesy of letters. I ask, indeed, and I request with every prayer that you deign to intercede and pray for me, as I am certain you will do, without ceasing. Both venerating and desiring them, I greet our sons.[5]

Sedatus of Nîmes, "Refecit me"

[1] *papae*: at this time the term *papa* was applied to any distinguished bishop. Only later did it come to be reserved for the bishop of Rome.

[2] *suscipiendo*: S; *suspiciendo*: edd.

[3] *nuntians*: Ruricius, therefore, had sent a verbal but not a written message.

[4] The letter carrier may have been Capillutus, who often carried Ruricius' correspondence to Provence (see *Epist.* 2.21); if so, the reference to him as *filius* rather than *frater* might suggest that this letter was sent prior to Capillutus' entry into the priesthood ca. 500/502 (*Epist.* 2.31).

[5] This comment seems more than purely conventional, so perhaps Sedatus means Ruricius' own

2.18 [ca. 495/500]

This letter easily could be the response to the previous letter.

BISHOP RURICIUS TO A SANCTIFIED AND MOST BLESSED LORD, AND A POPE TO
BE ESTEEMED SPECIALLY BY ME WITH PERSONAL WORSHIP AND AFFECTION,
BISHOP SEDATUS[1]

You often censure me and repeatedly charge that until now I have not written to Your Beatitude, a lord intimate with me in Christ the Lord. Would that,
just as there is the will to write, there would be the opportunity for doing so, so
that the love that is conceived in the heart might be proclaimed[2] with the
mouth. But, when speech[3] is lacking affection is silent, and, within the refuge
of the heart it is content in its self-awareness that it is not blameworthy with
regard to esteem, even if it does not perceive itself as evenhanded in the dis-
pensing of duties, for affection has faith that, just as it senses[4] in itself a brother's love through the very connection with him, likewise a loving brother can
discern it by means of his own affection, because in no way can we assess better the secrets of the hearts of others than by the contemplation of our own
hidden thoughts. Indeed, we believe ourselves to be loved by another with as
much charity we love him.

Therefore, I obey your plea, I obey your order,[5] that I send to you writing
composed in any kind of speech[6] at all. If, as I trust, you love me totally, you
either will immediately destroy it, lest that which is dear to your heart begin to
be contemptible to others,[7] for love and loathing do not listen with the same
discernment; or you at least will preserve it only to be reviewed by yourself, so
that, however many times the fire of charity in you burns to see me you will
temper your desire with the discourse of these words. Nay rather, so that you
might in fact comprehend more fully the sincerity of my love for you, I presume to inflict an injury <upon your ears>[8] because I am certain that they wish

---

sons, whom he therefore may have actually met.

2.18

[1] *Sedato episcopo*: edd.; *Sedatus episcopus*: S. Perhaps the copyist's error reflects an awareness
that the corpus included letters written by Sedatus.

[2] *promatur*: Demeulenaere, Hagendahl (p.33); *promitur*: S; *promeretur*: edd.

[3] *effatus*: S, edd., *affatus*: Demeulenaere.

[4] *persentit ita*: edd., *persententia*: S.

[5] "parui itaque petitioni vestrae, parui iussioni": Cassian, *De incarnatione*, praef. 3.

[6] *qualibuscumque sermonibus*: probably not this letter itself, but more likely the poem that follows this letter in the corpus and probably accompanied it.

[7] See *Epist.* 1.2 for another reference to possible circulation of Ruricius' writing.

[8] Something is missing here; some editors suggest the words "auribus vestris."

to hear words that are not as learned as they are forceful, not as pleasurable as they are truthful. I therefore trust that neither the length of my page will make you bored nor the rustic speech will make you disdainful, knowing that by however much you meditate upon me more fully, by that much you will hunger for me more ardently.

2.19 [ca. 495/500]

This is Ruricius' only extant verse, the quality of which is probably what one would expect from the average educated aristocrat (cf. Sid.Apoll. *Epist.* 9.13.4-6). It probably accompanied the preceding letter.

THE CLIENT RURICIUS, obeying your paternal admonitions,
Intones his gratitude and renders greetings
TO HIS SANCTIFIED PATRON SEDATUS,[1]
Whom he beseeches with flattering pleas on behalf of one who is fearful
Lest, perchance, his feeble muse[2] might be displeasing,   5
Diminished in the judgment of such a great teacher.
Pore over it freely with your eyes;
Turn it over[3] often in your sanctified hands;
While you study it, be mindful of me.
May your tongue always recollect and sing of me,   10
May your mind grasp me, your sleep retain me,
May your lips[4] always resound with me.
Conceal these words in your pious innards,[5]
Recite them while sitting at home or taking a journey,
Recite them while reclining on a couch amid the cups   15
And the frugal fare and the dainty morsels,
Enclosed in the grotto of your breast
And the midpoint of your heart, with a singing[6] spirit.

2.19
[1] The poem lacks a stand-alone salutation, which is incorporated into the first two lines of verse:
Sancto Ruricius cliens patrono
Sedato monitis parens paternis...
The verses are hendecasyllabics, that is, with eleven syllables per line of which the first, third, sixth, eighth, and tenth are long.
[2] *camena.*
[3] *revolve*: perhaps this means that it was written on both sides of the page.
[4] *labellum*: edd.; *bellum*: S.
[5] Cf. *Epist.* 2.18, "preserve it only to be read by yourself."
[6] *canente*: edd.; *cante*: S.

Thus may God, the giver[7] of all good things, and
Christ, ruling with the eternal Father,   20
Grant that we might see our respective visages
And express in living words those things
That now weary the secret places of the heart
As hymns fitting for the Holy Spirit.

THE VERSES CONCLUDE[8]

2.20 [ca. 490/500]

PLRE II, p.964, describes Rusticus as "in office under the Visigoths," and im-
probably suggests an identification with Rusticus, bishop of Lyon, who died in
501. He is more likely to be the *vir inlustris* ("illustrious gentleman") Rusticus
who was a friend of Sidonius and lived some distance away (Sid.Apoll. *Epist.*
2.11), who in turn may be the Rusticus who lived at Bordeaux (ibid. 8.11.3.35-
36. Here, Ruricius intercedes on behalf of Baxo, probably one of Rusticus' dependents, who had taken refuge at a church in Userca (Uzerche), which was located on the Vézère River, where Rusticus owned property (see *Epist.* 2.54). For
other letters of intercession addressed to laymen, see *Epist.* 2.7, 2.21, and 2.48.

BISHOP RURICIUS TO A SPECIAL AND ALWAYS MAGNIFICENT LORD SON, RUSTI-
CUS

Our mutual friendship creates disquietude in me caused by others and in
you caused by me because those who have faith in my influence with you, I
will not say in much but in everything, flee to our little church[1] for their own
safety. I am unable not to share their grief or comply with their pleas, so I zea-
lously entreat Your Authority on behalf of the guilt of these same individuals, to
be sure, but also equally for your own benefit. Nor should you marvel that I
said that their guilt could redound to your benefit, inasmuch as leniency toward
them would become pardon for you, just as the privation of the needy is under-

---

[7] *largitor*: edd.; *largior*: S.
[8] The verses are not parsed in the manuscript, and one wonders whether the *Sangallensis* copyist
would have realized that these were verses; unlike the occasional "finit" (see *Epist.* 1.1), the
words "finiunt versus" are written as if the copyist thought they were part of the text. And if
these two editorial words came from the exemplar, then it may be that the "finit"s did as well.
2.20
[1] *ecclesiolam*: subsequent discussion indicates that the parish church at Uzerch is meant; in 987
an *ecclesiola* of St. Eulalia of Barcelona (another Spanish connection, cf. the cult of St. Martin
at Brive-la-Gaillarde) was built there, perhaps replacing an earlier church (see Aubrun, *Limoges*,
p.261). Extant fragments of Pyrenaean marble and mosaic tessellae with gold and silver leaf
have been identified as coming from this late fifth-century church (*CAG* 19, p.187).

stood to be the prosperity of their benefactors. For whatever we dispense in this life will in fact be repaid to us in the Judgment, as our Lord himself says, "Forgive and you will be forgiven, give and it will be given to you";[2] or again, "If you forgive men, your Father likewise will forgive you your sins."[3]

For this reason we clearly recognize that our God has determined our own sentence on the basis of the judgments we issue. This merciful and just hearer of our prayers exercises His own authority on the basis of our own leniency, so that, in some manner, He will not impose a decree of severity against those whom He does not see to be greedy for vengeance, because He wishes us to be like Himself.[4] He is compassionate, and He seeks out those who are compassionate, saying, "Be perfect, just as your Father is perfect."[5] He grants pardon to sinners and suppliants every day; therefore He also demands indulgence from sinners. For this reason we also repeat His teaching in our Sunday prayer, "Forgive us our debts, as we also forgive our debtors."[6] On the basis of these words we would shackle ourselves in the most enduring chains if we did not fulfill what we promise, because through the prophet He also says, "Man holds anger against man, and seeks a remedy from the Lord."[7] For this reason, I approach you hopefully as an intercessor on behalf of Baxo,[8] who fled to the church at Userca,[9] so that you might deign to spare him first of all for fear of God, and then out of regard for my intercession. By absolving him, you can remove my apprehension and obtain a reward for yourself.

2.21 [ca. 485/502]

Capillutus was a friend of Ruricius and served as a regular letter-carrier between Limoges and Provence; indeed, he seems to have been a one-man postal service; see *Epist.* 2.40 and Caesarius, *Epist.* "Dum nimium." In this letter, Ruricius encourages Capillutus to adopt the religious life, advice he seems to have taken, for by 502, when he received *Epist.* 2.31, he had become a priest at Arles, although his regular visits suggest that he had family ties in the area of Limoges.

---

[2] Luke 6.37.
[3] Matthew 6.14.
[4] Cf. Leo Magnus, *Tractatus* 43.4: *CCL* 138A.256.
[5] Matthew 5.48.
[6] Matthew 6.12.
[7] Ecclesiasticus 28.3.
[8] Otherwise unknown, but given that Baxo's delict had occurred in the very area where Rusticus had property (*Epist.* 2.54), it may be that the matter concerned a lord and his dependent, not a state official and an accused criminal.
[9] Modern Uzerche, located on the Roman road south of Limoges on a bluff overlooking the Vézère River, about halfway between Limoges and Brive-la-Gaillarde; see L. Bournazel, G. Reboul, J.-M. Desbordes, "Les origines d'Uzerche," *TAL* 2 (1981) pp.97-104.

BISHOP RURICIUS TO HIS SON CAPILLUTUS, GREETINGS

Your recurring illness[1] is distressing to me; indeed, it seems to me to be a divine warning,[2] by means of which Our Lord chooses[3] to correct rather than to condemn sinners on account of His most generous kindness,[4] so that those whom the lengthy age of their years does not convert,[5] or infirmity does not convince to put down the scarlet cloak[6] of the world and assume the garb of the church, which is the hair shirt, the sign of contrition, "Because God does not spurn a contrite and humble heart."[7]   Indeed, whoever dashes himself upon the ground journeys to heaven, because, "Whoever exalts himself shall be humbled, and whoever humbles himself shall be exalted."[8]   For this reason that perfected penitent also says, "My soul cleaves to the dust; revive me according to Your word":[9] what is "according to Your word" if not according to Your promise? Because, whoever, remorseful in this world, repents his sins in Your presence, him You will lead into Your kingdom, where he then can confidently sing, "The Lord heard and took pity on me. The Lord has become my supporter. For me, You changed my grief into gladness; You shredded my sackcloth and garbed me in joyfulness."[10]   For this reason I encourage Your Piety to implement quickly, with the help of God, what you have contemplated,[11] because death does not delay, as the Lord Himself says, "Do not be tardy turning to God and do not delay from day to day. For His anger will come suddenly and will destroy you at the time of vindication."[12]   And therefore, while we still have the chance let us turn to God, so that we are not condemned along with this world, because without doubt a merciful God will offer comfort to one whom He perceives to be mindful of His precepts.

2.21

[1] *frequentior aegritudo*: edd.; *frequentiosa egritudo*: S. Another example of Ruricius' obsession with physical ailments.

[2] *commonitio*: edd.; *commotio*: S.

[3] *qua mavult*: edd.; *quam vult*: S.

[4] For the same theme, see *Epist.* 2.23 to Verus and 2.32 to Agricola.

[5] *convertit*: Demeulenaere, Hagendahl (pp.103-104); *convenit*: S; *convincit*: Krusch; *convicit*: Engelbrecht. *Convenit*, however, in the legal sense of "indict", may yet be correct.

[6] *byrrhum*: government officials wore scarlet cloaks, so this may be an indication that Capillutus had been in secular service.

[7] Psalms 50.19.

[8] Matthew 23.12.

[9] Psalms 118.25

[10] Psalms 29.11-12.

[11] A clear indication that Capillutus had not yet adopted the religious life.

[12] Ecclesiasticus 5.8-9.

Euphrasius of Clermont, *Epistula* "Taediosam pietatem" (*SG* no.11) [ca. 495/506]

> Euphrasius was bishop of Clermont ca. 490-515 (Duchesne, *Fastes* 2.35), the successor of Sidonius' successor Aprunculus (cf. *Epist.* 2.49, 55-58; Gregory of Tours, *HF* 3.2). He, in turn, was succeeded by Sidonius' son Apollinaris (*Epist.* 2.26-27, 41). He received *Epist.* 2.22 and 2.29 from Ruricius, two of whose sons, Ommatius and Eparchius, apparently were clerics of his. He also received *Epist.* 43 from Avitus of Vienne. In 571 the priest Euphrasius of Clermont, a probable descendent of this Euphrasius, lost the episcopal election to Avitus (Greg.Tur., *HF* 4.35). Text: *CCL* 64.401-402; *MGH AA* 8.274-275. Additional translation: I.N. Wood, "Letters and Letter-Collections from Antiquity to the Early Middle Ages: The Prose Works of Avitus of Vienne," in M.A. Meyer ed., *The Culture of Christendom* (London, 1993) pp.29-43 at p.30.

EUPHRASIUS TO A HALLOWED LORD, MOST BLESSED IN MERITS, AND A POPE TO BE RECEIVED WITH THE WORSHIP OF HONOR AND AN APOSTOLIC FATHER, LORD BISHOP RURICIUS

I learned from a vague rumor that Your Piety was ailing,[1] thus I sent the bearer of these words[2] so that you could quickly relieve my anxiety over the harshness of this report, because the divine piety knows that I share both your sorrow and your infirmity with the grief not of a sympathizer but of a fellow sufferer. Thus, let the divine compassion now concede that it grant to me for many years the vigor of your exterior self and the liveliness of your overall health, because then I truly [will] feel[3] that I am sound, if I learn quite quickly of your yearned-for well-being.

2.22 [ca. 495/506]

> This seems to be a reply to the previous letter. Ruricius discusses his health; the words "germanitati vestrae" suggest that he had a blood tie with Euphrasius.

BISHOP RURICIUS TO BISHOP EUPHRASIUS

I give thanks to Your Brotherhood, most sincere in Christ the Lord, because, after enduring my wearisomeness to you, you immediately thought it important to visit me with your letter. When you are solicitous of my illness, you attest to the wholesomeness of your heart, because, as you yourself know even better,

---

Euphrasius of Clermont, "Taediosam pietatem"

[1] The manuscript reading begins "plllll taediosam," with the first word erased after the letter "p"; Krusch suggests "postquam."

[2] *sic harum*; *sed harum*: S; *Sicharium*: Krusch.

[3] *sentio.*

"The purpose of the commandment is charity from a pure heart and from a good conscience and from faith unfeigned,"[1] and whoever visits the infirm is strengthened in love. In this regard, I particularly hope that he whom you seek out with your words you will aid with your prayers. Therefore, as the letter carriers return, I render the reciprocal responsibility of salutation and, just as the news has come to you,[2] I confirm that I have undergone tribulation that suffices for the divine mercy, although not for my deserts, because the same one who feeds on tears[3] in a threatening measure defines a limit to our punishment because of His kindness on behalf of our weakness, lest our infirmity grow weak because of the chastisement of His hand. And therefore, I report that I am more comfortable because of His propitious pity. Transmitting comfort for your concern to you by means of this communicating page, I ordain that you, who share the suffering of my labors on account of love, should share, in the name of God, the happiness in reading about the return of my health. Pray for me.[4]

2.23 [ca. 495/498]

> This may be the Verus who ca. 498 succeeded his relative Volusianus (*Epist.* 2.64) as bishop of Tours (*PLRE II*, p.1157; Duchesne, *Fastes* 2.305; Gregory of Tours, *HF* 2.26, 10.31). If so, then Ruricius' friend, like Volusianus, had connections to Clermont. And if this letter was sent to Verus of Tours (and Caesarius of Arles does attest [*Epist.* "Dum nimium"] that this Verus and Ruricius were acquainted), then it must have been written before ca. 498, when Verus became bishop, for in his salutation Ruricius calls himself "bishop," but not Verus (see *Epist.* 2.52 for discussion). Ultimately, Verus of Tours, like Volusianus, was suspected by the Goths of collaboration with the Franks and exiled (Greg.Tur. ibid.). In 506 he was represented at the Council of Agde by his deacon Leo (see Introduction), and he died ca. 508. See also Mathisen, "Bishops of Tours." This letter picks up on the theme of recovered health from the previous letter.

BISHOP RURICIUS TO THE MOST STEADFAST AND ALWAYS MAGNIFICENT LORD VERUS

After reading the letter of Your Piety I gave thanks to God because I learned that you had recuperated before learning, through its report, that you

---

2.22
[1] 1 Timothy 1.5.
[2] About his illness; see the previous letter. Ruricius' words, "sicut ad vos rumor pervenit," reprises Euphrasius' comment, "tenui rumore cognovi," from the previous letter, clearly indicating that the two letters followed one upon other.
[3] Cf. Psalms 79.6.
[4] "Ora pro me": the first of several "farewell salutations" in Ruricius' corpus (see Introduction). As noted above, this version was often used by Euphrasius' predecessor Sidonius.

were ailing.[1] I confide to you that I am confident that this happens to you so often because God is well-disposed rather than indignant,[2] because "the Lord disciplines him whom He loves and chastises every son whom He receives."[3] This sedulous and gentle admonition demonstrates, therefore, that you have been accepted into the divine discipline, because the paternal clemency prefers to correct a neglectful son through manifold annoyances rather than to punish one who sins, it prefers to draw one who is wayward and unsure to its servitude with reins[4] of reverent moderation <rather than>[5] to coerce with a harsher blow one who is error-ridden and stumbling through the pitfalls of the world.

Indeed, He Himself is a most indulgent father of a family,[6] one who lays down his life for the sake of his flock. He Himself is the good shepherd, who conscientiously prefers to return a lost sheep to the sheepfold of the Lord on his own shoulders rather than to recall it constrained by insistent blows. He Himself is the dutiful father, who not only does not impute previous sins to a sinfully prodigal[7] son[8] who has spent all the property he had received in advance and tardily returns to him, but[9] even multiplies the bounty that was lost, while he embraces him with his arms, caresses him with his kisses, enriches him with his largess, and confirms with his teaching that he was not as indignant at his departure as he is elated at his return. Indeed, He Himself undertook unto Himself the activities and passions of all these personalities,[10] so that, just as the apostle says,[11] multifariously in manifold manners, He might educate us with words, instruct us with teaching, encourage us with kindnesses, enlighten us with examples, reconcile us through prayer, redeem us through the passion, enliven us through death, endow us with immortality, justify us through the resurrection, uplift us through the ascension, and, when we have been restored, recreate us through His blood in that grace of the Father from which we departed. He Himself is our ceaseless appeasement[12] in the presence of the Father, appealing to His kindness, "Father, I do not pray for these alone, but for them also

---

2.23

[1] Another example of Ruricius' fascination with illness.

[2] For the same theme, see *Epist.* 2.21 to Capillutus and 2.32 to Agricola of Clermont.

[3] Hebrews 12.6-7.

[4] *habenis*: edd.; *habens*: S.

[5] *quam*: added by editors.

[6] *pater familias*, the traditional Roman term for the male head of the household.

[7] *male prodigo*: edd.; *male pro*: S[1]; *malo pro*: S[2].

[8] Luke 15.11-32; cf. *Epist.* 1.1, 2.58.

[9] *verum*: edd.; *veruerum*: S.

[10] *nominum.*

[11] Cf. Hebrews 1.1.

[12] *propitiatio.* Cf. 1 John 2.2.

who shall believe in Me through their words. Father, I wish that wherever I am, they also might be with Me. Father, forgive them, for they know not what they do."[13] He Himself proclaimed daily through His apostle, "Love not the world, nor the things that are in the world. If any one loves the world, the love of the Father is not in him. For all that is in the world, the lust of the flesh, and the lust of the eyes, and the pride of life, this is not of the Father, but is of the world. And the world passes away, along with its lust, but one who does the will of God abides forever,"[14] just as God abides forever.

He Himself in the Gospel invites with cajolery, encourages with blessings, sollicits us with exhortation,[15] saying, "Come to me all who labor and are heavy laden,"[16] and the rest,[17] so that submitting to his salutary precepts, as if to a yoke,[18] we might harness[19] our necks to His salutary chariot and in this way we might dare to follow Him who summons, to hear Him who proclaims, and not to spurn now Him who cajoles, lest we later experience Him who judges. In this judgment, just as He Himself deigned to foretell and instruct in the Gospel, "When He shall sit in His own seat of majesty,"[20] when He will not only weigh one's merits and deeds,[21] but even will assess one's words and wishes: one whom He now sees to neglect His salutary precepts and, with a proud spirit, disdain His must salubrious admonitions, He not only will exclude, along with the witless, from the door of the heavenly kingdom, but He also will sentence this person to the lot of the faithless, so that he might share eternity with those whose company he shared in this world.

2.24 [ca. 495/500]

In the following two letters Ruricius takes his son Constantius to task for irresponsibility and attempts to recall him to his duty. Constantius' devotion to popular forms of entertainment seems to have caused his otherwise indulgent father some distress. Because Ruricius calls himself "bishop," the letter must have been written after ca. 485; and like the other letters in this section, it may have been written after ca. 495, but perhaps not by much. Constantius, although addressed as a young man, apparently is living in his own household. He may be the unnamed son mentioned in *Epist.* 2.1-2 and 2.4 who married a daughter of

---

[13] John 17.20,24; Luke 23.34.
[14] 1 John 2.15-17.
[15] *adhortatione*: edd.; *adoratione*: S.
[16] Matthew 11.28.
[17] "et reliqua."
[18] *iugo*: Engelbrecht; *iugum*: S.
[19] *subiungamus*: Engelbrecht; *subiungemus*: S[1]; *subiungimus*: S[2]; *subiugemus*: Krusch, Mommsen.
[20] Matthew 19.28.
[21] Cf. *Epist.* 2.17.

Namatius and Ceraunia (see Introduction). His proximity to Briva may indicate
that he resided on the family's property at Gurdo/Decaniacum.

BISHOP RURICIUS TO HIS SON CONSTANTIUS

Even though I know that you are given to Bacchus, serenades, and diverse
musical activities, and in fact even to girls' choruses,[1] nevertheless, because
while adolescence mightily seethes[2] it is good occasionally to retreat from such
things and to spend time more with the Lord than with Liber, and to pay attention to parents rather than to melodies, I direct that tomorrow, which will be the
fourth celebration,[3] you hasten to fast with me at Briva,[4] and in a timely manner, which I do not at all think that you are planning to do.

2.25 [ca. 495/500]

This letter suggests that Ruricius' complaints had gone for nought, and that he
himself was indulgently supporting Constantius' life of ease.

2.24

[1] Such activities were attested, and specifically prohibited to clerics, at the Council of Agde: "nor
are they to be present at those gatherings where amorous and bawdy tunes are sung, or where
obscene motions of bodies are presented by choruses and dancing" (can.39: *CCL* 148.209-210).
[2] "pervalde fervet adulescentia"; cf. *Epist.* 2.17, where "adulescentiae regnet cupido" even in
mature people.
[3] *quarta feria*: in general, Wednesday, the fourth (counting inclusively) day after Sunday; and, in
particular, after Easter each day had its own liturgy, viz. "Legenda feria IV paschae" (*MGall* 40:
PL 71.201); "Item missa paschalis, quarta feria" (*MGoth* 40: ibid. p.281). If this was an Easter
service, Constantius' revelry would have been all the more reprehensible in Ruricius' eyes.
[4] The *vicus* of Briva Curretia (Brive-la-Gaillarde) lay in the territory of Limoges to the south-
south-west of the city on the Corrèze river just east of its confluence with the Vézere, where the
road from Limoges to Cahors crossed that from Clermont to Périgueux. In imperial times it was
a center of ceramic production, and it later boasted the cult of a Spanish St. Martin, believed to
have been a disciple of Martin of Tours: see Gregory of Tours, *HF* 7.10; and M. Gady, "Saint
Martin martyr de Brive," *BSSHAC* 68 (1946) pp.46-70. The late fifth-century church of St.
Martin, presumably the one to which Ruricius invited Constantius, was quite small, measuring
only about five by eleven meters. In 584, Gundovald was proclaimed king there and the church
was burned, but it was soon rebuilt by bishop Ferreolus of Limoges; extant column fragments of
white marble from St-Béat (cf. *Epist.* 2.64) have been found in the existing church of St. Martin
and may date to this reconstruction. A chalice supposedly was dedicated to Martin by Valentinian III (425-455) inscribed, "VALENTINIANUS AUGUSTUS DEO ET SANCTO MARTINO
MARTYRI BRIVENSI VOVIT ET REDDIDIT": see Le Blant, *ICG* 2 (1865) p.344. A solidus
of Valentinian III was discovered at Brive in 1907; a gold coin of Majorian (457-461) and a
gold hoard dating to the reign of Honorius (395-423) also have been found; all attest to continued vitality of the place at the end of the Roman period. It served as a mint during Merovingian
times. See *CAG* 19, pp.70-77.

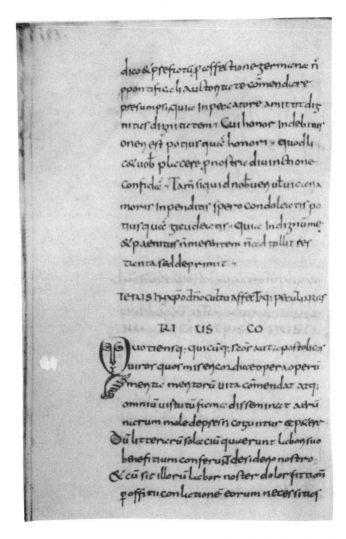

Fig.5: The *Codex Sangallensis* 190, p.183. The end of *Epist.* 2.7 to Elaphius, and the beginning of *Epist.* 2.8 to Aeonius of Arles. The elaborate salutation reads, with Aeonius' name misspelled, "D[omi]no s[an]c[t]o et apostolico ac mihi prae ce I teris in Xp[ist]o d[omi]no cultu affectuq[ue] peculiarius I excolendo patrono et papae Aenio I Ruricius episcopus." The first three lines are in alternating red and black ink, and in the fourth, alternating pairs of letters are in red and black. The ornate letter "Q" that begins the text is typical. See p.145 above. Reproduced by permission of the Stifts-bibliothek, St. Gallen.

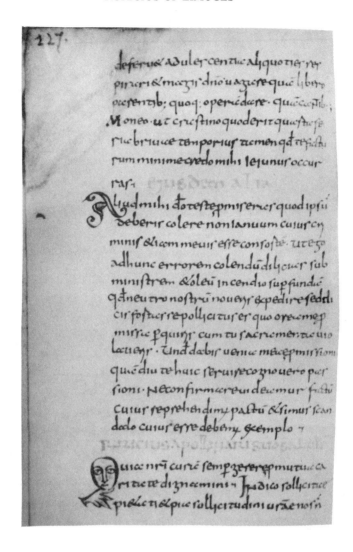

Fig.6: The *Codex Sangallensis* 190, p.227. The end of *Epist.* 2.24 to Constantius; followed by the complete text of *Epist.* 2.25, likewise to Constantius, as indicated by the heading "eiusdem alia" ("Another of the same person"). At the bottom is the beginning of *Epist.* 2.26 to Apollinaris, with the salutation "Ruricius Apollinari suo salute[m]" ("Ruricius to his Apollinaris, Greetings"). It begins with the same kind of ornate latter "Q" as *Epist.* 2.8 (see Fig.5). See p.180 above. Reproduced by permission of the Stiftsbibliothek, St. Gallen.

ANOTHER OF THE SAME PERSON

[Bishop Ruricius to his Son Constantius][1]

With God as your witness, you promised me something different, that you would worwhip Him, not Iacchus; you even want me to be a participant in this crime, so that I would provide delicacies for the cultivation of this error and pour oil on the fire, which you know would benefit neither of us. But perhaps you say, "You promised."[2] With what effrontery do you seek that promised by me, when you have violated your own oaths? Whence you will grant discharge to my promise, as long as I know that you serve your own appetite, lest I seem to encourage the activity, whose manner I rebuked, and lest I serve as an stumbling-block for one to whom I should be an example.

2.26 [ca. 502?]

Apollinaris (*PLRE II*, p.114) was the son of Sidonius Apollinaris, from whom he received *Epist.* 3.13. He also received *Epist.* 2.27 and 2.41 from Ruricius, and *Epist.* 43 and 51 from Avitus of Vienne. He fought on the Visigothic side in 507 at the battle of Vouillé (Gregory of Tours, *HF* 2.37), and in 515 became bishop of Clermont (Duchesne, *Fastes* 2.35), dying only four months later. This letter concerns a copy of some of Sidonius' writings that Apollinaris had sent to Ruricius to review, although it is unclear what they were. Sidonius already had edited and circulated his poems and letters, so perhaps Apollinaris had made a new edition. Or perhaps this was a selection of Sidonius' letters, such as the 27 listed in the index of the *Codex Sangallensis* 190. But a more intriguing possibility is that the work being discussed is some other now-lost work of Sidonius, such as the "masses that he composed" (Gregory of Tours, *HF* 2.22), some of which may survive in the so-called "Eusebian corpus" of sermons. An edition of something other than the readily available letters or poems might explain why Apollinaris had to borrow something written by his own father from Ruricius, and, given Ruricius' praise for Sidonius' preaching (*Epist.* 1.8), it would not be surprising if Sidonius had sent his protégé a sample. The next four letters all were sent to Clermont, apparently at about the same time, and the next six letters have the same form of salutation, "Ruricius ... suo salutem," the preferred form of Sidonius, suggesting not only that Ruricius had Sidonius on his mind, but also that they were written at about the same time. Several considerations, such as the implication that Sidonius had been dead for some time, place these letters in the early years of the sixth century.

2.25

[1] The salutation is reconstructed from the previous letter.

[2] Ruricius apparently had promised money to Constantius.

RURICIUS TO HIS APOLLINARIS, GREETINGS

Because you always deign to take concern for me because of our mutual affection, I report to your solicitous piety and to your pious solicitude[1] that, having returned from you,[2] I have undertaken[3] an enterprise that, although it is
not at all trivial, is yet, God willing, pleasurable. This project could be particularly profitable for me if either my intellect is equal to my intention or my talent
is equal to my intellect. Even a blind man, without any justification, awaits the
rising of the sun, which, indeed, always rises for the sighted, but whose radiance[4] is always concealed from the non-seeing as if by clouds. I have in fact
received to be read our lord and shared father Sollius,[5] which I said that I gave
to Your Exaltedness to be transcribed.[6] Just as reading him restores my past
affection for him, it likewise, because of the obscurity of his locutions,[7] does
not fire my own talent: let us awaken, if you please, with its own sparks and
with puffing breaths, this little flicker of love itself, which is glowing, so to
speak, in the midst of the embers of forgetfulness after so great a space of lengthy time[8] and let us sometimes drench it with sweet tears,[9] whereby, soaked by
this shower, the more that flicker is moistened the more it flares up, because
flames erupt, rather than subside, through an abundance of tears and desires and
affection. I hasten, therefore, if the Lord will grant support to your dutiful di-
rective,[10] to examine this work, created in your presence,[11] and to change
from a teacher into a pupil, because it is not shameful[12] for me at this age nor
is it an annoyance to exercise the industry of a pupil so long as I gain the mas-

---

2.26

[1] The rhetorical figure of *chiasmus*.

[2] Perhaps the same trip mentioned in *Epist.* 2.28 to Ommatius.

[3] *reversos sumpsisse*: Engelbrecht, Demeulenaere; *reversu/sumsisse*: S[1]; *reversum sumsisse*: S[2];
reversum sumpsisse: edd.

[4] *iubar*: edd.; *iubari*: S.

[5] That is, Gaius Sollius Apollinaris Sidonius. Only one's intimates used one's first names.

[6] "quem transcribendum sublimitati vestrae dedisse me dixeram, legendum recepi." It seems that
Ruricius has received back from Apollinaris a copy of something written by Sidonius that he had
lent him to copy, and that Ruricius now proposes to read, or proof-read, it himself.

[7] "prae obscuritate dictorum": a candid, and valid, admission by Ruricius that Sidonius was not
always easy to follow.

[8] An indication that this letter was written some time after Sidonius' death, which seems to have
occurred in the mid 480s.

[9] *flatibus ... fletibus*.

[10] "piae definitioni vestrae"; Engelbrecht and Demeulenaere suggest "nostrae." Ruricius seems to
be referring to Apollinaris' request that he review the text.

[11] That is, written by Sidonius when Apollinaris was young.

[12] *pudet*: edd.; *putet*: S.

tery of a chosen[13] discipline. Indeed, anyone at all ought to learn before teaching, because one too quickly[14] adopts the haughtiness of the scholar unless one initially has endured the servitude of the student. What, indeed, is more just than that you should be the interpreter of the paternal eloquence,[15] you who can produce everything that he wrote not so much from the leaves of a book[16] as from the pages of your heart? You confirm that you[17] are his son not only by the generosity of your birth, but in particular both by the flower of your eloquence and by every kind of virtue. You have been endowed with these goodnesses not so much by instruction as by nature, because a stream bursting forth from a fountain, even if it advances by flowing and acquires fullness by flooding, nevertheless also owes its merit to the source from which it receives its name.[18] If the Divine Clemency had permitted him to survive all the way to the present time, just as he once took pleasure in your imitation,[19] thus now he would rejoice in your perfection, because he would see that his hopes had been fulfilled, nor would he envy as an equal one who he had hoped would be his better.

2.27 [ca. 502]

A brief note complaining about Apollinaris' failure to write.

LIKEWISE, ANOTHER OF THE SAME SORT

[Ruricius to His Apollinaris, Greetings][1]

Although I did not merit the receipt, through the deacon Justus,[2] of a letter from your kind heart and your eloquent mouth with which my intellect might have been enlightened and my desire satiated, I, who prefer to be considered a pretentious rustic rather than an impious sophisticate, nonetheless have not permitted[3] this opportunity to be lost for me to write, inasmuch as I am one who

---

[13] *affectatae*: edd.; *affecta te*: S.

[14] *praepropere*: edd.; *praeponere*: S.

[15] For Apollinaris as the literary heir of Sidonius, see also Avitus of Vienne, *Epist*. 43.

[16] "de codicis membrana": a parchment book, as opposed to a papyrus one, such as that mentioned by Taurentius (*Epist*. "Litterae sanctitatis" above).

[17] *vos*: edd.; *nos*: S.

[18] This exemplifies the commonplace that literary ability, like other talents, was inherited.

[19] See, e.g., Sid.Apoll. *Epist*. 4.12.1-2, for Apollinaris' study of Terence with Sidonius.

2.27

[1] Hypothetically reconstructed from the previous letter.

[2] Possibly the Justus who was the physician to Sidonius' children (Sid.Apoll. *Epist*. 2.12.3).

[3] *passus sum*: edd.; *passum*: S.

would not wish[4] to lose, I would not say the opportunity of writing, but even of seeing you for the space of just a single hour. And therefore I send my warmest greetings, and ask that you deign always to honor me when the opportunity for writing is extended, avoiding mutual anguish, and to the advantage of us both, because you do not expend what you grant to me in affection, you do not lose what you bestow, and you shall retain in your heart whatever you forward to me in your letter.

2.28 [ca. 502]

This letter was written after Ruricius' had returned from a visit to Clermont, perhaps at the same time as *Epist.* 2.26. Ommatius had adopted the religious life (see *Epist.* 1.18) and risen to the office of *presbyter* (priest).

RURICIUS TO HIS OMMATIUS, GREETINGS

I departed <from>[1] Your Piety in such a manner that I have not withdrawn from you within. I maintained you in the same part of the human interior in which I remained for you. I know that I remained there, whence neither an ancient plotter nor a new counsellor[2] could exclude me. For this reason, I indeed admonish you with this observation of the most wise Solomon, "Son, do not abandon your old friend, indeed, a new one will not be like him. A new friend is new wine; when it has aged,[3] you may drink it with pleasure."[4] And therefore let us grow old[5] in our friendship and from day to day let us be renewed through our affections. And if a friend is not to be abandoned, by how much more not a father, who taught you,[6] who nourished you, who with the help of the Lord brought you all the way to the priesthood,[7] to whom is owed, perhaps, even the enjoyment of the light, according to the divine pity.

But I[8] write this to Your Beatitude[9] not, so to speak, blaming you for anything or finding fault, but as to a dearest son, whom I want to walk in this

---

[4] *nolim*: edd.; *inolli*: S.

2.28

[1] *a*: added by editors.

[2] *consiliator*: S; *conciliator*: Engelbrecht, Demeulenaere. These are probably references to Satan.

[3] *veterascet*: *Vulgate*, Engelbrecht, Demeulenaere; *veteriscat*: S; *veterescat*: Krusch.

[4] Ecclesiastes 9.14-15.

[5] *veterascamus*: Engelbrecht, Demeulenaere; *veteriscamus*: S; *veterescamus*: Krusch.

[6] Ruricius, therefore, undertook Ommatius' education, at least in his early years.

[7] "ad sacerdotium," presumably the office of *presbyter* (priest), a senior position that ranked just below bishop. Ruricius' wording suggests that he was taking credit for Ommatius' appointment which, however, probably owed at least as much to the influence of Hiberia's family.

[8] *ego*: edd.; *ergo*: S.

[9] The *vestra pietas* at the beginning can be contrasted with the more intimate *tua beatitudo* here.

world without any blemish of impiety, and to appear both pure and immaculate on that day of judgment in the presence of God and His angels and the congregation of all the flesh. I therefore greet Your Single-Mindedness and ask that you deign to pray for me, and, at the same time, when you have the chance, that you consider it important[10] to visit me. Farewell.[11]

2.29 [ca. 502]

The next three letters all relate to episcopal consultations. Like the previous one, this one to Euphrasius, who also received *Epist.* 2.22, was sent to Clermont.

RURICIUS TO HIS EUPHRASIUS, GREETINGS

I marvel that Your Sanctity,[1] after seeking the judgments rather than the replies[2] of so many and such great[3] men, seeks even the opinion of My Ignorance. Which I surmise that you have done more because of our relationship[4] than because of necessity, lest you seem to have passed over in a professional matter the opinion of one whose well-being you deem it particularly important to keep in mind. Whence I give thanks to Your Brotherhood,[5] inseparable for me in Christ, that you deign to judge and presume thus about me, so that we shall have nothing guileful, in the simplicity of love, or disguised,[6] in the purity of truth. I render, therefore, the due obligation of compliance, and regarding the matter about which you deign to write to me, I declare that I feel the same as our brothers.[7] But, as to what the actual need is or what in particular seems to me ought to be done, I have in good faith disclosed verbally through your deacon that which is too lengthy[8] to be explained in a letter.[9] Pray for me.[10]

---

[10] "tanti habeatis."

[11] *vale*: one of only two times (the other being *Epist.*2.30) that Ruricius uses this traditional form of farewell salutation. The manuscript is damaged in the margin here, and the words "saluto ... pro ... opportunum ... vale" appear only as "s||||| ... p|| ... opportun|| ... val|."

2.29

[1] *sanctitatem*: edd.; *sanitatem*: S.

[2] *rescripta*: technically, rescripts were replies written at the bottom of petitions and then returned to the sender.

[3] *talium*: edd.; *alium*: S.

[4] *necessitudine*: edd.; *necessitate*: S; parallel to the *necessitate* that follows.

[5] *germanitati vestrae*; this, and the preceding reference to *necessitas*, suggest that a blood relationship of some degree existed between the two.

[6] *fucatum*: edd.; *fugatum*: S.

[7] That is other bishops, suggesting some ecclesiastical matter was concerned. Clermont and Limoges were in the same ecclesiastical province, so perhaps an episcopal election was at issue.

[8] *longum*: edd.; /////m: S.

[9] "verbo ... intimavi, quae longum fuit litteris indicari"; repeated in the next letter, with "manda-

2.30 [ca. 502?]

Heraclianus probably was the bishop of Toulouse who attended the Council of Agde in 506 (Duchesne, *Fastes* 1.307); another Heraclianus was buried at Auch, next to bishop Orientius, in the sixth year of an unidentified king (*CIL* 13.498). In this case, it is of no moment that Ruricius does not address Heraclianus as "bishop," for he used a similar salutation in the previous letter to Euphrasius, who certainly was a bishop. The salutation form could suggest, however, that this letter was written at about the same time as the others in this section, when Ruricius' was using the Sidonian form of greeting. Here, Ruricius belatedly writes on a matter as mysterious as that of the previous letter.

RURICIUS[1] TO HIS HERACLIANUS, GREETINGS

He who knows himself to be culpable with regard to his duty ought to supplicate before he dares to salute, because, just as there is resistance against one who rudely[2] reproaches, there likewise is exoneration for one who courteously confesses. And therefore I place my sin in the open, so that I might more easily come to pardon, because no place is left for reproach when an entrance for a remorseful one lies open, according to that observation, "Recount first your iniquities so you might be justified."[3] Nor, indeed, will the antipathy of the accuser prevail when anticipated by the humility of the suppliant. For this reason, if I now have atoned for my fault by my apology, let me come to be judged. I therefore offer as much of a greeting to Your Piety as affection can comprehend but speech cannot pronounce,[4] as much as I feel but have not the ability to express, as much as the mind of the interior man can conceive when its desire has been aroused but the tongue of the exterior man cannot convey.

In this regard, giving thanks to the author of this very love, who deigned to insert it into our hearts, let us pray that He will deign always to safeguard and constantly to augment the special gift of his generosity in us, because according to the apostle Paul, the road that leads to life is more exalted. For the rest, I particularly petition that you pray daily to our common patron on my behalf, because, as you read, "The prayer of a righteous man has great power in its ef-

---

vi" for "intimavi."

[10] "ora pro me": six of the next twelve letters use this Sidonian form of farewell; otherwise, its only use is in *Epist.* 2.22, also to Euphrasius, which confirms the association with Clermont.

2.30

[1] *Ruricius*: edd.; ///*icius*: S.

[2] *inportune*; repeated at the end of the letter.

[3] Isaiah 43.25-26.

[4] Cf. Jerome, *Epist.* 130.6.1: *CSEL* 56.181.

fects,"[5] and just as our Lord Himself said in the Gospels[6] about the one who rudely but salubriously <sought>[7] three loaves of bread from his friend at night, what was denied to a demanding friendship was granted to an insistent troublesomeness. I have verbally entrusted the rest,[8] which would take too long to explain in writing, to the bearer; therefore, as noted at the beginning of my letter, I ask that you deign to pardon me for my tardiness.[9] Farewell.

2.31 [502]

> In this letter, Ruricius is consulted by Capillutus regarding the election of Caesarius as bishop of Arles at some point after the death of Aeonius in 502 (see Krusch, *MGH AA* 8.422). The election was very contentious, as indicated by Ruricius' references to "falsity," "perdition," "discord," "cupidity," and "rapine," and it even appears that a certain Johannes briefly held the see before being replaced by Caesarius (see Mathisen, *Factionalism*, p.276 n.9). The nature of Ruricius' involvement is unclear, but as seen in the correspondence with Aeonius (*Epist.* 1.15, 2.8-9), he did have interests and perhaps influence in Arles. If the consultation involved Caesarius' election, then Ruricius' comment to him in *Epist.* 2.33 about how he used to "merit being courted" would have been most pertinent. Ruricius' enthusiasm over the choice seems somewhat muted.

BISHOP RURICIUS TO HIS SON CAPILLUTUS, GREETINGS

I give thanks to Your Piety because you deign to consult with[1] me about the ordination in your city[2] even though, with the favor of God, you are able to act on your own fully and sufficiently. And therefore, because he who pleases you and your brothers[3] ought not to displease me, you do well to ordain a man whom common consensus selects. But admonish him to cultivate truth, not falsehood; peace, not perdition; discipline, not discord; the public good, not private greed; justice, not rapine. Let him safeguard the good and emend the culpable, let him protect the miserable not create them, let him reform the guilty and defend the innocent, acting in such a way that he shall be able to be more suitable for the future judgment rather than the present one.

---

[5] James 5.16.

[6] Cf. Luke 11.5-8.

[7] A word is missing, perhaps *petiit* (Mommsen).

[8] "The rest," of course, being the heart of the matter. Cf. the previous letter; perhaps both discussions concerned the same matter.

[9] *tarditate*: edd.; *tardita*: S.

2.31

[1] *consolare*: S, edd.; *consulere*: Canisius; cf. *Epist.* 2.58.

[2] *civitatis*: S, edd.; *antistitis*: Lütjohann; *civis talis*: Mommsen.

[3] "fratribus vestris"; cf. *Epist.* 2.29, "fratres nostros."

2.32 [ca. 502/506 or later]

Agricola was the son of the emperor Avitus (455-456) and the brother of Papianilla, who was herself the wife of Sidonius Apollinaris, from whom he received
two letters (*Epist.* 1.2, 2.12). His daughter Papianilla married Parthenius, the
grandson of Ruricius (see Introduction; *PLRE II*, pp.830, 833-834; and Mathisen,
"Epistolography," pp.102-103). Here, Ruricius provides another example of his
fixation on illness, followed by an exhortation on the value of adopting the religious life.

BISHOP RURICIUS TO HIS ILLUSTRIOUS[1] LORD AND ALWAYS MAGNIFICENT
SON, AGRICOLA

After I read the letter of Your Exaltedness I gave thanks to God because,
through its ordered arrangement, I learned that you had recovered before I knew
that you had been ill,[2] so that[3] it forestalled anxiety for me and yielded good
health for you. I conjecture, nevertheless, that this infirmity was imposed bene-
volently upon you by our Lord Himself, favorable rather than angry,[4] in accordance with His accustomed graciousness. Thus indeed we read that "the Lord
disciplines him whom He loves and chastises every son whom He receives."[5]
This is demonstrated in you, as I hear, so that, when your feelings were composed, His feeling penetrated into you, and after your apparel and attitude had
changed,[6] He imposed the yoke of his gentleness upon you, so that, submitting
your neck to His wholesome chariot,[7] you discard the heavy load of your sins
as you lightly bear the burden of His precepts.

Indeed, "This is the changing of the right hand of the Most High,"[8] when
He deigns to make for Himself just men from sinners, natives from foreigners,
and friends from slaves. It now remains to certify in your heart the conversion
that you profess in your garb,[9] and that this change in your clothing be felt also

---

2.32

[1] *inlustri*: unlike many of Ruricius' honorifics, this represents a formal title, that of *vir inlustris*,
the highest normal aristocratic rank.

[2] "Relictis litteris sublimitatis vestrae gratias Deo egi, quod vos prius revaluisse ordinatione
ipsius, quam infirmatos esse cognovi": cf. *Epist.* 2.23 to Verus, "Relictis litteris pietatis vestrae
gratias Deo egi, quod vos prius revaluisse quam infirmatos esse earum relatione cognovi."

[3] *ut*: edd.; *et*: S.

[4] For the same theme of illness as a blessing in disguise, see *Epist.* 2.21 to Capillutus and *Epist.*
2.23 to Verus.

[5] Hebrews 12.6.

[6] *animoque mutato*: edd.; *animo quae mutatu*: S.

[7] *currui*: edd.; *curui*: S.

[8] Psalms 76.11.

[9] It seems, therefore, that Agricola has in fact become a penitent, perhaps convinced to do so by

in your spirit, so that, just as until now it had blackness under its white garments, now it might shine by the light of its deeds under charcoal vestments.[10] Indeed, the sinner will weep on the day he is converted; then he will be saved, as long as, according to the saying of the sanctified apostle Paul,[11] just as we demonstrated hitherto that our bodies served the world and iniquity for the sake of iniquity, thus we now show that our members serve justice in sanctification; nor, fearing God, should we be,[12] so to speak, flaunting one thing with our words while having something different in our character, displaying one thing by our garments and endorsing something different in our deeds,[13] lest that utterance of the Lord rend us if we conceal the savagery of wolves under the skin of lambs, because that divine eye, as it is written, spies out good and evil men everywhere, and without doubt, with regard to one whom it sees crossing over to itself whole-heartedly, it itself descends into the heart of that person in a perpetual occupancy, so that one who has prepared himself as a little dwelling shall not lack this dweller within. Therefore, for His such indescribable goodness let us jointly render thanks to our Lord, who prefers to instruct His servants rather than to destroy them, to correct rather than to punish, and to grant a kingdom of perpetuity[14] in exchange for the temporary enjoyment[15] of a short life.

For the rest, I greet especially and commend to you with personal regard your maiden[16] — even though, thanks to your own saving piety, she does not stand in need of this — so that, to the extent that[17] you considered it worthwhile to receive her with affection, you may always cherish her with permissiveness, she who by divine generosity has made us both subservient to herself, making you grandparents and us great-grandparents[18] by her fruitfulness.[19]

---

his illness.

[10] *sub pullibus vestibus*: the muted apparel of penitents, also used for mourning garb.

[11] Cf. Romans 6.19.

[12] *simus*: edd.; *scimus*: S.

[13] For this theme, see Faustus' letter "Admiranda mihi" to Paulinus in Appendix I below.

[14] *perpetuitatis*: edd.; *perpetatis*: S.

[15] *usura*.

[16] "ancillam vestram vobis peculiari insinuatione commendo": it once was assumed that this young woman was an otherwise unknown daughter of Ruricius who was married to Agricola. But if this were the case, Ruricius most likely would have said "ancillam nostram." And Ruricius was in fact related to Agricola through the marriage of his grandson Parthenius to Agricola's daughter Papianilla (*Epist.* 2.36-37; see Introduction), and it is she to whom this passage refers.

[17] *quo eam*: edd.; *coeam*: S.

[18] "nos proavos": if this is a true plural, then it would indicate that Ruricius' wife Hiberia was still alive.

[19] For discussion of these relationships, see Introduction.

I bless my lady daughter[20] with longing and honor, as is fitting. For the purpose of beholding her, if I had the ability to get about,[21] my will to see you would be most immediate, so that I also could regard her with my exterior eyes, she whom I gaze upon with my interior eyes through the memory of our bond, for the sake of the intimacy of our very affinity.[22] I trust that you are doing well.[23]

Caesarius of Arles, *Epistula* "Dum nimium" (*SG* no.14)[1] [Autumn, 506]

Caesarius rebukes Ruricius for not attending the Council of Agde on 10 September 506, and advises him of plans for another council, at Toulouse, the following year. This and several of the subsequent letters date to ca. 506 and concern three bishops of Provence: Caesarius of Arles, Sedatus of Nîmes, and Victorinus of Fréjus. Text: *CCL* 64.402-403; *CSEL* 21. 448-449; *MGH AA* 8.274-275; Morin, *Caesarii* 2.6-7. Additional translation: W. Klingshirn tr., *Caesarius of Arles: Life, Testament, Letters* (Liverpool, 1994) pp.83-84.

BISHOP CAESARIUS TO A SANCTIFIED LORD, MOST DESERVING, TO BE PREFERRED AMONG THE LUMINARIES OF CHRIST AND ESPECIALLY TO BE DESIRED IN CHRIST, THE MOST PIOUS LORD BISHOP RURICIUS

At the time that my spirit was excessively troubled as to why we did not merit your presence at the synod, my sanctified lord the bishop Verus[2] deigned to mention to me that he had sent your letter[3] with his deacon on to me at Agde,[4] which I maintain that, through some misfortune or negligence, I did not

---

[20] "domnam filiam meam ... sospito": not the "ancilla," who already had been acknowledged, but Agricola's wife: cf. Faustus of Riez, *Epist.* "Gratias domino," "domnam filiam meam ... saluto," referring to Ruricius' wife Hiberia.

[21] *ambulandi*: another indication of Ruricius' poor health, and an indication that this letter was one of the latest in the collection.

[22] *adfinitatis*, referring to a relationship by marriage, and appropriate, therefore, in referring to Agricola's wife.

[23] "obto bene agatis": a typically secular form of farewell otherwise used by Ruricius only in *Epist.* 2.37 and 2.39. Canisius, Krusch, Engelbrecht, and Demeulenaere all wrongly read "opto bene agas"; but see Fig.9. The use of the plural would indicate, again, that Agricola's wife was being addressed as well.

Caesarius of Arles, "Dum nimium"

[1] Letters 12-13 in this group in the *Sangallensis* are by Faustus of Riez, viz. "Quaeris a me" and the letter to Paulinus. Their insertion in the midst of the letters to Ruricius suggests, again, that Ruricius preserved some of the letters of Faustus to other individuals.

[2] Verus, like his predecessor Volusianus, had been exiled from Tours after being accused of collusion with the Franks (Gregory of Tours, *HF* 10.31). He eventually died in exile. He may be the Verus who received Ruricius' *Epist.* 2.23.

[3] This letter of Ruricius does not survive.

[4] Verus had sent his deacon Leo to represent him (*CCL* 148.214-219), and this presumably is the

receive. But nevertheless, I most certainly believe my sanctified lord,[5] your brother, and I prefer to attribute this [misfortune] to the negligence of the carrier. But, although you did send your holy and desirable words, nevertheless, as you yourself well know, it would have been most proper if you had sent a representative who would have subscribed in your place and who would have confirmed, as your representative, what your holy brothers decreed.[6]

But because I knew how much, with holy and constant and pious desire, that you wished to be present,[7] I made clear your prayer and holy will to all your brothers, in consideration of which we either can or ought to cast no blame upon Your Piety. But, although we did not have your desirable presence, we felt thoroughly that we merited nevertheless the support of your prayers. And therefore, with this letter I convey my best regards with such affection and honor as is fitting and I ask that you commend me to the Lord with your sanctified and illustrious prayers and, likewise, merits. And at the same time I note to Your Piety that,[8] because your son Eudomius[9] desires to work on this, if he is able to arrange it, we also shall have in the upcoming year,[10] if Christ is favorable, a synod at Toulouse, where, if he is able, he also wants to convene the Spanish bishops. And therefore, pray that the Lord may deign to grant the accomplishment[11] of His so[12] holy desire.

I commend, indeed, to Your Holiness, with all the influence I have, my holy and most dear brother, the priest Capillutus,[13] your admirer and glorifier, and I

---

deacon who delivered Ruricius' letter.

[5] That is, Verus.

[6] Poor attendance at councils was a problem. The thirty-fifth canon of Agde specified that after notification, "Let them put everything aside and not delay being present on the determined day, except in case of grave bodily infirmity or royal command..." (*CCL* 148.208). The penalty was excommunication until the next synod. Ruricius would have based his absence on the illness clause (*Epist.* 2.33), and Verus would have been covered by the "royal command" provision.

[7] As Ruricius had told Caesarius at Bordeaux: see the next letter.

[8] *ut*: edd.; *et*: S.

[9] *filius vester*: S, edd; *filius noster*: Demeulenaere, Engelbrecht. The reading *vester* makes it clear that the courtier Eudomius (*PLRE II*, p.409) was one of Ruricius' own parishoners, and that he is to be identified as the Eudomius of *Epist.* 2.39. Nor was Eudomius a bishop, as assumed by Krusch (*MGH AA* 8.lxv), for a bishop would never be referred to as another bishop's *filius* (see Morin, *Caesarii* 2.6).

[10] Consistent with the final canon of Agde, "It is pleasing that a synod be gathered yearly according to the decrees of the fathers" (can.49: *CCL* 148.212). Such rules, however, were often mere wishful thinking. For discussion of this proposed synod, see Introduction.

[11] *dignetur effectum*: Engelbrecht, Demeulenaere; *dignaretur affectum*: S; *dignaretur effectum*: Krusch.

[12] *tam*: edd.; *tamen*: S.

[13] For the messenger Capillutus, now a priest at Arles, see *Epist.* 2.21, 31, 33, 40.

give great and rich thanks to you for his sake because, however much he himself requests, your pious and sincere benevolence applies itself on his behalf,
with a result that no one can describe. Now, therefore, because, aroused by his
desire for you, he has set out to visit Your Piety, I judge it proper to send a letter of My Humility through him, on whose return, Christ willing, I long to be
deserving of your words, like a celestial gift. Pray for me.[14]

2.33 [Autumn, 506]

> Like any aristocratic bishop, Ruricius was sensitive to slights, and no amount of
> subsequent kind words by Caesarius could make up for the initial rebuke. In his
> reply, therefore, Ruricius scored some points of his own. He also noted that he
> had met Caesarius at Bordeaux during the winter of 505/506. He did not reveal
> what the purpose of that trip was, but it may have concerned the deliberations
> preceding the issuance of the *Lex Romana Visigothorum* ("Roman Law of the Vi-
> sigoths") in February, 506 (see Introduction); Ruricius' legal expertise would
> have been particularly valuable. For the text of this letter, see also Caspari, *Cae-
> sarii* 2.6-7. Additional translation: Klingshirn, *Letters*, pp.84-75.

RURICIUS TO BISHOP CAESARIUS, A SANCTIFIED AND APOSTOLIC LORD AND A
BROTHER <TO BE ESTEEMED>[1] SPECIALLY BY ME WITH ALL HONOR AND LOVE

Our brother[2] and fellow-priest Capillutus[3] appeared on this occasion doubly
pleasing to me, both because he himself, long awaited, visited me now, and because he represented for me, through your letter, a certain presence of yourself.
Now that he is returning, I hastened to send these words, through which I reimburse the duty of kindness that is owed to Your Beatitude. As to what you
write, regarding why I did not come to the council[4] as we had discussed,[5] my
illness, not my desire, was the cause. Indeed, you yourself can recollect how
wearied you saw that I was at Bordeaux,[6] and this in the winter, when I nor-

---

[14] "ora pro me": the same kind of Sidonian farewell salutation used by Ruricius at this time.
2.33
[1] *excolendo*: restored from the salutation to *Epist.* 2.36.
[2] Ruricius' reference to Capillutus as *frater* rather than *filius* would have been an indication of
the high esteem in which he was held.
[3] For Capillutus, see also Caesarius, *Epist.* "Dum nimium," and *Epist.* 2.21, 31, 40, which begins
with these same words.
[4] *synodum*: edd.; *sydonum*: S. The Council of Agde.
[5] "sicut conlocutio habuit nostra": at Bordeaux, Ruricius and Caesarius apparently had discussed
Ruricius' projected attendance at Agde; Ruricius' failure to attend, therefore, would have been
doubly dissapointing to Caesarius.
[6] Caesarius was in exile at Bordeaux in 505, and, as seen in this letter, in early 506 as well, after
being charged with treason: see the *Vita Caesarii* 1.21, "in Burdigalensem civitatem est quasi in
exilio relegatus" ("[he was] removed to Bordeaux as if into exile"). Ruricius may have used his

mally am stronger than usual. I, who during summer days am scarcely strong enough to sustain this same chronic infirmity[7] even in my own lodging[8] and in cool places, cannot say that I could have[9] tolerated the scorching heat[10] of that area if I had come. For this reason, I hope all the more that you will deign to pray for me and <if>[11] you wish me to come at another time, as you hint, if God grants me life, you might warn me earlier[12] through your man because I point out that your letters come to me only very late. I ought not to be informed by them later than others, if not for the sake of my dignity, at least for the sake of my age, I who, perhaps, as I might imprudently[13] say, used to merit being courted,[14] because if for others the authority of their cities enhances their name, for me the humbleness[15] of my city does not detract from my authority — if indeed it is much better and much more outstanding to know a city by its bishop than a bishop by his city.[16]

2.34 [ca. 502/506 or later]

Ruricius commends several family members, perhaps Parthenius and Papianilla, to Sedatus of Nîmes (see also *Epist.* 2.18-19, 2.35), in which case this letter would have been sent at the same time as *Epist.* 2.36-37 (qq.vv. for discussion).

---

good offices with the Visigoths to help secure Caesarius' release: see Introduction.

[7] Ruricius' "infirmitas consuetudinaria," whatever it was, was aggravated by summer weather.

[8] *in hospitio meo*; cf. *Epist.* 1.12, *hospitioli mei*: perhaps at Gurdo/Decaniacum (*Epist.*1.7, 2.63).

[9] *quiverim*: S, edd.; *nequiverim*: Demeulenaere, Hagendahl (p.106).

[10] *aestus*: Engelbrecht, Demeulenaere; *coetus*: S, Krusch. If the manuscript readings are retained, Ruricius would be saying, rather impolitely, "I cannot say that I could have borne those meetings in that area if I had come."

[11] *si*: added by Demeulenaere, Engelbrecht.

[12] Ruricius had a point. The September 10 meeting date was earlier than other attested regular southern councils. Note the Councils of Riez (439) on November 18, Orange (441) on November 8, Vaison (442) on November 13, Angers (453) on October 4, Tours (461) on November 18, Epaon (517) on September 15, Carpentras (527) on November 6, Vaison (529) on November 5, and Clermont (535) on November 8. Impromptu councils, held on occasions such as the dedication of a church, however, could meet at anytime, e.g. the Council of Orange, on 3 July 529. Sixth-century Frankish councils, perhaps because of concerns over the weather, often met earlier in the year, e.g. Orléans (511) on July 10, Orléans (533) on June 23, Orléans (538) on May 7, and Orléans (541) on May 14, but Orléans (549) on October 28; note also the Council of Marseille (533) on May 26. Qq.vv. in *CCL* 148-148A.

[13] *minus prudens.*

[14] Perhaps an allusion to Ruricius' advice being sought about Caesarius' own election, see *Epist.* 2.31 above. Ruricius here goes on the offensive in order to cover up his own culpability.

[15] *humilitas*: Ruricius' turn of phrase may reflect an underlying feeling that he deserved better.

[16] Ruricius suggests, quite fittingly, that Caesarius' own stature resulted from the status of his city. Ruricius also may have indicated his pique by the omission of the usual farewell salutation, given that in this section of the corpus farewell salutations generally are included.

BISHOP RURICIUS TO HIS SANCTIFIED AND APOSTOLIC LORD, A PATRON TO BE
PREFERRED BY ME TO OTHERS IN CHRIST THE LORD WITH SPECIAL WORSHIP
AND AFFECTION, BISHOP SEDATUS

Whereas my spirit, thirsting for you, frequently seeks an opportunity for
writing to you, the lord of my heart, once in a while, occupied in lengthy meditation, it discovers a suitable bearer, through whom it might both shatter the
long silences[1] and demand spiritual delicacies for itself, desiring to be sprinkled
with the dew of your tongue. Concerning this thirst, I believe, the sanctified
psalmist used to say, "For you, my soul is like a land without water";[2] it longs
to extinguish the dryness of the body with the temperate intoxication,[3] of
course, of that water, concerning which our Lord in the Gospel deigned to ex-
claim, "If anyone thirsts, let him come to Me and drink. Out of his heart will
flow rivers of living water."[4] Indeed, the Lord himself offered this water to the
Samaritan, that is, to the church gathered from the gentiles, saying, "The water
that I will give him shall become in him a spring of water welling up to eternal
life."[5] If any of the faithful drinks this water, not just with a taste only with
the tip of the tongue, but like an eager guest soaks it up with all the innards of
the spirit, immediately he bursts forth in praise of the omnipotent Lord and begins to belch out what he drank, just as the most blessed evangelist, His disciple, who earned a resting place at the breast of the Lord, quaffed[6] the mysteries
of the celestial kingdom and in that voice, which no one had heard before, ex-
claimed, "In the beginning was the word, and the word was with God, and the
word was God."[7]

This was that word, which, timelessly born from the Father, was created in
time from the mother,[8] so that the creator would come into being, so that a certain portion of humanity[9] would be able to be the fullness of total divinity, and
so that this same portion of humanity might redeem by its passion the fullness
of humanity, while the image of invisible God took[10] the form of a servant, so
that, incapable of suffering He suffered, incapable of capture He was captured,

---

2.34

[1] Ruricius expressed a similar sentiment to Sedatus at the beginning of *Epist.* 2.18.

[2] Psalms 142.6; cf. *Epist.* 2.62.

[3] "sobria ebrietate"; cf. Augustine, *Confessions* 5.13, "sobriam vini ebrietatem", Ruricius' only
identified possible citation of Augustine.

[4] John 7.37-38.

[5] John 4.14.

[6] *haurivit*: Krusch; *aurivit*: S; *audivit*: Engelbrecht.

[7] John 1.1.

[8] That is, the virgin Mary.

[9] That is, Christ.

[10] *fit*: edd.; *sit*: S.

immortal He died, He who destroyed death by perishing, so that He would restore life by rising. But, forgetful of myself, greedy for you, as if conversing with you on such matters and thence burning ardently in desire of you, hastening to quench my thirst as if with a kind of rivulet of affection, pondering inscrutable and inaccessible matters, why do I not consider why I speak, who I am to speak, and with whom I speak? But piety, which affection arouses, will, I trust, give pardon, because "love endures all things."[11]

I offer, therefore, a most fervent greeting to your heart, special to me, and I ask that you deign to pray incessantly for me. And likewise I commend with particular cajolery even a portion of my body, by means of whom I deliver these words to you, so that you might demonstrate how completely you love me by how you treat them.[12] I think that they will be more dear to you because they bear part of me to you with themselves. Whatever affection you deign to expend upon them, know that you confer it upon me, that is, if, according to the sanctified apostle, the least member shares in suffering with the greatest,[13] and the greatest doubtless rejoices in the well-being of the least. And thus, it ultimately happens that when all the members are settled unceasingly in peace and quiet, the head, as the guide and ruler[14] of the whole body, rejoices. All the members of the body are instructed to observe by means of the head, with the prophet saying, "The eyes of a wise man are in his head,"[15] which another prophet clearly explained, saying, "My eyes are always on the Lord, because He plucked my feet from the snare,"[16] and again, "I lifted my eyes to You, who dwell in heaven."[17]

Therefore, let us direct the eyes of our heart to Christ and, in the night of this world, let us lift up our hands to the Lord in fruitful works and may He Himself deem it suitable to be our head and may we deserve to cling to our head as useful[18] members of His body, so that, departing from this age as if in the exodus[19] of Israel from Egypt, we might be able to say to our redeemer, "My soul clings to You, Your right hand upholds me,"[20] because it meditated in the prison of this body for days and nights, so that it would not be shamed once it was led forth. Pray for me.

---

[11] 1 Corinthians 13.7.

[12] Perhaps Ruricius' grandson Parthenius and his wife Papianilla; see also *Epist.* 2.36.

[13] 1 Corinthians 12.26.

[14] *dominator*: edd.; *donator*: S.

[15] Ecclesiastes 2.14; cf. Faustus, *Epist.* "Gratias domino."

[16] Psalms 24.15.

[17] Psalms 122.1.

[18] *utilia*: Engelbrecht, Demeulenaere; *ut ill a*: S; *ut utilia*: Krusch.

[19] *exitu*: S; *in* prefaced by Lütjohann, Engelbrecht, Demeulenaere.

[20] Psalms 62.9.

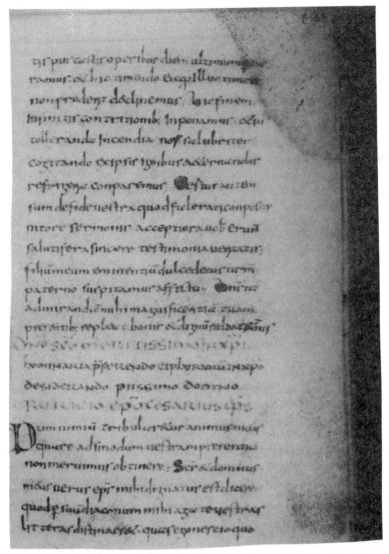

Fig.7: The *Codex Sangallensis* 190, p.126. The end of Faustus of Riez' letter "Admiranda mihi" to Paulinus of Bordeaux; and the beginning of Caesarius of Arles' letter "Dum nimium" to Ruricius. Caesarius' elaborate salutation reads "D[omi]no s[an]c[t]o meritissimo in Xp[ist]i I luminaria p[rae]ferendo et plurimu[m] in xp[ist]o I desiderando piissimo domno I Ruricio ep[iscop]o C(a)esarius ep[iscopu]s," and begins and ends with a line in red. See p.192 above. Reproduced by permission of the Stiftsbibliothek, St. Gallen.

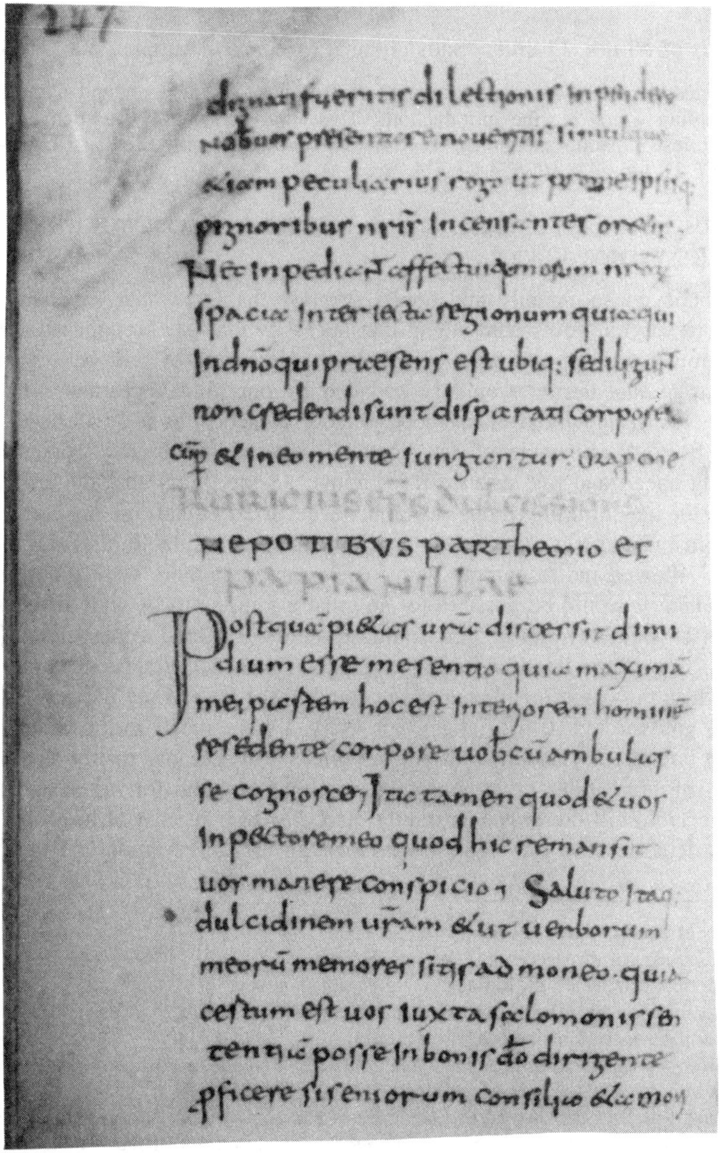

Fig.8: The *Codex Sangallensis* 190, p.247. The end of *Epist.* 2.36 to Caesarius, with the farewell salutation "ora p[ro] me" ("pray for me"); followed by nearly the entire text of *Epist.* 2.37 to Parthenius and Papianilla, with the salutation, "Ruricius ep[iscopu]s dulcissimis | nepotibus Parthemio et | Papianillae," with the first and third lines in red ink. See p.204 below. Reproduced by permission of the Stiftsbibliothek, St. Gallen.

Sedatus of Nîmes, *Epistula* "Satis credidi" (*SG* no.9) [Autumn, 506]

Sedatus expresses his disappointment at Ruricius' failure to attend a meeting, regarding which see the Introduction. This letter presumably was delivered by the priest Palladius mentioned in Ruricius' following reply. Text: *CCL* 64.400; *CSEL* 21.446-447; *MGH AA* 8.274-275.

SEDATUS TO A SANCTIFIED LORD AND POPE TO BE RECEIVED WITH AN APOSTOLIC REVERENCE, RURICIUS

I believed sufficiently and hoped strongly that, to whatever extent it was laborious to you, you would attend that necessity that has brought us here,[1] and that through this opportunity I would also be deserving of your benediction and that our mutual desire[2] would be satisfied by our joint appearance; and truly, after I was disappointed in my hope of your presence, as if I had been thrown down from the pinnacle of my hopes, I <feared>[3] both the work that was looming ahead and my absence from home: all the things that the anxiety and sorrow of an unfulfilled hope accumulate occurred equally in my mind. And the Lord only knows that if the opportunities were available or if the infirmity of age[4] allowed me to comply with my desires or if there were transportation[5] with which it would be possible for so great a journey to be undertaken at such a time, I would not return from Toulouse[6] before I earned a most desired benediction from Your Beatitude and that singular charity. But because these considerations that were mentioned above stand in the way of my desires, I beg and exhort you through Christ[7] that Your Piety always recall me to yourself, nor should you allow yourself to diminish your charity because of my delay in fulfilling my obligations or to consign it to oblivion. But, for my sake, just as I am sure you will do, pray incessantly[8] and, however often you have the opportunity, deign to visit with your servant through the conversation of letters.[9]

Sedatus of Nîmes, "Satis credidi"

[1] For discussion of this "necessity," see Introduction.

[2] "desiderium commune"; cf. Ruricius' reply, "communia vota."

[3] At least one word is missing here; Krusch suggests *odi* or *fastidio*.

[4] Here Sedatus uses Ruricius' own stock excuse.

[5] *animalia*. Perhaps Sedatus is letting a hint drop here; if so, the next letter indicates that Ruricius took him up on it.

[6] It seems that after the Council at Agde Sedatus had continued to Toulouse to conduct some kind of protracted business, which he had hoped Ruricius too would attend: see Introduction.

[7] "per Christum vos adiuro"; cf. the "Bee benediction" on pp.1 and 37 of the *Codex Sangallensis* 190, "per ... filium dei te adiuro."

[8] "incessanter oratis": this concluding sentence seems to take the place of the more conventionally brief farewell salutation "ora pro nobis."

[9] "servum vestrum per conloquia litterarum visitare," apparently a signature phrase of Sedatus, cf. his *Epist.* "Reficit me," "servum tuum litterarum munere visitare"

2.35 [Autumn, 506]

Ruricius' reply incorporates the horse portrayal that also appears in *Epist.* 1.14; repeated sections are enclosed in quotation marks. One might wonder why this letter was not placed after *Epist.* 2.33, which also deals with the Council of Agde.

RURICIUS TO BISHOP SEDATUS, A BLESSED LORD AND APOSTOLIC LORD FOR ME IN CHRIST, A PATRON TO BE PREFERRED TO OTHERS WITH SPECIAL WORSHIP AND AFFECTION

I received through the physician Palladius[1] letters of your fruitful heart and fluent tongue, which invited us to a mutual rendezvous in keeping with our hearts' desire. But what can I do? Because various infirmities[2] of the limbs resist the desires of my spirit, while you are excessively robust, I am impeded by the weakness of a worn-out body; whereas four feet belonging to another are hardly able to bear your weight, my own two are scarcely able to sustain even me without exhaustion. As a result, I cannot fulfill our shared desires.[3] Indeed, with the Lord as my witness, if I but had the strength I would have come to the scheduled synod[4] with all eagerness, but the necessity of weakness inhibited me from the intention of the planned journey, because I can hardly tolerate the atmosphere of that region[5] especially at this time.[6] Which I have faith that you believe and I do not doubt that the perverse ascribe to something else.[7]

Therefore, with these things sufficiently discussed, as far as I can, having given the salutation of an eager spirit, if you consider it proper, I have sent to you a steed of the sort that I know is necessary for you, "placid in gentleness, strong in limbs, hardy in strength, excelling in appearance, well-proportioned in form, temperate in spirit," that is, neither, lazy in lethargy nor excessively swift in speed: "the use of the bit and goad is at the will of the rider, and in the carrying of burdens it is both willing and able, with the result that it neither succumbs to the one placed atop nor drops a burden."[8] It remains for you to indi-

---

2.35

[1] Palladius is otherwise unknown; see *PLRE II*, p.822. It seems appropriate that Ruricius, with all his infirmities especially at the end of his life, received a letter carried by a physician. Perhaps Palladius was a medical specialist of some kind, like, perhaps, Justus (*Epist.* 2.27).

[2] Ruricius' ailments again.

[3] "communia vota," reprising Sedatus' "desiderium commune."

[4] "synodum condictam": the Council of Agde of AD 506; see Caesarius, *Epist.* "Dum nimium."

[5] "venissem... aeres regionis illius ... ferre non poteram"; cf. *Epist.* 2.33 to Caesarius, "aestus regionis illius ferre nequiverim, si venissem."

[6] In the summer, a result of the unseasonably early meeting time of the council, cf. *Epist.* 2.33.

[7] See Caesarius' letter "Dum nimium" for questions regarding Ruricius' absence. Perhaps some "perverse" persons attributed Ruricius' absence to some kind of personal animus.

[8] The quoted sections are repeated in Ruricius' letter to Celsus (*Epist.* 1.14), which surely must

cate in your reply how you like it, to whatever extent I can presume, based upon your personal affection for me, that the dreadfulness I have committed — I won't say transmitted — suits you. Indeed, the intensity of absolute affection is so great that nothing is displeasing in a friend,[9] although wickedness from a friend ought to displease more. And it is for this reason that men's judgment is influenced by affection or hatred,[10] so that they do not evaluate accurately.[11] You, truly, whom hatred does not exasperate and jealously does not inflame, tolerate my humor[12] agreeably and inform me abundantly about your health and activities so that, when I read your letter later, I will be instructed more fully. Pray for me.

Sedatus of Nîmes, *Epistula* "Equum quem" (*SG* no.15) [Autumn, 506]

> Sedatus' parody of the previous letter indicates that he not only received Ruricius' horse, but also appreciated his humor. But, one wonders, if Sedatus actually did visit Ruricius, what was the point of the letter? It may be that it was a literary tour-de-force, and that the two of them had a good chuckle reading it when Sedatus arrived. Text: *CCL* 64.403-404; *CSEL* 21.449-450; *MGH AA* 8.274-275.

BISHOP SEDATUS TO BISHOP RURICIUS, A SANCTIFIED AND BLESSED LORD AND PATRON TO BE RECEIVED WITH APOSTOLIC REVERENCE

I have received the horse that you sent through our brother priest,[1] loaded[2] with the magnificent trappings[3] of your words, vile on the hoof,[4] precious in the letter, moving itself when it is goaded with spurs or urged with blows, and[5] moving forward not at all. Most discouraging in form, most vile in color, more flabby than feather-down, more slow-moving than statues,[6] trembling at solid bodies, lacking an inbred fear only, I believe, of shadows, a runaway when it is

---

be earlier.

[9] *in amicum:* S; *in amico:* Krusch; *amicum:* Mommsen.

[10] The manuscript includes in the margin here the comment, "nunc exultationis mundus."

[11] *praeferebant:* S; *proferant:* edd.

[12] *iocos:* edd.; *locos:* S.

Sedatus of Nîmes, "Equum quem"

[1] "fratrem nostrum presbyterum": presumably not the physician Palladius who had brought Sedatus' previous letter to Ruricius, but perhaps Capillutus, who had delivered Caesarius' letter to Ruricius at this same time, and who elsewhere was referred to as "frater et conpresbyter noster" (*Epist.* 2.33).

[2] *onoratum:* Engelbrecht, Demeulenaere; *honeratum:* S; *honoratum:* Krusch.

[3] *phaleris:* decorative ornamentation worn by horses.

[4] *via:* S; *vita:* Engelbrecht, Demeulenaere.

[5] *et:* edd.; *ex:* S.

[6] *statuis:* edd.; *status:* S.

let loose, immobile when it is calmed, standing still on level ground, falling down in the rough: it does not know how to be held, it is unable to walk. Before I saw it, while I was perusing your letter, I believed it to be of the race of those,

> whom ingenious Circe bred as bastards[7]
> from the stolen mare she had mated.[8]

I thought then that it would be shrewd in spirit, energetic in running, blowing fire, when it is displayed, from its flaring nostrils, about to strike the ground with a solid hoof, an outstripper of the winds and rivers in speed. Such, indeed, did the most splendid description of your letter promise me. I believed then that two very strong men, lest it escape, would restrain it as it gnawed at the reins and crushed the iron with its bites. And it did not disappoint me, for several pulled it, others pushed it, and more pummeled it. When I saw it displayed thus, I wished that you always would send to those who are dear to you gifts just as they were, not such as my letter contains. Nevertheless, because you did not leave to me anything which I could say in praise of the gift you sent, lest I altogether [...][9]

2.36 [ca. 502/506 or later]

The letters involving the journey or journeys of Ruricius' grandson Parthenius to Arles (*Epist.* 2.34, 36-37) seem to be some of the latest in the collection, having been written no earlier than 502, when Caesarius of Arles became bishop. In this letter to Caesarius, Ruricius commends Parthenius, who − if this was the same journey that was discussed in *Epist.* 2.32, 37 − was accompanied by his wife Papianilla. The reasons for the journey are unspecified, but if it took place ca. 507, before or even after the battle of Vouillé, it could attest to an exodus of members of Ruricius' to the south: two sons of Ruricius, Leontius and Aurelianus, also departed for Provence at about this time (*Epist.* 2.40). For such departures, see R. Mathisen, "Emigrants, Exiles and Survivors: Aristocratic Options in Visigothic Aquitania," *Phoenix* 38(1984) pp.159-170. The first section of this letter is copied from *Epist.* 2.5 to Namatius, which almost surely was written before this one. Text: see also Caspari, *Caesarii* 2.8. Additional translation: Klingshirn, *Letters*, pp.85-86.

---

[7] *nothos*: edd.; *notus*: S. Another example of the limitations of a copyist's vocabulary.

[8] From Vergil, *Aeneid* 7.282-283. Circe was the daughter of the sun: his horses were immortal, her mare was mortal.

[9] The text breaks off here and there follows in the manuscript, without any break at all, the concluding section of Sidonius' *Epist.* 2.1 to Ecdicius. The seventeenth-century scholar Henricus Canisius noted (*PL* 58.869-870), "How this error occurred ... I cannot easily ascertain, unless the scribe came upon a codex in which certain pages were missing... This place has bothered me for a long time."

BISHOP RURICIUS TO BISHOP CAESARIUS, A SANCTIFIED AND APOSTOLIC LORD
AND A BROTHER TO BE ESTEEMED SPECIALLY BY ME IN CHRIST THE LORD

We who seek out occasions for writing reciprocally to each other because of
our mutual affection ought not to disregard them when they are offered, so that
our correspondence, as a mediator, might confer upon us a kind of shared presence: it is sent forth but is not lost, it is bestowed and yet retained, it seems to
depart and yet does not withdraw, it is sent by me and received by you, it is
written by me and read by you, and it is not detached, when, as if detached, it is
whole in each of our hearts, because, like the divine word, it is relinquished and
does not depart, it is conferred upon the needy and is not taken from the author,
as profit for the recipient without loss to the donor, enriching the pauper without
impoverishing the landlord.

And therefore, with the departure of my dearest grandson Parthenius I have
not delayed sending this letter though him and commending him at the same
time. You should know that you accord to me whatever affection you deign to
bestow upon him. And at the same time I also ask in particular that you ceaselessly pray for me and for my own progeny, nor should the intervening distances of territories[1] impede the tenderness of our love, because those who love
each other in the Lord, who is present everywhere, should not be thought to be
disparate in body, for they are equally[2] joined in the same spirit. Pray for me.[3]

2.37 [ca. 502/506 or later]

Ruricius' grandson Parthenius married Papianilla, a daughter of Agricola, the son
of the emperor Eparchius Avitus (455-456) (see *Epist.* 2.32). This letter may
have been written at the same time as *Epist.* 2.34 and perhaps 2.36. It reads as if
Parthenius and Papianilla are going off to "seek their fortune." After the Ostrogothic occupation of Provence in 508, Parthenius served on an embassy to the
Ostrogothic court at Ravenna and there met the poet Arator, whose *Epistula ad
Parthenium* ("Letter to Parthenius") (*PL* 68.250-255) survives. By ca. 540 he had
become a patrician under the Franks, and in 544 he held the office of *magister
officiorum* ("Master of Offices"). In 548 he was attacked by a mob in Trier and
murdered after the imposition of heavy taxes (Gregory of Tours, *HF* 3.36). As
for Papianilla, Parthenius suspected her of engaging in adultery with his friend
Ausanius and murdered them both (ibid.). He may be the "Partemius" who was
related to Apollinaris, bishop of Valence, the brother of Avitus of Vienne;[1] this

---

2.36

[1] A common theme among the isolated Gallo-Romans; cf. *Epist.* 2.52 to Stephanus.

[2] *pariter*: Demeulenaere; *per et*: S; *pari*: Krusch.

[3] Being on better terms with Caesarius in this letter (cf. *Epist.* 2.33), Ruricius deigns to include
the farewell salutation.

2.37

would be consistent with his known relationhip to the families of Avitus and thence to Sidonius Apollinaris (see Mathisen, "Epistolography").

BISHOP RURICIUS TO HIS DEAREST GRANDCHILDREN PARTHENIUS[2] AND PAPIA-NILLA

After Your Piety departed, I felt that I was halved, because I know that my greatest part, that is the interior man, has traveled with you even as my body remains here. Thus likewise I see that you, you,[3] remain because you also are in my heart, which remains here. Therefore, I salute Your Sweetness and, so that you might be mindful of my words, I suggest that it is certain that you will be able to profit in good things, under the direction of God, according to the observation of Solomon,[4] if the counsels of your elders are heeded both in affection and in practice. I trust that you are doing well.[5]

2.38 [ca. 500/506]

Petrus (Peter) might be the bishop of Saintes of that name who attended the Council of Orléans in 511 (Duchesne, *Fastes* 2.73). But a more intriguing possibility is that this is the "Petrus episcopus de palatio" ("Bishop Peter from the palace") who subscribed to the Council of Agde in 506 (*CCL* 148.213). If the word "palace" refers to the Visigothic court, and it is difficult to see what else it could mean, the question then arises of whether Petrus was an Arian representative of Alaric II, or a Nicene "bishop-without-portfolio" who was somehow attached to the court at Toulouse. The positioning of this letter immediately before that to Eudomius, a Visigothic courtier, and in the midst of letters involving persons associated with the Council of Agde, could lend support to this hypothesis. Yet another Petrus, a priest from Aire (Vicus Iulii), also attended Agde (ibid.). The farewell salutation and placement also suggest a date in the early sixth century.

BISHOP RURICIUS TO HIS BROTHER <BISHOP> PET<ER>[1]

Because obedience is preferable to sacrifices,[2] I therefore prefer to produce my rusticity rather than to lose your affection. Indeed, "knowledge puffs up,"

---

[1] "a consanguineis suis Partemio et Ferreolo assiduo veneratur" ("He was assiduously admired by his relatives Parthenius and Ferreolus") (*Vita Apollinaris Valentinensis* 10: *MGH SRM* 3.201). This Ferreolus also has been suggested as a relative of Ruricius (see Introduction).

[2] Parthenio: edd.; Parthemio: S.

[3] *vos ... vos*: S; most editors delete the second *vos*.

[4] Proverbs 12.15.

[5] "Opto bene agatis," cf. *Epist.* 2.32, 2.39.

[1] *Petro episcopo*: edd; *Pet<ro ep>*: S. The end of the salutation was blurred by the stain that affects the upper corner of the entire manuscript; a later hand traced in the letters "ro ep.".

[2] Cf. 1 Samuel 15.22.

and "love," as you yourself know very well, "builds up."[3] For this reason, because you commanded that on individual occasions I both inform you about my
activities and temper with conversation[4] your longing, which you expend upon
me not because of my merit but because of a general affection inherent within
you, I indicate that I am in fact stronger,[5] with the favor of <God>,[6] but that,
alas, my entire little household[7] is in distress, full[8] of diverse annoyances.[9] I
especially ask that you entreat the Lord assiduously, so that He who has rendered me healthy through your prayers also might confer the resources and[10]
relief of His divine pity through the patronage of your intercession. Pray for
me.

2.39 [ca. 502/506]

Eudomius (*PLRE II*, p.409) probably is to be identified with the courtier Eudomius who was in charge of organizing a church council scheduled for Toulouse in
507 but never held (see Caesarius, *Epist.* "Dum nimium"). Melanthia (*PLRE II*,
p.752) is otherwise unknown. Ruricius writes after the death of their son.

BISHOP RURICIUS TO HIS SUBLIME LORDS AND MAGNIFICENT CHILDREN EUDO-
MIUS AND MELANTHIA

Because I cannot express myself in words to Your Discernment,[1] God, who
knows my heart, is a witness to how terrible the sorrow for your loss is for me.
For the passion of your grief wounded my spirit in such a way as if I had lost
one of my own dear ones, because you have made me intimate with you and in
some sense a relation by dealing well with me. And therefore, because you frequently take my labors and troubles upon yourself because of your regard for
me, it is fitting that when they happen to you, I likewise share in your tribula-

---

[3] 1 Corinthians 8.1.

[4] *alloquio*: edd.; *alioqui*: S.

[5] Another reference to Ruricius' infirmities, and perhaps an indication that he was late in life.

[6] *Deo*: added by Engelbrecht.

[7] *hospitiolum*: cf. *Epist.* 2.2, perhaps Gurdo/Decaniacum.

[8] *plenum*: S²; *planum*: S¹; *plane*: Krusch.

[9] "diversis incommodis": perhaps another difficulty involving one of his sons, if not a typically
vague allusion to the political situation, which at this time would include the Frankish attacks
upon the Visigothic kingdom.

[10] *ac*: edd.; *a*: S.

2.39

[1] *subtilitati*: Engelbrecht, Demeulenaere; *subtilitatis*: S, Krusch; *sublimitati*: Basnage. Assuming
that the manuscript is correct, this is Ruricius' only use of the curious appellation "subtilitas vester"; it also was used by Avitus of Vienne to address the Frankish king Clovis at the beginning
of his *Epist.* 46, "Vestrae subtilitatis."

tions. If indeed, according to the observation of the apostle,[2] the members of a single body have compassion and agonize for each other in turn, it is fitting that we likewise often experience the misfortunes of these <...>[3] I grieve, therefore, at your calamity, and I believe that I am present in your sorrows. But what are we doing,[4] lord children, for we neither are able, nor ought we, to resist the divine will, and we [ought] to take care with all solicitude lest,[5] if we weep for our dear children with excessive grief, we become, so to speak, blasphemers and injurers of the Lord, and lest the author of this same death, having found the opportunity, stab our spirits more sharply than He smote us through the loss of our dear ones.

Therefore, in all our distress and grief we must flee to God and our misfortunes must be delivered to Him wholeheartedly, He who heals the wounded, who lifts up the despondent, who consoles the afflicted, and that observation of the blessed Job must be spoken: "The Lord gave, the Lord has taken away, and it has been done as it was pleasing to the Lord; blessed be the name of the Lord."[6] And he, when he said this, had lost ten sons with all his property, nor was he constrained to blaspheme either with condemnation or with grief, as the scripture says, "In all that happened to him, Job did not sin with his lips."[7] I presume to write this to Your Piety because of our mutual affection, so that I might moderate in some way with divine eloquence your spiritual grief, which I cannot assuage with my letter. And truly,[8] if you believe in me, as if in your own heart, you can take, not least of all, solace from the will of Christ the Lord, because, to whatever extent an untimely end awaited this very one,[9] He deigned to receive him[10] as such a one as those whom He taught are the kingdom of heaven, so that you even would have a patron from a son and would grieve less at your lost one, whom you see received by the Lord. I trust that you are doing well.[11]

---

[2] 1 Corinthians 12.26; cf. *Epist.* 2.3, 2.34.

[3] A few words seem to have dropped out of the text here.

[4] The following section is repeated or paraphrased from *Epist.* 2.3 to Namatius and Ceraunia.

[5] "voluntati divinae resistere nec possumus nec debemus et omni sollicitudine praecavere..."; cf. *Epist.* 2.3, "divinae resistere iussioni, sicut virtute non possumus, ita nec voluntate debemus et ... praecavere..." In *Epist.* 2.3, which seems to be the earlier version, *possumus* controls *resistere* and *debemus* controls *praecavere*. It appears that in *Epist.* 2.39 either the second *nec* should be emended to *et*, or a verb similar to *debemus*, to control *praecavere*, has dropped out after *et*.

[6] Job 1.21.

[7] Job 1.22.

[8] *moderarer et vere*: Engelbrecht, Demeulenaere; *moderare revere*: S; *moderarer vere*: Krusch.

[9] That is, their son.

[10] Eudomius' and Melanthia's son.

[11] "Obto bene agatis": cf. *Epist.* 2.32, 2.37.

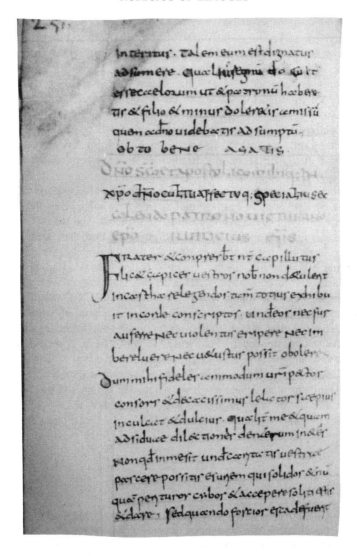

Fig.9: The *Codex Sangallensis* 190, p.251. The end of *Epist.* 2.39 to Eudomius and Melanthia, with the farewell salutation "obto bene agatis" ("I trust you are doing well"); followed by the beginning of *Epist.* 2.40 to Victorinus, with the salutation "D[omin]o s[an]ct[o] et apostolico mihiq[ue] in I xp[ist]o d[omi]no cultu affectuq[ue] specialius ex I colendo patrono Victorino I ep[iscop]o Ruricius ep[iscopu]s," and the first, third, and fourth lines in red ink. See pp.206 above and 211 below. Reproduced by permission of the Stiftsbibliothek, St. Gallen.

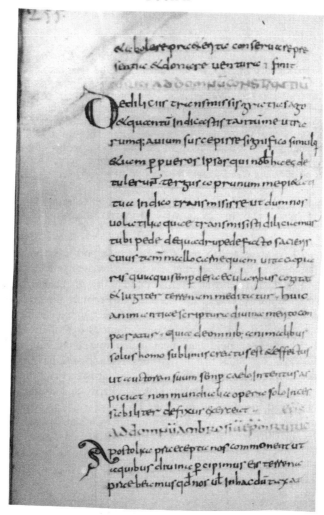

Fig.10: The *Codex Sangallensis* 190, p.255. The end of *Epist*. 2.42 to Leontius, with the word "finit" ("It is finished") at the end; followed by the complete text of *Epist*. 2.43 to Constantius, with the heading "Rurici ad domnu[m] Constantiu[m]" ("Of Ruricius to the lord Constantius"); followed by the beginning of *Epist*. 2.44 to Ambrose, with the salutation "Ad domnu[m] Ambrosiu[m] ep[iscopu]m Ruric[ius] ep[iscopu]s: it is clear that the black text was written first and the red headings (or "rubrics") were entered later, for in this instance the rubricator underestimated the amount of space needed and awkwardly had to abbreviate "Ruricius" and squeeze in the abbreviation for "episcopus" at the end of the preceding line. See p.214 below. Reproduced by permission of the Stiftsbibliothek, St. Gallen.

Victorinus of Fréjus, *Epistula* "Cum beatitudinem" (*SG* no.7) [ca. 500]

Like Ruricius, Victorinus, the bishop of Fréjus (Duchesne, *Fastes* 1.286), was a no-show at the Council of Agde in 506, although he did send his priest Johannes to represent him (*CCL* 148.214). In this letter he renews his acquaintance with Ruricius, whom he had met only once and very briefly, perhaps during Ruricius' visit to Arles ca. 500 (see *Epist.* 2.9), and commends to him a hapless refugee. Segments of the wording repeat Ruricius' *Epist.* 2.9 to Aeonius of Arles, and suggest not only that Victorinus had seen the letter, but also that he was consciously repeating it as a compliment to Ruricius and a means of securing his good will (assuming, of course, that it was not Ruricius repeating Victorinus). Text: *CCL* 64.397-398; *CSEL* 21.443-444; *MGH AA* 8.274-275.

VICTORINUS TO A LORD MOST BLESSED AND REVEREND, AND A PATRON IN CHRIST TO BE RESPECTED SINGULARLY BY ME WITH FITTING WORSHIP, BISHOP RURICIUS

Although I have deserved to see Your Beatitude both for a very short time and only in a single instance,[1] nevertheless you so watered my senses with the purest fountain of a kind heart at my first opportunity of recognizing and contemplating you, that however much I was unable to capture the precious gifts of your words,[2] I possessed nevertheless your presence within the depths of my mind,[3] so that even if I did not receive opportunities externally of refreshing my desire, I nevertheless could find them within myself as long as I remembered Your Grace. Nor, indeed, is it right that this blessing have need of reinforcement only from chance circumstances, because it is constant, infused within my marrow. For this reason, it happens that the charity that sweetens in my innards at the renewed memory[4] of our bond promises a reciprocatation of your charity toward me. And thus my affection toward you stands forth for me as a guarantor of your spirit and in some way my interior conscience assists, as a witness for me of your affection; and I question[5] my mind, which burns with

---

Victorinus of Fréjus

[1] Perhaps, as suggested above, on the occasion of the "Second Council of Arles," ca. 500.

[2] This would seem to suggest that at their first meeting they had scarcely spoken.

[3] "brevissimo ... vestrae ... contemplationisque ... sensus meos fonte purissimo benigni pectoris inrigastis, ut, quamlibet ... munera pretiosa ... praesentiam tamen vestram intra mentis ... possideam"; cf. *Epist.* 2.9, "brevissimos ... contemplatione vestra ... munera pretiosa ... praesentiam tamen vestram intra mentis ... possideam."

[4] "iugi recordatione": Victorinus reorganized Ruricius' thoughts a bit so that this phrase appeared earlier than in *Epist.* 2.9.

[5] The section beginning "For this reason..." is essentially repeated from *Epist.* 2.9, although Victorinus did make a few changes, such as altering the words "dilectio ... amoris" to "caritas ... caritatis," emphasizing, perhaps, that he wished Ruricius to exercise his specifically Christian love on behalf of the suppliant.

the full ardor of love toward you, regarding how much I might presume for myself about you.

For this reason, offering my greetings and beseeching intercession on behalf of the bearer of this letter, I render insufficient thanks. And because the labor of this poor unfortunate, on account of which he has been tossed about in exile through diverse regions for the sake of the release of his wife, was negated by her death immediately after her redemption, and now, again, his paternal anxiety is aroused for the sake of the redemption of his daughter, may you command that he be accompanied by your letters,[6] for the sake of the accumulation of the richness of your reward.

May the dutiful Lord deign to endow Your Beatitude with both years and merits to the profit and ornament of His church, lord most blessed and reverend, and a patron in Christ to be respected singularly by me with fitting worship.[7]

2.40 [ca. 495/506 or later]

> Ruricius subsequently seems to have availed himself of his burgeoning friendship with Victorinus by sending to him two of his sons, Aurelianus and Leontius (see Introduction), who perhaps became junior members of the clergy at Fréjus. The salutation to this letter is very similar to that of *Epist.* 2.36 to Caesarius of Arles, which recommended Ruricius' grandson Parthenius; if the two letters were written at about the same time, it would be another indication that members of Ruricius' family were retreating south. This is the last letter in the corpus to have a farewell salutation, and also the last in the group that was sent to Provence.

BISHOP RURICIUS TO A SANCTIFIED AND APOSTOLIC LORD AND A PATRON TO BE ESTEEMED SPECIALLY BY ME IN CHRIST THE LORD WITH WORSHIP AND AFFECTION, BISHOP VICTORINUS

Our brother and fellow-priest Capillutus,[1] although he did not deliver your words to me relegated to a written letter,[2] nevertheless exhibited them instead[3] written in his heart, whence no thief can steal them nor brigand snatch them nor tempest eradicate them nor old age erase them, as long as a fully faithful

---

[6] Ruricius apparently was not being asked to do anything more than show hospitality and provide an additional letter of reference; but, such letters counted for a lot.

[7] Like Faustus of Riez, Victorinus repeats his salutation in his farewell.

2.40

[1] For Capillutus, see *Epist.* 2.21, 31, 33, and Caesarius, *Epist.* "Dum nimium." This letter would have been written after Capillutus became a priest.

[2] *charta*: a sheet of papyrus, the usual material for writing letters. This makes it clear that this is not a reply to the previous letter.

[3] *potius*: edd.; *totius*: S; *totos*: Lütjohann.

consort of your heart and a most eloquent[4] informer apprises me, often and
sweetly, just as you, so to speak, chew upon me with the tooth[5] of your so constant affection, not because there is in me anything with which you, who are accustomed to give and receive solid and never perishing food, can nourish the
hunger of your affection, but because, when more robust food is lacking, you
gulp down my weakness in place of a draught of milk, so that you soothe the
desire of your pious and pure heart with the nourishment of innocence.

Nor, in fact, is this marvel anything remarkable in your virtue, that you love
those who venerate you — you who are accustomed to love the hateful, inasmuch as, in order to augment your love for me, you detain my two lights, I
speak of Aurelianus and Leontius.[6] I beg that you ceaselessly supplicate the divine pity, as I have faith you are doing, on behalf of my hope for and satisfaction in them, and that you always pray with them again for my sake, because I
faithfully believe that nothing is denied to your development[7] and to their de-
but[8] by our Lord the nourisher on behalf of their recent youthfulness itself.[9]
Therefore, I greet Your Piety richly, as much as the words of my mouth can express, not as much as the affection of my heart demands, and I ask in our[10]
name that you nurture the aforementioned sweetest stimuli of my breast,[11] and
that you drench me with the deluge of your benediction, however often the
chance of a carrier presents itself. Pray for me.

2.41 [ca. 494/502?]

In this brief letter to Apollinaris (see also *Epist.* 2.26-27), Ruricius makes a rare
references to contemporary disorders, which in this case were interfering with travel between Limoges and Clermont and which perhaps date the letter to after ca.
494. Ruricius' openness to travel, moreover, would seem to put it rather before
the end of his life.

---

[4] *dicacissimus*: Engelbrecht, Demeulenaere; *decacissimus*: S; *dicatissimus*: Krusch.

[5] Cf. *Epist.* 1.13.

[6] Generally thought to be Ruricius' sons (see Introduction). The word *detinetis* suggests that
they were staying with Victorinus for an extended period; perhaps Ruricius wished to put them
out of harm's way. If so, this letter could been written ca. 494-498, during the Frankish raids on
Aquitania, or ca. 506/507, just before or even after the battle of Vouillé.

[7] *profectioni*: S; *perfectioni*: Demeulenaere.

[8] *incipientiae*: contrasted with the *profectioni* of Victorinus, and perhaps an allusion to the beginning of the boys' careers in the clergy at Fréjus.

[9] Another indication that the boys were Ruricius' two youngest children.

[10] *nostro*: edd.; *non*: S.

[11] "pectoris mei nostro nomine": the contrast between the singular and the plural suggests that
the "nostro" refers to both Ruricius and Hiberia.

BISHOP RURICIUS TO HIS APOLLINARIS, GREETINGS

Affection for Your Exaltedness is a fierce enforcer[1] in my innards[2] and compels me to favor my love for you rather than my own modesty, because it has no thought for the kind of language or the kind of page with which I obey your commands. You force me to impose recurrent injury upon the ears of your expertness with my rustic words because you desire to receive my words often. I obey your will, I obey your command.[3] Indeed, I prefer to put faith in you yourself rather than in myself regarding myself, because what you command is a manifestation of piety not power. And therefore, you will doubtless emend rather than execrate whatever is displeasing, because nothing is more commanding than affection; whoever surrenders[4] to it wholeheartedly will freely both suffer its anchored chains and bear its imposed burdens, as long as one not unwillingly accepts[5] the authority of its tutelage and devotedly obeys it. Therefore, the divine pity will concede that in the tumults and necessities of this time,[6] whether drawn out[7] into perpetuity or suppressed for a time, it will quickly allow us to secure the profit[8] of each other's presence,[9] so that the desire that is aroused by our words might be assuaged by our shared presence.[10]

IT IS FINISHED[11]

2.42 [ca. 485/490]

> This Leontius seems to be Ruricius' biological brother, after whom one of Ruricius' sons was named (see *Epist.* 2.40, and Introduction). He also is mentioned in *Epist.* 1.8 as having borrowed a book from Sidonius Apollinaris, and in *Epist.* 2.49. In this letter Leontius, apparently in middle age, has undertaken the life of a penitent.

2.41

[1] *exactor*: a tax collector.

[2] Cf. the letters to Julianus Pomerius, *Epist.* 1.7, 2.10-11.

[3] "pareo voluntati vestrae, pareo iussioni": cf. Cassian, *De incarnatione*, praef., "pareo obsecrationi tuae, pareo iussioni"; cf. *Epist.* 2.18.

[4] *se dederit*: edd.; *sederit*: S.

[5] The ms. adds another *non* before *excipit*.

[6] "tumultibus temporis huius vel necessitatibus": Krusch, *MGH AA* 8.lxv, sees an allusion to the battle of Vouillé in 507, but the reference seems to be to troubles more chronic in nature.

[7] *dilatis*: S², Engelbrecht; *dilectis*: S¹; *deletis*: Krusch.

[8] *citius fructus nos*: edd.; /*itius* /f/ct/s /os: S.

[9] "fructus nos faciat de nostra capere praesentia," cf. *Epist.* 1.16, 2.64, and pseudo-Sulpicius Severus, *Epist. ad Claudiam sororem*, "de nostra nos fructum faciat capere praesentia."

[10] "incitantur affatibus, aspectibus mitigentur": the rhetorical figures of assonance and chiasmus.

[11] "Finit": this addendum appeared after the end of *Epist.* 1.1 (q.v. for discussion), but then disappeared until this letter and several of the subsequent ones.

RURICIUS TO HIS MOST INTIMATE LORD AND BROTHER, VENERABLE WITH ALL
HONOR, LEONTIUS

I give thanks both because you have concern for me and because you considered it important to replenish me with the novelty of your foliage,[1] which you
know I accept gladly and which you provide equally through habit and affection. And therefore, with your lad[2] returning, I render the reciprocal responsibility of salutation, and I recommend that you think ceaselessly about the responsibility, agreeable to God, that you have undertaken, because God is recognized as assessing not the beginning of a good work, but its end, saying, "He
who endures to the end will be saved."[3] His pity provides, as we believe, that
He Himself, who deigns to inspire the spirit of penitence in you, will grant us
full remission as a result of His pity, both to augment and to consummate our
virtue. He alone is able to restore the defiled and to revive the fallen, to annul
our deeds and to erase our past, to preserve our present and to grant our future.

IT IS FINISHED

2.43 [ca. 500/506]

> If this Constantius is Ruricius' son (see *Epist.* 2.24-25), then he continued in his
> pursuit of pleasures of the flesh, in spite of Ruricius' suggestion that he give less
> attention to *mundialia opera* ("worldly concerns"). The following three letters all
> are concerned with the dispatching of various kinds of delicacies. By now Con-
> stantius is living independently, suggesting an early sixth-century date for the let-
> ter.

RURICIUS TO HIS LORD CONSTANTIUS

I give thanks for the delicacies[1] you sent and I declare that I have received
the same quantity of both birds that you indicated,[2] and likewise that I have
sent to Your Piety, through the same lads who delivered the birds to me, a side
of bacon, so that, while I enjoy the winged creatures that you sent, you may be
satiated with a biped made from a quadruped.[3] I would prefer you to be captivated by its meat rather than by its life, because he who always thinks about

---

2.42
[1] Cf. *Epist.* 1.11 to Freda.
[2] Perhaps the same *puer* of Leontius mentioned in *Epist.* 2.49 to Aprunculus of Clermont,
although it might be too much to suggest that both letters were sent on the same occasion.
[3] Matthew 10.22.
2.43
[1] *de deliciis*: edd.; *de diliciis*: the reading of S, noted only by Engelbrecht.
[2] Presumably in a verbal message.
[3] That is, only half of the pig was sent.

temporal matters and constantly meditates on worldly things is rightly compared to this animal from the divine scripture,[4] because only man of all the animals is a sublime creation and constructed so that he always may gaze intently upon his creator in heaven, not so that, focused ceaselessly upon the ground, he may pursue worldly concerns.

2.44 [ca. 485/506]

This is quite likely the bishop Ambrose with whom Sidonius Apollinaris corresponded (*Epist.* 9.6). He may have been from Rodez (Segodunum), just west of Cahors, where the earliest dated bishop is Quintianus, who attended the Council of Agde in 506 (ibid. 2.40). The sending of perishables would suggest that Ambrose lived nearby, and if Ruricius was writing from Gurdo/Decaniacum, Rodez would have qualified. For other Ambrosii in the area, note also a bishop Ambrose of Albi, southwest of Rodez, attested in 549 (Duchesne, *Fastes* 2.42), and Ambrose, bishop of Cahors ca.550-575: see P. Bonnassie, "L'évêque, le peuple et les sénateurs: Scènes de la vie à Cahors, d'après la Vita Ambrosii," *Annales du Midi* 102 nos.189-190 (Jan.-June 1990) 209-217. Bardy, however, assumes ("Copies et éditions," p.50) that Ambrosius was bishop of Sens.

BISHOP RURICIUS TO THE LORD BISHOP AMBROSE

The apostolic precepts counsel us that we should offer earthly things to those from whom we have received divine things.[1] Observing these rules even in this instance in exchange for the celestial banquets that you bestow upon me both in living speech and in the words of the fathers, I have sent you fruits of the sea,[2] attesting through them that I have nothing of my own, because in fact I am alien from the divine goods that you grant, and I[3] send alien things. Therefore, because I recognize that I am an exile from the celestial seas[4] and dwell in a terrestrial earthly residence, I demand particularly from you that you accept these foreign things from me gratefully and deign to grant yours frequently to me. The one provides an example of affection, the other of ministry; the one of learning,[5] the other of favor.

---

[4] Cf. 2 Peter 2.22.

2.44

[1] Cf. 1 Corinthians 16.48.

[2] *legumina marina*: it is unclear just what these are; apparently some kind of vegetable. Ruricius' forwarding of perishables suggests that Ambrose lived relatively closeby. This is the second place where Ruricius alludes to being near the ocean; cf. *Epist.* 1.11, "frigus oceani." Perhaps, given his dislike of hot weather, he spent time in the summer near the coast; it was seen above (*Epist.* 2.1) that Namatius had interests near Saintes.

[3] *nos*: Engelbrecht, Demeulenaere; *vos*: S; *vobis*: Krusch.

[4] *marinis*: S, Engelbrecht; *mannis*: Krusch; *mensis*: Lütjohann.

[5] *doctrinae*: S, edd.; *coquinae*: Mommsen.

2.45

Hispanus is otherwise unknown; he lived near the Dordogne river, probably fairly close to Ruricius' estate at Gurdo/Decaniacum. The next three letters have the salutation in the genitive, "Ruricii episcopi," a form otherwise unknown in Ruricius' corpus.

OF BISHOP RURICIUS, TO THE LORD HISPANUS

I give thanks because, when you send me the spoils of the Dordogne,[1] you confirm your most sincere piety toward me, in which I delight more than in your treats, because with the one I suppress the hunger of the body, and with the other that of the heart. With the one I provide a transitory meal for my stomach,[2] with the other, truly, a permanent affection for my spirit. Accordingly, I salute Your Piety all the more, remitting reciprocal[3] thanks as much for your love as for your gift. And because you deign to be solicitous about my health,[4] in response to the concern of Your Piety I signify that I am well, and I likewise request that you inform me when your people return where you are going to celebrate the sanctified Pasch.[5]

IT IS FINISHED

2.46 [ca. 485/506]

The words "germanitatis vestrae" indicate that Albinus was in some way related to Ruricius. Given that Ruricius comments on Albinus' performance of his priestly duties, and that Albinus lived nearby, he probably was a priest of Limoges. Ruricius advises him on how to deal with a woman who had lost her husband. This letter reprises some of the sentiments from *Epist.* 2.4.

2.45

[1] *spolia Doranonia*: cf, Gregory of Tours, *HF* 7.28, 32, "Dornonia"; and Ausonius, *Mosella* 464, "Duranius" *PLRE II*, p.566, fails to realize that "Doranonia" refers to the Dordogne river; it also sees in the *spolia* allusions to "military activity," but they surely refer merely to fish.

[2] *ventri*: edd.; *vestri*: S.

[3] *reciprocas*; *reciprocis*: S; Lütjohann suggests adding *obsequiis*.

[4] Again, Ruricius' ailments.

[5] Attendance at the Easter service was important, for laypersons who did not take communion at Easter, Christmas, and Pentecost, were "not considered to be Catholic" (Council of Agde, can.18: *CCL* 148.202). Given that Hispanus was one of Ruricius' parishoners, he must have been living in the area of Brive-la-Gaillarde, the only region where the Dordogne enters the territory of Limoges. Ruricius also seems to have celebrated Easter there in *Epist.* 2.24.

OF BISHOP RURICIUS, TO THE PRIEST ALBINUS

When I learned of our common grief through the hearsay of a messenger, which in fact amazed me because I had not learned of it before from a report of Your Brotherhood, I would have come immediately to seek you out if the reverence for these days[1] had not held me back. I have sent this letter, through which I hope that you will deign to excuse me and that in my place, by means of your reason as much as your influence, you will console our daughter, who I hear is severely distressed, because our Lord did with His servant both what He wished and when He wished.[2] And therefore, one would seem[3] to go against the will of the Lord, one for whom the divine precept, which assuredly is divine, was displeasing, because He alone who pours our spirit into our body can lead it from the body, whenever He wishes. And therefore that grief is excessive which, seeming to come from piety, derives more from the counsel of the devil than from piety, with the result that it loses its soul because of its lack of faith, when, with its impious complaints, a grief that cannot abide consolation blames God, who sent His Son through the human condition.

Let those who are dead, who presume that the soul perishes with the flesh, grieve for their dead,[4] whom they do not believe will be resurrected. For such people there is no faith in[5] the happiness of the soul or in the restoration of the body. As for us, however, who have hope of the resurrection in Christ, who believe that our spirits are laid in the lap of the saints according to the promise of the Lord Himself, let us entrust ourselves to Him with our heart and prayers and let us take consolation from His promise, because He allows those believing in Him to live with Him and no one, except for the faithless, is judged dead by Him. And thus let us temper our grief for our own, as the scripture teaches us, saying, "The wise grieve for seven days, but the impious all the days of their lives."[6] Just as we know that he is dead[7] in body, we know that his soul truly

---

2.46

[1] If this is a reference to the period around Easter, then this letter may have been written about the same time as the previous one, an inference also suggested by the similar forms of salutation.

[2] Cf. *Epist.* 2.4. Later discussion indicates that this woman had lost a male relative. Because only she is mentioned as being distressed, one might have thought that a husband or father had died, but the reference to the "innocence" of the deceased could indicate that it was a child who had died.

[3] *videbitur*: edd.; *indebitur*: S.

[4] Cf. *Epist.* 2.4; and Luke 9.60.

[5] *de*: added by editors.

[6] Ecclesiasticus 22.13; the text reads *mortui*; Ruricius, *sapientis*.

[7] "illum mortuum," making it clear that it was a male who had died.

lives in God because of his innocence, thus <let us beware lest>[8] we, living in
our bodies, perish in our hearts.

IT IS FINISHED

2.47 [ca. 485/506]

Ruricius here deals with some unspecified legal business involving one of Taurentius' dependents. See also *Epist.* 2.17; Taurentius, *Epist.* "Litterae sanctitatis."

OF BISHOP RURICIUS, TO TAURENTIUS

I give thanks for your most ready devotion to the Lord and your most
sincere affection for me, which, as an imitator of the divine goodness, <grants>
what[1] it sees for itself is going to be requested by me before it is sought, and
hastens to anticipate my favors with its own benevolence, while it acts not only
to maintain but even to augment in <me> that[2] affection which it therefore
gladdens by anticipating favors, because it fears to sadden in the least amount.
And therefore it prefers to offer consideration to one who is silent rather than to
give it to one demanding, knowing that there is certainly more merit in this, in
what is bestowed with spontaneous kindness rather than what is conceded to
pleas, because one of them is given to necessity only[3] by necessity, and the
other is often granted even to the perseverance of a persistent pleader. For this
reason, speaking a reciprocal greeting secure in the assurance of Your Piety, I
signify that I have endorsed[4] your maid, having instructed your lads in the
matter. I trust that, according to your promise and out of regard for my
intercession you will grant to her not only your pardon but even your favor.

---

[8] "viventes corpore <...> corde moriamur": A word or two seem to have dropped out at a page
break, perhaps an alliterative "caveamus ne"; Hagendahl (*Ruricius*, pp.107-108) and Demeulenaere suggest "videamus ne." Cf. *Epist.* 2.4.

2.47

[1] The ms. reads only *id quod me* and is missing a verb. Most editors emend to *a me*, but
suggestions for verbs range from *dat* (Krusch) to *suppeditat* (Engelbrecht).

[2] The exmplar may have been mutilated here, for the copyist clearly had problems: a sentence
break was put after the word *augere*, and the next words, *id istum*, were awkwardly altered,
immediately it seems, to read *in* (or *im*) *ipsum*. Engelbrecht and Lütjohann suggest *in me istum*;
whereas Mommsen and Krusch prefer *initum*.

[3] *non nisi*: S; *non sine*: Hagendahl (p.77), Demeulenaere.

[4] *consignasse*: a legal term referring to a formal signature to a document (see Dirksen, *Manuale*,
p.198). It seems that the fulfilment of some promise to the woman, perhaps forgiveness for an
unspecified delict, was contingent upon the receipt of Ruricius' legal attestation to something,
which Ruricius granted. Ruricius' prefatory remarks were intended to encourage Taurentius to
fulfil his side of the agreement.

2.48 [ca. 485/506]

Ruricius twice uses the word *tua*, suggesting that he knew Johannes very well. The titles *venerabilis* and *frater*, plus the sending of *commendaticiae*, could suggest that Johannes was a bishop, in which regard one notes the Johannes of Chalon-sur-Saône (see Sid.Apoll. *Epist.* 4.25), who became bishop after being archdeacon, a cleric who oversaw finances and would have had the financial experience to engage in money-lending. Note also a short-lived bishop of Arles in 502; and bishops of Fréjus and Sisteron in the early sixth century (Duchesne, *Fastes* 1.286, 288). But Ruricius' failure to call Johannes *episcopus* in his salutation strongly suggests that Johannes was not a bishop. Other persons of this name include a grammarian in the early 470s (Sid. Apoll. *Epist.* 8.2); an aristocrat involved in litigation (ibid. 2.5.1-2); and a priest of Ruricius' friend Victorinus of Fréjus (*CCL* 148.214). This rather lengthy letter (the longest of the final 31 letters) begins *in medias res*, without the customary preamble.

BISHOP RURICIUS TO HIS VENERABLE LORD BROTHER JOHN

Magnus, our shared responsibility,[1] now does compelled by necessity what he ought to have done voluntarily, with the result that he pressures me for letters of attestation[2] to Your Reverence. And even if he was thankless in the past on account of his own negligence,[3] now, in spite of this, in an attempt to ingratiate himself he intrudes upon Your Grace through my cajolery. I readily acquiesced to his petition for this reason, because I believed, as I also trust, that you will freely assent to my petition.[4] In this regard, having dispensed my greeting, I hope that you will consider it important[5] to receive him on account of my intercession and, because he has repaid what he owed,[6] that you will deign to remit the interest on the same *solidi*[7] not so much because of my pleas as out of consideration for the divine teachings. Because without doubt you will prosper with regard to your own conversion, in which I hear that you are

---

2.48

[1] Or "Our great shared responsibility", with the borrower unnamed; knowing Ruricius, he probably meant it both ways. Cf. Faustus, *Epist.* "Magnum pietatis" for a similar introductory play on a name.

[2] *commendaticias*: see *Epist.* 2.7.

[3] That is, he had failed to pay the debt.

[4] "petitioni ... petitioni": by using the same word, Ruricius ties his own petition to that of the debtor.

[5] "tanti habeatis."

[6] That is, he had repaid the principal only.

[7] The *solidus* was a large gold piece, struck 72 to the pound. Three would provide a decent living for a year, so, Magnus' debt was quite large. In Merovingian Gaul, the *tremissis*, or one-third *solidus*, was much more common. For a similar request for the remission of interest, in this case from a priest, see Sid.Apoll. *Epist.* 4.24, where it seems that neither the principal nor the interest had been repaid.

making progress day-to-day with the favor of God,[8] because you yourself know
that he will see the kingdom of God with joy and thanksgiving and will ascend
in glory to the mountain of the Lord who exacts interest from his money not in
the present age from those close to him, but awaits it from the Lord in the age
to come. Nor, with grievous kindness,[9] does He cast the snares of unpayable
debts about those in difficulty, but He is their benefactor and creditor, the one
who says, "Give and it will be given to you,"[10] and, "The measure you give
will be the measure you get."[11]

He who does not want to have in perpetuity what he thinks is most to be
coveted is at the least faithless, and unjust even to himself. In fact, whoever
accumulates however much, gathers much, and acquires infinite things with
diverse mercantile activities[12] departs[13] as a beggar from this world unless he
first of all sends his own portion of his property ahead to the eternal beatitude,
with the Lord saying through the prophet, "Be not afraid when one becomes
rich, when the glory of his house increases, for when he dies he will carry nothing away, his glory will not go down[14] after him,"[15] and likewise, "They slept
their sleep and all[16] found nothing of their riches <in>[17] their hands."[18]   If
they were bounteous in spirit, they should rather have entrusted their assets to
Him who is the rightful guarantor of paupers and the most generous remitter of
interest. Therefore, may you not yearn, dearest brother, to receive two-fold[19]
that which the Lord promises that He will return to you a hundred-fold; for this
reason, you need neither to fear any destruction[20] by a moth[21] nor to dread
loss to a thief,[22] because our Lord Himself is the bestower and guardian of His
treasures.

IT IS FINISHED

---

[8] This suggests that Johannes either was only in the process of taking up the religious life, or
had but recently done so, and does not seem like what one would say to a bishop.

[9] That is, the kindness of the initial loan was offset by the burden of the resultant interest.

[10] Luke 6.38.

[11] Matthew 7.2.

[12] *nundinationibus*: perhaps Johannes was some kind of merchant.

[13] *discedit*: Mommsen; *discendit*: S; *discedet*: Krusch; *descendet*: Engelbrecht, Demeulenaere.

[14] *descendet*: edd., with the *Vulgate*; *discendit*: S.

[15] Psalms 48.17-18.

[16] *omnes*: the *Vulgate* adds *viri*.

[17] *in*: added by editors, with the *Vulgate*.

[18] Psalms 75.6.

[19] Apparently the interest had grown to equal the principal, so Ruricius was asking Johannes to
bear quite a significant financial loss.

[20] *exterminium*: presumably of his account-books.

[21] *a tinea*: edd.; *catena*: S.

[22] Cf. Matthew 6.19, Luke 12.33.

2.49 [485/490]

Originally bishop of Langres, Aprunculus was expelled by the Burgundians (Gregory of Tours, *HF* 2.23) and fled to Clermont where he served as bishop from the death of Sidonius ca. 485 until his own death ca. 490 (Duchesne, *Fastes* 2.35).

BISHOP RURICIUS TO BISHOP APRUNCULUS

The affection of mutual love compels me to send[1] letters to Your Sanctity, indivisible from me, solely for that reason, even if an opportune occasion does not present itself. For this reason, I have imparted this letter to Your Apostlehood through the lad[2] of my son Leontius, through which, having offered my salutation, I ask how, in your opinion, you fare, with the favor of God, because you yourself know that your good health is my happiness. I hope that, when the aforementioned fellow returns, with the blessing of the divinity, you will reassure me, whom you see concerned <for>[3] your welfare, about your activities.

2.50 [ca. 495/506]

Ruricius asks Ceraunia to send him an unidentified item that, based upon his predilections, may have been an edible delicacy or, perhaps more likely, something with medicinal value. The appellation "tua veneratio" suggests that Ceraunia had adopted the religious life and therefore that her husband Namatius had died, thus dating the letter to later in Ruricius' life. The abbreviated form of address here and in *Epist.* 2.62 (to Namatius), as compared to *Epist.* 2.1-5, 15, could have resulted from a change in Ruricius' style, from Ruricius' archiving practices, or from later editorial changes (see Introduction).

BISHOP RURICIUS TO CERAUNIA, GREETINGS

Trusting to your most sincere charity, with which[1] you deign to cultivate me in the Lord because of the kindness of your spirit, not because of my own qualities, I have confidently forwarded this letter to Your Reverence.[2] Conveying in it a lavish greeting in our Lord and God, I ask particularly that you deign to provide to me without delay, if it is possible, those things that I have been expecting,[3] per my request, through your servant Amandus,[4] both because

---

2.49

[1] *destinare*: edd.; *destinati*: S.

[2] For a *puer* of Leontius, see also *Epist.* 2.42.

[3] *de*: added by editors.

2.50

[1] *a qua*: S; *qua*: edd.

[2] *ad venerationem*: edd.; *adventionem*: S.

[3] *speravi*: S, Engelbrecht, Demeulenaere; *reseravi*: Mommsen, Krusch.

this item can relieve me and because nothing that I would consider to be the greatest favor can cause any expense for you. Again, regarding what you command or necessity demands, I will endeavor to reimburse you in turn with reciprocal kindnesses.

2.51 [ca. 485/500]

Censurius was bishop of Auxerre in the late fifth century (Duchesne, *Fastes* 2.445): the "Deeds of the Bishops of Auxerre" give his tenure as ca. 470-508 (*PL* 138.230). Circa 480 Constantius of Lyon sent him a copy of his "Life of St. Germanus of Auxerre" (*Sources chrétiennes* 112.114), and he received *Epist.* 6.10 of Sidonius Apollinaris. Ruricius' letter raises some questions of legal and political jurisdictions. All of the other letters of Ruricius whose addressees can be identified were sent to individuals resident in the Visigothic kingdom. Auxerre, however, is generally assumed to have lain in a kind of no-man's land to the northeast, on the far side of the Loire, which is thought to have marked the northern boundary of Visigothic territory. Yet, this letter suggests that Censurius and Ruricius lived in the same legal jurisdiction. It may be, therefore, that at some point Visigothic authority extended as far as Auxerre. Perhaps the territorial cessions made by the emperor Julius Nepos in 475 included not only the Auvergne, but areas further north as well.

BISHOP RURICIUS TO BISHOP CENSURIUS, GREETINGS

I rejoice that I have received the letter of Your Sanctity, even if on a business matter. For it makes no difference whether [our correspondence] occurs from necessity or from personal preference, as long as those who esteem one another communicate reciprocally among themselves and as long as a true conversation of their minds and senses links those whom spatial distances separate in body, because the virtue of the divine[1] piety has granted even this greatest thing to our kind, so that we who are unable to scrutinize each other in the flesh can see with a spiritual gaze. For this reason, as the bearer of your letter returns, I have endeavored to reply to it as you enjoined, so that I respond equally both to your concern and to our mutual esteem.

I offer greetings, therefore, to Your Apostlehood, and, regarding that matter, which you wished to investigate in writing through my peoples' testimony,[2] You should know that I have diligently conducted an examination of my men, as to where they were, that is, whether Sindilla[3] lost his pigs with Foedamius'

---

[4] Otherwise unknown.

2.51

[1] The manuscript reads "virtus divi" at the end of one page and "acte pietatis" at the beginning of the next. For "divilacte" editors suggest "divinae."

[2] "apicibus meorum testimonio": this sounds like a formal written affidavit.

[3] It would appear that Sindilla was the manager of an estate located in the territory of Limoges

knowledge.[4] But, just as I already ascertained before, I learned that Sindilla and the laborers[5] were primarily responsible, and that he himself lost the pigs <through>[6] his own disobedience, even though he claimed that he was in another place. But the aforementioned Foedamius was in no way culpable. For, of all these people, [Sindilla] ought to blame no other one for what he has suffered except <for himself>.[7] How much I have labored in this matter, out of regard for you, so that your men might be freed from custody and recover your pigs, you will be able to learn more fully <from>[8] their reports,[9] because, in this matter, there was no need to discuss that in this letter. It is up to you to defend your man justly from the charge of this false accusation,[10] which you know, from my letter, that he unjustly[11] suffered.

2.52 [ca. 500]

A Stephanus who was bishop of Lyon in the early sixth century received *Epist.* 26, 28, and 58 of Avitus of Vienne and *Epist.* 3.4 and 3.12 of Ennodius of Pavia. But this is unlikely to have been the Stephanus of Ruricius' letter. For one thing, Lyon was in the Burgundian kingdom, and, as just seen, Ruricius' extant letters seem to have been addressed almost exclusively to recipients in the Visigothic kingdom. Moreover, the salutation reads "Ruricius episcopus Stephano suo salutem," and it would have been a curious breach of etiquette for Ruricius to refer to himself, but not to the recipient, as a bishop if the recipient was also a bishop. Indeed, when using this form of salutation, Ruricius always addresses a bishop as "bishop" (e.g. *Epist.* 2.22, 38, 44, 49, 64-65), and in no case where he does not do so can the recipient be identified as a bishop (e.g. *Epist.* 2.21, 2.31, 2.37, 2.41, 2.46-48, 2.50, 2.53-54, 2.59-63). Stephanus, therefore, rather may have been a cleric, or perhaps an elderly layman who had adopted the religious life. The letter is cobbled together from sections of other letters sent to Arles (one to Aeonius and two to Julianus Pomerius) so it may be that Stephanus, too, who may have seen them, likewise lived in or near Arles.

---

that belonged to the church of Auxerre. There seem to have been ready communications between Auxerre and the southwest: Sidonius' letter to Censurius (*Epist.* 6.10) concerned a deacon of Clermont who fled to Auxerre in the early 470s in order to escape the Visigoths.

[4] *prudente Foedamio*: edd.; *prodente Foedamio*: S. For the priest Foedamius, see *Epist.* 2.14.

[5] *laborem facientes ac Sindillam*: Engelbrecht, Demeulenaere; *laborem faciente faci sindilae*: S; *laborem faciente facinore Sindillae*: Mommsen, Krusch.

[6] *per*: added by editors.

[7] *sibi*: added by editors.

[8] *per*: added by Engelbrecht, Demeulenaere.

[9] *ipsos iam referentes*: S, Engelbrecht, Demeulenaere; *ipso iam referente*: Mommsen; *ipsis iam referentibus*: Krusch.

[10] *calumnia*: a formal legal charge of making a false accusation: see the *Theodosian Code* 9.34. Another manifestation of Ruricius' legal training.

[11] *quam eum iniuste*: edd.; *qua meum inustae*: S.

BISHOP RURICIUS TO HIS STEPHANUS, GREETINGS

The piety of Your Sanctity captivated me so much for a very few days[1] in admiration of it that, when, with the blessing of God, I hold you in my heart and gaze upon you with my mind's eye,[2] I in fact always examine it carefully, at the constant instigation of my affection, because just as everything pleasant seems brief, likewise everything which is of the flesh cannot be satiated. And I give thanks[3] to omnipotent God for such an admirable gift, which He deigns to grant so freely to His servants with an unspeakable generosity, so that those who are distant in body are joined in spirit,[4] nor is there anything so laboriously distant[5] that it[6] impedes the gaze of our minds, for those who love reciprocally see each other there, where love itself exists, in the contemplation of their affection through the perception of their hearts. Whereby it happens[7] that Your Steadfastness, which is augmented in my innards by constant recollection because it is renewed every day, promises an interchange of your love for me <and>[8] my spirit stands by for me as a guarantor of your spirit as it dares to presume for itself upon your affection as much as it desires to expend upon you.

I give many greetings, therefore, to Your Beatitude, and I beg you to beseech our shared Lord ceaselessly so that, according to the wealth of His goodness and virtue, in whom we confess that all things are possible, even if we are unable to see each other often in this age on account of the whirlwinds and storms of this life[9] and the intervening regions,[10] he might make us meet in that city, "which is built as a city,"[11] to which the Lord is able to bring me by mercy, you by merit.[12]

2.52
[1] "paucissimus diebus"; cf. *Epist.* 2.9 to Aeonius of Arles, "paucis diebus"; cf. also Victorinus, *Epist.* "Cum beatitudinem," "brevissimo tempore et una tantum vice." Ruricius may be speaking of his visit to Arles, possibly ca. 500, when he met Aeonius, and perhaps Victorinus.
[2] "oculis mentis": for this theme, see *Epist.* 2.17.
[3] This section, down to "of their hearts," recurs in *Epist.* 2.10 (to Julianus Pomerius), and Faustus, *Epist.* "Gratias domino."
[4] "qui disparantur corpore, animis iungerenter"; cf. the previous letter, "quos corpore locorum intervalla discriminant, animorum ac sensuum conloquia fida coniungant," perhaps an indication of a temporal connection between these two letters.
[5] *tam longinquum difficile*: S; *tam longinquum tamque difficile*: edd.
[6] Editors add *non* here.
[7] This entire section, down to "expend upon you," is repeated from *Epist.* 2.9, to Aeonius of Arles; cf. also Victorinus, *Epist.* "Cum beatitudinem."
[8] *et*: added by editors.
[9] "vitae istius turbidines ac procellas": perhaps another vague allusion to political conditions.
[10] Another suggestion that Stephanus lived some distance away; cf. *Epist.* 2.36.
[11] That is, Jerusalem: Psalms 121.3.
[12] Repeated from the end of *Epist.* 1.17.

2.53 [ca. 490/500]

This letter is either a copy or an extra draft of *Epist.* 2.12 (q.v. for Biblical citations, and see Introduction). Differences include their different forms of salutation and that the Lupus of this letter is called Lupicinus in the other.

BISHOP RURICIUS TO HIS SON PRAESIDIUS, GREETINGS

Several persons, because they are confident that I have much influence with Your Inseparable Exaltedness, not because of the merit of my life but because of the privilege of friendship, seek from me letters of attestation by means of which they might be excused to you. The responsibility of my office does not allow me to deny these letters, not because of any audacity of presumption but because of the discipline of ministry, so long as I desire to provide solace[1] in the present life for them and in the eternal for you, both so that they might be preserved for penitence through your forbearance and so that you might come to pardon through pity, just as the scripture says, "For there will be judgment without pity <for him>[2] who does not have pity," because He <who>[3] said, "Forgive and you will be forgiven," doubtless in the future will restore what he promised to one whom he sees doing here what he orders. Indeed, for you[4] His truth is ready at hand if[5] our faith in Him is not lacking. For this reason, you are most manifestly able to realize that the pardon of sinners is equivalent to the absolution of your own afflictions, and that whatever you grant[6] to the prayers of others must be granted to your own, according to the saying of the same person in the Gospels, "You will be judged on the basis of the judgment you pronounce." And therefore, on behalf of Ursus and Lupus,[7] who, as I said above, came to me, as one who is particularly bound to you by the bond of love, with respect to intercession for their crimes, I approach you as a suppliant, so that you might impart,[8] first to God and then to me, that which they have done, and so that you might not put me to shame regarding the punishment of those who believed that they already[9] had been absolved when they were escorted to My Humility.

2.53

[1] *solatium*; *Epist.* 2.12 reads *solatia*.
[2] *illi*: omitted here, restored from *Epist.* 2.12.
[3] *qui*: omitted here, restored from *Epist.* 2.12.
[4] *vobis*; *Epist.* 2.12 reads *nobis*.
[5] *si*: added by editors.
[6] *praestatis*: *Epist.* 2.12 reads *praestiteritis*.
[7] *Lupicino*; *Epist.* 2.12 reads *Lupo*.
[8] *Epist.* 2.12 adds *et infieri* here.
[9] *iam tum*: omitted in *Epist.* 2.12.

2.54 [ca. 485/506]

The addressee probably is the aristocrat Rusticus (*Epist.* 2.20), not the priest Rusticus, the son of Taurentius (*Epist.* 2.17), because the Rusticus below lived near the Vézère river, and he of *Epist.* 2.20 lived near Userca, which is on the Vézère.

BISHOP RURICIUS TO HIS SON RUSTICUS, GREETINGS

Beyond your accustomed and approved affection, you also deign to expend your humanity upon me, so long as you withhold from your own use that which you lavish upon expenditures on my behalf, for I learned, from the report of your lad, that you ordered that the delicacies of the fishing in the Vézère[1] should minister to us on your behalf. For this reason, having dispensed my salutation, I give many thinks, praying the divine pity that, because of the honor that you have bestowed upon me for its sake, it will grant to you good fortune in the present days[2] and confer happiness in the future.

IT IS FINISHED

2.55 [ca. 485/490]

There follows a dossier of four letters to Aprunculus, bishop of Clermont ca. 485-490. Even though Ruricius does not call himself "bishop" in the salutation, he must have been one because he became one while Aprunculus' predecessor Sidonius Apollinaris. The following three letters lack the original salutations, perhaps indicating that Ruricius composed drafts on the same piece of writing material, and did not see fit to repeat the salutations. Here Ruricius indicates that he had not visited Clermont for some time.

RURICIUS TO BISHOP APRUNCULUS, GREETINGS

Just as I received the letter of Your Sanctity through the Venerable Gentleman[1] Eulogius[2] with pleasure, thus I sent mine gladly when he returned. I forward[3] with it the duty of salutation owed to Your Apostlehood and I request at the same time that you deign to pray for me and to ask this in particular from

---

2.54

[1] *Visera*: edd.; *vestra*: S.

[2] *praesentium dierum*: edd.; *presenti rerum*: S; *praescntium*: Mommsen.

2.55

[1] The title *vir venerabilis* suggests that he was a cleric, most likely a priest. He presumably was from either Clermont or Limoges, probably the former.

[2] Eulogius; Elogius: S, edd. The name "Elogius" is otherwise unknown, but an Eulogius (or Eulodius) was bishop of Bourges in the mid fifth century and perhaps the father of Simplicius, bishop of Bourges as of ca. 470 (Duchesne, *Fastes* 2.22, 27).

[3] *dependo*: edd.; *deponendo*: S.

our common Lord, that we now, at last, deserve to meet for a while and see each other, so that the affection, which, according to the lordly observation,[4] unfortunately[5] cools in our breasts through absence, might be revived again from its sleeping[6] cinders through our presence, and so that the reborn flame of our ancient love might be rekindled by our living voices as if by new breaths, a flame that by custom and by virtue of the fire of Him whom the Lord sent to earth both burns away the thorns of our negligence and idleness by the force of potent nature and[7] illuminates the shadows of a slumbering heart.[8]

IT IS FINISHED

2.56 [ca. 485/490]

> Ruricius refers to Aprunculus the priest Maxentius who had been commended to him by a third, unnamed, bishop. Gregory of Tours (*HF* 2.37) reports that in 496 an abbot Maxentius lived in a monastery in the territory of Poitiers, in a place later called "The Cell of St. Maxentius." If this is the Maxentius mentioned by Ruricius, and Gregory indicates he was still there in 507, then the "brother" who had recommended him would be the bishop of Poitiers (whose identity at this time is unknown: Duchesne, *Fastes* 2.82). Apparently Maxentius had some some kind of legal difficulty in Clermont.

LIKEWISE, ANOTHER OF RURICIUS TO THE SAME BISHOP

[Ruricius to Bishop Aprunculus, Greetings][1]

The persistence of suppliants supplements the duty of reciprocal benevolence in us, so that whatever we ought to do because of[2] the affection of mutual esteem, we do because of the demand of an external necessity, while we grant to the petition of another what we know is owed to our own affection. As a result, this necessity for a letter was pleasant, a natural result of our relationship, and was not <in fact>[3] extorted by the misfortune of a postulant. Moreover, just because I neglect the spontaneous courtesy of writing, at least I ought not to pass it by when it is offered. Therefore, I have sent [my letter] through our bro-

---

[4] Cf. Matthew 24.12.

[5] *quod peius est*: edd.; *quod peris est*: S.

[6] *sopitis*: edd.; *sospitis*: S.

[7] *et*: added by editors.

[8] See *Epist.* 2.6 for the use of the same metaphors, sent, presumably not accidentally, to another Arvenian correspondent.

2.56

[1] This and the following salutations are hypothetically restored from the previous one.

[2] *per*: edd.; *super*: S, Mommsen.

[3] *non vero*: Engelbrecht, Demeulenaere; *novo*: S; *non iuvet*: Mommsen; *non ex*: Krusch.

ther and fellow priest[4] Maxentius, whom our brother[5] commended to us in his own letters.[6] Having extended my salutation, I report to Your Apostlehood as he requested, for he says that he has[7] friends and acquaintances there who can explain his situation more fully in the presence of Your Beatitude, and by their testimony it might be possible to believe that which perhaps is not[8] to be believed by his own assertion.[9]

2.57 [ca. 485/490]

> At this time Ruricius' sons Ommatius and, it seems, Eparchius were clerics in the church of Clermont. Given that they would have been nearly twenty years old at the very least, they would have been born by the mid 460s, and this would seem to make them Ruricius' eldest children. In this letter, Ruricius asks Aprunculus to forgive some "foolishness" (*ignorantia*) of Eparchius, the nature of which is unspecified.

LIKEWISE, TO THE SAME PERSON

[Ruricius to Bishop Aprunculus, Greetings]

Our sons Ommatius and Eparchius have sent to me letters full of tears and lamentation, begging in particular that I serve as an intercessor with Your Sanctity because of our son Eparchius' own foolishness, and trusting that you are bound to deny me nothing because of our mutual regard. And therefore I have directed my priest Eusebiolus[1] to Your Piety in this matter. Through him I extend particular greetings, and I request that out of regard for my pleas you deign,[2] after first having fittingly admonished him,[3] to grant indulgence for Eparchius' error, because, just as in the defense of a transgression it is <not>[4] fitting that blame be relaxed for one who resists stupidly and faithlessly until he

---

[4] "per fratrum et compresbyterum nostrum"; Ruricius again refers to a priest as "brother."
[5] That is, Maxentius' bishop.
[6] *epistulis*: Engelbrecht, Demeulaenere; *episcopis*: S; *episcopus*: Krusch.
[7] *habere*: edd.; *hare*: S.
[8] *non*: S, edd.; *nos*: Demeulenaere (typographical error).
[9] At this time, the Germanic practice of multiple oath-taking as a means of settling disputes was becoming more and more widespread.
2.57
[1] A priest of Limoges, otherwise unknown.
[2] *supplicatione <digne>mini qu<i>a*: Mommsen, edd.; *supplicationem iniqua*: S; *supplicatione mini<me ini>qua*: edd.; *supplicatione <non> iniqua*: Gustafson.
[3] The language in this and the following letter suggests that Aprunculus' authority over Eparchius is more than merely that of a bishop over a parishoner, and that he, like Ommatius (see *Epist.* 2.28), was a junior member of Aprunculus' clergy.
[4] *non*: added by editors.

acknowledges his guilt, likewise it is fitting for the acknowledgement of a transgression to confer[5] pardon on one who confesses.[6] Indeed, an unfeigned confession of wrongdoing is the remedy for sin, nor is there a place left for public punishment when the guilty one is punished by a torturing conscience.

2.58 [ca. 485/490]

In a subsequent letter Ruricius continued to intercede on Eparchius' behalf. It turned out that Aprunculus had written to Ruricius on the same matter, reporting that Eparchius' delict had been serious enough to merit excommunication, something that the two brothers apparently had neglected to mention in their earlier letter. In 506, the Council of Agde cited several clerical crimes that could result in excommunication. Canon two noted, "contumacious clerics ... are to be disciplined by bishops, and if any [clerics] of a superior rank, incited by pride, perhaps disdain communion or are absent from church or fail to fulfil their duty, let the communion of the strangers (*communio peregrina*) be permitted them, to the extent that when penitence has corrected them, reentered onto the rolls they might recover their rank and office" (*CCL* 148.193). Clerics who committed a theft received the same punishment (can.5: ibid. p.194). (The *communia peregrina* perhaps also was offered to strangers who had not presented the proper letters of commendation from their bishops.) Drunkards suffered a thirty-day excommunication (can.41: ibid. pp.210). The nature of Eparchius' fault might be found in the report of Gregory of Tours (*Glor.mart.* 86) that a priest "Epachius," who was of noble ancestry and stationed in the *vicus Ricomagensis* (Riom), just north of Clermont, was a habitual drunkard and even conducted Christmas Eve services in an inebriated condition; such behavior could have merited excommunication. Moreover, the third canon of Agde advised, "Indeed, bishops, if... they presume to excommunicate those who are innocent or culpable for petty reasons and perhaps decline to receive those eager for grace, should be warned by letters of neighboring bishops of the respective province..." (ibid. 193-194). Ruricius' letter, as polite as it is, could fall into this last category by suggesting to Aprunculus that he had overreacted.

LIKEWISE, ANOTHER OF RURICIUS TO THE SAME PERSON

[Ruricius to Bishop Aprunculus, Greetings]

The day before I received the letter of Your Sanctity, I sent my fellow priest,[1] as you will have been able to recognize when he himself reports, to Your Brotherhood[2] in the same cause in which you wrote to me, so that, as not

---

[5] *conferre*: erased in S.
[6] Ruricius repeats his words: "peccati... agnoscat... peccati agnitio."
2.58
[1] Presumably Eusebiolus, who had delivered *Epist.* 2.57.
[2] *germanitatem vestram*, suggesting a blood tie, perhaps to Hiberia's family.

only our son Eparchius himself but also his brother tearfully implored in letters to me,[3] I — who[4] granted indulgence because of the confession of the transgression and the plea for pardon and the tie of blood, because I had no idea that you were going to write to me about this matter — might approach Your Apostlehood as a suppliant. But because you deign to consult[5] My Humility on account of that fondness which, God willing, exists between us, so that[6] I might indicate in my own words[7] to you, in particular, whether your punishment was just, Lord knows that I approve and praise and ardently admire your action[8] because, at the same time that you have inflicted pain upon a single desperate individual through the application of the spiritual sword in order to return him to health, you have brought sanity to many who were languishing. In fact, many in the church who cannot be cured by word are cleansed by example.

For the rest, let pity follow severity, with the result that you might receive with the gentleness of a father the one whom you chastised by your episcopal authority; and invoking that Gospel teaching[9] it is fitting for us to follow and imitate in all things the one who not only clemently granted pardon to the son, the waster of the paternal substance, confessing his sin, but even freely yielded his original good standing; and let us grieve with the fallen, support the ruined, embrace him who has returned, rejoice that he has been found. And I am certain that Your Apostlehood has acted for this reason: you exclude from the mother[10] a son who is a bit infirm so that, after a little while, you will have restored him to her recovered, and you punish in the present one over whom you desire to rejoice in eternity.

2.59 [ca. 490/500]

> The Severus to whom Ruricius writes here, the son of an old friend, is otherwise unknown, unless he is to be identified with the priest Severus who dwelt in the *vicus Sexciacensis* (St-Justin) near the *urbs Bigorritana* (St-Lézer) (Gregory of Tours, *Glor.conf.* 48-49) near the Pyrenees. Given the proximity of this place to the famous marble quarries, it may be that Severus' "kindnesses and favors" involved help in securing the columns for Ruricius' church (see *Epist.* 2.64). He is omitted from *PLRE II*, but see Mathisen, *Studies*, p.385.

---

[3] Eparchius and Ommatius would have ensured that their letters reached Ruricius first.
[4] *qui*: S, Engelbrecht, Demeulenacre; *quibus*: Lütjohann, Krusch; *cui*: Mommsen.
[5] *consulare*; cf. *Epist.* 2.31, *consolare*.
[6] *ut*: edd.; *et*: S.
[7] "potissimum apicibus": perhaps in the nature of a formal deposition, cf. *Epist.* 2.51.
[8] Ruricius tactfully accepts that Aprunculus already had excommunicated Eparchius without consulting him, and before he had the opportunity to intercede.
[9] For the prodigal son, see Luke 15.11-32; and *Epist.* 1.1 and 2.23.
[10] This makes it clear that Eparchius had been excommunicated.

BISHOP RURICIUS TO HIS SON SEVERUS, GREETINGS

At the same time[1] that you excuse my negligence and idleness[2] you draw attention to them, and I acknowledge that I am in your debt for your kindnesses and favors. But I know that you do this with a sincere and perfect love, with which you esteem me, because what you bestow upon me is not too much for Your Charity, seeing that you desire also to grant yourself[3] totally and daily to me. But, as for me, the good will of a spirit as eager as possible is more than sufficient, even if an assiduousness[4] of obedience[5] is lacking. For this reason, having extended my greeting I give the richest thanks to Your Piety because you not only retain but even overcome the affection of your well-remembered father toward me.

2.60 [ca. 490/500]

A Storacius was Prefect of Rome in 443 and of Italy in 453; *PLRE II*, p.1033, suggests, on the basis of the rarity of the name, that he might have been the father or grandfather of the Storacius addressed by Ruricius. If so, given Ruricius' own distant connections to the Italian aristocracy, he might have been a relative of Ruricius as well. Here Ruricius apologises for failing to send something that he had promised, apparently a rather large item.

BISHOP RURICIUS TO HIS SON STORACIUS, GREETINGS

I bear and I extend copious gratitude to Your Piety because you have reminded[1] me about the negligence of my servants[2] at the same time that your kind affection furnishes a fitting conveyance,[3] which a crafty enemy[4] pilfered[5] from me. Therefore, the Lord permitted him to impose this upon me at this time, so

---

2.59
[1] *dum*: Engelbrecht, Demeulenaere; *non*: S; omitted by Krusch.
[2] Cf. the end of *Epist.* 2.55.
[3] *vos*: edd.; *suos*: S.
[4] *etiamsi assiduitas*: Lütjohann, Engelbrecht, Demeulenaere; *etiam siduitas*: S; *etsi assiduitas*: Mommsen.
[5] "assiduitas ... obsequii"; cf. *Epist.* 2.56, "assiduitas supplicantium."
2.60
[1] *rescire*: edd.; *nescire*: S.
[2] For a different outcome regarding the behavior of Ruricius' servants, see *Epist.* 2.65.
[3] *subvectionem*: it seems that Ruricius had been expected to deliver a bulky item to Storacius; cf. Ruricius' concern for providing conveyance for the delivery of marble columns in *Epist.* 2.64, not to mention his sending of a horse to Celsus and Sedatus. In this case, it is Storacius who eventually provided the transportation.
[4] "callidus inimicus": an allusion, perhaps, to Satan, that is, "the devil did it."
[5] "subvectionem... subtraxerat... subministravit"

that He might validate both my suffering through my injury and your affection toward me through your compassion, and so that He might provide without any loss[6] to my property profit to you for your labor because of the kindness of your esteem.[7]

2.61 [ca. 490/500]

Vittamerus seems to have been a Goth, perhaps an Ostrogoth; the title *sublimitas* shows that he was, or had been, a secular official; see *PLRE II*, p.1178, which suggests that he was the Ostrogothic leader Videmer, who had invaded Italy with his father in 473/474 (ibid.1164-1165; Jordanes, *Getica* 282, *Romana* 347; see P. Périn, "L'armée de Vidimer et la question des dépôts funéraires chez les Wisigoths en Gaule et en Espagne," in F. Vallet, M. Kazanski eds., *L'armée romaine et les barbares* [Paris, 1993] pp.411-414). Ruricius' sending of perishables suggests that Vittamerus did not live far away; he also received *Epist.* 2.63.

BISHOP RURICIUS TO HIS SON VITTAMERUS, GREETINGS

Your Worthiness[1] makes me your intimate because what is offered gladly by me is accepted gratefully by you, because a gift is approved as suitable and sweet which size does not recommend but affection commends. This consideration brings it about that, in order to fulfill my dispensation of spontaneous devotion to you, I, in fact, have in my prayers what I do not have in my words. Therefore, having extended my greeting, <I add>[2] that I have presumed to send a hundred pears to Your Exaltedness and another hundred to my daughter,[3] which, if they perhaps are displeasing in the tasting of their flavor, will be pleasing, I trust, through the affection of the sender.

2.62 [ca. 490/500]

Namatius, the husband of Ceraunia, had died (see, e.g., *Epist.* 2.50) well before the latest letters in the collection were written, another indication that these final letters are not in chronological order. For another letter to Namatius alone, see *Epist.* 2.5

---

[6] *dispendio*: edd.; *dubio*: S.

[7] For a similar sentiment, with Ruricius as the beneficiary, see *Epist.* 2.50.

2.61

[1] "vestra dignatio."

[2] A word is needed: Leutjohann suggests "significo"; or perhaps "indico."

[3] Figuratively speaking, presumably; probably Vittamerus' wife. The pears would suggest that this letter was written in the summer.

BISHOP RURICIUS TO HIS BROTHER NAMATIUS

I greet you effusively and I hope that, if you should be unable the day after tomorrow,[1] you still will deign to visit us for the third celebration,[2] because I am alight with desire for Your Charity and I say with the prophet, "My soul, for you, is like a land without water; my spirit fails. Hide not thy face."[3] Do not delay your arrival, so that with the comfort of a short visit you might extinguish the fire that you have kindled[4] in my breast.[5]

IT IS FINISHED

2.63 [ca. 490/500]

In a second letter to Vittamerus Ruricius mentions an estate called Decaniacum. M. Aussel, "Première mention de Dégagnac dans l'histoire écrité à l'occasion du passage de Ruricius," *Bulletin de la Société des Etudes du Lot* 109 (1988) pp. 221-228, suggests that it is to be identified as Dégagnac (Lot). If so, then this would have been the name of Ruricius' property near Gurdo, which is located just 8 kilometers to the northeast.

BISHOP RURICIUS TO HIS SON VITTAMERUS

I give thanks to Your Exaltedness, most considerate toward me, because you have put me at ease by the diligence of your letters regarding your activities and ill health,[1] which you know had made me concerned, with the favor of God, as a result of the injunction of friendship.[2] For this reason, with this letter I render a reciprocal duty of salutation to Your Nobility and I report that I have sent you this letter from Decaniacum,[3] likewise indicating to you my[4] own good health, with the favor of the divinity, which I trust pleases you. The Lord will provide that having quickly returned from here[5] I will merit being presented to

---

2.62

[1] "secundo crastino."

[2] *tertia feria*: Wednesday, perhaps the one after Easter, cf. the celebration of the *quarta feria* at Briva (*Epist.* 2.24). Namatius seems to have been living nearby.

[3] Psalms 142.6-7; cf. *Epist.* 2.34.

[4] Cf. *Epist.* 2.26, 55.

[5] *pectoris*: edd.; *peccaris*: S.

2.63

[1] More concern over health.

[2] "pro amicitiarum iure."

[3] In the Carolingian period, the *decania* were the ten subsidiary churches under the authority of a larger church (Aubrun, *Limoges*, p.236, who does not mention Decaniacum or Dégagnac).

[4] *meam quoque*: Lütjohann, Krusch; *meamque*: S, Engelbrecht, Demeulenaere.

[5] Vittamerus, therefore, may have lived near Limoges, if that was indeed the place that Ruricius planned to "return" to.

your gaze so that you might stir up in person the affection of him whose longing you excite with your kindness.

2.64 [ca. 490/500]

Clarus was bishop of Eauze (Elusa) and attended the Council of Agde in 506
(Duchesne, *Fastes* 2.95). In this letter Ruricius confirms his order for some
marble columns, perhaps for use in the church that he built for St. Augustine (see
Introduction). The columns probably came from the famous quarries of St-Béat,
Sost, and elsewhere in Novempopulana, whose marble, during the sixth century,
continued to be used for the production of the distinctive Aquitanian sarcophagi
and other objects: see E. James, *The Merovingian Archaeology of South-West
Gaul* (Oxford, 1977) pp.29, 234-238, and passim; B. Sapene, "Autels votifs, ateliers de marbriers et sanctuaire gallo-romains decouverts a Saint-Béat en 1946,"
Revue de Comminges 69 (1946) pp.283-325; and J.B. Ward-Perkins, "The Sculpture of Visigothic France," *Archaeologia* 87 (1938) pp.79-128. I.N. Wood, however, suggests ("The Audience of Architecture in Post-Roman Gaul," in L.A.S.
Butler, R.K. Morris eds., *The Anglo-Saxon Church* [London, 1986] pp.74-79) that
by this time the Pyrenaean quarrying industry had failed, and that the "columns
had been taken from an earlier building" and were "a gift" from Clarus.

BISHOP RURICIUS TO HIS BROTHER BISHOP CLARUS

I should not speak reciprocally to Your Apostlehood[1] regarding that affection which you expend upon me as a result not of my merits but of the benevolence of your spirit; I am unable to reimburse you for your kindnesses, but neither can I express in words thanks as great as you deserve. Nevertheless, I extend through my letter the due duty of salutation and I forward through the
communication of my page part of my heart, into which I have admitted affection through desire of you, and likewise I beseech that you pray to our shared
Lord that He quickly cause us to clasp the reward of each other's presence,[2]
and that those whom He connected by the stimulus of His inspiration may join
their visages in a shared view, so that vision may inflame in us the desire that
our words kindle.

I truly give thanks for the columns and, as you ordered, because I am presently unable to send vehicles there because of the approaching winter, I will
send them after the sanctified Pasch,[3] the divinity willing. Concerning the les-

---

2.64

[1] A title of honor often used by Ruricius even for ordinary provincial bishops; cf. *Epist.* 2.51 to
Censurius of Auxerre and *Epist.* 2.56, 58, to Aprunculus of Clermont.

[2] "fructum de nostra capere praesentia"; cf. pseudo-Sulpicius Severus, *Epist. ad Claudiam
sororem*, "de nostra nos fructum faciat capere praesentia"; cf. also Ruricius, *Epist.* 1.16, 2.41,
and Faustus, *Epist.* "Propitia divinitate."

[3] That is to say, Ruricius was delaying by a good four months at least.

ser ones, as you confided verbally,[4] if they can be found,[5] I note that I need ten of them.[6] But if the Lord allows everything to prosper, I will send a man to you before I send the vehicles.[7]

2.65 [ca. 495]

Bishop Volusianus of Tours was a native of the Auvergne and a relative of his predecessor Perpetuus. He was said to have been suspected of collaboration with the Franks and sent into exile, where he died ca. 498 (see Introduction). He was succeeded by Verus. He also received a letter from Sidonius (*Epist.* 7.17). In Ruricius' waspish letter, the last in the collection and almost an epitaph for his times, Ruricius complains about some unspecified maltreatment that his letter carriers had suffered at the hands of Volusianus' wife.

BISHOP RURICIUS TO HIS BROTHER BISHOP VOLUSIANUS

Thus,[1] what is worse, long forgetfulness has destroyed the ancient and inherent affection in us, caused partly, as[2] it must be confessed, by our own negligence, partly by the exigencies of the times,[3] partly by infirmity of the body, so that having become completely forgetful, we demand from ourselves[4] not only no reciprocal duties but not even letters. I marvel that Your Nobility[5] sends a letter to me like to a son, because without any regard for religion or family ties my injuries are so pleasing to you that you do not wish to make up for

---

[4] A verbal message of Clarus, presumably relating to technical details. Clarus, it seems, was functioning in the capacity of a commercial middle-man, much like the reader Amantius of Clermont discussed by Sidonius (*Epist.* 6.8).

[5] "si inveniri possunt", that is, if they can be made ready for this shipment.

[6] Perhaps implying that at least ten large ones were needed as well.

[7] *vehicula*. It would appear that the Roman road system continued in use until well into the sixth century; see, e.g., J.-M. Desbordes, "Enquête sur le tracé de la voie antique de Limoges à Saintes," *TAL* 12 (1992) pp.120-121. Assuming the columns were to be delivered from Eauze, they would have had to be conveyed some 330 km. if the primary roads via Auch, Agen, Trajectus (Bergerac, on the Dordogne river), and Périgueux were used. The distance could be cut a bit by taking secondary roads directly north from Eauze to the Garonne, and then backtracking to Agen to pick up the main road north to Limoges. Circa 450/475 Euphronius of Autun sent marble to Tours for the tomb of St. Martin (Greg.Tur., *Virt. Mart.* 1.2).

2.65

[1] The letter seems to begin *in medias res*; perhaps only a partial draft survived, of a section to which Ruricius had given extra attention.

[2] *quoniam*: Engelbrecht, Demeulenaere; *quam*: S, Krusch.

[3] "necessitate temporis"; in this case, perhaps an allusion to the Frankish raids of ca. 494-498.

[4] *nos*: S; *vos*: edd.

[5] "nobilitatem tuam": Volusianus was, of course, an aristocrat, but for Ruricius to address a bishop with this honorific is a bit unusual, and it may be another indication of his pique.

them. For this reason, if I had not taken heed of my status and office, I would have sent back to you the bearer of your letter in such a state as my men were rendered not by your wife, but by an excessively froward and unrestrained governess,[6] whose manners — even if you tolerate them for so long, either voluntarily or by compulsion, to the diminution of your reputation — you should know that others neither wish nor are content to bear. For — because you write that you are rendered stupefied by fear of the enemy[7] — he who is accustomed to endure a domestic enemy ought not to fear a foreign one.

IT IS FINISHED[8]

THE LETTERS OF LORD RURICIUS, BISHOP OF LIMOGES, END[9]

---

[6] "domina procax nimium et effrenata."

[7] "metu hostium": the Franks would seem to be the only people who could be referred to in this manner in this context. Volusianus' trepidation does not suggest a person actively colluding with the enemy he purported to fear, so perhaps his "collusion" with the Franks was more circumstantial in nature: he did own property deep in Frankish territory at Baiocasses (Bayeux) (Sidonius Apollinaris, *Epist*.7.16), and all of his suffragan sees were located to the north, in territory that, if not under Frankish rule, was certainly under Frankish influence.

[8] "Finit": given that the word "finiunt" immediately follows in the concluding sentence at the end of the collection, this "finit," which otherwise have been superfluous, must have been seen as part of this particular letter.

[9] "Finiunt epistul(a)e domni
    Ruricii episco   pi
    Le mo vi ce ni",
with the first and third lines in red letters. The collection ends on p.277, the letter collection of Desiderius of Cahors begins on the next page with an ornate title similar to the one that began Ruricius' letters.

APPENDIX I

OTHER LETTERS BY AND TO FAUSTUS OF RIEZ

Several other letters of Faustus of Riez survive besides those written to Ruricius. Some are more in the nature of religious tracts presented in epistolographic form rather than letters-qua-letters. Two of them, "Quaeris a me" and a letter to Paulinus of Bordeaux, are preserved in the *Sangallensis* in the midst of the other letters to Ruricius. They probably were gathered up from Ruricius' archives when the collection was originally assembled. Ruricius could have acquired them when the exiled Faustus was staying with him. The letter to Paulinus might have been of particular interest, for it dealt with the concerns of an aristocrat who, like Ruricius, was just embarking on the adoption of the religious life.

Three more of Faustus' letters, those to Felix, Graecus, and Lucidus, also appear in the *Sangallensis*. They are found in a separate set of quaternions near the beginning of the manuscript and probably were not part of Ruricius' archive. Indeed, these three letters circulated as a separate collection which also included the letter from Paulinus (omitted from the *Sangallensis* 190) that had resulted in Faustus' reply. Manuscripts in which one or more of these four letters appear are the sixth/seventh-century *Codex Parisinus* 12097, also known as the "Corbie Collection" ("C"); the eighth-century *Codex Parisinus* 1564, also known as the "Pithou Collection" ("Q"); and the ninth-century *Codex Parisinus* 2166 ("P"), the sole source of Faustus' *De gratia* ("On Grace"). The last of these also includes another letter, to Leontius of Arles, which survives as the preface to the *De gratia*. In addition, a fragment of a possible lost letter of Faustus ("Whoever wishes to fulfil the duty of a married man loses the grace of consecration") survives in a letter of Pope John II to Caesarius of Arles in 534 (*CSEL* 21.220).

For the sake of completeness, translations of selected sections of these additional letters of Faustus, along with the letter of Paulinus, are included below. In general, only the sections that might qualify as "personal" are translated, whereas the lengthy "religous tract" sections are not. In addition, because the published editions of the letters of Faustus are completely inconsistent with regard to their organization and numbering, the following table is included to assist in sorting them out; the other letters addressed to Ruricius, the editions of which are equally incompatible, are included as well. Also included in the table are references to the edition of Canisius,[1] which was reprinted in the *Patrologia latina*, but with different numbering, and to the numbers that appear in the mar-

---

[1] H. Canisius, *Antiquae lectiones*, vol.5 (Paris, 1604).

gin of the *Sangallensis* next to some of the letters of Faustus. The letters are cited in the order in which they appear in the *Sangallensis* using, if available, the *Sangallensis* index entries.

CONCORDANCE OF LETTERS OF FAUSTUS AND LETTERS TO RURICIUS

	Sg190 pages	Ms. prov.	No.in Sg190	Cani-sius	PL 58	MGH 8	CSEL 21	CCL 64[2]
Epist. tres Fausti ad Felicem	27- 33	SQ	---	2	5	16	*6*[3]	-
et ad Graecum	33- 44[4]	SQ	---	3	6	17	7	-
et ad Lucidium	44- 48	SP	---	4	1	18	*1*	-
								[5]
Epistulae V Fausti ad Ruricium	66- 71	S	om.	5	7	1	*8*	2.1
	71- 77	S	om.	6	8	2	*9*	2.2
	77- 80	S	III	7	9	3	*10*	2.3
	80- 82	S	IIII	8	10	4	*11*	2.4
	82- 83	S	V	9	11	5	*12*	2.5
Epistula Graeci ad Ruricium	83- 84	S	VI	10	12	6	1	1.1
Epistula Victorini ad Ruricium	84- 86	S	VII	11	13	7	2	1.2
Epistula Taurencii ad Ruricium	86- 89	S	VIII	12	14	8	3	1.3
Epistulae Sedati ad Ruricium II	89- 91	S	VIIII	13	15	9	4	1.4
	91	S	X	14	16	10	5	1.5
Epistula Eufrasii ad Ruricium	91- 92	S	XI	15	17	11	6	1.6
Epist Fausti "Quaeris a me"[6]	92-111	S	XII	16	3	20	*3*	-
Epistula Paulini ad Faustum	---	QC	N/A	--	--	14	*4*	-
Epistula Fausti ad Paulinum	111-26	SQ	om.	17	4	15	*5*	-
Epistula Caesarii ad Ruricium	126-28	S	om.	18	18	12	7	1.7
Epistula Sedati ad Ruricium	128-30	S	om.	19	19	13	8	1.8
Exemplar epistulae Lucidi	328-32	SP	om.	20	2	19	2	-
Epist. "Quod pro sollicitudinis"[7]	---	P	om.	--	--	--	--	-

---

[2] In Appendix I and II.

[3] The letters of Faustus (in italics) (pp.161-219) and to Ruricius (pp.443-450) are numbered separately.

[4] In the *Sangallensis*, page 37 was initially skipped and later used for a bee benediction.

[5] In the Sg 190 the preceding letters are in a separate set of quaternions.

[6] This letter survives complete only in the *Sangallensis*; the third section of this letter, beginning with the words "ut respondeam praecipis," is preserved in manuscripts of the *De statu animi* of Claudianus Mamertus; in general, the Sg 190 preserves the best text (see *CSEL* 11.viiii, 2-17).

[7] The prologue to Faustus' *De gratia*, addressed to bishop Leontius of Arles.

Faustus, *Epistula* "Quaeris a me" (*SG* no.12) [ca. 468]

This lengthy document is more properly described as a theological tract than a letter. Except for conventional introductory protestations of lack of ability, it contains nearly nothing of a personal nature, and it ends merely with the word, perhaps a later addition, "amen." It is prefaced only by the words "Epistula sancti Fausti," but this clearly was not original, and may have been supplied by an editor or scribe who merely assumed that the text was an "epistula" because the other items in the collection were. The unnamed recipient, addressed as "reverentissime sacerdotum," presumably was a bishop. He had asked Faustus three theological questions, the last of which was, "In human affairs, which things must be considered corporeal and which incorporeal?" Faustus responded, among other things, that the soul was corporeal, and this led to a response, ca. 469/470, from the priest Mamertus Claudianus of Vienne, who denounced Faustus' views in his *De statu animae* ("On the Nature of the Soul") (*CSEL* 21), which then circulated along with the appropriate section of Faustus' letter. It is probably only this section of the letter that was seen by Gennadius of Marseille, who reported regarding Faustus (*De viris inlustribus* 86), "I read ... another [little book] against those who say that there is anything incorporeal in living things, in which he proves both by scriptural testimony and by the testimony of the fathers that nothing can be considered incorporeal except God." See Elg, *Studia*, pp.47, 90-91, 111-121; Krusch, *MGH AA* 8.lx; Mathisen, *Factionalism*, pp.235-241; and B. Rehling, *De Fausti Reiensis epistula tertia. Commentatio historica* (Münster, 1898). Preserved complete only in ms. "S"; partially in manuscripts of the *De statu animae*. Text: *CSEL* 21.168-181; *MGH AA* 8.292-298.

A LETTER OF ST. FAUSTUS

You ask me, most reverend of pontiffs,[1] how one should respond to the Arians, who with a blasphemous tongue attempt to assert: "He[2] is unable," one says, "to exist unless as a junior created from one who was not created."[3] Regarding such matters, I might assume total silence, as if I had been ordered to explain not so much for the sake of instruction in a topic but for the sake of a confession of faith, observing this first of all, that I not discuss matters in themselves obscure out of a desire for organized speech, but I put forth certain indications of the sense of a pauper, which might seem to serve not so much as ornamentation as for the intellect. I reasons, therefore, just as students are accustomed to respond to questioning teachers. Therefore, I speak at the request of Your Beatitude so that I might be put to the test, and I testify to my ignorance so that I might be taught. For if I am silent in the presence of the most learned,

---

Faustus, "Quaeris a me"

[1] "reverentissime sacerdotum."

[2] That is, Christ.

[3] One of the primary Arian tenets.

I hardly will be able to learn what I do not know.

Regarding the matter of "not created," we must understand that the substance of things is one thing, and the name of things is something different...

[*Faustus went on to argue that Christ is not "lesser" than God. He then turned to his questioner's second concern: whether God was affected by "human" feelings.*]

After this, in the second place, you ask me how it can be written in a certain letter, with regard to the substance of God, "He feels nothing with the feeling of a sufferer, but He feels through His connection with a fellow-sufferer"[4]
...

[*After dealing with this issue, Faustus went on to the third, the one subsequently dealt with by Claudianus*]

If, therefore, this simple and concise response is sufficient for an inquiring teacher, let us pass on to the third question, to which I respond as you command: which things[5] in human affairs must be considered corporeal and which incorporeal? Regarding this question, I will put forth some thoughts not in accordance with the presumption of my own feelings but in accordance with the opinion of the blessed elders...

[*In this, the lengthiest section of the document, Faustus presented his view that the soul was incorporeal, saying, for example:*]

With this being the case, you therefore make the claim to me that the soul is not corporeal, because, as it has been said, it neither is localized nor does it exist in quality or quantity. But the danger of believing this will be demonstrated in the following arguments. Now, truly,[6] in this matter the value of my argumentation in the ensuing discussion will depend on this: if the soul neither is localized nor is subjected to quantification, I certainly must concede that it is incorporeal. But if I demonstrate that it can be defined by quantity or location, I consequently demonstrate that it is in fact contained within the body, and you yourself no longer should have any doubt[7]...

---

[4] Faustus is being coy here, for this is a direct quotation from his own *Epist.* "Honoratus officio" to the deacon Graecus of Marseille (see below), which also dealt with the issue of the nature of God and Christ, and, like others of Faustus' "letters", had an independent circulation.

[5] The remaining portion of the letter is preserved in manuscripts containing Claudianus Mamertus' "On the Nature of the Soul."

[6] The words "credere in subsequentibus demonstrabitur. nunc vero..." are omitted, apparently inadvertently, from the *Sangallensis* 190.

[7] It is only by defining the parameters of the discussion in this manner that Faustus is able to

Paulinus, *Epistula ad Faustum* "Scribere vobis" (*SG* --) [ca. 465/470]

In this letter, lacking in the *Sangallensis*, Paulinus asked Faustus several theological questions, to which Faustus responded in a long letter that is included in the *Sangallensis*. Paulinus is referred to as *magnificentia tua*, indicating that he was an aristocrat of high rank. This letter also circulated independently, and Avitus of Vienne, in a refererence to it, indicates that Paulinus was from Bordeaux (*Epist.4: MGH AA* 6.2.29). As a result, it has been suggested that he is to be identified as Paulinus the son of Pontius Leontius (*PLRE II*, pp.674-675, 847), a *vir inlustris* of Bordeaux and good friend of Sidonius Apollinaris (*Carm.* 22). Like Ruricius, Paulinus was on the verge of adopting the religious life. He had been terrified by the picture painted by the hermit Marinus, and asked for Faustus' guidance. In addition, like the anonymous bishop of the previous letter, Paulinus was interested in the nature of the soul, and this suggests a date for the later of the late 460s. See Elg, *Studia*, pp. 47-48, 131-132. Preserved in mss. "C" and "Q". Text: *CSEL* 21.181-183; *MGH AA* 8.275-276.

PAULINUS TO A LORD, EQUALLY FATHER AND PATRON, THE POPE FAUSTUS

On the one hand, the fear of writing to you has held me back, but on the other, affection compels me, and thus my uncertain mind is tossed between one alternative and the other, just as a fearful sailor entrusts his sails to fickle fortune. But I, who have a dependable port in you, often presume for myself upon the outcome of an uncertain voyage, and I have chosen moreover to create loathing rather than guilt. Indeed, I recognize best of all that my lord Faustus will receive my letters without disdain. But because my lord the hermit Marinus,[1] a saintly man and one to be feared because of his excessive rigor, with enormous severity manifested in me such a great fear, I inquisitively approach you. While I fulfil the daily human destiny, I am entwined in carnal sins, I engage in every activity that can be called sinful. I have undertaken a sudden penitence;[2] I desire to know whether it eradicates sin wholly or in part; or, if those believing in the unified trinity, who do not sin through corporeal delicts in their spirit, are tortured by perpetual punishments and tortures, by flames and every kind of torment.

---

make a convincing argument.
Paulinus, "Scribere vobis"
[1] The hermit Marinus, who also is mentioned in Faustus' subsequent reply, is otherwise unknown. In the mid fifth century, an aristocrat Marinus was a resident of Narbonne; Sidonius Apollinaris (*Carm.* 23.479-482) mentions his *sedulitas* ("zeal"), a characteristic consistent with the monk's hard-nosed approach; perhaps Marinus was yet another Gallic aristocrat who took refuge in the religious life.
[2] Penitence involved a public acknowledgment of one's sins, followed by a period of penance. Penitents then were expected to adopt the "religious life" and to attempt to live without sin.

This is my own opinion, that, if a Christian is exposed to all these things, then an Arian cannot suffer anything more, regardless of whether the soul, enclosed in a corporeal bond, is contained in some sort of custody or is held by a closed prison, or whether it is tossed about uncertainly among the winds. And because I know that in this hour[3] all thought perishes, if you permit me, I respectfully ask whether both good and bad thought descends from the soul, which is considered to be immortal, or whether it comes from some sort of sense and intellect, or whether it senses something from upright feeling. And because we know that all things are granted to those who are good, so that even greater things are available after death than in life, I would like to know what is given to or taken away from the wicked, and I would like to be instructed regarding whether the the soul itself is better described as corporeal or incorporeal, and, because "the flesh is weak but the soul is ready"[4], I would like to know what is immortal, and how it can be tormented for mortal sins, or whether the soul and the spirit are the same, or in what way they are separate.

For the aforementioned man terrified me in this way, [saying] that even with the interposition of the sacrament, one who succumbs to corporeal sins cannot be promised any pardon, but is retained in these punishments until the very resurrection, nor can he be shriven of diabolic torments, because he had accumulated fixed [punishments] through his corporeal sins. In spite of this, I most miserably believe that he who never, knowledgeable of the evil in himself or as a tricky falsifier, violates the sign, once accepted, of the divine name and the mark[5] of our Lord fixed on the forehead, with torments freely accepted for the purpose of expiating sin, produces on the ultimate day a pure aerial sense and fire in a simple spirit. For if we, as sinners, incur all those things that my lord Marinus threatens, I do not know what more an impious person can suffer. Grant me pardon, for I impose injury on Your Piety, because as a new and someday future disciple I wish to be instructed by a veteran teacher.[6]

---

[3] That is, the hour of death.

[4] Matthew 26.41; Mark 14.38.

[5] *character*.

[6] It was possible for laypersons to seek instruction from any bishop they chose: Note can.55 of the Second Council of Arles (ca. 500) (*CCL* 148.125), "If any layperson through love of religion believes that he should commit himself to a certain bishop, this same person shall claim for himself the one whom he received for the sake of instruction."

Faustus, *Epistula ad Paulinum* "Admiranda mihi" (*SG* no.13) [ca. 465/470]

In another lengthy letter, Faustus enthusiastically responded to Paulinus' string of theological questions. In the margin, the *Sangallensis* numbers the different sections of Faustus' response, from i to xii. See Elg, *Studia*, pp. 24-25, 33-34, 39, 48-51, 91-92, 113-114, 121-122, 133. Preserved in mss. "S" and "Q." Text: *CSEL* 21.183-195; *MGH AA* 8.276-282.

FAUSTUS TO A LORD NOTABLE AND TO BE SPECIALLY CULTIVATED BY ME WITH THE GREATEST HONOR, PAULINUS

The page of your letters, which is always admirable for me, now gleams more abundantly with the double light of eloquence and faith, because it questions regarding the nature of the soul[1] and sighs over the future judgment with an anxious trepidation. In a certain place, the divine speech says, "Rightly does wisdom reflect upon the questioner."[2] In fact, it is a certain part of knowledge to know what one does not know, and prudently to inquire regarding those matters that one unknowingly does not know.

In the first place, you think that it must be asked whether it is possible for those lying in the constraints of extreme necessity to expiate capital offenses with a penitence of brief duration. One who believes that sins contracted over a long period can be erased through sudden and now ineffectual tears deceives himself with an inimical persuasion...

[Faustus went on to discuss in depth each of Paulinus' questions, often quoting Paulinus' words before responding to each one. Regarding the nature of the soul, he responded:]

That which coincides with God, this alone is incorporeal... [But] the soul is enclosed in a localized space... What is that which, removed from its supernal home, submits to a place, if not corporeal?

[Faustus then dealt with the issues raised by the monk Marinus, the twelfth and final topic enumerated in the margin of the Sangallensis:]

... regarding what you clearly stated, "For if we, as sinners, incur all those things that my lord Marinus threatens, I do not know what more an impious person can suffer": for those who are everlastingly wicked, punishments have their own categories, so that one who is guilty of serious sins is tormented by ever-

---

Faustus, "Admiranda mihi"

[1] Even though this question was not Paulinus' primary concern, it is the one that Faustus picks up on first.

[2] Cf. Ecclesiastes 24.46.

lasting albeit, so to speak, somehow bearable punishments, but the impious person by unheard of ones. Futhermore, the grace of baptism is able to free a man from eternal death, if his integrity and honor does not perish because of certain things. The refusal of a heretic to accept it[3] is a serious sin, but for a Christian to accept it and lose it is no less serious. In addition, one who as a defiler rushes into the fellowship of the sacred gathering through the nuptial faith of baptism is expelled, having lost the brightness of purity, from the illustrious convocation of the just and is thrown out into the exterior shadows. Or should we believe that one who is unchaste, venal, and bloodstained might possess the snowy whiteness of saintly regeneration or one who, shortening his life by a headlong tumble or by hanging himself, crosses over to the side of the impious?

We read that inextinguishable flames are readied for capital crimes, but we do not read that a man living in his wickedness can be saved through baptism alone. An inimical security promises, perilously for itself, that which the celestial scripture does not affirm, and much more perilously it does not believe those things that the truth advocates. The most blessed man Marinus taught otherwise,[4] as you say, but just as that thing, which the Lord promised to those who love Him, cannot, according to the testimony of the apostle,[5] enter into the human heart on account of the magnitude of the issue, thus the immensity of future torments exceeds the limitations of the human mind; the shadow of an ephemeral penitance cannot remove these punishments, faith without works cannot repel them, the rush into inextinguishable flames of the hastening centuries has not the strength to prevent its end, in the midst of this inexhaustible smoke the soul tardily both senses and sees that it is corporeal. And therefore let us rush toward the last day with just, pious, and chaste works, and let us let us alter our course by fearing here those things that it does not profit us to fear there. Let us now impose an end to infinite chastisment and to intolerable burning; by salubrious contemplation let us prepare for ourselves an eternal refuge from these flames.

I am certain, moreover, regarding your faith, that these health-giving testimonies of sincere truth will be acceptable to you. I salute my son Eminentius,[6] our sweet ornament, with paternal affection. May Our Lord fill Your Magnificence, so admirable to me, with good things in the present, and render you worthy for things eternal.

---

[3] That is, Nicene baptism.

[4] That is, Faustus respectfully disagreed with him. Avitus of Vienne, moreover, thought that even Faustus was too harsh, although he purported to believe that the letter had been written by an African bishop, Faustus the Manichee.

[5] 1 Corinthians 2.9.

[6] Otherwise unknown, Eminentius would seem to be a son of Paulinus. He is omitted from *PLRE II*, but see Mathisen, *Studies*, p.372.

Faustus, *Epistula ad Felicem* "Magnum pietatis" (*SG* no.1*[1]) [ca. 477/485]

This letter on abstinence to Magnus Felix of Arles (*PLRE II*, pp.463-464) was written during Faustus' exile (see Krusch, *MGH AA* 8.lvii). It was cited by Gennadius of Marseille in his entry on Faustus (*De viris inlustribus* 86): "He also wrote later to the praetorian prefect Felix, a man of patrician rank and the son of the consul Magnus, a letter now exhorting him to the fear of God and suited for a person disposing himself to undertake penitence with a devoted spirit." Felix served as prefect of Gaul ca. 469, his father having been consul in 460. Some of the wording recurs in Faustus' letter "Propitia divinitate" to Ruricius, and, indeed, aside from the letters to Ruricius, this is the only letter in which Faustus makes any extensive references to his personal circumstances. Preserved in mss. "S" and "Q". Text: *CSEL* 21.195-200; *MGH AA* 8.282-284.

FAUSTUS TO THE LORD FELIX, A LORD MOST PIOUS AND A BROTHER TO BE EXTEEMED WITH SPECIAL DUTIES,[2] AS I TRUST, ETERNALLY AND THROUGH ALL THINGS[3]

It is a great[4] testimony to faith and piety that you extend the breadth of your charity through the vast intervals of such extensive regions and through the intervening divisions of so many circumstances. In this exile of mine, the artful pity of our God performs a double function: it tends to my affliction with paternal sedulity, and it illuminates your faith and endorses your piety toward me. His benign ingenuity abrades me and uplifts you, it salubriously confines me and augments you, it castigates me and supports you. My own misfortunes are transformed into your benefits. When you make profit from me, you begin to be my debtor, because I am the cause of your devotion and the material for your gain. Your exploits take profit from me, your merits render gain from my sufferings. The affection of your sollicitude reaches me, and its fruit reaches the Lord; and thus, we are obliged to the divine benefactions in a two-fold manner, for my punishment and for your remuneration. The perfection of your commiseration, however, nearly enjoined upon me a silence in response. For your very solicitude in questioning already <exemplifies>[5] a manner of life that you sufficiently draw daily from the efficacious teachings and present examples of my

---

Faustus, "Magnum pietatis"

[1] The following three letters of Faustus appear in the first section of quaternions in the *Sangallensis*, and do not seem to have been part of the collection of Ruricius. Their sequence numbers are indicated with an asterisk.

[2] *officiis*: edd.; *officiiciis*: S.

[3] "Domino piissimo et specialibus officiis excolendo, ut confido, in aeternum fratri et per omnia domno Felici Faustus."

[4] The first word, "Magnum," plays upon Felix' name.

[5] *prodit*: added by Engelbrecht.

lord and your father, the saintly bishop Leontius.[6] However, I do not marvel if you also require some sort of superfluous advice from me, whose singular affection toward you you know well...

[The tract continues for several pages, and concludes rather abruptly:]

... It is fitting that one who wished to be transformed to glory there first be transformed to life here.

Faustus, *Epistula ad Graecum diaconum* "Honoratus officio" (*SG* no.2*) [ca. 450/455]

> In an unusually harsh letter, Faustus rebuked the deacon Graecus of Marseille for misinterpreting Augustine. Faustus also accused him of being tainted with Nestorianism (the belief that the divine and human natures of Christ were separate), as seen in Gennadius of Marseille's summary of the letter (*De viris inlustribus* 86): "There also is his letter in the style of a little book addressed to a certain deacon, Graecus by name, who, departing from the catholic faith had approached to the Nestorian impiety. In this letter he advises him to believe that the blessed virgin Mary did not give birth only to a man who afterwards became divine, but to God truly in man." Gennadius here purports not to know that Graecus later was a distinguished bishop of Marseille (ca. 460-475) (see R.W. Mathisen, "Episcopal Hierarchy and Tenure in Office: A Method for Establishing Dates of Ordination," *Francia* 17 [1990] pp.125-140 at p.137), placing this letter, written when he was still a deacon, perhaps ca. 450/455, which would mean that Faustus himself had not yet become bishop of Riez, but was still abbot of the monastery at Lérins. See Elg, *Studia*, pp.1-2, 28, 32-33, 122-124, 136; and Mathisen, "Specialists," passim. Preserved in mss. "S" and "Q". Text: *CSEL* 21. 200-207; *MGH AA* 8.284-288.

FAUSTUS TO A SAINTLY LORD AND A BROTHER MOST STEADFAST IN CHRIST, THE DEACON GRAECUS

Honored by your respect for me, honored by your regard for me, having been summoned in affection I speak with you in sincere humility, in benevolent candor, with unfeigned charity, in the word of truth. And although you had the opportunity to indicate to me a reason for keeping silent, when with a kind and excessively naive spirit you attributed nearly as much learning and erudition to me as I attribute to you, nevertheless through your persistent requests you have imposed upon me the necessity of responding,[1] in which regard I think that I

---

[6] Bishop of Arles ca. 460-485; see *Epist.* 2.8 above.

Faustus, "Honoratus officio"

[1] Faustus works himself up to an unpleasant task that he had hoped to avoid: pointing out to his young friend Graecus, in no uncertain terms, the errors of his ways.

must speak with one who is absent[2] not without trepidation, because concerning matters which are so profound and which exceed both your and my abilities there is no less danger in responding than in entrusting such great mysteries to my inelegant style, and therefore, in these matters which he too rashly puts forth, I ought to castigate one who is dear to me more by keeping silent. Moreover, in your consultation on such an important issue, regarding which you have deviated greatly from the royal road,[3] you ought to question other men of expert wisdom, elders in erudition and age, whom you might be able to believe more easily, according to that saying of the prophets, "Ask your father, and he will show you; your elders, and they will tell you."[4] But without doubt, whatever kind of guide one seeks, one ought to choose to avoid error. Finally, regarding these matters which we consider, and which we discuss, and which, in the end, we commit to paper: we ought to await fruitfulness and profit in the result. In this little composition[5] that you think it proper to send to me, however, there appears no eloquence, no wisdom, no good sense, no constuction of ordered or punctuated speech, but rather testimonies heaped up in great confusion with respect to ease of recollection indict the temerity of a rash heart. God knows that, in astonishment, I say these things out of desire for your salvation, and thus may it serve the common good for you to have consulted me and for me to have responded.

Even if something in the writings of the blessed bishop Augustine is thought to be suspect by the most learned men, you should know that there is nothing reprehensible in those sections that you thought should be condemned, but know that, in particular, the sense of faith in the Catholic church regarding the two substances or natures of God, and of the Lord as man, and of our redeemer not only is accepted by the authority of the fathers but also is confirmed by apostolic pronouncements...

[In a lengthy exegesis, Faustus then proceeded to condemn Nestorianism. One point was picked up by the recipient of the letter "Quaeris a me" above:]

It follows that you say that there is a single nature of God and man, [and that] in this manner God has a single substance.[6] You would have spoken rightly if you had spoken about the Trinity alone, where the nature is one and the same in the distinction of the three persons. But when it comes to the In-

---

[2] Cf. Faustus' letter "Grandis caritatis" to Lucidus below.

[3] "viam regiam": cf. Faustus' letters "Grandis caritatis" to Lucidus and "Quod pro sollicitudine" to Leontius of Arles below.

[4] Deuteronomy 32.7.

[5] "scripturula": a disparaging dimunitive.

[6] The words "et hominis unam esse naturam, hoc modo unam dei" are missing from the Sg 190.

carnation of the assumption of human form, just as we confess that there is a single person of man and God, we likewise know that there was a double substance... God experienced all these things not through Himself, but through the nature He had assumed as a man. For God feels nothing with the feeling of a sufferer, but he feels through his connection with a fellow-sufferer...

[*Faustus concluded by giving Graecus some advice:*]

It is difficult for me to produce speech that asserts a matter in such an outspoken manner. I know that I briefly and cursorily have rashly entrusted the aforementioned opinions both to my letter and to your feelings. But, so long as you submit yourself to healthy questioning with earnest humility, you give much promise to me for the correction of your error. Withdraw, I beg you, your foot from this danger before you are swept away by an irrevocable torrent of pride, and constrain your upright mental intellect, which a weight of much reading does not sustain and which does not know how to disburse a treasury of knowledge, more by an occupation in labor. Temper an excessive rigor of abstinence, which in fact engenders mental infirmity, and which I think is the source from which arises a presumption in writing.[7] Return to the royal road; flee the earnest nurturer of pride. And because we read, "It is not good to eat much honey,"[8] knowledge in fact bloats rather than edifies an intellect that is insufficiently well-founded; thus, avoid excessive reading, so that you might remove the dangerous intoxication, similar to that of wine drunken immoderately, of a spirit whose capacity is too small. But, never trusting to your own thoughts, you should instead read things to be imitated rather than write things to be read, and in your mind you should say to the Lord, "I have laid up thy word in my heart, that I might not sin against thee."[9] And if you are not going to fail to evade threatening dangers, I know of nothing more useful for you than that you fortify your life under some most upright abbot[10] and that you surrender your wilfulness to the restrictions of someone senior, and that you fear for yourself so that you might be able to overcome the traps of an adversary.[11]

I think that this little composition[12] must be retained, or rather suppressed, lest it later come into the possession and cognizance of some other catholic who

---

[7] Even the ascetic Faustus thinks it is possible to be too ascetic, if doing so results in a false sense of superiority.

[8] Proverbs 25.27.

[9] Psalms 118.11.

[10] An office that Faustus seems to have held at the time he wrote this letter, but in this case he would be referring to an abbot at Marseille, and he may have had in mind Eutropius, abbot of the monastery of St. Victor at Marseille and later bishop of Orange.

[11] Probably a reference to Satan.

[12] "scripturulam" again.

is less well disposed toward you. Moreover, from this you should be able to acknowledge that the innermost parts of your heart are sound if from now on,
free, so to speak, until now,[13] you listen earnestly and willingly to me, your
admirer, as I humbly and lovingly advise you. Before you sought my advice,
your opinion will seem to have been merely imprudent, but after my response it
will appear as inexcusable excessiveness. But if, in the midst of this, you think
that any blame[14] must be laid against me, who believes that your soul can be
saved by severity rather than by sweetness, remember that I prefer the wounds
of charity to wickedly caressing kisses.

IT IS FINISHED.[15]

Faustus, *Epistula ad Lucidum* "Grandis caritas" (*SG* no.3*) [ca. 470]

> Graecus, it seems, followed Faustus' advise and did not publish his tract. Other
> clerics, however, were less accommodating, or prudent. Faustus wrote this letter
> just before the Council of Arles, ca. 470, in an attempt to induce the priest Luci-
> dus to recant his predestinarian views. Lucidus refused to capitulate, and shortly
> thereafter was condemned at Arles. His reply, "Correptio vestra," addressed to
> the bishops who attended the Council of Arles, also survives (*CSEL* 21.165-168).
> See Elg, *Studia*, pp.109-112. Preserved in mss. "S" and "P", also in Hincmar of
> Reim's *De praedestinatione dei et libero arbitrio* ("On the Predestination of God
> and Free Will") (*PL* 125.79). Text: *CSEL* 21.161-165; *MGH AA* 8.289-291.

FAUSTUS TO A MOST STEADFAST LORD AND A BROTHER TO BE VENERATED
AND RECEIVED BY ME WITH SPECIAL AFFECTION, THE PRIEST LUCIDUS

It is a great charity to wish to cure the error of a brother who has been insufficiently careful, rather than, as the greatest priests[1] are considering, to sus-
pend him from oneness.[2] What can I say to Your Singlemindedness about this
matter, as you wish, in correspondence, when in much sweet and humble discussion I was unable to draw you to the road of truth? Therefore, speaking about
the grace of God and the obedience of man, we must see to this in every way,
that we walk along the royal road[3] neither leaning toward the left nor inclined
toward the right. I marvelled, however, that Your Reverence said that no one

---

[13] "Free" because no one but Faustus had seen his tract and it had not been publicly condemned.
[14] Cf. the end of *Epist.* 2.15 above.
[15] "Finit"; in the *Codex Parisinus* 1564 but not in the *Sangallensis* 190.
Faustus, "Grandis caritatis"
[1] "summi antestites": a common circumlocution for referring to bishops.
[2] That is, Lucidus is being threatened with excommunication.
[3] Cf. Faustus' letters to Graecus above and Leontius below.

had ever, under the guise of religion, written or preached against the catholic faith, because many individuals, who nevertheless glory in the Christian name, have believed that their manifold and profane errors ought to be inserted even into the records of scripture. I therefore will discuss briefly, to the extant that I can speak with one who is absent,[4] what you ought to believe along with the catholic church, that is, that you always must link the actions of a baptized servant with the grace of the Lord, and that, along with the teaching of Pelagius, you must detest the one[5] who asserted predestination, to the exclusion of the labor of man.

[Faustus then presented a number of statements that Lucidus was asked to anathematize. He concluded:]

I am keeping with me a copy of this letter to be presented, if such should be necessary, in the council of the holy bishops. If Your Fraternity thinks it should be acknowledged, you should either return it quickly signed by your own hand, or respond in a subsequent answer that you reject it altogether. But if you choose not to return it signed, as I said, you will attest with your very silence that you persist openly in your error and thus you will create the necessity for me of exposing your person to a public meeting. And therefore write back, having removed equivocations, regarding those matters that I have sent, whether, you either acknowledge or reject them.

Then in another hand[6]: I, Faustus, have read and subscribed to this copy of my letter.

Faustus, *Epistula* "Quod pro sollicitudine" = *De gratia, prol. (SG --)* [ca. 470]

> This letter to bishop Leontius of Arles is not included in the *Sangallensis* 190, and has been transmitted independently as the preface to Faustus' *De gratia*, which was written after the Council of Arles of ca. 470 (see Mathisen, *Factionalism*, pp.256-264). See Elg, *Studia*, p.71. Preserved only in ms. "P". Text: *CSEL* 21.3-4.

---

[4] Cf. Faustus' letter "Honoratus officio" to Graecus above.

[5] That is, Augustine: see Introduction.

[6] *Item alia manu*: a phrase added to copies of documents by scribes to indicate that a document was signed by a person other than the one who had written it. This was a common practice, especially with official documents. In the *Sangallensis* 190, the conclusion of the letter proper appears on p.48, but Faustus' subscription not until p.328.

FAUSTUS TO THE MOST BLESSED AND REVERED BISHOP LEONTIUS

Because, through your solicitude, blessed pope Leontius, you have gathered a council of the highest priests for the condemnation of the error of predestination,[1] you have been outstanding among all the churches of Gaul. Because truly, for the ordination of those matters which you have presented most learnedly in a public gathering, you have entrusted the labor and care to infirm shoulders, you have considered, I think, such an important matter too little, your own holy opinion too little: you have burdened me with the judgment of charity, yourself with the danger of making a choice. Because, therefore, you also recognize that your person toils under the burden we have imposed, you pursue a common goal in this instance if you extend the hand of sufferance to the one whom you see as unequal to your expectations.

One undertakes the desire of defending grace competently and salubriously who links the obedience of a servile labor, just as an attendant clings to his patron or lord, inseparably following in his footsteps. But if there should be one without the other, either the lord will appear to be ignoble without the slave, or the slave, unmindful of his status, will occupy the place of the lord. Rightly, therefore, is such an arrangement preserved between the helper and the struggler equally, so that the former holds his position of power by full right and the latter renders servitude with total subjection. The dignity of the master will be magnified, moreover, if there is always in him a diligence of indulgence. Let the lowest things be associated with the highest, but associated in such a way that they are made subject in some way, not equal. But just as it is not proper for the helmsman to be lacking his rower, the bishop his minister, the general his soldier, thus it is fitting that service, as a foster child, be connected to obedience through an inseparable servitude.

Truly, because Pelagius improperly exalted labor alone and, as a madman, stupidly believed that human weakness can fend for itself without grace, and he impiously spoke out, having attempted to erect to the sky a tower of elation, we have judged it necessary to summarize and refute his blasphemies in a short discussion, lest, perhaps, someone, who excludes the gift of labor, that is, the precept of the one ordering, ignorant of discretion place a broad interpretation upon the teaching of Pelagius and having left the royal road to the right and falling to the left, believe that we are deviationist because of our assertions that the pity of God must be brought forth through faith and good works, and lest we seem to have placed a small obstacle before the feet of a blind man when we speak of labor as a servant of grace. When, moreover, we make mention of work and la-

---

Faustus, "Quod pro sollicitudine"
[1] For the controversy over predestination, see Introduction and previous letter.

bor, we do so in the words and sense of the prophet, apostle, and evangelist. If anyone presumes to contradict them, he will be attempting not to destroy our reasoning but without doubt to dissolve the celestial laws and to undermine the foundations of faith. We have published this discussion of prescience and predestination as widely as possible so that whatever is thought to be obscure may be rendered more concrete for those who are more slow-witted. Let it not offend some who delight in quivers of words, because, contented with the virtue of our evidence without loftiness of speech, we have put forth the light of truth. Indeed, after the council of Arles was signed new errors were detected and the synod of Lyon[2] demanded that a few matters be added to this work.

---

[2] ca. 470/471: see Mathisen, *Factionalism*, pp.264-268.

Appendix II

Epitaph of Ruricius and Ruricius II Proculus

Venantius Fortunatus, *Carmina* 4.5, "Epitaphium Ruriciorum episcoporum civitatis Lemovicenae" [ca. 590]

> Toward the end of the sixth century, Venantius Fortunatus, later bishop of Poitiers, composed a metrical epitaph for Ruricius and his homonymous grandson, Ruricius II Proculus (ca. 520-550). He also wrote an epitaph for Exocius (ca. 550-565), the successor of the younger Ruricius (*MGH AA* 4.1.83). If the person who commissioned the epitaph was a bishop of Limoges, it would have had to have been either Exocius' successor Ferreolus (ca. 565-591), or Asclepius (ca. 591-625). Along with the usual platitudes, the epitaph notes that the Ruricii were related to the Anicii of Rome and that each built a church. Text: B. Krusch ed., *MGH AA* 4.1.82-83.

Epitaph of the Bishops Ruricius of the City of Limoges

> Spiteful death, however much you threaten with a rabid maw,
>> you will never be able to hold sway over the saints.
> Not after Christ, returning, tamed the Tartarean terrors:
>> you will lie underfoot, overcome by the merits of the just.
> Here, a tomb covers the blessed bones, gleaming throughout the world,
>> of our bishops; their spirit worships the heavens.
> The twin Rurician flowers, to whom Rome was joined
>> through the parental eminence of the Anicii,
> Linked in deed, in spirit, in rank, in hopes, in name, in blood,
>> they rejoice equally, here the grandfather and there the grandson.
> Each in his own time built a dutiful church for a patron:
>> this one for Augustine, and that one for Peter.
> This one upright, that one responsible, this one serious, that one serene,
>> competing equally as to who was greater than whom.
> Bestowing more upon paupers than their precious wealth,
>> they sent to the heavens things that follow upon riches,
> They whom, redeeming the sins of the world with their bestowing hand,
>> we believe to be among the apostolic choirs.
> Happy are those who in this way, fleeing their nobility,
>> have senatorial rights in the assembly in heaven.

Appendix III

Hagiographical Sources Referring to Ruricius and Limoges

A number of saints' lives and other hagiographical sources contain information relating to both Ruricius and Limoges. Even though they date to the ninth century or later, they preserve material from much earlier periods. They are discussed in context in the Introduction, and more lengthy relevant selections are presented here.

Vita Juniani confessoris Comodoliacensis [ca. 850]

The ninth-century *vita* of Junianus not only mentions Ruricius and his grandson, but also describes Aquitania in the time of Alaric II. Virtually the only event reported at any length is Junianus' encounter with a member of the family of Ruricius, attesting to the importance that was attached to this connection. To some extent, the *vita* is corroborated by Gregory of Tours (*Glory of the Confessors* 101), who reports that Junianus was a hermit who resided west of Limoges circa the late fifth and early sixth century. Text: *MGH SRM* 3.376-379.

THE LIFE OF JUNIANUS, CONFESSOR OF COMODOLIACUS

... (2) When the savage Arian heresy was present within the borders of Gaul and the province of Aquitania under Alaric, the prince of the Goths, and when the nation of the Franks was held, at that time, by the error of paganism, St. Remigius, bishop of the church of Reims, preached, and Clovis, the king of the Franks, flew to the grace of baptism with many superstitious and funereal bands of pagans. Soon, he began to exhort the entire nation of the Franks to a share of baptism, so that under the gentle yoke of Christ they might constrain their gallant necks with a sweet burden. Soon, after having reached a decision with the bishops of Christ, under the guidance of grace, that the heretical people should be expelled by the power of the Christians, Clovis joined battle with the aforementioned king Alaric in the territory of Poitiers. With his allies he ejected the teaching of this superstition from the borders of Gaul and Aquitania and instituted all in the teachings of the one true Christian faith and in the catholic religion. (3) At nearly the same time a nobleman named Amandus, born of illustrious parentage, a not insensible harkener to the Gospels, abandoned his posessions and was seen to have built himself a hut, not at all immense, where he could live a more isolated life in a place of enormous solitude, on the prop-

erty (the word of whose name is said to have been Comodoliacus[1]) of a certain
most noble individual: the bishop Ruricius[2] of blessed memory... (4) Then the
aforementioned[3] devout boy Junianus, having left his parents in a desire to a-
bandon this world so that he would in no way be deprived of the inheritance of
the eternal homeland, and desiring, through the teachings of Christ, to bring
himself to the notice of the aforementioned man Amandus, began to pound on
the doors so that he would open them to him... (6) Moreover, at the same time a
certain man, born of illustrious parents, the nobleman Ruricius, who was called
Proculus by another name,[4] enriched by an abundance of material goods, when
he was uplifted in his arrogance of pride was not undeservedly handed over to a
judgment dispensed from omnipotent God; he who first uplifted himself in
pride, after he had been humbled realized how much he had lost through his arrogance. <...>[5] But after he had been taken, in fact, by members of his own
household to physicians and even, which is worse, to sorcerers and enchanters,
and after he had wasted part of his substance upon such persons, who, in fact,
when they wished to restore him to health, tormented him more seriously, for
when they wished to expel a single [demon] from him, soon, as it is said, a le-
gion of demons entered into him. (7) As a result, a salubrious plan was undertaken, and he was directed to the man of God. He was exhorted greatly by the
man of God to undertake fasts and prayers and nightime vigils, and to disperse
great benefactions from his property to the poor, because this kind of demon
could be expelled in no other way than by according to what was confirmed by
the sentiment that was put forth by our Lord Jesus Christ... After Junianus had
prayed for a long time, and had beseeched the Lord for the return of [Proculus']
health in many fasts and vigils, he was restored to pristine health by Junianus'
merits, and thus, in a display of the divine mercy, he was rendered so healthy
that subsequently, in the face of the power of the aforementioned servant of
God, not one from that horde of malignant spirits dared to return to his body.
Rather he was returned to good health in body and mind by the prayer and
chastisement of the aforementioned blessed man Junianus to such an extent that
after the death of his uncle,[6] Ruricius, once bishop of blessed memory, he was

---

Vita Juniani
[1] Now St-Junien in the département of Haute-Vienne.
[2] That is, the elder Ruricius.
[3] "praedictus": in fact, Junianus only had been "aforementioned" in the preface and title.
[4] This is the only evidence for any of the Ruricii having a cognomen.
[5] A discussion of Ruricius' illness seems to have dropped out here. One can only note the elder
Ruricius' preoccupation with his own illnesses.
[6] *patruelis*: in classical Latin, "descended from a father's brother or sister," i.e. a cousin, but in
medieval Latin, an uncle: see R.E. Latham, *Revised Medieval Latin Word List* (Oxford, 1965)
p.336. Proculus may have been considered to have been an uncle here because of Venantius'

made bishop of the city of Limoges.[7] (8) Moreover, the aforementioned man of God, empowered with many virtues, led a solitary life in the aforementioned place for the space of forty years.... (9) But the aforementioned man Ruricius, known as Proculus, not forgetful of how many benefits of the aforementioned holy man had accrued to him, ordered a basilica to be built, where it is seen that the holy bones of the most blessed Junianus were placed...

Vita Vincentiani confessoris Avolcensis [ca. 900]

St. Vincentianus was said to have been born in the territory of Angers and to have been educated by Desiderius of Cahors. Ca. 670 he built a church at Avolca (St-Viance), located midway between Limoges and Cahors, and he died ca. 672. His *vita* was composed by the deacon Ermenbertus during Carolingian times, and reflects the close ties that existed between Limoges and Cahors in the post-Roman period. Text: B. Krusch ed., *MGH SRM* 5.116-128.

THE LIFE OF VINCENTIANUS, CONFESSOR OF AVOLCA

(1) „„„ I, Ermenbertus, the most humble of all the deacons, have brought forth the spirtual memory regarding the most blessed Vincintantus: how he lived his life when he was place in this world and how he instructed several others with saintly examples, and what he taught by word, and demonstrated by his life and character... (2) ... In the province of Angers, in a villa with the name Nantogilo which was located above the Oudon river,[1] belonging to the estate and family of the duke Beraldus,[2] the man of God Vincentianus was born and raised under his care... (5) The aforementioned man Beraldus, moreover, traveled to the city named Cahors together with his son Barontus. After he had supped with the bishop of this same city, Desiderius by name, a book was offered to the blessed Vincentianus to be read in front of the table in the presence of all. And truly, when the reading had been completed, Desiderius said to the duke Beraldus, "Lord, if this seems a good thing to you, let the hair be cut from the head of Vincentianus and let him remain with us among the ranks of the clerics." The duke replied, "Let it be as you suggest"... [*Time passed*] (11) He, truly, arising

---

reference to him as the elder Ruricius' *nepos*, which by this time generally meant "nephew" (ibid. p.312) rather than the classical meaning of "grandson."

[7] It is possible that the author of the *vita* has conflated two persons into one and that Ruricius Proculus, who apparently engaged in some unchristian behavior, is different from Ruricius II, who became bishop.

Vita Vincentiani

[1] "super fluvium Olda": The Oudon is a tributary of the Mayenne, in the département of Maine-et-Loire.

[2] The *Dux Aquitaniae* ("Duke of Aquitania").

at dawn, having with him Savinianus, began a journey and returned to Exando [Yssandon][3] in the hamlet of Avolca [St-Viance], and there above the Vézère river he ordered a church to be built and he sent the priest Genesius to the bishop of Limoges, Rusticus[4] by name, to ask him, for his part, under his episcopal authority, to send him relics, so that the aforementioned place and the church itself might be dedicated in honor of these same relics. Departing once again from Avolca, and coming to the hamlet of Lintiacum [Lentillac],[5] he found his entire family there, just as he himself had left them... [More time passed; Vincentianus continued to wander] (17) ... Then a certain individual, Ambrosius by name,[6] encountered him and asked him, "What are you up to, Vincentianus? Where do you come from, and where are you going"? And he replied, "I am fleeing from the face of my Lord from the territory of Poitiers...." Ambrosius said, "Come with me." Therefore, they continued together seeking solitude and arrived above the Vienne river and there they remained for several days. (18) ... Then Ambrosius sought the city of Cahors and died there, ending his temporal life[7]... (21) In addition, at the same time bishop Rusticus obtained the pontificate of the city of Limoges[8] and, having received a message from an angel, quickly hastened to that place[9] with his people. Furthermore, at the eighth hour of the day the most blessed Vincentianus heard a voice calling to him and saying, "Depart, man of God, and come to the company of your brothers, where you are called"... And he died, in peace, three days before the Nones of January.[10]

Vita Sacerdotis episcopi Lemovicensis [ca. 1100]

The vita of St. Sacerdos, who may have succeeded Ruricius as bishop of Limoges (see Introduction), likewise describes Aquitania in the late fifth and early sixth

---

[3] On the Vézère river, southwest of Brive-la-Gaillarde, located midway between Limoges and Cahors.

[4] Bishop of Limoges ca. 670; see Introduction. The church, therefore, was under the ecclesiastical jurisdiction of Limoges.

[5] Lentillac, or Lintillac, between Brive-la-Gaillarde and St-Viance.

[6] For a possible connection between this Ambrosius and a poorly known Ambrosius who was bishop of Cahors, who can be dated only to the sixth or seventh century, see P. Bonnassie, "L'évêque, le peuple et les sénateurs: Scènes de la vie à Cahors, d'après la Vita Ambrosii," Annales du Midi 102 nos.189-190 (Jan.-June 1990) pp.209-217.

[7] Krusch (MGH SRM 3.122 n.3) notes that an Ambrose, bishop of Cahors, is commemorated on 16 October (AASS October VII, pt.2, p.1031); see also Ruricius, Epist. 2.44.

[8] This doublet of the Rusticus already mentioned might account for the duplication of Rusticus' name in the episcopal catalogues (see Introduction).

[9] After his travels, Vincentianus was back in the territory of Limoges.

[10] 3 January; a later section places his death in the fifteenth year of King Chlothar, or AD 672.

century, and provides further testimony to the close connection between Limoges and Cahors. It may be significant that Sacerdos' had property in the same area as Ruricius. Text: *AASS* May I, pp.12-18.

THE LIFE OF SACERDOS, BISHOP OF LIMOGES

Sacerdos was born in the province of Aquitania of an aristocratic family... His father, therefore, the *vir clarissimus* Laban, stood out as one of the first men of the city of Bordeaux, whereas his mother was called Mundana... At the same time, a most Christian king, Anticius[1] by name, reigned in Aquitania. It happened, moreover, that this same king came to a certain village, named Calabrum,[2] which was located between the territories of Cahors and Périgueux, not far from the Dordogne river.[3]

[Sacerdos then was baptized.]

And immediately the king, raising the boy from the sacred water, granted him the aforementioned village of Calabrum, in which all this happened, to be possessed by hereditary right, for this same village was royal property... (2) After this had been done, the venerable lad was turned over to Capuanus,[4] bishop of Cahors, so that he might instruct him in letters and in Christian teaching. This Capuanus was, at that time, was most renowned[5] among the religious prelates of Aquitania. Truly, this happened by the will of omnipotent God, in order that the most blessed boy might drink the purest fount of doctrine from a perfected and catholic master of sanctity, so that, having become an eminent teacher, he might irrigate the minds of the faithful, and lest anyone, encircled by heretical depravity, of which there was at this time in that region a great abundance,[6] deviate from the correct path of faith...

[Sacerdos then was made a deacon by Capuanus]

(4) There was at that time in the already mentioned village of Calabrum a mon-

---

Vita Sacerdotis
[1] Perhaps Ecdicius, the son of Eparchius Avitus (see Introduction). In 474 Ecdicius was appointed by the emperor Julius Nepos (474-475) as Patrician and Master of Soldiers.
[2] The name survived in the seventeenth century as a lake near the Dordogne river known as "l'estang de Calabre," where a tower called "la Tour de Calabre" remained from a church where the surrounding territory was known as the "Bordar of St. Sacerdos" (*AASS* May II, p.12).
[3] And also not far, apparently, from Ruricius' property at Gourdon.
[4] The connection of Sacerdos with Cahors is consistent with the family property in the territory of Cahors, and parallels Ruricius' own possession of property in the same area.
[5] Albeit now being otherwise unknown.
[6] A recollection, perhaps, of the Arian faith of the Visigoths.

astery, in which forty or more monks were tarrying. As a result, Sacerdos, beloved of the Lord, ministered to them most diligently, to such an extant that any of his own property that he did not expend upon them he immediately considered to be a total loss. And after he first had rebuilt the basilica there, which by then had nearly collapsed as a result of its great age, he then built a suitable habitation for the monks. He even granted to the same monastery the very village of Calabrum, along with all its appurtanences, which, as has been said, he had received from king Anticius by hereditary right... He served the Lord under the rule of the abbot for nearly seven years before he passed to the order of the priesthood...

[*(5) Subsequently, Sacerdos was chosen abbot.*]

(13) ... then, after the bishop of Limoges, Aggericus of blessed memory, died, the man of God Sacerdos was lifted to the episcopal seat of the same church, to the honor of God, by the election of the clergy and the favor of the people, and with the approval even of Clovis the Elder, king of the Franks and ruler of that province.[7] And thus, for several turns of the years he governed the same church through the providence of God. But, seeing that I might seem tedious to some persons, I here avoid verbosity and apply my spirit to brevity: let us now turn the page to his death. (14) Therefore, the most blessed Sacerdos, sensing, as a revelation to him from Holy Spirit, that his last day was approaching, bid farewell to his brothers and departed from the city of Limoges, desiring to return to his native soil... While he was making his journey, he came to a certain villa which is called Argentacum,[8] and there, already having been weakened for a long time by ill health, he was stricken by a grave acuteness of fever... (15) ... On the third day before the Nones of May[9] he rendered his spirit to heaven...

Translatio Asclepii [ca. 1100]

This late account of the translation of the relics of St. Asclepius, bishop of Limoges ca. 571-625, from the church of St. Paul to the monastery of St. Augustine tells of the monastery's establishment. Text: J. Becquet, "L'évêque Asclèpe à Saint-Augustin de Limoges (VIe siècle)," *BSAHL* 122 (1994) pp.12-22 at pp.19-21.

---

[7] The author distinguishes between Clovis' position as king of the Franks, and successor to the Romans as administrator of a Roman province. "Chlodovaeo seniore" must be a reference to Clovis I (481-511), who did not come into possession of Limoges until ca. 507/508, so Sacerdos must have become bishop between 507 and 511.

[8] For the vicus of Argentacum (modern Argentat), south of Limoges, see Introduction and J.-M. Courteix, "Aux origines d'Argentat," *TAL* 12 (1992) pp.143-151.

[9] 5 May.

THE TRANSLATION OF ASCLEPIUS

.. and there, when no other regular career then existed in the primitive church during the times of the emperor Claudius,[1] he devotedly instituted priests living communally who oversaw the matters regarding the duty of ecclesiastical burial. Living communally and devotedly serving God, they have overseen the present place all the way back to the times of the most blessed bishop of Limoges, Ruricius, the first of that name, Indeed, at the present place this Ruricius was the first to institute regular canons, whom he established in honor of St. Augustine; from them all the way to the present the same monastery has retained the name of St. Augustine.   In fact, the aforementioned Ruricius was the twenty-third bishop of the see of the church of Limoges after the blessed Martial.   After a blessed life, his body was buried in the aforementioned monastery and rests in peace, uplifted in the reliquary of the greater altar with the blessed Flavia[2]...

Stemma Aredii [ca. 850]

> Along with the *vita* of Pelagia, the mother of St. Aredius, the *Codex Parisinus* 5365 preserves a curious *Stemma Aredii*, a genealogy of Aredius.   Although the *stemma* has several obvious errors and inconsistencies, it also has some instructive elements: for example, before and after the name "Ruricius" appear, within the space of a few lines, the names (italicized below) [He]sperius, Ambrosius, Severus, Bassulus, Clarus, Hispanus, and Leontius — all of which are found in Ruricius' correspondence, being the recipients of *Epist.* 1.3-5, 2.44, 2.59, 1.7, 2.64, 2.45, and 2.42 respectively.   This may be more than mere coincidence, and it may be more than mere speculation to suggest that the author of the *stemma* might have seen Ruricius' letter collection.   Text: B. Krusch ed., *MGH SRM* 3.611-612.

THE GENEALOGY OF AREDIUS

In the name of Our Lord Jesus Christ, the narration of the genealogy of the famous abbot Aredius begins thus:

The noblewoman Waldeca, daughter of king Childebert (511-558) and queen Matilda, bore Astidius,[1] bishop of Limoges, who, born at Trier by the favor of

---

Translatio Asclepii
[1] The emperor Claudius reigned from AD 41 to 54, clearly far too early for the events described here.
[2] An Italian martyr; see Introduction.
Stemma Aridii
[1] In the *fasti*, Astidius appears just before the elder Ruricius, that is, in the third quarter of the fifth century; see Introduction. This demonstrates at once the unreliability of at least this part of

God, was later elevated to be bishop of the city of Limoges. Then, Astidius himself had a gracious wife, Thecla by name, before his episcopate, whose sister was the wealthy Frontonia, whose property was at Nataliacum. Astidius, therefore, and his wife Thecla begot Liverius, Adtecus, Dulcitius, Adteca, and Austiliniana. Liverius, truly, begot *Sperius*[2] and Pientia. Adtecus begot Eustachius, *Ruricius*, and Peladia. Dulcitius, moreover, begot *Ambrosius*, the most blessed *Severus*, whom the people of Bourges above the Loire river revere, and *Basolus*[3] of Ravenna. Adteca, moreover, bore *Clarus* and the martyr *Hispanus*. Pientia, moreover, bore *Leontius* of Périgueux. *Ambrosius*, truly, begot Julius, Industrius[4] and Eusebia. Eusebia, truly, bore Savina, [and] Salica. Savina bore Optatus the venerable archbishop of Bourges.[5] Optatus, therefore, begot Pomponia, the wife of Godefredis of Flandelum, and Ocilus, the most noble prelate of Soissons.[6] Peladia, truly, bore Carteria and Euladia and Mummulus. Carteria, moreover, bore the most blessed Pelagia and Savina, the aunt of the abbot Aredius. Pelagia, therefore, the niece of king Theodebert (534-548), and her husband Jocundus, a most noble leader[7] of Limoges, begot the learned man Aredius, chancellor of the king mentioned above, and his brother Eustachius and his sister Consortia. Consortia, moreover, bore Astidius, Pientia, and Basilia. Pientia bore Ocilus. Basilia, the wife of Dodo, a leader of Bourges, begot Pugia and Carissima.

---

the genealogy. Another tradition has an Astidius, the nephew of Aredius, as the abbot of the monastery at Vosia (*Gallia christiana* 2.593).

[2] That is, Hesperius?

[3] I.e. Bassulus.

[4] Note the Industrius who received *Epist.* 4.9 of Sidonius Apollinaris.

[5] No Optatus is attested as bishop of Bourges (Duchesne, *Fastes* 2.22-31). Note, perhaps, in this context the Ruricius who was bishop of Bourges in the early sixth century (see Introduction).

[6] No Ocilus is attested as bishop of Soissons (Duchesne, *Fastes* 3.88-92).

[7] "princeps."

BIBLIOGRAPHY

PRIMARY SOURCES

SELECTED TEXTS RELATING TO LATE ROMAN GAUL AND THE TIME OF RURICIUS OF LIMOGES

Ado of Vienne, *Chronicon* and *Martyrologium*: PL 123.23ff.

Agroecius, *Ars de orthographia*: H. Keil ed., *Grammatici latini* 7 (Leipzig, 1880) 113-125

Alcimus Ecdicius Avitus of Vienne, *Carmina, Epistulae*, and *Sermones*: R. Peiper ed., *MGH AA* 6.2 (Berlin, 1883)

Arator, *Epistula ad Parthenium*: PL 68.250-255

Johannes Cassianus, *Conlationes*: E. Pichery ed., *Jean Cassien, Conférences* (3 vols.) *SC* 42, 54, 64 (Paris, 1955-1959); E. Petschenig ed., *CSEL* 13 (Vienna, 1886)

Cassiodorus, *Variarum*: Translations: S.J.B. Barnish, *The Variae of Magnus Aurelius Cassiodorus Senator* (Liverpool, 1992); T. Hodgkin, *The Letters of Cassiodorus* (London, 1886); *De institutis coenobiorum*: J.-C. Guy ed., *Jean Cassien, Institutions cénobitiques*, *SC* 109 (Paris, 1965), M. Petschenig ed., *De institutis coenobiorum et de octo principalium vitiorum remidiis*, *CSEL* 17 (Vienna, 1888).; *De incarnatione Christi*: PL 50.9-273

Caesarius of Arles: G. Morin ed., *Sancti Caesarii Arelatensis, Opera varia. Epistulae, concilia, regulae monasticae, opuscula theologica, testamentum, vita ab eius familiaribus conscripta* (Maretioli, 1942), and *Sermones, CCL* 103-104 (Turnholt, 1953). Translations: W. Klingshirn tr., *Caesarius of Arles: Life, Testament, Letters* (Liverpool, 1994); C. McCarthy tr., *The Rule for Nuns of Caesarius of Arles. A Translation with a Critical Introduction* (Washington, 1960), M.M. Mueller tr., *Saint Caesarius of Arles. Sermons I-II* (New York, 1956)

Chronica gallica anno 452: T. Mommsen ed., *MGH AA* 9.615-662

Chronica gallica anno 511: T. Mommsen ed., *MGH AA* 9.662ff.

Claudianus Mamertus, *De statu animae* and *Epistula ad Sapaudum*: A. Engelbrecht ed., *CSEL* 11 (Vienna, 1885)

Codex theodosianus: T. Mommsen, P.M. Meyer, P. Krüger eds., *Theodosiani libri XVI cum constitutionibus Sirmondianis et leges novellae ad Theodosianum pertinentes* (2 vols.) (Berlin, 1905)

Conciliae: C. Munier ed., *Concilia Galliae a.314-a.506, CCL* 148 (Turnholt, 1963); C. de Clercq ed., *Concilia Galliae a.511-a.695, CCL* 148A (Turnholt, 1963); J. Sirmond ed., *Concilia antiqua Galliae* vol.1 (Paris, 1629)

Constantius of Lyons, *Epistula ad Patientem, Epistula ad Censurium*, and *Vita s. Germani episcopi Autessiodorensis*: R. Borius ed., *SC* 112 (Paris, 1965); W. Levison ed., *MGH SRM* 7 (Hanover and Leipzig, 1920) 225-283. Translation: F.R. Hoare tr., *Sulpicius Severus et.al. The Western Fathers: Being the Lives of Martin of Tours,*

Ambrose, Augustine of Hippo, Honoratus of Arles and Germanus of Auxerre (New York, 1954)

Cyprianus Gallus: R. Peiper ed., *Cypriani Galli poetae Heptateuchos, CSEL* 23 (Vienna, 1881)

Magnus Felix Ennodius of Pavia, *Carmina, Epistulae* and *Vita s. Epifani episcopi Ticinensis*: F. Vogel ed., *MGH AA* 7 (Berlin, 1885); G. de Hartel ed., *CSEL* 6 (Vienna, 1882); *Vita Antonii monachi Lerinensis*: *PL* 63.239-246. Translation: G.M. Cook, *The Life of Saint Epiphanius by Ennodius. A Translation with an Introduction and Commentary* (Washington, 1942)

Epistulae Arelatenses genuinae: W. Gundlach ed., *MGH Epist.* 3 (Berlin, 1892) 1-83

Epistulae austrasicae: W. Gundlach ed., *MGH Epist.* 3 (Berlin, 1892) 110-153.

Eucherius of Lyons, *De laude heremi, Formulae spiritalis intellegentiae, Instructionum ad Salonium, Epistula ad Salvium*: C. Wotke ed., *CSEL* 31.1 (Vienna, 1894) 177ff; S. Pricoco ed., *De laude heremi* (Catania, 1964); *Epistula paraenetica ad Valerianum cognatum de contemptu mundi et saecularis philosophia*: *PL* 50.701-726; *Passio Acaunensium martyrum*: B. Krusch ed., *MGH SRM* 3 (Hanover, 1896) 20-41

"Eusebius Gallicanus": F. Glorie ed., *Eusebius 'Gallicanus', Collectio homiliarum, CCL* 101-101B (Turnholt, 1970)

Faustus of Riez, *De gratia, De spiritu sancto, Epistulae, Sermones*: A. Engelbrecht ed., *CSEL* 21 (Vienna, 1891); B. Krusch ed., *MGH AA* 8 (Berlin, 1887) 265-298; *Sermo de sancto Maximo episcopo et abbate*: F. Glorie ed., *CCL* 101 (Turnholt, 1970) 401-412; S. Gennaro ed. (Catania, 1966) 131ff.

Gennadius, presbyter of Marseilles, *De viris inlustribus*: E.C.Richardson ed., *Texte und Untersuchungen zur Geschichte der altchristlichen Literatur* 14 (Leipzig, 1896); *PL* 58.1059-1120; *Liber ecclesiasticorum dogmatum*: *PL* 58.970-1054. Translation: E.C. Richardson tr., *Jerome and Gennadius, Lives of Illustrious Men* (New York, 1892)

Gesta episcoporum Autissiodorensium: G. Waitz ed., *MGH, Scriptores* 13 (Berlin, 1881) 393-400; *PL* 138

Georgius Florentius Gregorius (Gregory) of Tours, *Liber in gloria confessorum, Liber in gloria martyrum, De virtutibus sancti Martini episcopi, Liber de passione et virtutibus sancti Juliani martyris*, and *Liber vitae patrum*: B. Krusch ed., *MGH SRM* 1.2 (Hanover, 1885); *Historia Francorum* (*Libri historiarum X*): B. Krusch, W. Levison eds., *MGH SRM* 1.1 (Hanover, 1951). Translations: O.M. Dalton tr., *The History of the Franks, by Gregory of Tours* (Oxford, 1927); L. Thorpe tr., *The History of the Franks* (Penguin, 1974); E. James tr., *Gregory of Tours: Life of the Fathers*[2] (Liverpool, 1991); R. Van Dam tr., *Saints and Their Miracles in Late Antique Gaul* (Princeton, N.J., 1993); *Idem* tr., *Glory of the Confessors* (Liverpool, 1988); *Idem* tr., *Glory of the Martyrs* (Liverpool, 1988)

Liber historiae Francorum: Translation: Bernard S. Bachrach, *Liber historiae Francorum* (Lawrence, Kans.: Coronado Press, 1973)

Meropius Pontius Paulinus of Nola, *Carmina*: G. de Hartel ed., *CSEL* 30 (Vienna, 1984); *Epistulae*: G. de Hartel ed., *CSEL* 29 (Vienna, 1894). Translation: P.G. Walsh tr., *The letters of Paulinus of Nola* (2 vols.) (London, 1966)

Paulinus of Périgueux, *Epistula ad Perpetuum* and *De vita sancti Martini episcopi libri VI*: M. Petschenig ed., *CSEL* 16 (Vienna, 1888) 1-190

Julianus Pomerius, *De vita contemplativa*: *PL* 59.415ff. Translation: M.J. Suelzer, *The Vita Contemplativa of Julianus Pomerius* (Westminster, 1947)

Prosper of Aquitania, *De grati dei et libero arbitrio contra collatorem* and *Epistula ad Rufinum de gratia et libero arbitrio*, also *Pro Augustino responsiones ad capitula obiectionum Gallorum calumniantium*, *Carmen de providentia dei* [?], *Epigrammata in obtrectatorem Augustini*, *Epitaphium Nestorianae et Pelagianae haereseon*, *De ingratis*, *Poema coniugis ad uxorem* [?], *De vocatione omnium gentium*: PL 51. Translations: M.P. McHugh, *The Carmen de providentia dei Attributed to Prosper of Aquitaine* (Washington, 1964); G.G. Walsh et.al. tr., *Niceta of Remesiana. Writings. Sulpicius Severus. Writings. Vincent of Lerins. Commonitories. Prosper of Aquitaine. Grace and Free Will* (New York, 1949)

Ruricius, *Epistulae*: A. Engelbrecht ed., *CSEL* 21 (Vienna, 1891) 349-450; B. Krusch ed., *MGH AA* 8 (Berlin, 1887) 299-350; R. Demeulenaere ed., *CCL* 64 (Turnholt, 1985)

Salvian of Marseilles, *De gubernatione dei*, *Ad ecclesiam sive adversus avaritiam*, and *Epistulae*: G. Lagarrigue ed., *SC* 176, 220 (Paris, 1971-1975); F. Pauly ed., *CSEL* 7 (Vienna, 1883); C. Halm ed., *MGH AA* 1.1 (Berlin, 1877). Translations: E.M. Sanford, tr. *On the Government of God*, (New York, 1930), J.F. O'Sullivan, *The Writings of Salvian, The Presbyter* (New York, 1947).

Sidonius Apollinaris, *Carmina* and *Epistulae*: A. Loyen ed., *Sidoine Apollinaire: Poemes* (Budé, 1960) and vols.2-3, *Sidoine Apollinaire: Lettres* (Budé, 1970); W.B. Anderson, *Sidonius Apollinaris: Poems and Letters I-II* (Loeb, 1936-1965); P. Mohr ed., *C. Sollius Apollinaris Sidonius* (Teubner, 1895); C. Leutjohann ed., *MGH AA* 8 (Berlin, 1887)

Sulpicius Severus, *Chronicorum libri II*, *Dialogi*, *Epistulae* and *Vita s. Martini episcopi Turonensis*: J. Fontaine ed., *Sulpice Sévère, Vie de saint Martin, vol.1. Introduction, texte et traduction* and vols.2-3, *Commentaire et index*, *SC* 133-135 (Paris, 1967-1969); C. Halm ed., *CSEL* 1 (Vienna, 1866). Translations: Gerald G. Walsh et.al. tr., *Niceta of Remesiana, Writings. Sulpicius Severus, Writings. Vincent of Lerins, Commonitories. Prosper of Aquitaine, Grace and Free Will* (New York, 1949); F.R. Hoare tr., *Sulpicius Severus et.al. The Western Fathers: Being the Lives of Martin of Tours, Ambrose, Augustine of Hippo, Honoratus of Arles and Germanus of Auxerre* (New York, 1954); A. Roberts tr., *The Works of Sulpitius Severus* (New York, 1894)

Venantius Fortunatus, *Carmina* and *Vitae*: B. Krusch ed., *MGH AA* 4.2 (Berlin, 1885, repr. Berlin, 1961); *Vita s. Severini Burdigalensis* and *Vita s. Germani Parisiensis*: W. Levison ed., *MGH SRM* 7 (Berlin, 1920) 219-224, 372-418. Translation: J. George tr., *Venantius Fortunatus: Personal and Political Poems* (Liverpool, 1995)

Verus of Orange, *Vita s. Eutropii episcopi Arausicensis*: P. Varin ed., "Vie de saint Eutrope évêque d'Orange," *Bulletin du Comité Historique des Monuments Ecrits de l'Histoire de France* 1 (1849) 52-64

Vincentius of Lerins: Translation: C.A. Heurtley, *The Commonitory of Vincent of Lerins* (New York, 1894)

Vita Apollinaris Valentinensis: *MGH SRM* 3.196-209

Vita Aridii: *MGH SRM* 3.576-612; *Testamentum Aridii*: Aubrun, *Limoges*, 413-417; *PL* 71.1119ff

Vita Desiderii episcopi Cadurcensis: W. Arndt ed., *MGH SRM* 4.553ff; R. Poupardin, *La vie de Saint Didier, Evêque de Cahors (630-655)* (Paris, 1900).

Vita Domnoli episcopi Cenomanensis: *AASS* May III, 606-612

Vita Eligii: *MGH SRM* 4.730-746

Vita Firmini: *AASS* October V, 641.

Vita Juniani: *MGH SRM* 3.377-379; *AASS* October VIII pt.2, 848-851
Vita Marcelli: F. Dolbeau, "La vie en prose de saint Marcel, évêque de Die. Histoire du texte et édition critique," *Francia* 11 (1983) 97-130
Vita Martialis antiquior: *AASS* June V 555.
Vita Sacerdotis episcopi Lemovicensis: *AASS* May II, 15ff; *PL* 163.985ff
Vita Segolenae abbatissae Troclarensis: *AASS* July V, 630-637
Vita Viviani episcopi Santonensis: B. Krusch ed., *MGH SRM* 3.92-100

Secondary Sources

Literature, History, and Society in Late Antiquity

J. Arbellot, "Saint Ferréol, évêque de Limoges au VIᵉsiècle," *Seminaire religieuse de Limoges* (1869) 475-479

M.T.W. Arnheim, *The Senatorial Aristocracy in the Later Roman Empire* (Oxford: Clarendon Press, 1972)

C.F. Arnold, *Caesarius von Arelate und die gallische Kirche von seiner Zeit* (Leipzig, 1894; repr. Leipzig, 1972)

A. Audin, "Alcimi Ecdicii Aviti Viennensis episcopi homilia dicta in dedicatione superioris basilicae: MS. sur papyrus, Paris, Bibl. nat. 8913+8914," in *Studi in onore de Aristidi Calderini e Roberto Paribeni*, vol.2 (Milan, 1957) 433-51

E. Auerbach, *Literary Language and its Public in Late Antiquity and the Middle Ages*, tr. by R. Manheim (New York: Pantheon Books, 1965)

A.A.R. Bastiaensen, "Le cérémonial épistolaire des chrétiens latins," in *Graecitas et Latinitas christianorum paimaeva* suppl.2 (Nimègue, 1964) 4-45

H.G.J. Beck, *The Pastoral Care of Souls in South-East France during the Sixth Century* (Rome, 1950)

W. Bergmann, *Studien zu einer kritischen Sichtung der sudgallischen Predigtliteratur des 5. und 6. Jahrhunderts* (Leipzig, 1898; repr. Aalen, 1972)

B. Bischoff, "Briefe des neunten Jahrhunderts," in B. Bischoff, *Anecdota novissima* (Stuttgart, 1984) 123-149

P. Bonnassie, "L'évêque, le peuple et les sénateurs: Scènes de la vie à Cahors, d'après la Vita Ambrosii," *Annales du Midi* 102 nos.189-190 (Jan.-June 1990) 209-217

B. Brennan, "Senators and Social Mobility in Sixth-Century Gaul," *Journal of Medieval History* 11 (1985) 145-151

P.R.L. Brown, *Society and the Holy in Late Antiquity* (Berkeley, 1982)

H. Bruhn, "De affectata modestia, qua in epistulis Symmachus Sidonius Ruricius Ennodius utuntur," chap. 2 in *Specimen vocabularii rhetorici ad inferioris aetatis latinitatem pertinens* (thesis, Marburg, 1911)

M.-B. Brugière, *Littérature et droit dans la Gaule du Veme siècle* (Paris, 1974)

M. Casquero, M. Antonio, "Epistolografia romana," *Helmantica* 34 (1983) 377-406

N.K. Chadwick, *Poetry and Letters in Early Christian Gaul* (London, 1955)

E. Clark, *John Chrysostom and Friends, Essays and Translations* (New York, 1979)

P. Courcelle, *Histoire littéraire des grandes invasions germaniques*³ (Paris, 1964)

E.R. Curtius, *Europäische Literatur und lateinisches Mittelalter*⁶ (Bern, 1967)

O.M. Dalton, *The Letters of Sidonius* (2 vols.) (Oxford, 1915)

E. Dekkers, A. Gaar eds., *Clavis patrum latinorum, qua in novum corpus christianorum edendum optimas quasque scriptorum recensiones à Tertulliano ad Bedam*[2] (Turnhout, 1961)

S. Dill, *Roman Society in Gaul in the Merovingian Age* (London, 1926; repr. New York, 1970)

M. Duchein, "Le premier écrivain limousin, Ruricius," *BSAHL* 36 (1955) 17-22

E.S. Duckett, *Latin Writers of the Fifth Century* (New York, 1930; repr. New York, 1969)

J. Durliat, "Les attributions civiles des évêques merovingiens: L'exemple de Didier, évêque de Cahors (630-655)," *Annales du midi* 91 (1979) 237-254

P.-M. Duval, *La Gaule jusqu'au milieu du Ve siècle* (Paris, 1971)

A. G:son Elg, *In Faustum Reiensem studia* (Upsala, 1937)

R. Etienne, "L'Hommage de la cité des Cadurques au Picton M. Sedatius Severianus," *Revue de l'agenais* 11 (1994) 89-94

A. Engelbrecht, "Beiträge zur Kritik und Erklärung der Briefe des Apollinaris Sidonius, Faustus und Ruricius," *Zeitschrift für die österreichischen Gymnasium* 41 (1890) 481-497

A. Engelbrecht, "Titel und Titulaturen in den Briefen des Ruricius und seiner Genossen," *Patristische Analecten* (Vienna, 1892) 48-83

A. Engelbrecht, *Studien über dei Schriften des Bischofes von Reii Faustus* (Vienna, 1889)

E.L. Fortin, *Christianisme et culture philosophique au cinquième siècle. La querelle de l'ame en Occident* (Paris, 1959)

P. Geary, *Before France and Germany. The Creation and Transformation of the Merovingian World* (New York, 1988)

F. Gilliard, "The Senators of Sixth-Century Gaul," *Speculum* 54 (1979) 685-697

E. Griffe, "L'épiscopat gaulois et les royautés barbares de 482 à 507," *Bulletin de littérature écclésiastique* 76 (1975) 261-284

E. Griffe, "La pratique religieuse en Gaule au Ve siècle. Saeculares et sancti," *Bulletin de littérature écclésiastique* 63 (1962) 241-267

T.J. Haarhoff, *Schools of Gaul. A Study of Pagan and Christian Education in the Last Century of the Western Empire* (London, 1920)

H. Hagendahl, *La correspondance de Ruricius*, Acta Universitatis Gotoburgensis Göteborgs Högskolas Arsskrift 58.3 (Göteborg, 1952)

J. Harries, *Sidonius Apollinaris and the Fall of Rome* (Oxford 1994)

M. Heinzelmann, "Gallische Prosopographie 260-527," *Francia* 10 (1982) 531-718

M. Heinzelmann, *Bischofsherrschaft in Gallien: Zur Kontinuität römischer Führungsschichten von 4. bis 7. Jahrhundert* (Munich, 1976)

Y. Hen, *Culture & Religion in Merovingian Gaul, AD 481-751* (Leiden, 1995)

Instrumenta lexicologica latina. Scriptores minores Galliae s.IV-V. Foebadius, Victricius, Leporius, Vincentius Lerinensis, Evagrius, Ruricius (Turnhout, 1985)

E. James, *The Franks* (Oxford, 1988)

E. James, *The Origins of France: From Clovis to the Capetians, 500-1000* (New York, 1982)

T. Janson, *Latin Prose Prefaces. Studies in Literary Conventions* (Stockholm, 1964)

G. Jouassard, "Saint Césaire d'Arles et Sedatus de Nîmes," *Science religieuse, travaux et recherches* (1943) 210-215

W. Klingshirn, *Caesarius of Arles and the Making of a Christian Community in Late Antique Gaul* (Cambridge, 1995)

W. Klingshirn, "Charity and Power: Caesarius of Arles and the Ransoming of Captives in Sub-Roman Gaul," *Journal of Roman Studies* 75 (1985) 183-203

A. Koch, *Der heilige Faustus, Bischof von Riez. Eine dogmengeschichtliche Monographie* (Stuttgart, 1895)

B. Krusch, "De Ruricio episcopo Lemovicensi," *MGH* 8 (Berlin, 1887) lxii-lxxx

H. Legier-Desgranges, *Les Apollinaires. Histoire d'une famille gallo-romaine pendant trois siècles* (Paris, 1937)

L. Levillain, "La crise des années 507-508 et les rivalités d'influence en Gaule de 508 à 514," *Mélanges offerts à M. Nicholas Iorga* (Paris, 1933) 537-567

A. Loyen, *Recherches historiques sur les panégyriques de Sidoine Apollinaire* (Paris, 1942)

A. Loyen, *Sidoine Apollinaire et l'esprit précieux en Gaule aux derniers jours de l'empire* (Paris, 1943)

M. Manitius, *Geschichte der lateinischen Literatur des Mittelalters. I. Von Justinian bis zur mitte des zehnten Jahrhunderts* (Munich, 1911)

J.R. Martindale, *The Prosopography of the Later Roman Empire. Volume II. A.D. 395-527* (Cambridge, 1980)

R.W. Mathisen, "Agrestius of Lugo, Eparchius Avitus, and a Curious Fifth-Century Statement of Faith," *Journal of Early Christian Studies* 2 (1994) 71-102

R.W. Mathisen, "Barbarian Bishops and the Churches 'in barbaricis gentibus' during Late Antiquity," *Speculum* 72 (1997) 664-697

R.W. Mathisen, "Clovis, Anastase, et Grégoire de Tours: Consul, patrice et roi,"in M. Rouche ed., *Clovis, le Romain, le chrétien, l'Européen* (Paris, 1998) 395-407.

R.W. Mathisen, *The Ecclesiastical Aristocracy of Fifth-Century Gaul: A Regional Analysis of Family Structure* (dissertation: University of Wisconsin, 1979; Ann Arbor, 1980)

R.W. Mathisen, *Ecclesiastical Factionalism and Religious Controversy in Fifth-Century Gaul* (Washington, D.C., 1989)

R.W. Mathisen, "Emigrants, Exiles and Survivors: Aristocratic Options in Visigothic Aquitania," *Phoenix* 38 (1984) 159-170

R.W. Mathisen, "Episcopal Hierarchy and Tenure in Office: A Method for Establishing Dates of Ordination," *Francia* 17 (1990) 125-140

R.W. Mathisen, "Epistolography, Literary Circles, and Family Ties in Late Roman Gaul," *Transactions of the American Philological Society* 111 (1981) 95-109

R.W. Mathisen, "The Family of Georgius Florentius Gregorius and the Bishops of Tours," *Medievalia et Humanistica* 12 (1984) 83-95

R.W. Mathisen, "For Specialists Only: The Reception of Augustine and His Theology in Fifth-Century Gaul," in J.T. Lienhard et al. eds., *Augustine. Presbyter factus sum* (Peter Lang, 1994) 29-41

R.W. Mathisen, *Roman Aristocrats in Barbarian Gaul: Strategies for Survival in an Age of Transition* (Austin, 1993)

R.W. Mathisen, "The 'Second Council of Arles' and the Spirit of Compilation and Codification in Late Roman Gaul," *The Journal of Early Christian Studies* 5 (1997) 511-554

R.W. Mathisen, "Sidonius on the Reign of Avitus: A Study in Political Prudence," *Transactions of the American Philological Association* 109 (1979) 165-171

R.W. Mathisen, *Studies in the History, Literature, and Society of Late Roman Gaul* (Amsterdam, 1991)

R.W. Mathisen, "The Theme of Literary Decline in Late Roman Gaul," *Classical Philology* 83 (1988) 45-53

R. McKitterick, "Script and Book Production," in *Eadem* ed., *Carolingian Culture: Emulation and Innovation* (Cambridge, 1993)

R. McKitterick, "The *scriptoria* of Merovingian Gaul: A Survey of the Evidence," in H. Clark, M. Brennan eds., *Columbanus and Medieval Monasticism* (Oxford, 1981) 173-207

P. Périn, "L'armée de Vidimer et la question des dépôts funéraires chez les Wisigoths en Gaule et en Espagne," in F. Vallet, M. Kazanski eds., *L'armée romaine et les barbares* (Paris, 1993) 411-414

H.W.G. Peter, "Ruricius (und Faustus)," in H.W.G. Peter, W.G. Hermann eds., *Der Brief in der römischen Literatur* (Leipzig, 1901; repr. Hildesheim, 1965) 158-162.

G.-C. Picard, *L'Ascension d'une dynastie Gauloise. La gloire des Sedatii* (Paris, 1990)

L. Pietri, *La ville de Tours du IVe au VIe siècle: Naissance d'une cité chrétienne* (Rome, 1983)

L. Pietri, "L'ordine senatorio in Gallia dal 476 alla fine del VI secolo," in *Società romana et impero tardoantico*, vol.1 (Rome-Bari, 1986) 307-323, 699-703

R. Pinchon, *Etudes sur l'histoire de la litterature latine dans les Gaules, les derniers écrivains profanes* (Paris, 1906)

B. Quintreau, *Sidoine Apollinaire et ses amis: La société gallo-romaine au Ve siècle* (Paris, 1964)

F.J.E. Raby, *A History of Secular Latin Poetry in the Middle Ages* (Oxford, 1934)

B. Rehling, *De Fausti Reiensis epistula tertia. Commentatio historica* (Münster, 1898)

P. Riché, *Education et culture dans l'Occident barbare, VIe-VIIIe siécles* (Paris, 1962) = *Education and Culture in the Barbarian West, Sixth through Eighth Centuries*, tr. by J. Contreni (Columbia, S.C., 1976)

P. Riché, "La survivance des écoles publiques en Gaule au Ve siècle," *Le Moyen Age* 63 (1957) 421-476

B. Rimini, "Sullo stile delle epistole di Ruricio," *Rendiconti. Instituto lombardo di scienze e lettere* 45 (1912) 569-590

M. Rouche, *L'Aquitaine des wisigoths aux Arabes 418-781. Naissance d'une région* (Paris, 1972)

P. Rousseau, "In Search of Sidonius the Bishop," *Historia* 25 (1976) 356-377

M. Schanz ed., *Die römische Litteratur von Constantin bis zum Gesetzgebungswerk Justinians*, in M. Schanz, C. Hosius eds., *Geschichte der römischen Litteratur bis zum Gesetzgebunswerk Justinians* vol.4.2 (Munich, 1920)

G. Scheibelreiter, *Der Bischof in merowingischer Zeit* (Vienna, 1983)

C. Settipani, *La préhistoire des Capétiens (481-987)* (Villeneuve d'Ascq, 1993)

C. Settipani, "Ruricius Ier évêque de Limoges et ses relations familiales," *Francia* 18 (1991) 195-222

D. Shanzer, "Dating the Baptism of Clovis: The Bishop of Vienne vs the Bishop of Tours," *Early Medieval Europe* 7 (1998) 29-57

H.S. Sivan, "Sidonius Apollinaris, Theodoric II, and Gothic-Roman Politics from Avitus to Anthemius," *Hermes* 117 (1989) 85-94

C.E. Stevens, *Sidonius Apollinaris and His Age* (Oxford, 1933)

K.F. Stroheker, *Der senatorische Adel im spätantiken Gallien* (Reutlingen, 1948, repr. Darmstadt, 1970)

K.F. Stroheker, *Eurich, König der Westgoten* (Stuttgart, 1937)

N. Valois, *De arte scribendi epistolas apud Gallicos medii aevi scriptores rhetores* (Paris, 1880)

R. Van Dam, *Leadership and Community in Late Antique Gaul* (Berkeley, 1985)

P.-P. Verbraken, "Traces d'un 'De consolatione peccatoris' attribuable à Sedatus de Béziers," *Revue Bénédictine* 90 (1980) 135-9

P.P. Verbraken, "Sermons jumeaux de Sedatus de Nîmes pour la fête de Nöel," *Revue Bénédictine* 88 (1978) 81-91

G. Weigel, *Faustus of Riez. An Historical Introduction* (Philadelphia, 1938)

A. Wilmart, "Une homélie de Sedatus, évêque de Nîmes, pour la Nativité de Notre-Seigneur," *Revue Bénédictine* 35 (1923) 5-16

I.N. Wood, "The Audience of Architecture in Post-Roman Gaul," in L.A.S. Butler, R.K. Morris eds., *The Anglo-Saxon Church* (London, 1986) 74-79

I.N. Wood, "The Ecclesiastical Politics of Merovingian Clermont," in P. Wormald ed., *Ideal and Reality in Frankish and Anglo-Saxon Society* (Oxford, 1983) 34-57

I.N. Wood, "Letters and Letter-Collections from Antiquity to the Early Middle Ages: The Prose Works of Avitus of Vienne," in M.A. Meyer ed., *The Culture of Christendom* (London, 1993) 29-43

F.A. Wright, T.A. Sinclair, *A History of Later Latin Literature. From the Middle of the Fourth to the End of the Seventeenth Century* (New York, 1931)

HISTORY AND ARCHAEOLOGY OF LIMOGES AND THE LIMOUSIN

J.-L. Antignac, "Deux fragments de poterie sigillée à Gourdon-Murat," *Lemouzi* 46 (1973) 256-257

M. Aubrun, *L'ancien diocèse de Limoges des origines au milieu du XIe siècle* (Clermont-Ferrand, 1981)

M. Aussel, "Première mention de Dégagnac dans l'histoire écrité à l'occasion du passage de Ruricius," *BSELSAL* 109 (1988) 221-228

J. Becquet, "L'évêque Asclèpe à Saint-Augustin de Limoges (VIe siècle)," *BSAHL* 122 (1994) 12-22

J. Becquet, "Les saints dans le culte en Limousin au Moyen age," 26-59

R. Bedon, "A propos du statut et de l'histoire de la civitas gallo-romaine des Lemovices et de sa capitale Augustoritum," *TAL* 15 (1995) 31-41

Ch.-F. Bellet, *L'ancienne vie de Saint Martial et la prose rhythmée* (Paris, 1897)

P. Bordier, J.-M. Desbordes, O. Hernandez, "La voie romaine du bois d'Ahun," *TAL* 2 (1981) 9-16

J.-P. Bost, "Elites urbaines à Augustoritum sous le Haut-Empire," *TAL* 13 (1993) 101-108

J.-P. Bost, J. Perrier, "Professeur de grammaire à Limoges sous le Haut-Empire," *BSAHL* 116 (1989) 55-66

L. Bournazel, G. Reboul, J.-M. Desbordes, "Les origines d'Uzerche," *TAL* 2 (1981) 97-104

R. Bulit, *Gourdon. Les origines, les seigneurs, les consuls et la communauté jusqu'à la fin du XIVe siècle* (Toulouse, 1925)

J.-P. Clapham, J.-M. Desbordes, "Les itinéraires antiques de Limoges à Saintes. Etat des recherches," *TAL* 9 (1989) 35-44

R. Couraud, "L'amphithéatre de Limoges. Premiers sondages: october 1966-mars 1967)," *BSAHL* 94 (1967) 49-63

R. Couraud, "Decouvertes archéologiques à la Place de la Republique à Limoges (1968-70)," *BSAHL* 97 (1970) 45-79

R. Couraud, "La voie de Burdigala-Augustoritum-Avaricum dans la traversée de la région d'Ambazac," *BSAHL* 89 (1962) 204-206

R. Couraud, F. July, "Voies romaines de la Haute-Vienne (VI): voies romaines et chemins antiques dans la région de Sauviat," *BSAHL* 95 (1968) 67-95

J.-M. Courteix, "Aux origines d'Argentat," *TAL* 12 (1992) 143-151

R. Crozet, "Les lieux de sép[ulture des évêques de Limoges, des origines chrétiennes à la fin du XIIIᵉ siècle," *BSAHL* 98 (1971) 149-152

M. Deloche, *Description des monnaies mérovingiennes en Limousin* (Paris, 1863)

J.-M. Desbordes, "Un ancien itinéraire de long parcours entre armorique et Mediterranée," *TAL* 3 (1982) 15-22

J.-M. Desbordes, "Enquète sur le tracé de la voie antique de Limoges à Saintes entre Aurence et Vienne," *TAL* 12 (1992) 113-121

J.-M. Desbordes, "L'oppidum de Villejoubert, commune de Saint-Denis-des-Murs (Haute-Vienne)," *TAL* 4 (1983) 25-28

J.-M. Desbordes, "Au premier millenaire: cultes chrétiens et voies antiques en Limousin," *TAL* 13 (1993) 91-8

J.-M. Desbordes, "La station routière de Praetorium dans la cité des Lemovices: Hypothèses et réalité," *TAL* 14 (1994) 17-22

J.-M. Desbordes et al, *Augustoritum. Aux origines de Limoges* (Limoges, 1990)

J.-M. Desbordes et al., "Les remparts de l'oppidum de Villejoubert (Commune de Saint-Denis-des-Murs, Haute-Vienne)," *TAL* 7 (1986) 63-74

J.-M. Desbordes, J. Dubois, S. Louradour, "La voie romaine de Lyon à Bordeaux dans le pays d'Eygurande (Corrèze)," *TAL* 13 (1993) 71-79

J.-M. Desbordes, C. Gautrand-Moser, G. Lintz, F. Moser, *Les origines de Brive* (Brive-la-Gaillarde, 1982)

J.-M. Desbordes, J. Perrier, "Aux origines de Rancon," *BSAHL* 109 (1982) 43-52

J.-M. Desbordes, J. Perrin, "Archéologie aërienne en Haute-Vienne: La recherche des anciens itinéraires et de leur équipement riverain," *TAL* 10 (1990) 7-16

M.-A. Dostes, "L'ancienne voie de Clermont à Limoges: Recherches à Saint-Agnant-pres-Crocq (Creuse)," *TAL* 6 (1985) 97-99

G.M. Dreves, *Prosarium Lemovicense. Die Prosen der Abtei St. Martial zu Limoges* (Leipzig, 1889)

P. Ducourtieux, "Decouvertes faites à l'emplacement de la ville gallo-romaine, à Limoges, et 1886," *BSAHL* 31 (1882) 229-238

P. Ducourtieux, *Histoire de Limoges* (Limoges, 1925)

H. Duplès-Agier, *Chroniques de Saint-Martial de Limoges* (Paris, 1874)

D. Dussot, "Nouvelles decouvertes dans le vicus gallo-romain de Bridiers," *TAL* 11 (1991) 97-102

P. Freytet, "La villa de la Védrenne (Commune de La Chapelle-Saint-Martial, Creuse): Nouvelles decouvertes," *TAL* 6 (1985) 105-110

P. Freytet et al, "Le site de la Védrenne (La Chapalle Saint-Martial, Creuse). Etude d'une villa gallo-romaine, et de son environnement," *TAL* 11 (1991) 33-43

P. Ganne, "Un carrefour d'anciens itinéraires aux confins de l'Auvergne et du Limousin (Commune de Flayat, Creuse)," *TAL* 14 (1994) 115-135

A. Gary, "Tombe à Prouilhac près de Gourdon," *BSELSAL* 22 (1897) 78ff.

A. Hochuli-Gysel, J.-P. Loustaud," La verrérie de la village de Brachaud, près de Limoges," *BSAHL* 121 (1993) 21-48

E. James, *The Merovingian Archaeology of South-West Gaul* (Oxford, 1977)

G. Janicaud, "Vestiges romains à La Vendrenne", *MSSNAC* 22 (1944) 27-29

F. July, P. Texier, "Cippe gallo-romain à Verneuil-sur-Vienne," *BSAHL* 99 (1972) 329

Y. de Kisch, "Vestiges des thermes gallo-romains de la Place des Jacobins à Limoges," *BSAHL* 102 (1975) 220-221

P. Labbé ed., *Nova bibliotheca manuscriptorum librorum* (Paris, 1657)

M. Labrousse, G. Mercadier eds., *Le Lot, Carte archéologique de la Gaule 46* (Paris, 1990)

C. Lacorre, "Les origines de Saint-Junien: Elements de recherche," *TAL* 1 (1979/80) 69-81

J. Lafaurie, "Les monnaies épiscopales de Limoges aux VIIe et VIIIe s.," *Bulletin de la société française de numismatique* 30 (1975) pp.778-782

J. Lafaurie, "Monnaies mérovingiennes. Atelier de Limoges," in *Musée municipal de Limoges. Catalogue édité à l'occasion des Journées de la Société Française Numismatique, Limoges, 7-8 juin 1975* (Limoges, 1975) 60-63

Ch. de Lasteyrie, *L'abbaye de Saint-Martial de Limoges* (Paris, 1901)

A. Leroux, "Les sources de l'histoire du Limousin," *BSAHL* 41 (1895-1896) 1-260

A. Leroux, E. Molinier, A. Thomas, *Documents historiques bas-latins, provençaux et Français concernant principalement la Marche et le Limousin* vol.1 (Limoges, 1883)

J. Levet, *Histoire de Limoges*, vol.1 (Limoges, 1974)

R. Limouzin-Lamothe, *Le diocèse de Limoges, des origines à la fin du Moyen-Age* (2 vols.) (Strasbourg, 1951)

G. Lintz ed,, *Carte archéologique de la Gaule romaine 16. Carte et texte du département de la Corrèze* (Paris, 1981)

G. Lintz ed., *La Corrèze, Carte archéologique de la Gaule 19* (Paris, 1992)

G. Lintz, "Les sépultures à inhumation du Bas-Empire en Limousin. Typologie et chronologie," *BSSHAC* 116 (1974) 39-51

G. Lintz, "Sépultures gallo-romaines de Sauviat-sur-Vige," *BSAHL* 106 (1979) 17-38

J.-P. Loustaud, "Emplacement du forum gallo-romain de Limoges," *BSAHL* 107 (1980) 245

J.-P. Loustaud, *Limoges gallo-romain* (Limoges, 1980)

J.-P. Loustaud, "Limoges, rue Sainte-Felicité, Théatre romain, Sondage," *TAL* 9 (1989) 148-149

J.-P. Loustaud, "Nouvelle inscription relative à un notable Lemovice à Lyon," *BSAHL* 111 (1984) 168

J.-P. Loustaud, "Sondage archéologique à l'ancien hôpital de Limoges, la première ville gallo-romaine," *BSAHL* 111 (1984) 183-184

J.-P. Loustaud, "Le théâtre gallo-romain de Limoges, premiers éléments archéologiques," *BSAF* 118 (1990) 17-30

J.-P. Loustaud, "Thermes antiques de la Place Franklin-Roosevelt," *BSAHL* 104 (1977) 186, 105 (1978) 194

J.-P. Loustaud, "Les Thermes de la villa gallo-romaine de Brachaud. Synthèse d'une évolution," *TAL* 3 (1982) 31-57

J.-P. Loustaud, "L'urbanisation gallo-romaine des versants du ruisseau d'Enjoumar à Limoges," *BSAHL* 116 (1989) 14-50

J.-P. Loustaud, "Vestiges du theatre d'augustoritum," *BSAHL* 116 (1989) 184-185

J.-P. Loustaud "La voirie d'Augustoritum," *TAL* 5 (1984) 57-80

J.-P. Loustaud, J. Perrier, "Les monnaies de la villa gallo-romaine de Brachaud, 1974-1986," *BSAHL* 122 (1994) 4-11

J.-P. Loustaud, J.-J. Viroulet, "Le forum de Limoges, première approche (1976-1980)," *BSAHL* 108 (1981) 40-53

F. Massicot, "Coupe d'une voie ancienne entre auvergne et poitou sur la commune de Payrat-de-Bellac (Haute-Vienne)," *TAL* 15 (1995) 113-118

J. Mathevet, "Villa gallo-romaine da La Vaclette (Magnac-Laval)," *BSAHL* 93 (1966) 216

J.-H. Moreau, "Cassinomagus, Chassenon" *BSAHL* 90 (1963) 285-286

F. Moser, "Les ateliers gallo-romains de Brive (Corrèze)," *TAL* 7 (1986) 77-89

C. Moser-Gautrand, F. Moser, "Les figurines Gallo-romaines en terre cuite de Brive," *TAL* 2 (1981) 17-58

J.-M. Pardessus, *Diplomata, chartae, epistolae, leges aliaque instrumenta ad res Gallo-Francicas spectantia,* 2 vols. (Paris, 1843-1849)

A. Perrier, "S. Goar, ermite d'origine Limousine," *BSAHL* 86 (1955) 198

J. Perrier, "Fouilles sur l'emplacement de l'abbaye de Saint-Martial. Limoges, Place de la République (13 juin - 15 september 1966)," *BSAHL* 94 (1967) 87-99

J. Perrier ed,, *Carte archéologique de la Gaule romaine 14. Carte et texte du département de la Haute-Vienne* (Paris, 1964)

J. Perrier ed., *La Haute-Vienne, Carte archéologique de la Gaule 87* (Paris, 1993)

J. Perrier, "Les monnaies de la basse antiquité à Limoges. Leur relation avec la topographie urbaine," *TAL* 11 (1991) 61-64

J. Perrier, "Partie d'un trésor monétaire antique trouvé à Bridiers" *TAL* 7 (1987) 175-177

J. Perrier, "Recherches sur les sepultures médiévales en Haut-Limousin: La nécropole de Saint-Martial de Limoges," *TAL* 1 (1979-80) 101-111

J. Perrier, M. Tandeau de Marsac, "Le 'petit rempart' de l'oppidum de Villejoubert, Commune de Saint-Denis-des-Murs (Haute-Vienne)," *TAL* 4 (1983) 29-40

G. Pichaud, "Vestiges gallo-romains à Brachaud (Limoges)," *BSAHL* 100 (1973) 288-291

F. Prevot, "Limoges," in F. Prevot, X. Barral i Altet eds., *Topographie chrétienne des cités de la Gaule des origines au milieu du VIIIe siècle. VI. Province ecclésiastique de Bourges (Aquitania Prima)* (Paris, 1989) 67-77

J.-F. Priot, "Coupe d'une voie d'origine antique au Nord de Compreignac," *TAL* 6 (1985) 101-103

J.-F. Priot, "La nécropole suburbaine et le carrefour de Saint-Cessateur à Limoges," *TAL* 1 (1979-80) 15-20

J.-F. Priot, "La voie romaine de Limoges à Ahun à la Vergnolle. Le Chatenet-en-Dognon (Haute-Vienne)," *TAL* 5 (1984) 77-80

B. Sapene, "Autels votifs, ateliers de marbriers et sanctuaire gallo-romains decouverts à Saint-Béat en 1946," *Revue de Comminges* 69 (1946) 283-325

P. Saumande, "Aqueduc du quartier des Arènes à Limoges," *BSAHL* 96 (1969) 97 (1970) 277

P. Saumande, "Chassenon. Problèmes hydrauliques," *BSAHL* 123 (1995) 11-22

H.S. Sivan, "Funerary Monuments and Funerary Rites in Late Antique Aquitaine," *Oxford Journal of Archaeology* 5 (1986) 339-353

Z. Tomieux, "Etude topographique d'un diplôme de 626," *BSAHL* 39 (1891) 431-440

Z. Tomieux, "Partage de terres en Limousin d'après un diplôme de 626," *MSSNAC* 7 (1892) 397-399

M. Villoutreix, "L'itinéraire antique de Limoges à Angoulème," *TAL* 4 (1983) 85-91

J.B. Ward-Perkins, "The Sculpture of Visigothic France," *Archaeologia* 87 (1938) 79-128

INDEX